TRANSLATION CHANGES EVERYTHING

In *Translation Changes Everything*, leading theorist Lawrence Venuti gathers fourteen of his incisive essays since 2000.

The selection sketches the trajectory of his thinking about translation while engaging with the main trends in research and commentary. The issues covered include basic concepts like equivalence, retranslation, and reader reception; sociological topics like the impact of translations in the academy and the global cultural economy; and philosophical problems such as the translator's unconscious and translation ethics.

Every essay presents case studies that include Venuti's own translation projects, illuminating the connections between theoretical concepts and verbal choices. The texts, drawn from a broad variety of languages, are both humanistic and pragmatic, encompassing such forms as poems and novels, religious and philosophical works, travel guidebooks and advertisements. The discussions all explore practical applications, whether writing, publishing, reviewing, teaching or studying translations.

Venuti's aim is to conceive of translation as an interpretive act with far-reaching social effects, at once enabled and constrained by specific cultural situations.

This latest chapter in his developing work is essential reading for translators and students of translation alike.

Lawrence Venuti, Professor of English at Temple University, USA, is a translation theorist and historian as well as a translator from Italian, French, and Catalan. He is the author of *The Translator's Invisibility* (second edition, 2008), *The Scandals of Translation* (1998), and *The Translation Studies Reader* (third edition, 2012), all published by Routledge.

TRANSLATION CHANGES EVERYTHING

Theory and Practice

Lawrence Venuti

Routledge
Taylor & Francis Group

LONDON AND NEW YORK

First published 2013
by Routledge
2 Park Square, Milton Park, Abingdon, Oxon OX14 4RN

Simultaneously published in the USA and Canada
by Routledge
711 Third Avenue, New York, NY 10017

Routledge is an imprint of the Taylor & Francis Group, an informa business

© 2013 Lawrence Venuti

British Library Cataloguing in Publication Data
A catalogue record for this book is available from the British Library

Library of Congress Cataloging in Publication Data
Venuti, Lawrence.
Translation changes everything : theory and practice / Lawrence Venuti.
p. cm.
Includes index.
1. Translating and interpreting. 2. Intercultural communication. I. Title.
P306.2.V454 2013
418'.02–dc23
2012026316

ISBN: 978-0-415-69628-9 (hbk)
ISBN: 978-0-415-69629-6 (pbk)
ISBN: 978-0-203-07442-8 (ebk)

Typeset in Bembo
by Taylor & Francis Books

For Karen Van Dyck

Es wird etwas sein, später,
das füllt sich mit dir ...

Later will be something
filling itself
                    with you

CONTENTS

ACKNOWLEDGEMENTS

Earlier versions of the essays that comprise this book, with one exception (chapter 13 is previously unpublished), appeared in edited volumes and in journals. I gratefully acknowledge the copyright holders for permission to reprint the material:

"Translation, Community, Utopia." In *The Translation Studies Reader*. Ed. Lawrence Venuti. 1st and 2nd editions. London and New York: Routledge, 2000/2004, pp. 468–88/482–502.

"The Difference That Translation Makes: The Translator's Unconscious." In *Translation Studies: Perspectives on an Emerging Discipline*. Ed. Alessandra Riccardi. Cambridge: Cambridge University Press, 2002, pp. 214–41. Copyright © 2002 by Cambridge University Press.

"Translating Derrida on Translation: Relevance and Disciplinary Resistance." *Yale Journal of Criticism* 16/2 (2003): 237–62. Copyright © 2003 by Yale University and The Johns Hopkins University Press.

"Translating Jacopone da Todi: Archaic Poetries and Modern Audiences." *Translation and Literature* 12/2 (2003): 231–45. Copyright © 2003 by Edinburgh University Press Ltd.

"Retranslations: The Creation of Value." In *Translation and Culture*. Ed. Katherine Faull. *Bucknell Review* 47/1 (2004); Lewisburg, Pennsylvania: Bucknell University Press, pp. 25–38.

"How to Read a Translation." *Words Without Borders: The On-Line Magazine for International Literature*, July/August 2004.

"Local Contingencies: Translation and National Identities." In *Nation, Language, and the Ethics of Translation*. Ed. Sandra Bermann and Michael Wood. Princeton: Princeton University Press, 2005, pp. 177–202.

"Translation, Simulacra, Resistance." *Translation Studies* 1/1 (2008): 18–35. Copyright © 2008 Taylor and Francis/Routledge.

"Translations on the Market." *Words Without Borders: The On-Line Magazine for International Literature*, February 2008.

"Teaching in Translation." In *Teaching World Literature*. Ed. David Damrosch. New York: Modern Language Association, 2009, pp. 86–96.

"The Poet's Version; or, An Ethics of Translation." *Translation Studies* 4/2 (May 2011): 230–47. Copyright © 2011 Taylor and Francis/Routledge.

"Translation Studies and World Literature." In *The Routledge Companion to World Literature*. Ed. Theo D'haen, David Damrosch, and Djelal Kadir. London and New York: Routledge, 2012, pp. 180–93.

"Towards a Translation Culture." *The Iowa Review* 41/2 (Fall 2011). Online.

I would like especially to thank the editors who enabled the first publication of this work: Sandra Bermann, Jessica Brantley, David Damrosch, Theo D'haen, Katherine Faull, Stuart Gillespie, Susan Harris, Djelal Kadir, Joseph Luzzi, Alane Salierno Mason, Alessandra Riccardi, Sherry Simon, Kate Sturge, Russell Valentino, Michaela Wolf, and Michael Wood. The sales figures cited in chapter 9 for publications by the Hogarth Press, Chatto and Windus, and Martin Secker Ltd are used with the kind permission of the Society of Authors in the United Kingdom and the Random House Group Ltd.

I am indebted to my editor at Routledge, Louisa Semlyen, for her support of what has proven to be an unusual project. Jonathan Gagas was of enormous help in preparing the electronic files and in suggesting revisions. Several essays were written in most favorable circumstances provided by Martha Tennent, who served as my first informant for matters Catalan.

My comments on English and Catalan words throughout rely on the online editions of the *Oxford English Dictionary* and the *Gran Diccionari de la Llengua Catalana*. I am responsible for all unattributed translations, which have been prepared in accordance with the interpretive occasions that they are intended to serve.

The dedication is taken from the opening lines of Paul Celan's poem "Es wird etwas sein, später," from *Zeitgehöft: späte Gedichte aus dem Nachlass* (Frankfurt: Suhrkamp, 1976). The English version is mine.

L.V.
New York City
June 2012

INTRODUCTION

This book gathers a selection of essays I have published since 2000. Although several were occasioned by invitations to contribute to journals and edited volumes, the issues I address are wide-ranging and consistently engaged with current trends and debates in translation studies as well as in literary and cultural studies. These issues include basic concepts like equivalence, retranslation, and reader reception, sociological topics like the impact of translations in academic institutions and in the global cultural economy, and philosophical problems like the translator's unconscious and translation ethics. Some essays propose guidelines for how to read and teach translations as translations, as texts in their own right, relatively autonomous from the source texts they translate. Others comment on trends in translation research, in translator training, and in publishing. Still others develop historical perspectives which extend from antiquity to the present. Every essay provides detailed case studies that seek to establish connections between theoretical concepts and their material realization, so that the discussions all have a bearing on practice, whether writing, publishing, reviewing, teaching, or studying translations. A number are devoted to considerations of my own translation projects. The genres and text types are varied, both humanistic and pragmatic. They include poems, novels, drama, philosophy, sociology, travel guidebooks, and advertisements. The translating language is English, for the most part, but the cases also involve such other languages as Catalan, Chinese, Dutch, French, German, ancient Greek, Italian, Latin, Russian, and Spanish.

Despite the appearance of randomness, the essays do not constitute a typical miscellany. Taking roughly the past decade as the time frame, the selection I present is intended to serve a dual purpose: to sketch the trajectory of my thinking about translation and to intervene into the main trends in translation research and commentary. These two aims are interrelated in the sense that they have exercised a reciprocal influence upon one another, but each is sufficiently distinct that it can be described separately. Insofar as they establish the overall coherence of this book, I will offer an account of them that also glances at future directions for my own work and for translation studies.

Abandoning instrumentalism

The essays reflect a significant change in my thinking. By the end of the 1990s, I had formulated an approach to translation that tried to synthesize divergent theoretical concepts. The core of the approach was Friedrich Schleiermacher's notion of a translation method that signals the linguistic and cultural differences of the source text, subsequently revised in Antoine Berman's notion of a translation ethics that respects cultural otherness by manifesting the foreignness of the source text in the translation (see Schleiermacher 1813 and Berman 1999, originally published in 1985). In my view, however, this respect was most effectively shown in an indirect way by questioning and upsetting the hierarchy of linguistic and cultural values in the receiving situation, where dominant values tend to suppress differences through assimilation or to marginalize them through neglect. I located two strategies of "foreignizing" (defamiliarizing and interrogating) these values: a selection of source texts that runs counter to the canon of the source literature already translated and a translation method that does not necessarily adhere closely to the source text, as both Schleiermacher and Berman had advocated, but rather cultivates an experimentalism as practiced by the nineteenth-century Italian writer I. U. Tarchetti and the modernist poet Ezra Pound (Venuti 2008: 15–16, 18–20, 125–26, 176–78).

These strategies were based on my understanding that, as the twentieth century unfolded, translators worldwide came to work under a discursive regime that values a narrowly defined fluency secured by relying on the most familiar form of the translating language, usually the current standard dialect. Hence innovative variations on the standard or the appropriate use of nonstandard items can release a foreignizing "remainder" (borrowing Jean-Jacques Lecercle's concept), effects that exceed a semantic correspondence according to dictionary definitions and register linguistic and cultural differences in the receiving situation (Lecercle 1990; Venuti 1998: 10–11; see also below: 37–38). My idea was not so much to abandon fluent translating as to widen its boundaries beyond the restricted lexicon and syntax allowed to translators. When the discursive regime involves a major language like English or French, "major" in terms of its cultural authority or prestige in the global hierarchy of languages, an experimental translation strategy can produce a minoritizing effect, "minoritizing" in Gilles Deleuze and Félix Guattari's sense of "deterritorializing" the major language and culture, taking it on an "escape" that challenges its authority (see Deleuze and Guattari 1987: chapter 4; Venuti 1998: 9–13). As applied to translation, the concept of minoritizing situates foreignizing practices in national and transnational frameworks.

I have no intention of abandoning the pursuit of foreignizing effects, whether in translation research or in my translation projects. The idea of mobilizing such effects to question dominant values in the receiving situation remains a pressing concern – or, more precisely, it has become for me the very definition of humanistic translation insofar as it traffics in linguistic and cultural differences and should not work to diminish them so as to sustain a status quo, regardless of whether the translating language and culture are central or peripheral, major or minor. No language can afford the stagnation that results from restricting or excluding contacts with other languages. No culture can afford the complacency of allowing the hierarchy of values that structure it to go unexamined and uncriticized (Venuti 2008: 19–20).

Nonetheless, I came to recognize that the Schleiermacher–Berman line of thinking, although apparently hermeneutic in its approach, although apparently treating translation as an interpretation, rests uneasily on an instrumental model of translation. Here translation is seen as the reproduction or transfer of an invariant contained in or caused by the source text, whether its form, its meaning, or its effect. For Schleiermacher and Berman, the foreignness of the source text is an invariant that inheres in its lexicon and syntax, style and genre, theme and discourse, and it is this foreignness that the translator must reproduce or manifest by adhering closely to those textual features. Thus Schleiermacher describes what he calls "the true goal of all translation" as "the fullest possible unadulterated enjoyment of foreign works" and as "the most direct enjoyment of the works themselves," where "unadulterated" and "direct" indicate that the translator provides not an interpretation of the source text but rather unmediated access to that text (Schleiermacher 1813: 61). Berman similarly argues that a translation ought "to disclose [d'ouvrir] the Foreign as Foreign in its own linguistic space," whereby he draws on Martin Heidegger's concept of truth as the disclosure of "being" (Berman 1999: 75, where the phrase is italicized; see below: 186–87). The assumption of the instrumental model in Schleiermacher and Berman sets up an unexpected resemblance to the rather different thinking of theorists like Jerome and Eugene Nida, whose respective notions of "sense-for-sense" translation and "equivalent effect" continue to be widely influential (see Venuti 2012a: 483–85).

Such formulations posit an unchanging essence inherent in or produced by the source text and freely accessible to the translator, regardless of the time and place in which the translating occurs. Instrumentalism does not take into account the transformative difference that translation inscribes in the source text, the ratio of loss and gain that can be glimpsed only indirectly, in the terms of the translating language and culture (hence my recourse to a literary discourse like modernist experimentalism to make the translator's work visible). Any sense of foreignness communicated in a translation is never available in some direct or unmediated form; it is a construction that is always mediated by intelligibilities and interests in the receiving situation. The linguistic and cultural differences that make up a source text are inevitably diminished and altered, even when the translator maintains a fairly strict semantic correspondence, because that text is much more than any such correspondence: its distinctive linguistic features are the support of meanings, values, and functions specific to its originary culture, and these features do not survive intact, without variation, the move to a different language and culture. Instrumentalism is, in a word, a falsehood that cannot offer an incisive and comprehensive understanding of translation.

I began to develop a more rigorously conceived hermeneutic model that views translation as an interpretive act, as the inscription of one interpretive possibility among others. This model assumes that the source text, regardless of whether its genre or text type is humanistic, pragmatic, or technical, is radically variable in form, meaning, and effect. The extent of variation is always controlled by the materials used to interpret the source text and by the institutions where the translation is carried out. In the case of technical texts in law and science (e.g. contracts and patents, medical research and pharmaceutical treatises), it is only the routine application of idiomatic usage, standardized terminologies, and precisely defined functions that serves to limit or preempt variation by fixing the form and meaning of the source text. I subsequently redefined the remainder as the creation of a new context: a translation recontextualizes the source text in the translating language and culture by applying a set of formal and thematic interpretants to inscribe an interpretation. Following Jacques Derrida's concept of inscription, I saw the source text not only as coming to the translation process as always already interpreted, traced with a cultural discourse, but also as undergoing a further, perhaps divergent inscription when translated; following Charles Peirce's concept of interpretant, I saw the translation process as the application of formal and thematic mediators that perform the inscription, turning the source into the translated text (Venuti 2012a: 495–99). The inscription and the interpretant became the key factors in a hermeneutic model that eschews the German tradition of hermeneutics – notably the work of Heidegger and Hans-Georg Gadamer – where the aim is to disclose an essentialist meaning in the source text. The different model I began to imagine opens up the interpretive possibilities of translation, allowing them to vary with the nature of the interpretants applied by the translator but enabling the interpretations to be described and evaluated with clarity and precision in the conditions – linguistic and cultural, social and political – under which the translation is produced and circulated. The concepts of inscription and interpretant increase the explanatory power of the remainder by refining it, facilitating an exact account of the different effects that a translation releases in the receiving situation – an account that of course is itself an interpretation grounded on a reconstruction of the values, beliefs, and representations that define that situation.

Treating translation as an interpretive act in this more flexible approach led me to an ethical reflection that acknowledges the inevitable loss of source-cultural difference as well as the exorbitant gain of translating-cultural difference, a trade-off that exposes the creative possibilities of translation. To reformulate a translation ethics, I turned to Alain Badiou's notion of the "event," the emergence of an innovative form or practice that breaks with cultural and social institutions by pointing to a lack in them (Badiou 2001: 67; see below: 184–85). The translation that sets going an event introduces a linguistic and cultural difference in the institution, initiating new ways of thinking inspired by an interpretation of the source text. As a linguistic and cultural practice, furthermore, translation is unique in initiating events on an international scale, potentially affecting not only the hierarchy of values, beliefs, and representations in the receiving situation, but also the global hierarchy of symbolic capital that theorists like Pascale Casanova (following Pierre Bourdieu's sociology) see as structuring relations between national literary traditions (Casanova 2004).

Recovering history, textuality, and agency

Over the past two decades, translation studies has undergone a phenomenal growth as an academic field. Linguistics-oriented approaches remain prevalent in the *training* of translators, where their formidable analytical tools are used to devise solutions to translation problems that arise primarily with pragmatic and technical texts. Corpus linguistics in particular has proven useful in analyzing translated texts and in building databases to assist translators. Yet since 2000, as even a cursory survey of journal articles, edited volumes, and book-length studies makes clear, various forms of literary and cultural studies have come to dominate translation *research* around the world. The most productive approaches in terms of methodology and findings have been social in orientation.

Sociological theories, notably the cluster of concepts formulated by Bourdieu, have increasingly been applied in translation studies. This trend appeared first in franco-phone sites, Quebec and France, where such scholars as Jean-Marc Gouanvic and Gisèle Sapiro have researched the important place of translations in the French lit-erary field. The focus here is on large-scale or systemic trends, examining huge cor-pora of translations, tabulating publishing statistics, and considering the assimilation of specific genres into French literary traditions. Gouanvic (1999; 2007) has studied two genres of United States literature, science fiction and the realistic novel, translated into French during the twentieth century. Sapiro has taken up such issues as the extent to which translation patterns promote "linguistic and cultural diversity" and "indicate a tendency toward denationalizing literary production in the world market of translation" (Sapiro 2010: 313–18).

Within literary studies, a second, related trend has coincided with the reformulation of the Goethean concept of "world" literature by such scholars as Casanova and Franco Moretti. Here too the focus is systemic: translation is seen as internationalizing literary relations, which are structured hierarchically according to an uneven dis-tribution of symbolic capital among languages and literatures. World literature has also been treated as the production of a distinctive form of textuality (foreign form joined to local content) and as a mode of reception (an accrual of meanings as texts cross linguistic and cultural borders). Translation figures prominently in both prac-tices. Theorists of world literature have tended to avoid the close reading of texts for what Moretti calls "distant" reading, paying attention either to the transmission of micro features like tropes and themes or to the development of macro structures like genres and traditions (Moretti 2000: 56–58).

A third research trend is frankly political, advocating translation practices that are activist, intervening in social and military conflicts and advocating a particular side. Mona Baker's effort to isolate ideologically charged narratives embedded in transla-tions, working from a concept of narrative formulated by social and communication theorists, has given a strong impulse to this line of inquiry (Baker 2006). The difficulty that the translator faces in maintaining neutrality in conflictual situations has been illuminated by Moira Inghilleri's theoretically nuanced exploration of the ethical and political stakes involved in interpreting in asylum adjudication and in war zones (Inghilleri 2011). Using a similarly sophisticated approach, Vicente Rafael has traced the repressive history by which a uniform American English was enforced in order to understand the compromised position of Iraqi interpreters during the United States military occupation (Rafael 2009).

The social orientation of these trends has made a significant contribution to translation research, not only advancing the field but also attracting the attention of scholars outside of it. Nonetheless, their commanding influence has meant that certain areas have been studied much less, in some cases neglected entirely. This unevenness is all the more conspicuous because translation is a linguistic as well as a cultural practice that has given rise to long traditions of theory and commentary around the world. The areas that have received less scholarly attention include history, textuality, and agency.

The past decade has witnessed relatively few projects in which translations have been studied in specific cultural situations at specific historical moments, contextualized with the help of extensive archival research. The prevalence of sociological applications and the concern with activism, driven by continuing conflicts and cataclysmic events, have instilled a presentism in translation studies whereby the emphasis has been placed squarely on recent publishing practices, political tensions, and military struggles. On the whole, the leading research trends have shown little interest in translation theories and practices, or in texts generally, produced before the twentieth or twenty-first centuries. As a result, the use of the past not merely as a source of theoretical concepts and practical strategies but as a means of understanding and criticizing the present has been less and less pursued.

The nature of the translated text, so important for practice as for training, and the implications that translated textuality carries for reading and analyzing translations, so important for research and teaching, have not been studied much at all. Close readings of translations are explicitly excluded in some recent theories of world literature. Most importantly, the shift to systemic explanations grounded in sociological concepts has tended to suppress the text as a unit of analysis, sometimes deliberately so (see, for example, the rejection of "interpretative" approaches in Heilbron and Sapiro 2007: 93–95). The emphasis on narrative in the ideological critique of translations has not so much remedied the neglect of translated textuality as drastically limited the possible interpretants that might be applied both in translating and in analyzing translations. If "narrative theory," as Baker states, "allows us to piece together and analyze a narrative that is not fully traceable to any specific stretch of text but has to be constructed from a range of sources," that theory demands an aggressive interpretation of translated texts which excludes other theoretical and critical discourses (Baker 2006: 4). We still do not understand the cultural and social implications of the translator's verbal choices, and no consensus has developed as to how translations might be written and read or even what sort of communicative act translation is.

Without a historical sense of the translated text, produced and received in a particular culture at a particular period, our understanding of the translator's agency has been impoverished. The study of broad developments through notions of the cultural and social field and various forms of capital has considerably illuminated translation patterns, showing how intercultural relations are structured hierarchically, whether between individual linguistic communities or on a global scale. Yet that approach has occluded the role played by the translator's specific verbal choices in favor of treating networks of agents in institutions as most important in the circulation of translations.

In this respect, the repeated invocation of Bourdieu's concept of *habitus*, an embodied "system of cognitive and motivating structures" that generate practices in a field, has not brought a finer discrimination to the translator's actions (Bourdieu 1990: 52). On the contrary, the application of the concept in translation studies has been extremely reductive, perhaps because the concept itself oversimplifies human behavior. Thus Gouanvic asserts that

> Translation as a practice has little to do with conforming to norms through the deliberate use of specific strategies; in other words, it is not a question of consciously choosing from a panoply of available solutions. Norms do not explain the more or less subjective and random choices made by translators who are free to translate or not to translate, to follow or not to follow the original closely. If a translator imposes a rhythm upon the text, a lexicon or a syntax that does not originate in the source text and thus substitutes his or her voice for that of the author, this is essentially not a conscious strategic choice but an effect of his or her specific *habitus*, as acquired in the target literary field.
>
> *(Gouanvic 2005: 157–58)*

Gouanvic is right to distinguish translation norms from conscious deliberation: norms are more likely to be dominant linguistic and cultural values that the translator learns and applies in a manner that is preconscious or unconscious, and therefore they may be assimilated to the Bourdieusian *habitus* (see below: 54). Yet to assume that the translator's verbal choices or strategies *all* lack deliberation or intentionality, as the reliance on the *habitus* implies ("The *habitus* is a spontaneity without consciousness or will" [Bourdieu 1990: 56]), betrays an utter lack of familiarity with the act of translation, with the myriad choices made during the composition of any literary translation. Gouanvic has in effect collapsed the translator into the literary field, although not without contradiction. The translator may indeed choose to impose a rhythm, lexicon, or syntax, but because such linguistic and literary forms are likely to be selected from the resources available in a literary field, they can be considered transindividual elements which can hardly be identified with an individual voice. In the end, the recourse to the *habitus* strips the translator's agency of the full complexity of human behavior, which encompasses not only intended actions but also a self-reflexive monitoring in relation to rules and resources (e.g. translation norms), not only a degree of consciousness but also an unconscious composed of unacknowledged conditions and unanticipated consequences (cf. Giddens 1979: chapter 2; see chapters 2 and 5).

Essaying a new approach

The fourteen essays that follow try to profit from concurrent research trends but tacitly take them in more productive directions by compensating for their limitations as I have defined them. Using a reconceived hermeneutic model as their base, the essays maintain the social and political orientation in translation studies, a feature of my work from the very beginning, while theorizing the translator's agency and the translated text in case studies that reconstruct the contexts of production and reception. My assumption has been that translation studies must work to link the social and the textual so as to advance, but that this link must be rooted in the concept of translation as an interpretive act.

The essays should not be read, however, as building a coherent argument in a sequence of chapters. They are rather essays in the strong sense of the word, discrete attempts to develop a recurrent set of theoretical concepts and to consider their practical implications. Hence each essay stages a different argument through the examination of various cases, and key concepts are formulated more than once, restated with differences that suit the changing contexts. Although the arrangement is chronological (the date of first publication appears within square brackets at the end of each text), the essays can be read individually, apart from any chronology. But if the reader chooses to proceed in chronological order, an intellectual trajectory emerges: a movement away from instrumentalism towards a hermeneutic model of translation, an abandonment of the remainder and an adoption of the inscription and the interpretant, and a rethinking of the ethics of respect which argues that the most decisive way for a translation to show respect is to make the source text the ground of an ethics of innovation in the translating culture.

Throughout, I have lost no opportunity to worry the questionable distinction between translation theory and practice, whether that practice is research or translating. In "The Name and Nature of Translation Studies" (1972), an essay that has been viewed as instituting the field but has come to be criticized as limited, James Holmes unfortunately divides research into three categories, "descriptive," "theoretical," and "applied" (Holmes 1988: 71, 77; see Chesterman 2009). He finally acknowledges that these "branches" are not as "distinct" as he makes them seem because the relations between them are "dialectical" or mutually determining (Holmes 1988: 78). He explains:

> Translation theory, for instance, cannot do without the solid, specific data yielded by research in descriptive and applied translation studies, while on the other hand one cannot even begin to work in one of the other fields without having at least an intuitive theoretical hypothesis as one's starting point.
>
> *(Ibid.)*

Here Holmes makes the empiricist assumption that knowledge is merely given to observation rather than constructed on the basis of theoretical concepts. Thus descriptive and applied research are said to supply "solid, specific data" from which theories are inferred: Holmes's model is scientific, deploying the inductive method. Not only is theoretical speculation reduced to a "hypothesis," but Holmes also seems not to have recognized that a conceptual basis is necessary even to determine which textual features, translation strategies, and pedagogical practices can be classified as data. In treating translation theory as derived from empirical fact, he shows no awareness that the same data can be processed with – and in support of – differing theories. Nor could he have anticipated subsequent developments in translation studies: over the past half-century, most of the theoretical discourses that have informed research have come from outside the field, mainly from such disciplines as linguistics, philosophy, and literary and cultural studies.

A similar sort of empiricism can be perceived in translators' comments about their work, where it devolves into an antipathy towards theory. A recent interview with Jonathan Galassi is especially pertinent since his work straddles so many cultural practices: he is a poet, a translator of Italian poetry, and the president and publisher of perhaps the most distinguished literary press in the United States, Farrar, Straus and Giroux. To the question "Are there particular types of translations or ways of thinking about translation that you're not interested in or find antithetical to your approach?" Galassi responded:

> I'm afraid I'm not very interested in the theoretical aspects of translation. I think that it's really a hands-on artistic practice – of course there's the business of translation, the economic business of it, but that doesn't really enter into what we're talking about. We're talking about vocational work here – the extension of the poet's work via an engagement with another writer in another language. And it's a really interesting question you're asking me. I think Mark Strand is a very wonderful translator. He has some of the same ability that [Elizabeth] Bishop has. His style is so cool that again, it's like looking through water.
>
> *(Fitzgerald 2012)*

Despite Galassi's demurral about translation theory, his response rests on certain assumptions about poetry translation, and I would call these assumptions a definite theory. He values not only the work of poets whose poetry informs the style of their translations, but a particular poetics that he finds in Strand and Bishop. Just before this response, Galassi had praised Bishop's translations of Brazilian poetry: "I would say that the limpidity of her own writing comes through in her translations really very beautifully. It's like seeing something through very clear water" (ibid.). This image of transparency points to Ezra Pound's modernist poetics, which he developed partly through his translations. In his essay "Cavalcanti" (1928), Pound indicates the linguistic features that attracted him to the work of the thirteenth-century Italian poet Guido Cavalcanti:

> We have lost the radiant world where one thought cuts through another with clean edge, a world of moving energies *"mezzo oscuro rade,"* *"risplende in sé*

> *perpetuale effecto*," magnetisms that take form, that are seen, or that border the
> visible, the matter of Dante's *Paradiso*, the glass under water, the form that
> seems a form seen in a mirror, those realities perceptible to the sense, […]
>
> *(Anderson 1983: 208)*

"The glass under water": the resemblance to Galassi's comment is remarkable. Following Pound's example, Galassi's translation theory evidently assumes modernist philosophical and poetic values like logical positivism and linguistic precision, perhaps ultimately the empiricist notion of language as direct expression and reference.

The thinking about translation that I would like to encourage is suspicious of any attempt to draw a sharp distinction between theory and practice. No practice of any kind can occur without theoretical concepts; every practice is at once enabled and constrained by assumptions that may remain unexpressed or unthought, but that nonetheless constitute the immediate conditions that make possible that practice. In the case of translation, the categories of "theory" and "practice" are closely interrelated and reciprocal in their effects. Innovative research in translation, whether theoretically or historically oriented, can lead to new translation practices, at once inspiring and justifying different ways to translate, while innovative practices, whether spurred by a specific cultural situation, the appearance of a unique text type, or the invention of a communications medium, can lead to new theoretical concepts and research. Without a theoretically based self-consciousness, translation research and practice remain incapable of developing their methods and of submitting their projects to a probing critique.

Finally, a word about my title. It points to a basic assumption that underlies every essay and is realized in the case studies: translation carries the potential to bring about multiple transformations. Translation changes the form, meaning, and effect of the source text, even when the translator maintains a semantic correspondence that creates a reliable basis for summaries and commentaries. Translation changes the cultural situation where the source text originated through an investment of prestige or a creation of stereotypes. Translation changes the receiving cultural situation by bringing into existence something new and different, a text that is neither the source text nor an original composition in the translating language, and in the process it changes the values, beliefs, and representations that are housed in institutions. Translation deals in contingencies open to variation. To cling to an instrumental model of translation, to insist on the existence of a source invariant, to suppress the translator's interpretation, and to neglect the cultural situation to which it responds must ultimately rest, then, on a fear of change.

1

TRANSLATION, COMMUNITY, UTOPIA

An antinomy in theory

Even though no one seems likely to deny that communication is the primary aim and function of a translated text, today we are far from thinking that translating is a simple communicative act. In contemporary translation theory informed by Continental philosophical traditions such as existential phenomenology and poststructuralism, language is constitutive of thought, and meaning a site of multiple determinations, so that translating is readily seen as investing the source text with a significance that is specific to the translating language and culture (see, for example, Heidegger 1975; Lewis 1985; Benjamin 1989). A translation never communicates in an untroubled fashion because the translator negotiates the linguistic and cultural differences of the source text by reducing them and supplying another set of differences drawn from the receiving situation to enable the translation to circulate there. The source text, then, is not so much communicated as domesticated or, more precisely, assimilated to receiving intelligibilities and interests through an inscription. This inscription begins with the very choice of a text for translation, always a very selective, densely moti- vated choice, and continues in the development of discursive strategies to translate it, always a choice of certain receiving discourses over others. Hence the inscription is totalizing, even if never total, never seamless or final. It can be said to operate in every word of the translated text long before that text is further processed by readers, made to bear other meanings and to serve other interests in the receiving situation.

Seen as domesticating inscription, never quite cross-cultural communication, translation has moved theorists towards an ethical reflection wherein remedies are formulated to signal the foreignness of the source text, what makes it linguistically and culturally different in relation to the receiving situation (see, for example, Berman 1999 and Venuti 1998). Yet an ethics that counters the domesticating effects of the inscription can only be formulated and practiced primarily in *domestic* terms, in the dialects, registers, discourses, and styles of the translating language and culture. And this means that the linguistic and cultural differences of the source text can only be signaled indirectly, by their displacement in the translation, through differences introduced into values and institutions in the receiving situation. This ethical attitude is therefore simultaneous with a political agenda: the domestic terms of the inscription become the focus of rewriting in the translation, the development of discursive strategies through which the hierarchies that rank receiving values are disarranged to set going processes of defamiliarization, canon reformation, ideological critique, and institutional change. A translator may find that the very concept of the domestic merits interrogation for its concealment of heterogeneity and hybridity, which can complicate existing stereotypes, canons, and standards applied in translation.

When motivated by this ethical politics of difference, the translator seeks to build a community with foreign cultures, to share an understanding with and of them and to collaborate on projects founded on that understanding, going so far as to allow it to revise and develop receiving values and institutions. The very impulse to seek a community abroad suggests that the translator wishes to extend or complete a particular receiving situation, to compensate for a defect in the translating language and culture. As Maurice Blanchot argues, the very notion of community arises when an insufficiency puts individual agency into question (Blanchot 1988: 56). The ethically and politically motivated translator cannot fail to see the lack of an equal footing in the translation process, stimulated by an interest in the foreign, but inescapably leaning towards the receptor. Such a translator knows that a translation can never simply communicate a foreign text because it makes possible only a domesticated understanding of that text, however much defamiliarized, however much subversive or supportive of the domestic.

In the absence of cross-cultural communication unaffected by receiving intelligibilities and interests, what kinds of communities can translation possibly foster? What communities can be based on the domestic inscription of the foreign that limits and redirects the communicative aim of translation?

Communication in translation

In the 1970s, the formalist theorist Gideon Toury tried to define translation as a communicative act while acknowledging the receiving values that come into play, the target norms that constrain communication. Translation, he wrote,

> is *communication in translated messages* within a certain cultural-linguistic system, with all relevant consequences for the decomposition of the source message, the establishment of the invariant, its transfer across the cultural-linguistic border and the recomposition of the target message.
>
> *(Toury 1980: 17, his emphasis)*

"The establishment of the invariant": if communication in translation is defined as the transmission of an invariant, does not the very need to establish the invariant mean that translating does something more and perhaps other than communicate? The source message is always interpreted and reinvented, especially in cultural forms open to interpretation, such as literary texts, philosophical treatises, film subtitling, advertising copy, conference papers, legal testimony. How can the source message ever be invariant if it undergoes a process of "establishment" in a "certain" target language and culture? It is always reconstructed according to different sets of values and always variable according to different languages and cultures. Toury ultimately reckoned with the problem of communication by sidestepping it altogether: he shifted the emphasis away from exploring a relation of equivalence between the translation and the source text and instead focused on the acceptability of the translation in the target culture. Thinking about the foreign is thus preempted in favor of research that describes receiving cultural norms.

But let us pursue this preempted line of enquiry. What formal and thematic features of a novel, for instance, can be described as invariant in the translation process? Since canons of accuracy vary according to culture and historical moment, definitions of what constitutes the invariant will likewise vary. Let us ask the question of current translation practices. Today, translators of novels into most languages seek to maintain unchanged the basic elements of narrative form. The plot isn't rewritten to alter events or their sequence. And none of the characters' actions is deleted or revised. Dates, historical and geographical markers, the characters' names – even when the names are rather complicated and foreign-sounding – these are generally not altered or only in rare cases (e.g. Russian names). Contemporary canons of accuracy are based on an adequacy to the source text: an accurate translation of a novel must not only reproduce the basic elements of narrative form, but should also do so in roughly the same number of pages.

In 1760, however, Abbé Prévost claimed that accuracy governed his French version of Samuel Richardson's *Pamela* even though he reduced the seven English volumes to four in French. "I have not changed anything pertaining to the author's intention," the Abbé asserted, "nor have I changed much in the manner in which he put that intention into words" (Lefevere 1992: 39). To us, such statements don't merely substitute a different canon of accuracy (founded on notions of authorial intention and style); they also seem to exceed the very practice of translation. Prévost's text involved abridgement and adaptation as well.

In current practices, a translation of a novel can and must communicate the basic elements of narrative form that structure the source text. But it is still not true that these elements are free from variation. Any language use is likely to vary the standard dialect by sampling a diversity of nonstandard or minor formations: regional or group dialects, jargons, clichés and slogans, stylistic innovations, archaisms, neologisms. Jean-Jacques Lecercle calls these variations the "remainder" because they exceed communication of a univocal meaning and instead draw attention to the conditions of the communicative act, conditions that are in the first instance linguistic and cultural, but that ultimately embrace social and political factors (Lecercle 1990). The remainder in literary texts is much more complicated, of course, usually a sedimentation of forms and themes, past as well as present (Jameson 1981: 140–41).

Any communication through translating, then, will involve the release of a domestic remainder, especially in the case of literature. The source text is rewritten in domestic dialects and discourses, registers and styles, which produce textual effects that signify only in the history of the translating language and culture. The translator may produce these effects to communicate the source text, trying to invent analogues for its forms and themes. But the result will always go beyond any communication to release target-oriented possibilities of meaning.

Consider a recent English translation of an Italian novel, *Declares Pereira*, Patrick Creagh's 1995 version of Antonio Tabucchi's *Sostiene Pereira* (1994). Creagh's English consists mostly of the current standard dialect. But he cultivated a noticeable strain of colloquialism that sometimes veers into underworld argot. He rendered "taceva" ("silent") as "gagged," "quattro uomini dall'aria sinistra" ("four men with a sinister air") as "four shady-looking characters," "stare con gli occhi aperti" ("stay with your eyes open") as "keep your eyes peeled," "un personaggio del regime" ("a figure in the regime") as "bigwig," "senza pigiama" ("without pyjamas") as "in his birthday-suit," and "va a dormire" ("go to sleep") as "beddy-byes" (Tabucchi 1994: 13, 19, 43, 73, 108, 196; 1995: 5, 9, 25, 45, 67, 127). Creagh also mixed in some distinctively British words and phrases. He rendered "orrendo" ("horrible") as "bloody awful," "una critica molto negativa" ("a very negative criticism") as "slating," "pensioncina" ("little boarding house") as "little doss-house," "sono nei guai" ("I'm in trouble") as "I'm in a pickle," "parlano" ("they talk") as "natter," and "a vedere" ("to look") as "to take a dekko" (Tabucchi 1994: 80, 81, 84, 104, 176; 1995: 50, 51, 54, 64, 115).

Within parentheses I have inserted alternative renderings to highlight the range and inventiveness of Creagh's translating. The alternatives should not be regarded as somehow more accurate than his choices. In each case, both renderings establish a lexicographical equivalence, a semantic correspondence to the Italian words and phrases according to dictionary definitions. Creagh's choices communicate meanings that can be called "invariant" only insofar as they are reduced to a basic meaning shared by both the Italian and the English.

Creagh's translation, however, varies this meaning. The variation might be called a "shift" as that concept has been developed in translation studies since the 1960s (see, for example, Catford 1965; Blum-Kulka 1986; Toury 1995). If Creagh's English is juxtaposed to Tabucchi's Italian, lexical shifts can indeed be detected, shifts in register from the current standard dialect of Italian to various colloquial dialects in British and American English. In response to my queries, Creagh admitted that "some phrases are more colloquial in English than in Italian," making clear that his shifts are not required by structural differences between the two languages, but rather motivated by literary and cultural aims: "I even tried," Creagh stated, "to use only idioms that would have been current in 1938," the period of the novel, "and to hand them to the right speaker, to make slight linguistic differences between the characters" (correspondence: 8 December 1998).

Yet the notion of a shift does not entirely describe the textual effects set going by Creagh's choices. His translation signifies beyond his literary and cultural intentions by releasing a peculiarly English remainder: the different dialects and registers establish a relation to English literary styles, genres, and traditions. In terms of generic distinctions, Tabucchi's novel is a political thriller. Set under the Portuguese dictator António de Oliveira Salazar, it recounts how one Pereira, the aging cultural editor of a Lisbon newspaper, is slowly radicalized over a few weeks, which climax when he prints an attack on the fascist regime. Creagh's polylingual mixture of standard and colloquial, British and American, gives his prose an extremely conversational quality that is consistent with Tabucchi's presentation of the thriller plot: Pereira's narrative takes an oral form, an official testimony to an unnamed authority (hence the curious title). Yet the slangy English also alters the characterization of Pereira by suggesting that he is less staid and perhaps younger than the elderly journalist presented in the Italian text.

At the same time, the British and American slang refers to moments in the history of English-language fiction – for the informed reader of that fiction. It can recall thrillers that address similar political themes, notably such novels of Graham Greene as *The Confidential Agent* (1939), which, like Tabucchi's, is set during the Spanish Civil War and involves an attempt to aid the Republican side against Franco. If this literary reference is recognized, Creagh's translation in effect invites the reader to distinguish between Tabucchi's leftwing opposition to fascism and Greene's more cautious liberalism (Diemert 1996: 180–81). Greene saw his thrillers as "entertainments" engaged in social and political issues, designed "not to change things but to give them expression" (Allain 1983: 81). The linguistic resemblances between Creagh's translation and Greene's novel highlight the ideological differences that distinguish Tabucchi's and Greene's treatments of the same historical event.

Thus although Creagh's translation can be said to communicate the form and theme of Tabucchi's novel, neither of these features escapes the variations introduced by the inscription of an English-language remainder. The remainder does not just inscribe a set of linguistic and cultural differences specific to the receiving situation; it also supplies the loss of the differences that constituted the source text. The loss occurs, as Alasdair MacIntyre observes, because in any "tradition-bearing community" the "language-in-use is closely tied to the expression of the shared beliefs of that tradition," and this gives a "historical dimension" to languages which often fails to survive the translating process (MacIntyre 1988: 384). MacIntyre argues that this problem of untranslatability is most acute with "the internationalized languages-in-use in late twentieth-century modernity," like English, which "have minimal presuppositions in respect of possibly rival belief systems" and so will "neutralize" the historical dimension of the source text (ibid.). In English translation, therefore,

> a kind of text which cannot be read as *the text it is* out of context is nevertheless rendered contextless. But in so rendering it, it is turned into a text which is no longer the author's, nor such as would be recognized by the audience to whom it was addressed.
>
> *(Ibid.: 385, his emphasis)*

Creagh's translation at once inscribed an English-language cultural history in Tabucchi's novel and displaced the historical dimension of the Italian text. This text occupies a place in a narrative tradition that includes resistance novels during and after the Second World War, as well as novels about life under fascism, Alberto Moravia's *Il conformista* (1951; *The Conformist*), for instance, and Giorgio Bassani's *Il giardino dei Finzi-Contini* (1962; *The Garden of the Finzi-Continis*). The very fact that Italian history contains a fascist tradition ensured that Tabucchi's readers would understand the Salazarist regime in distinctively Italian terms, not merely as an allusion to Mussolini's dictatorship, but as an allegory of current events. *Sostiene Pereira* was written in 1993 and published the following year, when a center-right coalition gained power in Italy with the election victory of Silvio Berlusconi's Forza Italia movement. As Tabucchi himself said of his novel, "those who didn't love the Italian political situation took it as a symbol of resistance from within" (Cotroneo 1995: 105, my translation). Invested with this peculiarly Italian significance, *Sostiene Pereira* sold 300,000 copies within a year of publication.

Although favorably received by British and American reviewers, Creagh's translation hardly became a bestseller. Within two years of publication, the American edition published by New Directions sold 5,000 copies. Creagh maintained a lexicographical equivalence, but the remainder in his translation was insufficient to restore the cultural and political history that made the novel so resonant for Italian readers, as well as readers in other European countries with similar histories, such as Spain.

Communication through inscription

Can a translation ever communicate to its readers an understanding of the source text that is available to readers who are natives of the source culture or at least proficient in its language and conversant with its forms and practices? Yes, I want to argue, but this communication will always be partial, both incomplete and inevitably slanted towards the receiving situation. It occurs only when the domestic remainder released by the translation includes an inscription of the cultural context in which the source text first emerged.

The form of communication at work here is second-order, built upon but signifying beyond a lexicographical equivalence, encompassing but exceeding what Walter Benjamin called "message," "information" or "content" (Benjamin 1923: 75). "Translations that are more than transmissions of a message," Benjamin wrote, "are produced when a work, in its continuing life, has reached the age of its fame" (ibid.: 77). I understand the term "fame" to mean the overall reception of a literary text, not only in its own language and culture, but also in the languages of the cultures that have translated it, and not only the judgments of reviewers at home and abroad, but also the interpretations of literary historians and critics and the images that an internationally famous text may come to bear in other cultural forms and practices, both elite and mass. A translation of a novel can communicate, not simply dictionary meanings, not simply the basic elements of narrative form, but an interpretation that participates in its "basically eternal continuing life in later generations" (ibid.). And this interpretation can be one that is shared by the source-language readers for whom the text was written. The translation will then foster a common understanding with and of the source culture, an understanding that in part restores the historical context of the source text – although for readers in a different language and culture.

Take, for example, Camus's novel *L'Étranger* (1942). As Camus himself acknowledged, the peculiarities of style, plot, and characterization that distinguish the French text were derived from American fiction during the early twentieth century, especially the writing of Ernest Hemingway, but more generally the hardboiled or toughguy prose of writers like James M. Cain. The stylistic features of Matthew Ward's 1988 translation, *The Stranger*, make this intertextual connection for the English-language reader much more effectively than Stuart Gilbert's 1946 version. The differences are apparent on the opening page:

> Aujourd'hui, maman est morte. Ou peut-être hier, je ne sais pas. J'ai reçu un télégramme de l'asile: "Mère décédée. Enterrement demain. Sentiments distingués." Cela ne veut rien dire. C'était peut-être hier.
>
> L'asile de vieillards est à Marengo, à quatre-vingts kilomètres d'Alger. Je prendrai l'autobus à deux heures et j'arriverai dans l'après-midi. Ainsi, je pourrai veiller et je rentrerai demain soir. J'ai demandé deux jours de congé à mon patron et il ne pouvait pas me les refuser avec une excuse pareille. Mais il n'avait pas l'air content. Je lui ai même dit: "Ce n'est pas de ma faute." Il n'a pas répondu. J'ai pensé alors que je n'aurais pas dû lui dire cela. En somme, je n'avais pas à m'excuser. C'était plutôt à lui de présenter ses condoléances. Mais il le fera sans doute après-demain, quand il me verra en deuil. Pour le moment, c'est un peu comme si maman n'était pas morte. Après l'enterrement, au contraire, ce sera une affaire classé et tout aura revêtu une allure plus officielle.
>
> *(Camus 1942: 1)*

> Mother died today. Or, maybe, yesterday; I can't be sure. The telegram from the Home says: YOUR MOTHER PASSED AWAY. FUNERAL TOMORROW. DEEP SYMPATHY. Which leaves the matter doubtful; it could have been yesterday.
>
> The Home for Aged Persons is at Marengo, some fifty miles from Algiers. With the two o'clock bus I should get there well before nightfall. Then I can spend the night there, keeping the usual vigil beside the body, and be back here tomorrow evening.
>
> I have fixed up with my employer for two days' leave; obviously, under the circumstances, he couldn't refuse. Still, I had an idea he looked annoyed, and I said, without thinking: "Sorry, sir, but it's not my fault, you know."
>
> Afterwards it struck me I needn't have said that. I had no reason to excuse myself; it was up to him to express his sympathy and so forth. Probably he will do so the day after tomorrow, when he sees me in black. For the present, it's almost as if Mother weren't really dead. The funeral will bring it home to me, put an official seal on it, so to speak.
>
> *(Camus 1946: 1–2)*

Maman died today. Or yesterday maybe, I don't know. I got a telegram from the home: "Mother deceased. Funeral tomorrow. Faithfully yours." That doesn't mean anything. Maybe it was yesterday.

The old people's home is at Marengo, about eighty kilometers from Algiers. I'll take the two o'clock bus and get there in the afternoon. That way I can be there for the vigil and come back tomorrow night. I asked my boss for two days off and there was no way he was going to refuse me with an excuse like that. But he wasn't too happy about it. I even said, "It's not my fault." He didn't say anything. Then I thought I shouldn't have said that. After all, I didn't have anything to apologize for. He's the one who should have offered his condolences. But he probably will day after tomorrow, when he sees I'm in mourning. For now, it's almost as if Maman weren't dead. After the funeral, though, the case will be closed, and everything will have a more official feel to it.

(Camus 1988: 3)

The English in both versions is cast in a fairly colloquial register, but once they are juxtaposed, the differences begin to proliferate. Gilbert translated freely. He added words for clarification, expanding "je pourrai veiller" ("I shall be able to keep vigil") into "I can spend the night there, keeping the usual vigil beside the body." He revised and softened the abruptness of the French phrasing, turning "Cela ne veut rien dire" ("That does not mean anything") into "Which leaves the matter doubtful." And he endowed his prose with a formality and politeness, rendering "maman" as "Mother," "patron" as "employer," and "Ce n'est pas de ma faute" as "Sorry, sir, but it's not my fault, you know." Ward, in sharp contrast, translated closely. He reproduced the lexical and syntactical peculiarities of the French, departing from Gilbert not only by making choices like "Maman" and "boss," but also by adhering to Camus's brief, precise sentences: "That doesn't mean anything," "It's not my fault." As a result, Ward endowed his prose with a familiarity and directness. Where Gilbert resorted to phrases like "two days' leave" ("deux jours de congé"), "Home for Aged Persons" ("l'asile de viellards"), and "I had no reason to excuse myself" ("je n'avais pas à m'excuser"), Ward used "two days off," "old people's home," and "I didn't have anything to apologize for." Ward himself described the difference between the two versions as dialectal: he called Gilbert's a "'Britannic' rendering" and saw his own as "giving the text a more 'American' quality" (Camus 1988: v–vi). And Ward knew that he was drawing a cultural difference as well, releasing a literary remainder that leads the English-language reader to an American narrative tradition, to "Hemingway, Dos Passos, Faulkner, Cain" (ibid.).

Gilbert's version, even though free in places, established a lexicographical equivalence that does in fact transmit the distinctive plot and characterization of Camus's novel. Hence his translation can also enable English-language readers to perceive the American literary origins of the French text even when they don't know its larger French context. The leading American critic Edmund Wilson reviewed Gilbert's version for the *New Yorker* the year it was published, offering a remarkable account of his response. He knew that Camus was "one of the principal exponents in literature of what is called the Existentialist philosophy," but he immediately added a confession of ignorance: "I have read very little of Sartre and nothing by Camus but this novel, and I am entirely unfamiliar with the philosophical background of their writing" (Wilson 1946: 99). Because of his limited knowledge Wilson headed straight for what was familiar and emphasized the domestic reference in Gilbert's translation: "One feels sure," he wrote, "that M. Camus must have been reading such American novels as 'The Postman Always Rings Twice'." And this reference ultimately prompted an unfavorable comparison. Wilson judged *The Stranger* as a failed imitation of Cain's novel, not as a French narrative that used American forms to explore European philosophical themes. The absence of the foreign context was supplied by the realism that has long dominated the American narrative tradition, so that Camus's main character was dismissed as "incredible; his behavior is never explained or made plausible" (ibid.).

Ward was fortunate in having a better-informed readership: he could rely on some four decades of literary criticism and history during which *L'Étranger* was studied, taught, and admitted to the canon of contemporary world literature – in the United States as well as in many countries worldwide. Gilbert's version undoubtedly helped the novel to achieve this status for English-language readers, but not until Ward's was there a translation that produced a stylistic analogue for Camus's experiment, a heterogeneous mix of linguistic and cultural forms, both American and French. In this way, Ward's version communicated an understanding of the French text that is available to French readers. This understanding motivated his decision, for example, to retain the French "Maman" in the opening sentence:

> In his notebooks Camus recorded the observation that "the curious feeling the son has for his mother constitutes *all* his sensibility." And Sartre, in his "Explication de *L'Étranger*," goes out of his way to point out Meursault's use of the child's word "Maman" when speaking of his mother. To use the more removed, adult "Mother" is, I believe, to change the nature of Meursault's curious feeling for her.
>
> *(Camus 1988: vii)*

Ward's writing released a remainder that inscribed American and French references, and for the English-language reader the result was truly defamiliarizing. Not only did American narrative forms acquire a philosophical density they did not possess in the American writers who used them, but also Gilbert's version was deprived of its authority as an interpretation of the French text. This was evident in a brief but appreciative notice that appeared, appropriately enough, in the *New Yorker*:

> The effect of the closer, simpler rendering is to make Meursault seem even stranger – more alien and diffident – than the explanatory confider of the British version. He becomes not so much an exponent of illusionless hedonism as a psychological study who is brought, through a gratuitous, sun-dazzled act

and its merciless social consequences, to a rapport with his dead mother and a recognition of his fraternity with "the gentle indifference of the world" – a palpable improvement upon Gilbert's grander phrase "the benign indifference of the universe."

(New Yorker 1988: 119)

The "improvement," judging from this anonymous reviewer's response, involved an increased plausibility. Ward gave Camus's character the psychological realism that Wilson found lacking in Gilbert, although for a later American readership. Ward's translation was more acceptable to his readers, partly because they knew more about French literature and philosophy, but also because of his writing: his style was more evocative of American and French cultural forms and therefore more communicative of the French text.

Heterogeneous communities

The domestic inscription in translating constitutes a unique communicative act, however indirect or wayward. It creates a community of interest around the translated text in the receiving situation, an audience to whom it is intelligible and who put it to various uses. This shared interest may arise spontaneously when the translation is published, attracting readers from different constituencies that already exist in the translating language and culture. It may also be housed in an institution where the translation is made to perform different functions, academic or religious, cultural or political, commercial or municipal. Any community that arises around a translation is far from homogeneous in language, identity, or social position. Its heterogeneity might best be understood in terms of what Mary Louise Pratt calls a "linguistics of contact," in which language-based communities are seen as decentered across "lines of social differentiation" (Pratt 1987: 60). A translation is a linguistic "zone of contact" between the source and translating cultures, but also within the latter.

The interests that bind the community through a translation are not simply focused on the source text, but reflected in the receiving values, beliefs, and representations that the translator inscribes in it. And these interests are further determined by the ways that the translation is used. In the case of source texts that have achieved canonical status in an institution, a translation becomes the site of interpretive communities that may support or challenge current canons and interpretations, prevailing standards and ideologies (cf. Fish 1980 and the criticisms in Pratt 1986: 46–52). In the case of source texts that have achieved mass circulation, a translation becomes the site of unexpected groupings, fostering communities of readers who would otherwise be separated by cultural differences and social divisions yet are now joined by a common fascination. A translation can answer to the interests of a diverse range of audiences, so that the forms of reception will not be entirely commensurable. Because translating traffics in the foreign, in the introduction of linguistic and cultural differences, it is equally capable of crossing or reinforcing the boundaries between domestic audiences and the hierarchies in which they are positioned. If the domestic inscription includes part of the social or historical context in which the source text first emerged, then a translation can also create a community that includes source intelligibilities and interests, an understanding in common with another culture, another tradition.

Consider the readerships that gather around a poetry translation. In 1958, the American translator Allen Mandelbaum published the first book-length English version of the modern Italian poet Giuseppe Ungaretti. It was warmly welcomed by Italian academic specialists at American universities, some of whom were themselves Italian natives. The reviewer for the journal *Comparative Literature*, Giovanni Cecchetti, wrote his review in Italian and concluded that Mandelbaum's translation "does honor to Italian studies in America and can be recommended to anyone who wishes to familiarize himself with the work of one of the major poets of our time" (Cecchetti 1959: 268, my translation). The "our" suggests the extent of Cecchetti's esteem for Ungaretti's poetry, an assertion of universal value. But since he was reviewing in Italian the first English translation of that poetry, the "our" couldn't be universal because it didn't yet include British and American readers lacking Italian. Cecchetti imagined a community that was partly actual, academic or professional, and partly potential, anglophone readers of poetry.

The Ungaretti project also applied a standard of accuracy consistent with the interpretation that prevailed in the Italian academic community. Mandelbaum maintained a fairly strict lexicographical equivalence and even imitated Ungaretti's syntax and line breaks. He read Ungaretti's achievement, like the Italian scholars, as an effort "to bury the cadaver of literary Italian" by developing a spare, precise poetic language devoid of "all that was but ornament" (Ungaretti 1958: xi). It was in these terms that the reviewers judged Mandelbaum's versions successful. "If one is tempted to observe that in many places the translation is too literal," wrote Carlo Golino, "further reflection will show that it would have been impossible to do otherwise and still retain the rich allusiveness of Ungaretti's words" (Golino 1959: 76).

Mandelbaum's translation was thus the site of an academic community's interest in Ungaretti's poetry, an American readership that nonetheless shared an Italian understanding of the text and in fact included Italian natives. In this context, the translation ultimately achieved canonical status. In 1975, almost two decades after its first publication, it was reissued in a revised and expanded edition from Cornell University Press.

All the same, it is possible to perceive an appeal to another community in Mandelbaum's translation, a domestic readership that is incommensurable with the interests of the Italian academics and the prevailing interpretation of Ungaretti. While Mandelbaum adhered closely to the terse fragmentation of Ungaretti's Italian texts, he also introduced a poetical register, a noticeable strain of Victorian poeticism. Mandelbaum rendered "morire" ("die") as "perish," "buttato" ("thrown") as "cast," "ti basta un'illusione" ("an illusion is enough for you") as "you need but an illusion," "sonno" ("sleep") as "slumber," "riposato" ("rested") as "reposed," "potrò guardarla" ("I can watch her") as "I can gaze upon her" (Ungaretti 1958: 7, 13, 25, 37, 145). He used syntactical inversions: some were added, while others were the results of literal translating, calques of the Italian. Both kinds amounted to poetical archaisms in English:

Lontano
Lontano lontano
come un cieco
m'hanno portato per mano.

Distantly
Distantly distantly
like a blind man
by the hand they led me.

Una Colomba
D'altri diluvi una colomba ascolto.

A Dove
Of other floods I hear a dove.

(Ungaretti 1958: 35, 53)

Sometimes the poeticism deviated from the otherwise simple language of the context, as in the last six lines of "Giugno" ("June"):

Ho perso il sonno

Oscillo
al canto d'una strada
come una lucciola

Mi morirò
questa notte?

I have lost slumber

Sway
at a street–corner
like a firefly

Will this night die
from me?

(Ungaretti 1958: 39)

On other occasions the poetical register swells with a lush Romanticism, usually to match a more expansive poetic line in Ungaretti. Compare Mandelbaum's version of the Virgilian sestina, "Recitativo di Palinurno," with Tennyson's "Ulysses." Both English texts were written in an Elizabethan pentameter (Shakespearean, Marlovian) pitched at an epic height:

> Per l'uragano all'apice di furia
> Vicino non intesi farsi il sonno;
> Olio fu dilagante a smanie d'onde,
> Aperto campo a libertà di pace,
> Di effusione infinita il finto emblema
> Dalla nuca prostrandomi mortale.

> I could not, for the hurricane at fury's
> Summit, sense the coming-on of slumber;
> An oil that overspread the raving breakers,
> Field open to the freedom that is peace,
> Of infinite outpouring the feigned emblem
> Thrusting at the nape downdashed me mortal.

> *(Ungaretti 1958: 145)*

> I cannot rest from travel: I will drink
> Life to the lees: all times I have enjoyed
> Greatly, have suffered greatly, both with those
> That loved me, and alone; on shore, and when
> Through scudding drifts the rainy Hyades
> Vex the dim sea: I am become a name [...]

> *(Tennyson 1972: 562)*

What made Ungaretti's poetry seem so innovative in Italy was the hard-edged language, a modernist precision that turned away from the ornate, rhetorical styles developed by decadent writers like Gabriele D'Annunzio. Mandelbaum's version reinscribed these styles in Ungaretti, restoring what the translator himself called the "cadaver of literary Italian" – although now transmogrified into archaic English poetries.

In releasing this domestic remainder, Mandelbaum's translation not only positioned Ungaretti in English-language poetic traditions, but also affiliated him with the dominant trends in contemporary poetry translation. For the fact is that during the 1950s a mixture of current standard English with poetical archaisms constituted the discourse for translating poetry favored by leading American translators. Richmond Lattimore's 1951 version of the *Iliad*, which became the most widely read translation in the United States, claimed to have avoided any "poetical dialect of English" because, "in 1951, we do not have a poetic dialect," and "the language of Spenser or the King James Version" seemed inappropriate to Homer's "plainness" (Homer 1951: 55). Yet Lattimore's text is dotted with Victorian poeticisms: "as when rivers in winter spate," "So he spoke, vaunting," "he strides into battle," "his beloved son," "that accursed night" (ibid.: 125, 131, 279, 438). John Ciardi's 1954 version of

Dante's *Inferno*, which for over five decades has been continuously available in a mass-market paperback, aimed for "something like idiomatic English" to evoke the anti-rhetorical character of the Italian; "sparse, direct, and idiomatic," wrote Ciardi, Dante's language "seeks to avoid elegance simply for the sake of elegance" (Dante 1954: ix–x). Yet this paradoxical understanding of Dante's Italian also describes Ciardi's text, which, although mostly in a plain register of current usage, is strewn with poetical words and phrases: "drear," "piteous," "fleers," "beset," "perils," "sorely pressed," "thy," "anew," "it seemed to scorn all pause," "bite back your spleen" (for "non ti crucciare": "don't be distressed"), "his woolly jowls" (ibid.: 28, 30, 36, 38, 39, 43, 44, 45).

Mandelbaum's version bridged the cultural gap between Ungaretti's actual Italian readership and his potential American audience. Translating a modern Italian poet into the discourse that dominated American poetry translation was effectively a canonizing gesture, a poetic way of linking him – for American readers – to canonical poets like Homer and Dante (not to mention the echoes of Tennyson, Shakespeare, Marlowe). Yet this domestic inscription deviated from Ungaretti's significance in the Italian poetic tradition, the view, as Mandelbaum put it, that "Ungaretti purged the language of all ornament" (Ungaretti 1958: xi). The ornate English version was addressing another audience, distinctly American, poetry readers familiar with British and American poetic traditions as well as recent translations that were immensely popular.

Indeed, Mandelbaum's translation discourse was so familiar as to be invisible to the reviewer for *Poetry* magazine, Ned O'Gorman, an American poet who published his first collection of poems in the same year. O'Gorman found Ungaretti's poetry "truly magnificent," while quoting and commenting on the translation as if it were the Italian text (O'Gorman 1959a: 330). What O'Gorman liked about (Mandelbaum's) Ungaretti was the fact that it was poetical: he praised the Italian poet for writing "of a world transformed into poetry" and proclaimed "the *Recitative*" as "his finest poem" (ibid.: 331). The poems in O'Gorman's first book reflected this judgment. They included "An Art of Poetry," where he wrote: "Poetry begins where rhetoric does" (O'Gorman 1959b: 26).

Mandelbaum's readerships were fundamentally incommensurable. Even though written in English, the translation was intelligible to each of them in different linguistic and cultural terms. The Italian academic community also did not recognize the Victorian poeticism. For them, however, this stylistic feature was invisible because English was not their native language and because, as foreign-language specialists, they were most concerned with the relation between the English version and the Italian text: lexicographical equivalence. Cecchetti noticed one of Mandelbaum's poetical turns, his rendering of "smemora" ("to lose one's memory," "to forget") with the archaism "disremembers" (Ungaretti 1958: 51). Yet this choice was seen as appropriate to "the rare and suggestive flavor" of the Italian and indicative of the translator's "poetic sensibility" (Cecchetti 1959: 267).

The fact that in English this sensibility might be alien to Ungaretti's modernist poetics seems to have been recognized – in print – only by a British reader, interestingly enough. A reviewer for the London *Times*, who agreed with Cecchetti that

Ungaretti was "one of the most distinguished poets alive," felt that "Mr. Mandelbaum translates with a quite exceptional insensitivity" (*The Times* 1958: 13C). There can be no doubt that the reviewer had Mandelbaum's poeticisms in mind, since he preferred to recommend a "good crib," the very close French version that Jean Lescure published in 1953 (where "D'altri diluvi una colomba ascolto" was turned into "J'écoute une colombe venue d'autres déluges" (Ungaretti 1953: 159)). Only a native reader of English poetry who also knew the Italian texts and their position in the Italian poetic tradition was able to perceive the English-language remainder in Mandelbaum's version.

The readerships that gathered around this poetry translation were limited, professionally or institutionally defined, and determined by their cultural knowledge, whether of the source language and literature or the literary traditions in the translating language. The translation became the focus of divergent communities, foreign and domestic, scholarly and literary. And in its ability to support their linguistic and cultural differences, to be intelligible and interesting to them in their own terms, the translation fostered its own community, one that was *imagined* in Benedict Anderson's sense: the members "will never know most of their fellow-members, meet them, or even hear of them, yet in the minds of each lives the image of their communion" (Anderson 1991: 6). In the case of a translation, this image is derived from the representation of the source text constructed by the translator, a communication domestically inscribed. To translate is to invent for the source text new readers who are aware that their interest in the translation is shared by other readers, foreign and domestic – even when those interests are incommensurable.

The imagined communities that concern Anderson were nationalistic, based on the sense of belonging to a particular nation. Translations have undoubtedly formed such communities by importing foreign ideas that stimulated the rise of large-scale political movements at home (see chapter 7). At the turn of the twentieth century, the Chinese translator Yan Fu chose works on evolutionary theory by T. H. Huxley and Herbert Spencer precisely to build a national Chinese culture. He translated the Western concepts of aggression embodied in social Darwinism to form an aggressive Chinese identity that would withstand Western colonial projects, notably British (Schwartz 1964; Pusey 1983).

The imagined communities fostered by translation produce effects that are commercial as well as cultural and political. Consider, for example, the mass audience that gathers around a translated bestseller. Because of its sheer size, this community is an ensemble of the most diverse domestic constituencies, defined by their specific interests in the source text, yet aware of belonging to a collective movement, a national market for a foreign literary fascination. These constituencies will inevitably read the translation differently, and in some cases the differences will be incommensurable. Yet the greatest communication gap here may be between the source and receiving cultures. The domestic inscription in the translation extends the appeal of the source text to a mass audience in another culture. But widening the range of that appeal means that the inscription cannot include much of the source context. A translated bestseller risks reducing the source text to what constituencies in the receiving situation have in common, a dialect, a cultural discourse, an ideology.

This can be seen in the reception that greeted Irene Ash's English version of *Bonjour Tristesse* (1955), Françoise Sagan's bestselling novel. In France, the French text had been acclaimed as an accomplished work of art: it won the Prix des Critiques and sold 200,000 copies. In the United Kingdom and the United States, the translation drew favorable comments on its style and likewise stayed on the bestseller lists for many months. But no reviewer failed to abandon considerations of aesthetic form for more functional standards, expressing amazement at the youthful age of the author (19) and distaste for the amorality of its theme: a 17-year-old girl schemes to prevent her widowed father from remarrying, so that he can continue to engage in a succession of affairs. The *Chicago Tribune* was typical: "I admired the craftsmanship, but I was repelled by the carnality" (Hass 1955: 6).

This general response varied according to the values of the particular constituency addressed by the reviewer. The Catholic weekly *Commonweal* sternly pronounced the novel "childish and tiresome in its single-minded dedication to decadence" (Nagid 1955: 164), whereas the sophisticated *New Yorker* referred simply to the "father's hedonistic image," subtly suggesting that at 40 he deserves "pity" (Gill 1955: 114–15). In the United States after the Second World War, where the patriarchal family assumed new importance and "husbands, especially fathers, wore the badge of 'family man' as a sign of virility and patriotism" (May 1988: 98), Sagan's pleasure-seeking father and daughter were certain to make her novel an object of both moral panic and titillation. The reviewer for the *New Statesman and Nation* was unique in trying to understand it in distinctively French terms, describing the youthful heroine as "a child of the *bebop*, the night clubs, the existentialist cafés," comparing her and her father to "M. Camus's amoral Outsider" (Raymond 1955: 727–28).

Ash's English version was of course the decisive factor that enabled Sagan's novel to support a spectrum of very different responses in British and American cultures. The translation was immediately intelligible to a wide English-language readership: it was cast in the most familiar dialect of current English, the standard, but it also contained some lively colloquialisms that matched similar forms in the French text. Ash rendered "le dernier des salauds" ("the last of the sluts") as "the most awful cad," "loupé" ("failed") as "flunked," and "ce fut la fin" ("that was the end") as "things came to a head" (Sagan 1954: 32, 34, 45; 1955: 25, 27, 35). She aimed for a high degree of fluency by translating freely, making deletions and additions to the French to create more precise formulations in English:

> Au café, Elsa se leva et, arrivée à la porte, se retourna vers nous d'un air languoureux, très inspiré, à ce qu'il me sembla, du cinéma américain et mettant dans son intonation dix ans de galanterie française: "Vous venez, Raymond?"

> (After coffee, Elsa stood up and, on reaching the door, turned back towards us with a languorous air, very inspired – so it seemed to me – by American cinema, and investing her tone with ten years of French flirtation: "Are you coming, Raymond?")

> *(Sagan 1954: 38, my translation)*

After coffee, Elsa walked over to the door, turned around, and struck a languorous, movie-star pose. In her voice was ten years of French coquetry:

"Are you coming, Raymond?"

(Sagan 1955: 30)

Here the translator cut down forty words of French to twenty-nine in English. The use of the popular "movie-star pose" (for "du cinéma américain") is symptomatic of the drive towards readability.

By increasing the readability of the English text, such freedoms endowed the narrative with verisimilitude, producing the illusion of transparency that permitted the English-language reader to take the translation for the foreign text (Venuti 2008: 1). The reviewer for the *Atlantic*, impressed that "the novel has such a solid air of reality about it," commented on Ash's writing as if it were Sagan's: "Simple, crystalline, and concise, her prose flows along swiftly, creating scene and character with striking immediacy and assurance" (Rolo 1955: 84, 85).

Ash's freedoms may have been invisible, but they inevitably released a domestic remainder, textual effects that varied according to the specific passage where they occurred, but that were generally engaging, even provocative. The reviewer for the *New Statesman and Nation* was also unique in noticing her freedoms ("she has not been afraid to pare and clip the text to suit the English reader"), and he discussed an example where the "distinct gain in English" consisted of "an added, elegiac dimension" (Raymond 1955: 728). With a different passage, Ash's rewriting might be not just sentimental or melodramatic, but steamy, exaggerating the erotic overtones of the French:

> il avait pour elle des regards, des gestes qui s'adressaient à la femme qu'on ne connaît pas et que l'on désire connaître – dans le plaisir.

> (for her he had looks [and] gestures that are addressed to the woman whom one does not know yet desires to know – in pleasure.)
>
> *(Sagan 1954: 378, my translation)*

> I noticed that his every look and gesture betrayed a secret desire for her, a woman whom he had not possessed and whom he longed to enjoy.
>
> *(Sagan 1955: 29)*

Ash's translation, however free in places, maintained a sufficient degree of lexico-graphical equivalence to communicate the basic narrative elements of the French text. Yet the addition of words like "betrayed" and "secret" in this passage shows that she made the narrative available to an English-language audience with rather different moral values from its French counterpart, a morality that would restrict sexuality to marriage or otherwise conceal it. This is a rather odd effect in a novel where a father does not conceal his sexual promiscuity from his adolescent daughter. Ash inscribed Sagan's novel with a domestic intelligibility and interest, addressing a community that shared little of the foreign context where the novel first emerged.

The utopian dimension in translation

The communities fostered by translating are initially potential, signaled in the text, in the discursive strategy deployed by the translator, but not yet possessing a social existence. They depend for their realization on the ensemble of cultural constituencies among which the translation will circulate in the receiving situation. To engage these constituencies, however, the translator involves the source text in an asymmetrical act of communication, weighted ideologically towards the translating language and culture. Translating is always ideological because it releases a domestic remainder, an inscription of values, beliefs, and representations linked to historical moments and social positions in the receiving situation. In serving domestic interests, a translation provides an ideological resolution for the linguistic and cultural differences of the source text.

Yet translating is also utopian. The domestic inscription is made with the very intention to communicate the source text, and so it is filled with the anticipation that a community will be created around that text – although in translation. In the remainder lies the hope that the translation will establish a domestic readership, an imagined community that shares an interest in the foreign, possibly a market from the publisher's point of view. And it is only through the remainder, when inscribed with part of the foreign context, that the translation can establish a common understanding between domestic and foreign readers. In supplying an ideological resolution, a translation projects a utopian community that is not yet realized.

Behind this line of thinking lies Ernst Bloch's theory of the utopian function of culture, although revised to fit an application to translation. Bloch's is a Marxist utopia. He saw cultural forms and practices releasing a "surplus" that not only exceeds the ideologies of the dominant classes, the "status quo," but also anticipates a future "consensus," a classless society, usually by transforming the "cultural heritage" of a particular class, whether dominant or dominated (Bloch 1988: 46–50).

I construe Bloch's utopian surplus as the domestic remainder inscribed in the foreign text during the translation process. Translating releases a surplus of meanings which refer to domestic cultural traditions through deviations from the current standard dialect or otherwise standardized languages – through archaisms, for example, or colloquialisms. Implicit in any translation is the hope for a consensus, a communication and recognition of the foreign text through a domestic inscription.

Yet the inscription can never be so comprehensive, so total in relation to domestic constituencies, as to create a community of interest without exclusion or hierarchy. It is unlikely that a foreign text in translation will be intelligible or interesting (or both simultaneously) to every readership in the receiving situation. And the asymmetry between the foreign and domestic cultures persists, even when the foreign context is partly inscribed in the translation. Utopias are based on ideologies, Bloch argued, on interested representations of social divisions, representations that take sides in those divisions. In the case of translating, the interests are ineradicably domestic, always the interests of certain domestic constituencies over others.

Bloch also pointed out that the various social groups at any historical moment are non-contemporaneous or non-synchronous in their cultural and ideological development, with some containing a "remnant of earlier times in the present" (Bloch 1991: 108). Cultural forms and practices are heterogeneous, composed of different elements with different temporalities and affiliated with different groups. In language, the dialects and discourses, registers and styles that coexist in a particular period can be glimpsed in the remainder released by every communicative act. The remainder is a "diachrony-within-synchrony" that stages "the return within language of the contradictions and struggles that make up the social; it is the persistence within language of past contradictions and struggles, and the anticipation of future ones" (Lecercle 1990: 182, 215). Hence the domestic inscription in any translation is what Bloch calls an "anticipatory illumination" (*Vor-Schein*), a way of imagining a future reconciliation of linguistic and cultural differences, whether those that exist among domestic groups or those that divide the foreign and domestic cultures.

In Mandelbaum's version of Ungaretti's poetry, the utopian surplus is the Victorian poeticism. This English-language remainder did not just exceed the communication of the Italian texts; it also ran counter to the modernist experiment that they culti-vated in the context of Italian poetic traditions. During the 1950s, however, Mandelbaum's poeticism projected an ideal community of interest in Ungaretti by reconciling the differences between two readerships, Italian and American, scholarly and literary. Today, we may be more inclined to notice, not the ideal, but the ideologies of this community: Mandelbaum's translation was an asymmetrical act of communication that at once admitted and excluded the Italian context, while sup-porting incommensurable responses among American constituencies. Yet the ideological force of the translation made it utopian in its own time, hopeful of communicating the foreign significance of the foreign text through a domestic inscription. And this utopian projection eventually produced real effects. The American readership latent in Mandelbaum's poetical remainder reflected a dominant tendency in American poetry translation, helping his version acquire cultural authority in and out of the academy.

Translating that harbors the utopian dream of a common understanding between source and translating cultures may involve literary texts, whether elite or mass. But usually it takes much more mundane forms, serving technical or pragmatic purposes. Consider community or liaison interpreting, the oral, two-way translating done for refugees and immigrants who must deal with the social agencies and institutions of the host country. Community interpreters perform in a variety of legal, medical, and educational situations, including requests for political asylum, court appearances, hospital admissions, and applications for welfare. Codes of ethics, whether formulated by professional associations or by the agencies and institutions themselves, tend to insist that interpreters be "panes of glass" which "allow for the communication of ideas, once again, without modification, adjustment or misrepresentation" (Schweda Nicholson 1994: 82; see also Gentile et al. 1996). But such codes do not take into account the cultural and political hierarchies in the interpreting situation, the fact that – in the words of a British interpreting manual – "the client is part of a powerless ethnic minority group whose needs and wishes are often ignored or regarded as not legitimate by the majority group" (Shackman 1984: 18; see also Sanders 1992). And of course the "pane of glass" analogy represses the domestic inscription in any translating, the remainder that prevents the interpreting from being transparent communication even when the interpreter is limited to exact renderings of foreign words.

In practice, many community interpreters seem to recognize the asymmetries in the interpreting situation and make an effort to compensate for them through various strategies (Wadensjö 1998: 36). Robert Barsky's study of refugee hearings in Canada demonstrates that the interpreter can put the refugee on an equal footing with the adjudicating body only by releasing a distinctively domestic remainder. The foreign-language testimony must be inscribed with Canadian values, beliefs, and representations, producing textual effects that work only in English or French. Legal institutions value linear, transparent discourse, but the experiences that refugees must describe – exile, financial hardship, imprisonment, torture – are more than likely to shake their expressive abilities, even in their own languages. "Restricting the interpreter's role to rendering an 'accurate' translation of the refugee's utterances – which may contain hesitations, grammatical errors and various infelicities – inevitably jeopardizes the claimant's chances of obtaining refugee status, irrespective of the validity of the claim" (Barsky 1996: 52). Similarly, the interpreter must reconcile the cultural differences between Canada and the refugee's country by adding information about the foreign context, historical, geographical, political, or sociological details that may be omitted in testimony and unknown to Canadian judges and lawyers. "Insisting upon an interpretation limited exclusively to words uttered evacuates the cultural data which could be essential to the refugee's claim" (Barsky 1994: 49).

Barsky provides a telling example of a Pakistani claimant who spoke French during the hearing, apparently in an effort to lend weight to his case with the Québec authorities. But his French was weak, and his claim was previously denied because of interpreting problems, as he tried to explain:

> Moi demander, moi demander Madame, s'il vous plaît, cette translation lui parle français. Vous demander, parle français. Parce qu'elle m'a compris, vous qu'est ce qu'elle a dit. Moi compris. Madame m'a dit, désolé Monsieur, seul anglais.

> (Literally: Me ask, me ask Madame, please this translation speak to him French. You ask, speak French. Because she understood me, you that is what she said. Me understand. Madam said to me, sorry sir, only English.)
>
> *(Barsky 1996: 53, his translation)*

The claimant was testifying with a Pakistani interpreter who rendered the broken French into intelligible and compelling English:

> He has a complaint with the interpreter there. He speaks better French than English, but the interpreter was interpreting from Urdu to English. He is not too good in English, better in French, which he could understand. An interpreter was provided to interpret the hearing into English, which he did not agree to. So he was having a hard time expressing himself or understanding the

CPO, lawyers, himself, and the interpreter. There is no satisfaction in the hearing. And that is one reason why I lost the case.

When effective, community interpreting provides a complicated ideological resolution for the linguistic and cultural differences of the refugee's or immigrant's speech. The interpreting inevitably communicates the foreign text in domestic terms, in the terms of the host country, but the domestic inscription also needs to include a significant part of the foreign context that gives meaning to the claim. This sort of interpreting, although seemingly partial to the client, is not in fact ideologically one-sided: it serves both foreign and domestic interests. The ideology of the resolution is fundamentally democratic insofar as the aim is to overcome the asymmetries that exist between the client and the representatives of the social agency within and outside of the interpreting situation. According to the British manual, the community interpreter permits "professional and client, with very different backgrounds and perceptions and in an unequal relationship of power and knowledge, to communicate to their mutual satisfaction" (Shackman 1984: 18). An important requirement for this mutual satisfaction, clearly, is the idea that a consensus as to the validity of the claim, shared by the two parties, has emerged in rational communication. Yet the communication can be seen as rational only when the interpreter so intervenes as to enable both the client to participate fully and the agency representatives to arrive at an informed understanding of the claim.

Community interpreting that takes an interventionist approach thus presupposes what Jürgen Habermas calls an "ideal speech situation," distinguished by conditions that are normally "counterfactual" because "improbable": they include "openness to the public, inclusiveness, equal rights to participation, immunization against external or internal compulsion, as well as the participants' orientation toward reaching understanding (that is, the sincere expression of utterances)" (Habermas 1998: 367). In presupposing such conditions, the community interpreter works ultimately to foster a domestic community that is receptive to foreign constituencies, but that is not yet realized – or at least its realization will not be advanced until the client is given political asylum, due process, medical care, or welfare benefits, as the case may be. Even then, of course, the receptive domestic community is primarily a utopian projection that does not eliminate the social hierarchies in which the refugee or immigrant is actually positioned. Still, it does express the hope that linguistic and cultural differences will not result in the exclusion of foreign constituencies from the domestic scene. Translating has of course been motivated by much more questionable things.

[2000/revised 2004]

2

THE DIFFERENCE THAT TRANSLATION MAKES

The translator's unconscious

I need hardly say that the description that follows is partial, perhaps even somewhat misleading, because I have tried to make conscious and logical something that is, most of the time, unconscious, instinctive. Faced with a choice between "perhaps" and "maybe," the translator does not put the words on trial and engage attorneys to defend and accuse. Most probably, he hears the words in some corner of his mind, and likes the sound of one better than the other. Of course, his decision is only apparently instinctive. His instinct will be guided by his knowledge of the author's work, by his reading in the period. It will almost certainly not be guided by any rules, even self-made ones.

William Weaver, "The Process of Translation" (1989)

William Weaver thus opens an essay in which he presents a detailed description of the choices he made in translating a paragraph from an Italian short story. By 1989, Weaver had come to be recognized as the premier English-language translator of modern Italian fiction, the author of roughly sixty translations and the recipient of prestigious awards from such cultural institutions as the American Translators Association and the PEN American Center. Given the extent of his experience, we must take seriously his view that translating is a largely unreflective process, where the grounds for the translator's choices remain not merely unarticulated, but unknown to him, "unconscious," with decisions taken "in some corner of his mind." Indeed, although in describing one such translation process Weaver gives reasons for his choices, none of these reasons takes the form of an explanation that extends beyond a brief semantic or stylistic comment on an Italian word ("*atti* is more 'deeds' than 'actions'") or on a possible English equivalent ("highfalutin," "too banal," "a pompous ring") (Weaver 1989: 119, 118, 120, 123). Many choices seem to be based either on linguistic and cultural values that remain unstated or on sheer personal preference: "[By choosing 'beat' over 'beating'] I can avoid the -ing, of which there are probably too many in this passage"; "the passage contains several words I hate";

"Literally translated ('An idea, an idea ... '), it sounds wrong to me" (ibid.: 122, 118, 119). Weaver's essay certainly documents his own translation process, even if he does not actually explain it. But he asserts something more, that "most of the time" translating is "unconscious," not only for him, or for translators of his generation, but for "the translator" in general.

This is a provocative hypothesis, but its implications have rarely been examined in translation studies (notable exceptions are the speculative projects of Gavronsky 1977 and Frota 2000). Translation scholars have studied the linguistic and cultural resources that a translator internalizes over the course of a professional career, resources that are used spontaneously in the translation process but can be articulated upon reflection and might therefore be said to constitute the translator's latent thinking, easily recoverable rather than repressed (see, for example, the treatment of "norms" in Toury 1995: 53–69). Yet although Weaver's essay clearly refers to such resources ("knowledge of the author's work," "reading in the period"), he stresses personal preferences or antipathies ("another word that always seems to cause me problems [...]"; "I dislike two plurals in a row": Weaver 1989: 119, 120) whose origins he does not identify. One inevitably wonders, then, not only whether such choices have been unconsciously motivated, but also whether the "rules" that Weaver denies applying are likewise unconscious, subliminal, or possibly repressed in his case yet nonetheless active in the translation process.

Scholars of psychoanalytic theory have likewise tended to overlook such considerations. They have instead chosen to follow Freud in understanding translation either as a psychic process (the translation of unconscious material into symptoms, for instance, or into the manifest content of dreams) or as the hermeneutic process that occurs during analysis (the translation of symptoms and dreams into the analyst's language) (see especially Mahony 1980; cf. the dissenting view of Amati Mehler et al. 1990: 297–301). Allan Bass (1985) presents an exceptional study of Freud as an interlingual translator, treating a linguistic error as the sign of an unconscious motivation. As this study suggests, more attention needs to be given to the idea that the unconscious, a universal category in psychoanalytic theory, might operate somehow in the translator's choices and be visible in the translated text, available for reconstruction.

My aim here is precisely to pursue this line of thinking. My point of departure, however, will not be psychoanalysis, not an exposition of basic psychoanalytic concepts, but rather translation theory, a formulation of the fundamental linguistic and cultural issues that translation raises. If the translator's unconscious is at work in the translation process, then it is important to understand how the distinctive linguistic and cultural practice that is translation gives a specific form and meaning to psychoanalytical concepts. This approach will enable distinctions to be drawn between different aspects of the translator's unconscious, between the translatorly and the personal, the cultural and the political. I will proceed, then, by presenting an exposition of theoretical concepts in translation and by illustrating them with a specific case so as to establish a textual basis for the development of a psychoanalytic approach.

The irreducible differences in translation

Despite what may seem to be analogous linguistic and discursive structures between a source text and its translation, no similarity of form and meaning or of reception pre-exists the translating process. Any such similarity is constructed on the basis of irreducible differences which are always already present before the translating begins, which the translator may work to resolve or simply mystify – as with the illusion of transparency produced by fluent translating – but which remain present in the translated text and complicate its communicative function (Venuti 2008: 1–5). The differences are those that exist between languages and cultures, and although they are what translating is supposed to negotiate or resolve in the first place, it ultimately winds up multiplying and exacerbating them, sometimes without the translator's awareness and in many cases without the awareness of the audience for whom the translation was produced and whom, increasingly from the nineteenth century onwards, has no access to the source text. We should study these differences, even when they occur unconsciously, but not in the hope of eradicating them. For they cannot be eradicated, and some in fact ought not to be because they are necessary for an understanding or awareness of the foreignness of the source text, that is to say, what makes that text different from texts originally written in the translating language and culture. The goal we should set for translation studies is rather the ultimately ethical one of developing methods of translation research and practice that describe, explain, and take responsibility for the differences that translation inevitably makes.

To explore these assertions, I will rely, first, on poststructuralist theories of language and textuality and specifically on the work of Jacques Derrida. It is these theories that have sought to take into account linguistic and cultural differences and have enabled us to think about them in the most incisive and sophisticated ways. Among Derrida's many suggestive comments on translation is a passage that refers to the materiality of the translated text:

> Or un corps verbal ne se laisse pas traduire ou transporter dans une autre langue. Il est cela même que la traduction laisse tomber. Laisser tomber le corps, telle est même l'énergie essentielle de la traduction. Quand elle réinstitue un corps, elle est poésie. En ce sens, le corps du signifiant constituant l'idiome pour toute scène de rêve, le rêve est intraduisible.
>
> *(Derrida 1967: 312)*

> The materiality of a word cannot be translated or carried over into another language. Materiality is precisely that which translation relinquishes. To relinquish materiality: such is the driving force of translation. And when that materiality is reinstated, translation becomes poetry. In this sense, since the materiality of the signifier constitutes the idiom of every dream scene, dreams are untranslatable.
>
> *(Derrida 1978: 210)*

In Derrida's view, the body ("le corps") of the source text, its materiality in the sense of the specific chain of acoustic or graphemic signifiers that constitute it, cannot be reproduced in translation and therefore is inevitably dropped by the translator. This displacement, to be more precise, involves a twofold loss: a loss of intratextual effects, what makes up the unique texture or signifying process of the source text, and at the same time a loss of intertextual relations, what invests it with significance for readers of the source language who have read widely in that language. In dropping the materiality of the source text, translation is radically decontextualizing: it dismantles the context that is constitutive of that text. This decontextualization is the first difference produced by the translating process itself.

Derrida also observes that, when translation restores a body, a materiality in the sense of another chain of signifiers in another language, translation is "poetry" ("poésie"). The term "poetry" can obviously be loaded with various meanings which depend on what materials the interpreter brings to bear on it, although we cannot be sure from this passage what load Derrida himself has given to it. Insofar as he is a philosopher conversant in the history of philosophy, I shall take the term in the ancient Greek philosophical sense of ποίησις (*poiesis*): writing a translation involves a particular act of making, of creativity or invention. Translation creates another signifying chain accompanied by intratextual effects and intertextual relations that are designed to reproduce the source text, but that also work in the translating language and culture. As a result, translation exceeds the communication of any univocal signified which the translator establishes in the source text, however reductive or decontextualized that signified may be. The creation of a different signifying chain proliferates semantic possibilities as the translator seeks to fix a signified that answers not only to the source text, but also to intelligibilities and interests in the receiving situation. In restoring a materiality, in creating a text, translation is radically recontextualizing and thus produces a second difference, in fact a set of linguistic and cultural differences that are inscribed in the source text.

These points can be illustrated by Alan Bass's English version of Derrida's French passage. Not only did Bass drop the chain of French signifiers, but he also did not carry over the French syntax, the placement of adjectives after nouns, for example, as in "un corps verbal" and "l'énergie essentielle," or the ablative construction that begins the last sentence: "le corps du signifiant constituant l'idiome [...]." Bass did not restore these material features of Derrida's writing because French and English signify differently, according to different linguistic and discursive structures. Placing adjectives after nouns is standard usage in contemporary French but archaic in English, restricted today to certain literary instances. Thus Bass was adhering to current standard English when he reversed the order of the French adjectives. The ablative construction is typical of what Philip Lewis has called "the looser, less forcefully determined relations that prevail in French," whereas English tends "to prefer a strict, precise, homogeneous set of relations" (Lewis 1985: 35). Here Bass was following a preference for precision and cohesiveness distinctive of the English language when he avoided the ablative and instead created a relative clause, inserting the connective word "since."

The same preference can be seen in Bass's lexicon. Yet here his choices reveal a more striking deviation from Derrida's passage: whereas the French is at once concrete and metaphoric in the use of words such as "corps" (body) to refer to language and "laisser tomber" (to let fall, to drop) to refer to the loss that translation forces upon the source text, the English is more abstract and precise in the use of words such as "materiality" and "relinquish." Bass has not just reinvented Derrida's French according to linguistic preferences distinctive of English; he has also shifted the style away from the literary towards the philosophical as this generic distinction has long been drawn in British and American philosophy, assimilating the language in the French text to the language that is customarily used in anglophone philosophical traditions. At least since the end of the nineteenth century, Continental philosophy has tended to blur the distinction between literary and philosophical writing: think not only of poststructuralism, but also of existential phenomenology, not only of Derrida, but also of Nietzsche and Heidegger. British and American philosophy, in contrast, has aimed to maintain the distinction by constructing technical terminologies on the model of scientific writing: think of symbolic logic and speech act theory, of Bertrand Russell and John Austin. This difference can be seen in the work of a single philosopher, Wittgenstein, perhaps because he was an Austrian who wrote in German but who long lived in England. Wittgenstein shifted from the rigorously logical style of the *Tractatus Logico-Philosophicus* (1922) to the conversational, occasionally figurative style of the *Philosophical Investigations* (1953) (Perloff 1996 discusses this shift).

Bass's rendering illuminates the peculiar materiality of the translated text, as well as the translator's intentionality in producing that text. He adheres to a norm that shapes most translation today, regardless of the language and culture, a prevailing expectation that an acceptable translation will be adequate to the source text by containing roughly the same number of words or pages. Although contemporary translators often depart from source-text syntactical constructions and lexical items because of the differences between languages, they nonetheless try to maintain a semantic similarity based on current dictionary definitions, or in other words a lexicographical equivalence. As Derrida argues elsewhere, this intention is a matter of "stay[ing] as close as possible to the equivalence of 'one word *by* one word' and thereby respect[ing] verbal quantity as a quantity of words, each of which is an irreducible body, the indivisible unity of an acoustic form incorporating or signifying the indivisible unity of a meaning or concept" (Derrida 2001: 181). The effort to maintain a lexicographical equivalence is thus based on a particular concept of meaning in language which, however, the very materiality of the translated text, even the very act of translating is constantly putting into question because translating displaces the signifiers constituting the source text and proliferates differences that answer to the receptors' language and culture. A lexicographical equivalence can be detected between Derrida's use of the French word "corps" and Bass's choice of the English word "materiality" – but only if the words are reduced to a common meaning, stripped of the variations, the formal and semantic differences, that enable them both to signify further possibilities in French and English and to affiliate the texts in which they appear to distinct philosophical traditions.

The remainder and the translator's unconscious

Translators, then, can never entirely avoid the loss that the translation process enfor- ces on the source text, on its meanings and structures, figures and traditions. And translators cannot obviate the gain in their translating, the construction of different meanings, structures, figures, and traditions and thereby the creation of textual effects that go far beyond the establishment of a lexicographical equivalence to signify primarily in the terms of the translating language and culture. Following the important work of Jean-Jacques Lecercle (1990), I call these effects the "remainder" in a translation.

As theorized by Lecercle, the remainder is ever-present in language use: it is a range of possible phonological, lexical, and syntactical variations on the current stan- dard dialect, which is by definition invested with such cultural and social value as to exclude or repress any nonstandard forms or to restrict them to particular uses and situations. Whereas the standard dialect pushes the language user towards homo- geneity, adherence to the rules of grammar, for instance, and to prevailing norms of signification, the remainder directs attention to the utter heterogeneity of language. The remainder consists of such variations as regional and social dialects, slogans and clichés, technical terminologies and slang, archaisms and neologisms, literary figures like metaphors and puns, stylistic innovations, and foreign loan words. In varying the standard dialect, the remainder complicates the communication of a univocal signified by calling attention to the linguistic, cultural, and social conditions of any commu- nicative act, to the fact that the standard dialect is merely one among a wide variety of possible forms. The remainder is not what is left over from the standard dialect or from a meaning communicated in that dialect, but is rather constitutive of the standard and of any communicated meaning – even if by exclusion or restriction.

In a translation, the remainder consists of linguistic forms and textual effects that simultaneously vary both the current standard dialect of the translating language and the formal and semantic dimensions of the source text. The variations that comprise the remainder complicate the establishment of a lexicographical equivalence with the source text because they work only in the translating language and culture and reflect the linguistic, cultural, and social conditions of the receptors. The remainder is the most visible sign of the domesticating process that always functions in translating, the assimilation of the source text to what is intelligible and interesting to readerships in the receiving culture. But the remainder can also be a significant point of foreignizing effects by deviating from the current standard dialect, the form of the translating language that is the most familiar to readers and the most frequently imposed on translators by editors. Bass's rendering of Derrida's French passage can be described as releasing a distinctive philosophical remainder whereby English lexical choices work to assimilate the French to British and American philosophical traditions. In the end, however, Bass's choices are not so much domesticating as foreignizing because the linguistic similarity that they establish between those traditions and Derrida's philosophy winds up enhancing what is different in his thinking.

The remainder can be intentionally released by a language user. A poet or novelist, for example, may wish to vary the current standard dialect for literary effect; a scientist or engineer may wish to develop specialized terms to describe a scientific law or technological process with greater precision. Similarly, a translator may decide to release a remainder, to vary the form and meaning of the source text, because a linguistic feature or literary effect can be no more than approximated in the translation or because it cannot be reproduced at precisely the same point where it occurs in the source text. This sort of intentional variation is sometimes called compensation, the creation of a feature or effect that compensates for a loss of some aspect of the source text resulting from linguistic and cultural differences (cf. Harvey 1995).

The remainder may also be released unintentionally. Conversation and writing can produce variations on the standard dialect that escape the language user's conscious control, but that nonetheless signify meanings grasped by interlocutors and readers. Lecercle suggests, in fact, that the remainder might be considered "the linguistic equivalent of the Freudian unconscious, excluded or repressed by the rules of grammar, but trying to return in jokes, slips of the tongue, solecisms, and poetry" (Lecercle 1990: 23). In translation, by the same token, a remainder may be unconscious on the translator's part, but highly significant in relation to the source text and the receiving culture. For example, a translator can unwittingly misconstrue a source-text lexical item or syntactical construction, and the error may reverberate with meanings that amount to a repressed interpretation of the source text.

Consider an error that appears in Bass's rendering, a misconstrual of the French syntax. In the fourth sentence of the passage, Derrida writes, "Quand elle réinstitue un corps, elle est poésie," which in a close English version might read, "When it [translation] reinstitutes a body, it [translation] is poetry." The repeated feminine pronoun "elle" I take as referring to the feminine noun "la traduction" ("translation"); the indefinite article "un" before "corps" refers to any verbal body or materiality in the *translating* language, any chain of signifiers in that language, which the translator might devise to render a source text. Bass's version introduces several departures from the French, two of which – namely, the reversal of the word order and the change of the verb from the active to the passive voice – are not incorrect renderings since they do not appreciably affect the meaning. The misconstrual occurs in the replacement of the indefinite article "un" with the demonstrative adjective "that," whereby "that" evidently refers to the materiality of the *source* text mentioned in the first three sentences of the passage. The shift from "un" to "that" is erroneous because it reverses the meaning: Derrida's first sentence in the English version, stating that the materiality of the source text cannot be carried over, is contradicted by the fourth sentence, which states that this materiality can in fact be carried over or "reinstated." For over two decades, apparently, readers did not perceive any error in this passage because they understood "that" as referring to the translated text. Yet such a reading disregards the deictic force of the demonstrative adjective, which refers back to the preceding three references to the "materiality" of the source text.

How do we explain this error? It is important to rule out sheer incompetence as the cause: Bass is an extremely knowledgeable translator of Derrida's writing who received a doctorate in French literature from the Johns Hopkins University and then trained as a psychoanalyst in New York, where he continues to practice. He has translated four of Derrida's books: *Writing and Difference* (1978), the source of the essay from which the passage under examination is taken; *Positions* (1981); *Margins of Philosophy* (1982); and *The Post Card: From Socrates to Freud and Beyond* (1987). Bass's translations always include illuminating annotations, and he has commented insightfully on Derrida's philosophy and psychoanalysis in his own writing. Bass is, moreover, a scrupulous translator who routinely consults previously published translations. In the case of the essay under discussion, he examined a previously published version by Jeffrey Mehlman, a professor of French at Boston University and a translator of French theoretical texts, including psychoanalytic theory (Derrida 1978: xx). Mehlman's version, however, contains the very same error, the same misconstrual of the syntax, even the same wording (Derrida 1972: 90–91).

Bass's error (and Mehlman's before him) might be dismissed as a mere oversight that went undetected in proofreading, whether by the translator himself or by the copyeditor at the University of Chicago Press, the publisher of this and Bass's other translations of Derrida. But I want to argue that more is at stake, even if we regard the error as an oversight. And this more is a remainder, obviously unconscious but nonetheless significant. Bass's (and Mehlman's) erroneous rendering reveals what can be called the translator's dream: that a translation will restore the source text in its entirety, in its materiality, without loss or gain, that the translation will establish such a similarity to the source text as to overcome the irreducible differences between languages and cultures. Translation is a dream scene in its own right, where the translator's unconscious can emerge through variations on linguistic and discursive structures, through a remainder. The signifying chain created by the translator does not translate any dream embodied in the source text, but rather replaces it with the translator's own unconscious desire, a desire for a particular meaning or, as in this case, a particular theory of meaning in translation. Yet this desire is implicit, not explicit, perceptible only through a misconstrual of the syntax.

I am reading the translator's error symptomatically, as a signifier that is unconsciously motivated, and in so doing I am relying on Freud's psychoanalytic treatment of such common phenomena as verbal slips and misreadings (Frota 2000 considers a similar method). The error in Bass's translation in fact constitutes a misreading of the French text. Freud notes that

> in a very large number [of misreadings] it is the reader's preparedness that alters the text and reads into it something which he is expecting or with which he is occupied. The only contribution towards a misreading which the text itself need make is that of affording some sort of resemblance in the verbal image, which the reader can alter in the sense he requires.
>
> *(Freud 1960: 112–13)*

Thus in translating a passage in which Derrida comments on translation, Bass altered the syntax by creating a similar construction that was able to convey a different sense, a sense that is actually opposed to Derrida's point. This opposition is essential to the psychoanalytic understanding of misreadings because, as Freud points out, the text "contains something which rouses the reader's defences – some information or imputation distressing to him – and which is therefore corrected by being misread so as to fit in with a repudiation or with the fulfillment of a wish" (ibid.: 114). A passage that casts doubt on the possibility of translation, that asserts the inevitability of an irrecoverable loss during the translating process, might well distress the translator who is rendering it into another language. Hence, I suggest, Bass's error, which in effect denies any loss in translation by assuming that the materiality of the source text can be restored. (The same can be said of the error in Mehlman's version.)

Bass's translation allows for a more precise account of the translator's unconscious. Perhaps the first point worth articulating is that the translator's unconscious is textual: it does not exist outside of the language of the translation, but rather comes into being when that language is used in the translating process. As Jacques Lacan has observed, "the unconscious is neither primordial nor instinctual; what it knows about the elementary is no more than the elements of the signifier" (Lacan 1977: 170). In producing a chain of signifiers to render the source text, the translator releases a remainder that exposes the workings of his or her unconscious – but only in relation to that text or even a particular passage in it. And this remainder may include various intertextual connections. Thus Bass demonstrates that Freud's unwitting mistranslation occurred "because it fits in too well with the related theories" which he was then discussing in articles and correspondence, and which colleagues such as Carl Jung were addressing in their own research (Bass 1985: 137).

Lacan argues, moreover, that the signifying chain is the site of a lack that produces the subject's desire (Lacan 1977: 256–65). Desire originates not in the subject, but in what Lacan calls the "Other," the signifiers which the subject internalized during language acquisition, including the signifiers used by the first person who desired the subject (i.e., the mother), but also the signifiers from which the subject expects a response to a demand for satisfaction (ibid.: 263). The Other is the symbolic order, the signifying chain that constitutes the subject through a process of identification. And this constitution in language occurs without the subject's awareness. In Lacan's formula, "the unconscious is the discourse of the Other"; or, in other words, "the presence of the signifier in the Other is, in effect, a presence usually closed to the subject, because it usually persists in a state of repression" (ibid.: 193, 200).

In the translator's case, the source-text signifiers are the stage upon which desire is produced. The source text creates a lack in the translator who unconsciously demands that this text satisfy the lack and who alters it so as to achieve satisfaction. The translator's desire, then, is revealed primarily in those instances where the language of the translation is dislocated or where the translation so deviates from the source text as to result in an error. Yet this means that the translator's desire never actually finds its object, is never satisfied. The dislocation in the translation and the deviation from the source text constitute the translator's "phantasy," which Lacan defines as "that by which the subject sustains himself at the level of his vanishing desire, vanishing in so far as the very satisfaction of demand hides his object from him" (ibid.: 272; cf. Easthope 1999b for the differences between Freud's and Lacan's theories on this point).

Thus Derrida's French text provoked an unconscious demand in Bass's translating, the desire that the source text be fully translatable. Yet this desire was denied on the thematic level of the text by Derrida's assertion of untranslatability, the idea that a verbal body cannot be carried over. And the denial was further manifested on the lexical and syntactical level of the translation, in Bass's recourse to terminology suggestive of British and American philosophy and in the very misconstrual that revealed his desire for translatability. The unconsciously released remainder was a phantasy that seemed to satisfy Bass's desire, yet concealed its actual frustration.

Although psychoanalytic theory aims to study individual psychology, my application of this theory to translation suggests that the translator's desire is not entirely personal, but transindividual as well, potentially shared by many different translators because it is informed by the theory and practice of translation. Thus the same error expressing the same sort of desire, an unconscious desire for a particular notion of translatability, occurs in translations made by two different translators at different moments: Mehlman and Bass. To be sure, a translated text can express a translator's personal desires as these relate to specific source texts and cultures and to specific passages in those texts. But since desire as theorized by Lacan originates in the Other, and the Other assumes a symbolic function, representing various people in the subject's experience, working through identification and transference or substitution (where, for example, an adult woman comes to replace the mother in a man's affection), we must acknowledge the probability that the translator's desire can take collective forms, determined by cultural traditions and social institutions (this view implicitly takes issue with the stress on the translator's individuality in Frota 2000). In such cases, the translator's desire may be not merely personal, but political as well.

Unintended sound effects and the political unconscious

In addition to misreadings, Freud considers slips of the tongue that involve a similarity in sound. A word or phrase that might be expected to occur at a certain point in an utterance is replaced or contaminated by others that sound similar yet are not part of the context and ultimately reveal a repressed anxiety or wish. Freud observes that "it is not the influence of the 'contact effects of sounds' but the influence of thoughts that lie outside the intended speech which determines the occurrence of the slip and provides an adequate explanation of the mistake" (Freud 1960: 80). Such slips have a direct bearing on translation: because the translating process substitutes another chain of signifiers for those that comprise the source text, the translation may produce unintended sound effects that work only in the translating language and culture, homophones or homonyms, rhymes or echoes that establish intertextual connections and thereby offer a glimpse of the translator's unconscious.

Consider the following translation, "In You The Earth," Donald D. Walsh's 1972 English version of Pablo Neruda's poem, "En Ti La Tierra":

> Little
> rose,
> roselet,

at times,
tiny and naked,
it seems
as though you would fit
in one of my hands,
as though I'll clasp you like this
and carry you to my mouth,
but
suddenly
my feet touch your feet and my mouth your lips:
you have grown,
your shoulders rise like two hills,
your breasts wander over my breast,
my arm scarcely manages to encircle the thin
new-moon line of your waist:
in love you have loosened yourself like sea water:
I can scarcely measure the sky's most spacious eyes
and I lean down to your mouth to kiss the earth.

Pequeña
rosa,
rosa pequeña,
a veces,
diminuta y desnuda,
parece
que en una mano mia
cabes,
que así voy a cerrarte
y llevarte a mi boca,
pero
de pronto
mis pies tocan tus pies y mi boca tus labios:
has crecido,
suben tus hombros como dos colinas,
tus pechos se pasean por mi pecho,
mi brazo alcanza apenas a rodear la delgada
linea de luna nueva que tiene tu cintura:
en el amor como agua de mar te has destado:
mido apenas los ojos mas extensos del cielo
y me inclino a tu boca para besar la tierra.

(Neruda 1972: 2–3)

Walsh's version makes quite clear the kind of translation strategy he intended to implement. For the most part, he chose to maintain a close adherence to the Spanish text, respecting Neruda's lexicon, syntax, and lineation. He also adheres to the current standard dialect of English, although with two exceptions that effectively serve to heighten the homogeneity of his language: the word "roselet," which might today be considered a slightly archaic poeticism, and the contraction "I'll," a colloquial form. Walsh's version is so close to the Spanish, and his English is so homogeneous and familiar, that he evidently aimed to efface his decisive intervention, to assume – as the poet and translator Ben Belitt once remarked in a critical review – "the role of being 'nobody in particular'" (Belitt 1978: 48). Walsh himself stated his aim while introducing his version of Neruda's collection *Residence on Earth*:

> The translator's double responsibility is to find out what the author has said in his language, and then to say this in the translator's own language with as much fidelity to the author's words and intent as is permitted by the differences between the two languages. He must, in short, make the language curtain as transparent as possible, letting the author speak for himself in a new tongue.
>
> *(Neruda 1973a: vii)*

From the vantage point of the argument I have been making, Walsh's statement of his intention is deeply questionable. He acknowledges that linguistic differences complicate the translating process, but he seems unaware that these differences make any transparency an illusory effect produced by the translator while insuring that Neruda cannot ever "speak for himself" in a translation. Walsh is also unaware that his practice contradicts his intention. His use of the poetical archaism "roselet," for example, does not reproduce Neruda's opening lines, "Pequeña/rosa,/rosa pequeña," which create a simple, repetitive, song-like effect enabled by the flexible positioning of Spanish adjectives. Here Neruda's simplicity is displaced by the artificiality of Walsh's poeticism, which because of its very archaic quality calls attention to itself as a word and so prevents the line from seeming transparent to an English-language reader.

Another deviation from the Spanish text occurs in Walsh's penultimate line, "the sky's most spacious eyes." Not only is "spacious" an unusual choice for the Spanish word "extenso," which might be more closely rendered as "wide" or "vast," but for American readers the English phrase can also release an acoustic remainder. It is likely to echo the opening line of Katharine Lee Bates's "America the Beautiful" (1893–1913), a very familiar anthem-like poem that is sometimes sung at public events:

O beautiful for spacious skies,
For amber waves of grain,
For purple mountain majesties
Above the fruited plain!

America! America!
God shed his grace on thee
And crown thy good with brotherhood
From sea to shining sea!

To test this echo in Walsh's translation, I showed the two texts to some accomplished translators of Spanish-language poetry, including Eliot Weinberger, the American translator of the Mexican poet Octavio Paz. Weinberger agreed, adding some illuminating observations:

> One never knows, but my guess is that "for spacious skies" was not conscious – but one of those things stuck in the back of the brain that just comes out. Certainly "spacious" is not the obvious way to translate "mas extenso." But you're right that the combination of skies and spacious cannot help but echo "oh beautiful." I often find song lyrics suddenly popping up in one of my translations, and I have to change it – even when it's the most literal rendering.
>
> *(Email correspondence, 9 October 2000)*

Weinberger's admission that similar unintended effects occur in his own translations should make us wary of merely dismissing Walsh's version as inadequate or incompetent. Walsh (1903–80) was a distinguished American educator who specialized in Spanish-language instruction, in addition to his work as a translator. He served as Head of the Spanish Department at the exclusive Choate School. He also directed the Foreign Language Program of the Modern Language Association of America and edited *Hispania*, the journal of the American Association of Teachers of Spanish and Portuguese. In the 1940s, he began to publish, producing a number of books in various genres: two manuals for teachers of Spanish, three Spanish textbooks, editions of eight Spanish literary texts for students, and translations of eight works of Latin American literature, both poetry and prose, by such writers as Ernesto Cardenal, Angel Gonzalez, and Pedro Mir, as well as Neruda. Despite Walsh's many professional accomplishments, he brought a literary and theoretical naiveté to his translating, whether we consider his work in the context of recent trends in translation studies or accept the judgment of contemporaries like Belitt ("a simplistic semantics and a misguided analogy with scientific method have led him to identify the truth of a poem substantively with its 'words,' and its 'intent' with its data" (Belitt 1978: 46). And Walsh was undoubtedly unconscious of the remainder released by his translation, the similarity in sound between his penultimate line and the opening of "America the Beautiful."

Following Freud's approach to verbal slips, I want to argue that this echo is symptomatic of the translator's unconscious desire, although here the desire carries larger, political implications. Neruda's "En Ti La Tierra" is a love poem in which the poet-lover concludes a sensual description of the woman he loves by comparing her to the earth. This sort of analogy occurs in many poetic traditions: the seventeenth-century English poet John Donne, for instance, was fond of metaphors in which love made two lovers entire worlds to one another. The analogy is certainly retained in Walsh's translation, but the acoustic remainder alters its significance: the lover leans down to kiss, not simply the earth, or the earth-likened woman he loves, but America the Beautiful, the United States, a nation that undergoes some degree of personification in Bates's poem. The unconscious desire in Walsh's translation is that a major Chilean poet, noted for his leftist attacks on American capitalism in such works as the 1966 play *Splendor and Death of Joaquín Murieta*, should instead express his affection towards the United States through an allusion to a nationalistic representation of this country.

The acoustic remainder thus reveals the translator's political unconscious, which can be brought more clearly into focus with additional historical details. The New York-based publisher New Directions had contracted Walsh to translate two of Neruda's books, *The Captain's Verses*, which contains the poem "In You The Earth," and *Residence on Earth*. Walsh delivered the completed manuscript of the first book in 1971 (email correspondence with Declan Spring, 16 February 2001). This means that he was working on these translations during the period when Neruda won the Nobel Prize for Literature (1971) and the socialist politician Salvador Allende, a close friend of the poet, was democratically elected to serve as the president of Chile (1970–73). Neruda himself had been nominated to serve as the presidential candidate of the Chilean Communist Party (1970), but he later withdrew because Allende's candidacy seemed more viable (Sigmund 1977: 84–85, 91).

Allende's election sent shock waves through the Western democracies, especially the United States. It provoked fears that were not only political – the spread of Communism in Latin America – but also economic – the end of foreign interests in Chile. The fears seemed to be realized when Allende quickly moved to reorganize the Chilean economy, instituting agrarian reform and nationalizing industries which in some cases were owned by American companies. Richard Nixon, the then president of the United States, responded by implementing international economic sanctions against Chile. Neruda ultimately produced a text that called for Nixon's death while praising the Chilean socialist "revolution" (Neruda 1973b).

The acoustic remainder in Walsh's translation can be described as a wishful resolution to a disturbing political reality, the opposition between Chile and the United States in which the very poet he was translating had intervened. Walsh's translation exemplifies the political unconscious that operates in literary texts, their ability to provide imaginary compensations for real social conflicts through formal and thematic features that constitute an ideological resolution (for this concept, see Jameson 1981: chapter 1). The ideology of Walsh's resolution was clearly conservative, filled with the hope that a leftist poet like Neruda would not simply accept, but also cherish the hegemonic position of the United States.

Walsh's translation in fact reflects the Cold War era, when the ideological conflict between American liberal democracy and Soviet state socialism was very tense. The cultural implications of his conservative stand in this conflict were evident in a report on foreign-language education which he co-authored as an administrator of the Modern Language Association of America (Starr et al. 1960). The report regarded foreign-language study as an important means of avoiding an ethnocentric approach to foreign cultures. "Learning a foreign language," the authors asserted, "involves the student in the culture of which the language is an expression and frees him from the ethnic-centered attitudes of his community and from the prejudices that he must overcome if he is to be a responsible citizen of the world" (ibid.: 20). Yet to be "a responsible citizen of the world" was to serve American interests in the current geopolitical situation. Walsh, in his signed preface, explicitly aligned the report with the National Defense Education Act of 1958, referring to "the professional and public realization that it is in the national interest that even larger numbers of Americans acquire proficiency in many foreign languages" (ibid.: 9; for the political significance of the Congressional Act, see Clowse 1981). During the 1950s, while working for the Foreign Language Program of the Modern Language Association, Walsh also helped to draft several policy state-ments in which the idea that "the United States now occupies a position of world leadership" is taken as a "commonplace" justifying increased foreign-language study (ibid.: 83).

This political conservatism could only be intensified during the controversial Allende presidency, making its pressure felt in Walsh's translation by triggering the acoustic remainder that functioned as an unconscious ideological resolution. The translation in fact unfolds this resolution in a climactic way through subtle deviations from the Spanish text, deviations that are especially noticeable in view of Walsh's deliberately close rendering. Whereas at the beginning of the poem Neruda uses verbs in the present tense to evoke the lover's tender intimacy with the woman, Walsh relies on the subjunctive mood and the future tense, suggesting – even if paradoxically in this context – that the intimacy has yet to be achieved. Thus

> parece
> que en una mano mia
> cabes,
> que así voy a cerrarte
> y llevarte a mi boca,

which might be translated closely as

> it seems
> that you fit
> in one of my hands,
> that I am going to clasp you like this
> and lift you to my mouth

becomes in Walsh's rendering

> it seems
> as though you would fit
> in one of my hands,
> as though I'll clasp you like this
> and carry you to my mouth,

Here, especially in the repeated "as though," the lover appears to be merely fanta-sizing about his physical contact with the woman. By revealing this contact more gradually than the Spanish text, Walsh's translation places a greater emphasis on the kiss in the line that resonates with the American anthem. That emphasis, I suggest, is symptomatic of the intensity of the translator's unconscious desire for a conservative ideological resolution to the Chilean crisis.

Walsh's translation shows, once again, that the source text produces the translator's desire by creating the stage whereon the unconscious can be revealed through textual effects, here a contamination through sound. But this case also points to the efficacy of an extensive intertextual network in the production of desire: the intertext of Walsh's translation encompassed not only "America the Beautiful," but also Neruda's other texts and the sensationalistic coverage of Allende's presidency in the print and electronic media. Walsh worked in a cultural and social situation that was volatile enough to weaken his conscious control over his announced strategy of close adherence to the Spanish text.

The unconscious motivation of false cognates

False cognates represent another kind of verbal slip or misreading that sometimes occurs in translations, and, depending upon the translator's experience and the source text to be translated, they may reveal an unconscious desire. A false cognate is a translating-language word that closely resembles a source-language word in form, often because of a shared etymology, but that nonetheless signifies a very different meaning because the two languages have undergone different historical developments (see Shuttleworth and Cowie 1997: 57–58). Because the resemblance tends to be superficial, usually based on sound or orthography, a false cognate is likely to be chosen by beginning translators whose knowledge of the source language may be imperfect and whose experience with translation problems is limited. Hence when a false cognate occurs in the work of a translator who has already produced a con-siderable number of translations, when it cannot be attributed simply to imperfect linguistic knowledge or limited translation experience or to what Freud calls "the laws of resemblance, of indolence or of the tendency to haste" (Freud 1960: 221), an unconscious motivation should be sought. In such cases, moreover, it may prove instructive to consider the relation of the false cognate to the meaning of the source text as a whole, since the error may be symptomatic of the translator's implicit commentary on that text.

Consider an example from my own work as a translator of Italian. In 1983, I published my fourth book-length translation, a selection of short stories by the twentieth-century writer Dino Buzzati. In one of the stories entitled "The Bogeyman" ("Il Babau"), an engineer who serves on the city council deplores a babysitter's effort to discipline his son with "foolish superstitions" ("stolte superstizioni") such as the title character (Buzzati 1983: 118). Ultimately, the engineer persuades his fellow councilors to order the execution of the imaginary being. After the execution is carried out, the story concludes with the narrator issuing a warning to any fantasy that still survives:

> Galoppa, fuggi, galoppa, superstite fantasia. Avido di sterminarti, il mondo civile ti incalza alle calcagna, mai più ti darà pace.
>
> *(Buzzati 1971: 12)*

> Hurry, fly away, superstitious fantasies. The civil world, eager to exterminate you, follows in hot pursuit. It will never let you rest.
>
> *(Buzzati 1983: 122)*

My translation of this passage contains a false cognate: I used "superstitious" to render the Italian word "superstite," which actually means "surviving." The error, of which I was completely unaware at the time and which also escaped the notice of the publisher's copyeditor, was subsequently pointed out by a reviewer, who observed that

> the fantasies addressed are those which have somehow managed to stay alive, furtively, beyond the pale, in what Buzzati considers our clinical and positivistic times. The superstitious ones, alas, are ourselves, who believe we are more real.
>
> *(Cary 1983: 120)*

My error, in effect, reverses the meaning of the story: whereas Buzzati aims to question the engineer's charge that the Bogeyman is a foolish superstition, my translation concludes by agreeing with that charge.

Since by the time of this project I had already gained substantial translating experience, and since no other false cognates had been discovered in this or previous translations of mine, I want to suggest that the linguistic error is an unconsciously motivated remainder that constitutes a critical commentary on Buzzati's story. It communicates my repressed judgment that his treatment of the Bogeyman should be seen as superstitious because the psychological processes that he represents as supernatural or magical can be given rational explanations. Indeed, Buzzati's representation of the Bogeyman is inconsistent: on the one hand, the imaginary being is called a "comic friend/enemy" and described as "a gigantic blackish animal whose shape seemed a cross between a hippopotamus and a tapir" (Buzzati 1983: 122, 118); on the other hand, it functions along the lines of what Freud theorizes as a distressing punishment dream, in which the dreamer fulfills a wish "to be punished for a repressed or forbidden wishful impulse" (Freud 1953: 710; see also 613, 708–13). Thus the Bogeyman is said to "arouse trepidation, even fear" in "the child who was to be reproached," and he also causes "the engineer a few moments of anxiety" by appearing with the face of a superior who poses a threat to his professional ambitions, his "eminent position" in the firm where he works (Buzzati 1983: 118–19). Buzzati's representation of the Bogeyman combines a Freudian concept of the psychological determinants of dreams with a superstitious notion of external influences upon human thought and action (Freud himself draws this distinction in 1960: 256–60). My use of the false cognate points to this inconsistency and at the same time repudiates it.

In this context, however, the remainder released by the false cognate continues to reverberate with meanings that turn out finally to be contradictory. In rendering the Italian word "fantasia" as "fantasies," my English version includes another semantic shift, not merely from the singular to the plural, but from general to specific, from the mental faculty "fantasy" or "imagination" to particular "fantasies," a term that can apply to every fantastic manifestation in the story, whether the imaginary Bogeyman or the punishment dreams experienced by the children and by the engineer himself. As a result, the mistranslation, "superstitious fantasies," amounts to a sweeping dismissal of the Freudian concepts that can be perceived in Buzzati's story, a repudiation of the dreamwork, even of the existence of the unconscious, and therefore a denial that it might affect any human thought or action, including the translator's work. What the mistranslation shows, then, is that I as the translator shared the engineer's repressive rationalism in questioning Buzzati's mournful celebration of fantasy. I was responding to the Italian writer's representation of the unconscious in the same way that analysands sometimes respond to psychoanalysis: by resisting it, here by choosing a signifier that mistranslates and so represses a key signifier in the Italian text, while at the same time revealing my own repression through the contradiction created by my mistranslation.

How can my interpretation of the same symptomatic errors in my translation both assume the pertinence of psychoanalytic concepts and repudiate them? Freud's theories in fact offer an explanation for this contradiction. He first observes that the revelation of repressed anxieties and wishes in phenomena like verbal slips and misreadings corresponds to "the mechanism of dream-formation": in both, "by unfamiliar paths, and by the way of external associations, unconscious thoughts find expression as modifications of other thoughts" (Freud 1960: 277–78). Second, Freud's study of dreams demonstrates that the unconscious lacks any form or process of negation or the reconciliation of logical opposites. On the contrary, it works by sheer juxtaposition:

> Thoughts which are mutually contradictory make no attempt to do away with each other, but persist side by side. They often combine to form condensations, *just as though there were no contradiction between them*, or arrive at compromises such as our conscious thoughts would never tolerate but such as are often admitted in our actions.
>
> *(Freud 1953: 755, his italics)*

The unconscious motivations that can be detected in translators' errors, then, may reveal multiple and conflicting determinations, depending on the remainder that the translation releases, on the textual effects and intertextual connections that are unintentionally produced by the error. And the error may be symptomatic of a desire, not simply to interrogate, but to challenge or resist the discourse that is unfolded in the source text. What may ultimately be at stake in the translator's desire is the very social authority and cultural prestige of the source-text author, if not, more generally, a desire to achieve an authorial recognition for the work of translation.

The translator, the Name-of-the-Father, and the mother tongue

This point can be developed further if we introduce, finally, the Oedipal triangle that lies at the heart of Freudian psychoanalysis, but rethink it according to Lacan's language-based theories. For Lacan, "it is in the *name of the father* that we must recognize the support of the symbolic function which, from the dawn of history, has identified his person with the figure of the law" (Lacan 1977: 67). Lacan uses the term "Name-of-the-Father" to designate not a real person, the subject's actual father, but the symbolic function that the father comes to assume in the chain of signifiers constitutive of the subject. The Name-of-the-Father represents various manifestations of the "law," figures and institutions, values and beliefs that carry social authority or cultural prestige, starting with the ancient prohibition against incest that regulates marriage.

In Lacan's linguistic revision of the Oedipus complex, the Name-of-the-Father is defined as a signifier that eventually replaces the "Desire of the Mother," a desire that emerged in the subject when the demand for love was detached from mere physical need and experienced as lack. As Lacan observes, moreover, "if the desire of the mother *is* the phallus," insofar as she desires the father, "the child wishes to be the phallus in order to satisfy that desire" (ibid.: 289). The phallus in Lacan's thinking is not a bodily organ, not a penis, but a signifier that marks sexual difference with the subject's entry into language. The Name-of-the-Father intervenes in the child's psychological development to redirect the incestuous desire for the mother into socially acceptable forms, constructing a sexual identity for the subject within language (whether Lacan's theories apply to women remains unclear and controversial: for a brief but incisive account, see Easthope 1999b). For the male child, the paternal intervention is in effect a threat of castration that drives the subject to locate the desire of the phallus in other objects.

In turning to translation, we can notice that the translator is positioned between two signifying points: (1) the Name-of-the-Father in the form of a source author and text, which not only represent an original creator and an original composition in relation to the second-order status of the translator's work, but which may also have accrued significant social authority and cultural prestige; and (2) the mother tongue and the translation produced in it, the language that is not only the most familiar to the translator but also overdetermined by a libidinal identification with the maternal figure who first taught it, the language that is not only the primary site of the translator's linguistic competence and cultural knowledge, but also the site of the translation theories and practices that currently prevail in the translating culture (for clinical evidence of the relation between mother and mother tongue, see Amati Mehler et al. 1990: 90–105). The source author and text symbolically lay down a law of translation by requiring that the translator show sufficient respect for the linguistic and discursive structures of that text so as to imitate and thereby communicate it; the mother tongue leads the translator towards language use that is familiar and competent, that has in the past satisfied the translator's demand for communicative effectiveness, especially in translations, and that is governed by translation norms in the receiving situation. The Name-of-the-Father represented by the source author and text intervenes to prevent the translator's investment in the mother tongue from assimilating that text too closely and with too much distortion to the translating language and culture. In Serge Gavronsky's psychoanalytic reflection on the translating process, the translator "is forced to curtail himself (strictly speaking) in order to respect the interdictions on incest. To tamper with the text would be tantamount to eliminating, in part or totally, the father-author(ity), the dominant presence" (Gavronsky 1977: 55).

The translating process may nonetheless reveal the translator's repressed desire to challenge the source author by releasing an unconscious remainder. This desire may be one to assume a position of authority in the translation, to emulate the source author's status as an original creator and – depending on the author – as a canonical figure by producing a translation that implicitly questions that status. Bass's translation of Derrida's essay, Walsh's translation of Neruda's poem, and my translation of Buzzati's story all contain verbal dislocations and deviations wherein the translators resisted the source authors' cultural prestige by revising their texts in ways that answered to the translators' unconscious desires – namely, to accept a theory of translatability, to advance a conservative political ideology, to dismiss a psychoanalytic explanation of fantasies. In each case, the translator's revision indicates a more fundamental and urgent desire to act as an original author in relation to the source text.

These translations clearly involve a gain of meanings that do not simply exceed a lexicographical equivalence, but run counter to the meanings signified in the source texts. Yet translations inevitably effect a loss of source-text form and meaning as well, and here too an unconscious motivation may be present. As Freud points out, the verbal slips that reveal the workings of the unconscious may include omissions of key words or phrases. And his example, appropriately enough, hinges on a translation of a legal document:

> In one of the sections of the law dealing with the financial obligations of Austria and Hungary, settled in the "Compromise" of 1867 between the two countries, the word "actual" was left out of the Hungarian translation; and [the psychoanalyst] Dattner makes it plausible to suppose that the unconscious desire of the Hungarian parliamentary draftsman to grant Austria the least possible advantages played a part in causing the omission.
>
> *(Freud 1960: 128)*

Freud's commentary suggests that the unconscious desire revealed in the omission was at once collective, possibly nationalist, clearly political. Omissions in a translation may also point to other, more personal motives or relate generally to the status of the translator and the translation in relation to the source author and text.

Consider an example from William Weaver's 1968 version of Italo Calvino's collection of short stories, *Cosmicomiche* (*Cosmicomics*). Calvino's narrative strategy here is to give an anthropomorphic form to scientific ideas, using science to explore and defamiliarize human experiences. The story entitled "Lo zio acquatico" ("The Aquatic Uncle") is based on the theory of evolution: two reptiles who live on land – a boy and a girl – meet and fall in love, but their relationship encounters difficulties when the girl is attracted to the boy's uncle, who, as the title suggests, has not yet reached an evolutionary stage that allows him to leave his watery environment. The text concludes with the boy reptile reflecting on the biological changes that he sees occurring around him:

> Ogni tanto, tra le tante forme degli esseri viventi, incontravo qualcuno che "era uno" più di quanto io non lo fossi: uno che annunciava il futuro, ornitorinco che allatta il piccolo uscito dall'uovo, giraffa allampanata in mezzo alla vegetazione ancora bassa; o uno che testimoniava un passato senza ritorno, dinosauro superstite dopo ch'era cominciato il Cenozoico [...]
>
> *(Calvino 1965: 83)*

> Every now and then, among the many forms of living beings, I encountered one who "was somebody" more than I was: one who announced the future, the duck-billed platypus who nurses its young, just hatched from the egg; or I might encounter another who bore witness to a past beyond all return, a dinosaur who had survived into the beginning of the Cenozoic [...]
>
> *(Calvino 1968: 81–82)*

Weaver's English version adheres closely to the Italian text, even following the Italian syntax with minimal variation. Yet there is a substantial omission, the phrase "giraffa allampanata in mezzo alla vegetazione ancora bassa," which in a very literal rendering might read: "the giraffe grown emaciated amid vegetation that is still low." This phrase refers to the evolutionary theory of the French biologist Jean-Baptiste Lamarck (1744–1829), whose treatise *Philosophie zoologique* (1809) argues that organisms develop anatomical traits in response to a need created by their environment. Thus according to Lamarck the giraffe's elongated neck resulted from the need to eat the foliage of trees in regions of Africa where grass was lacking. Lamarck was eventually discredited by Darwin's theory of natural selection, which forms the basis of Calvino's story. Yet in the concluding passage Calvino's allusion is characteristic of his wry humor: here the Lamarckian giraffe has ironically grown taller than the vegetation.

How do we explain Weaver's omission of this phrase? It is important to observe, first, that the omission was certainly unconscious. By the mid-1960s, Weaver was not just a highly experienced translator who had been working with Italian fiction for more than a decade; his translations were also very accomplished, much in demand among American and British publishers and favorably received by readers. His version of *Cosmicomiche* in fact won the American National Book Award for translation in 1968. In a phone conversation (13 March 2001), Weaver himself described the omission as unconscious, "just an oversight" which he could not explain.

He also provided some additional information that illuminates the circumstances under which he was working. He said that, although Calvino's writing had been translated into English since the 1950s, *Cosmicomiche* was the first of the Italian writer's books that he himself translated. And Weaver remarked, interestingly, that Calvino had chosen him after rejecting another English translator as inadequate to the task. After noting that the omission is "too large to be done on my own," Weaver mentioned that Calvino sometimes revised previously published Italian texts before they were translated into English. But Weaver had no way of telling whether the omission was due to such a revision, and he did not remember it, a point that seems significant since, as Freud noted, "distressing memories succumb especially easily to motivated forgetting" (Freud 1960: 147). For the fact is that an authorial revision seems improbable, given the humor that characterizes so much of Calvino's work and hence the likelihood that he would want to preserve it here. None of the Italian editions of *Cosmicomiche* shows any alteration of the passage in question.

To these details must be added the fact that Weaver's version of Calvino's text is extremely confident, distinguished by a slangy lexicon and syntax that is somewhat free, but generally consistent in maintaining a lexicographical equivalence. Common Italian expressions – "Vedrà che ci si trovava bene" ("You'll see how well you'll get along"), "Mica storie" ("[It is] not a lie"), "Se ci stai stella" ("If you stay with us, beautiful") – are replaced by colorful English colloquialisms: "You'll be nice and snug," "I'm not fooling," "If you're game, sweetie" (Calvino 1965: 74, 77, 81; 1968: 74, 77, 79). Weaver's translating throughout shows an impressive command of various registers and styles of English. Thus with a phrase like "mi precipitai a riconquistarla," which could be rendered simply as "I hurried to win her back," Weaver resorts to a more literary eloquence: "I hastened to woo her back" (Calvino 1965: 81; 1968: 80). And the translation is endowed with a greater explicitness than the Italian text in accordance with the preference for precision and cohesiveness distinctive of English. For instance, the phrase "all'asciutto" ("in the dry place," "on the dryness") is rendered as "on dry land," the phrase "i nostri vecchi" ("our elderly") as "our ancestors," and the verb "viene?" (in this context meaning "Will you come?") as "Won't you come home with us?" (Calvino 1965: 71, 72, 74; 1968: 71, 72, 74). Weaver's translation displays such enormous control, it is so fluent and expressive, that the omission becomes all the more conspicuous and difficult to explain away as a mere oversight.

I want to argue that the omission is symptomatic of the translator's unconscious desire to compete against the foreign author. The circumstances surrounding the translation – notably that *Cosmicomics* was Weaver's first translation of Calvino's acclaimed writing, that the Italian author chose the translator after rejecting another one, and that the translator executed the project with such confident control – all suggest that the translator was seeking Calvino's approval of his work. Yet in so doing he was also emulating Calvino's authorship and even, in the increased precision and explicitness of the English version, surpassing the linguistic and stylistic features of the Italian text. The omission, more specifically, was subtly provocative: by deleting an allusive phrase that is so characteristic of the Italian author's wryly humorous style, Weaver subliminally challenged Calvino's identity as a writer, as well as the cultural prestige that his writing had already acquired in Italy and elsewhere at that time.

Insofar as the giraffe's elongated neck constitutes a phallic image, the omission can be viewed as a symbolic castration of the paternal author, which was supplied by a greater fluency in the mother tongue. To improve coherence and enhance the readability of the English, Weaver inserted the phrase, "I might encounter," absent from the Italian and repetitive of the earlier phrase, "I encountered."

Some conclusions

The notion of "similarity" in translation can be understood as two different kinds of relationship: first, as a resemblance between the source and translated texts and, second, as a resemblance between the translation and other values and practices in the receiving situation. These two relationships are not simply opposed, but often mutually undermining. Yet they work together to guide every translation practice. Neither of them pre-exists the translating process; both are rather constructions. The similarity between the source text and the translation that is most commonly established today is a lexicographical equivalence; it is always constructed on the basis of irreducible differences, structural and discursive differences between languages, axiological and ideological differences between cultures. A similarity between the translation and the receiving situation is always constructed on the basis of equally irreducible differences, a difference between the form and theme of the source text and texts originally written in the translating language and culture, but also a different network of connections – intratextual and intertextual – than those that constituted the source text in the source culture. In translation, difference always precedes similarity. It is difference that motivates the reductive search for similarities, even with the paradoxical hope of communicating the originary difference.

A cause of the irreducible differences in translation is the translator's unconscious. It must first be distinguished from the preconscious, from what the translator has learned but does not formulate consciously during the translating process. The preconscious includes the translator's knowledge of the source and translating languages, but also what Gideon Toury (1995) would call the cultural and social norms that shape the translating process, especially the translating traditions, conventions, and practices that currently prevail in the receiving situation. Although this body of knowledge is applied automatically in translating, it can be made conscious and articulated if the translator steps back from the process or product and examines either with critical detachment. The unconscious, however, remains by definition beyond the translator's cognitive grasp and is available only to another investigator – or perhaps to the translator at a later moment and in another, analytical situation.

The translator's unconscious inexorably introduces differences into the translation because it emerges within the translating language and culture and in relation to the source author and text, a relation that may well be oppositional. The unconscious, especially in the case of a writing practice like translating, is fundamentally linguistic and textual, "already," as Derrida puts it, "a weave of pure traces, differences in which meaning and force are united – a text nowhere present, consisting of archives which are *always already* transcriptions" (Derrida 1978: 211). The translator's unconscious is "nowhere present" because it comes into being in the translating process and is revealed through the remainder in the translation, through textual effects and intertextual connections created by the translator in an effort to render the source text.

Some effects and connections may in fact be intentional; others exceed even the experienced translator's conscious intention, taking the form of misconstructions or misreadings that are symptomatic of an unconscious motivation, a repressed anxiety, an unsatisfied desire. These errors may be motivated by the source text, by its formal and thematic features, by the particular passage in which the errors occur. Yet they may also be triggered by something that lies outside of the immediate context of the error but is nonetheless connected to it, the larger cultural and social situation in which the translation is produced. In such cases, the symptomatic errors may reveal the translator's political unconscious, a repressed desire to resolve a social conflict on the imaginary level of a translation. The errors in question are symptomatic, not cognitive, not merely mistakes or oversights, because they are made by experienced translators and when given a detailed contextualization they reveal the unconscious operation of transindividual factors (cf. Timpanaro 1976, from whom I dissent). These factors insure that the unconscious will always work against the similarities that the translator seeks to establish and prevent the translation from ever being a simple act of communication.

My examination of the translator's unconscious must nonetheless remain provisional in the absence of more cases. And significant issues remain to be considered, although they can only be formulated generally here. Thus the cases I have presented all involve male translators, and this limitation, especially given the feminist reflections on psychoanalysis (see, for example, Mitchell 1975 and Mitchell and Rose 1982), poses the question of whether the gender identity of the source author or the translator has a bearing on the nature and significance of the symptomatic textual features that might occur. Would a source text by a canonical female writer release errors of a particular kind in a male translator's text? In view of the centuries-old representations of authorship as male (see Chamberlain 1988), would a female translator unconsciously make an authorial challenge in translating a male writer? The clinical evidence that establishes a link between the libidinal investment in the maternal figure and a subject's relation to the mother tongue raises questions about the translator's use of his or her mother tongue. Does the depth of the libidinal investment carry implications for the translator's inclination to experiment with his or her mother tongue? Does this investment affect translating from the translator's mother tongue into a second language? These questions need to be addressed; I state them in this rapid way only to suggest the extent to which a psychoanalytic approach to translation might be productive and illuminating.

Finally, a word about translation research methods. In order to study the translator's unconscious, the translation scholar must obviously bring to the translation process or product a set of theoretical assumptions drawn from the psychoanalytical tradition. Without such assumptions, the translator's unconscious does not become visible or available for analysis, and errors, even in translations produced by the most accomplished of translators, will not acquire any significance beyond their status as errors. Moreover, if psychoanalytic assumptions are not accepted as working hypotheses, no amount of empirical evidence is likely to incline a translation scholar to accept an argument based on them. Of course, psychoanalysis offers an explanation for the refusal to accept key assumptions like the existence and operation of the unconscious: the resistance to analysis is a form of repression. And we may well wonder what exactly the repression is concealing in an academic discourse, what individual or institutional interests are being served. Perhaps what most recommends the psychoanalytic tradition to translation studies is that it can help translators and translation research and practice to avoid being held hostage to such hidden agendas.

[2002]

3

TRANSLATING DERRIDA ON TRANSLATION

Relevance and disciplinary resistance

The unique and the exemplary

This is the story of my struggle as an English-language translator and student of translation who questions its continuing marginality in the United States. Yet this can also be read as the story of your struggle, you who have an interest in translation, who wish to study and practice it and who therefore can be affected adversely by the cultural and institutional marginality that limits the opportunities to do both in this country, as well as elsewhere. For since American economic and political dominance sustains the global hegemony of English, insuring that it is the most translated language worldwide but relatively little translated into, the marginality of translation in the United States inevitably produces adverse effects abroad, notably by maintaining unequal patterns of cultural exchange (for translation figures, see Venuti 2008: 11–12). Thus, in the particular instance of translation, the "you" for whom I claim to speak – and hence the "I" who speaks – may be taken as universal.

Nevertheless, my shift from "I" to "you" must not be so rapid, must not appear so seamless, because my story is fairly unique, occasioned by a translation project. I want to discuss the circumstances surrounding my translation of a lecture by Jacques Derrida on the theme of translation. To be sure, translating the work of this contemporary French philosopher requires that one be a specialist in a certain sense, possessing a knowledge not only of the French language, but also of Continental philosophical traditions, and not only of translation practices between French and English, but also of the discursive strategies that have been used to translate Derrida's writing for several decades. Yet these different kinds of specialized knowledge are not sufficient for the task: one must also *desire* to translate Derrida. Indeed, scholars who admire his work, who teach, research, and edit it may decline to translate it, both because his playful, allusive writing poses numerous difficulties to the translator and because translation continues to rank low in the scale of scholarly rewards. Of course, if the hand is willing, it may still be tied by the legal factors that always constrain translation (see Venuti 1998: chapter 3). Derrida's French texts have accrued such immense capital – symbolic, cultural, and economic – that academic presses have tended to purchase exclusive world rights from his French publishers and from the author himself. This means that a translator must not only receive permission to translate Derrida's work, but must also negotiate with presses to avoid copyright infringement. The many complicated factors that play into translating Derrida seem to make such a project so special as to undermine any effort to treat it as exemplary. How, then, can I presume to do so?

Derrida can help to answer this question. He has called attention to the "interbreeding and accumulating [of] two logics" ("croisant et accumulant" in Derrida 1996: 40) that occur in any testimony seeking to be representative, the simultaneous coexistence of empirical individuality – in this case, a marginalized individuality – and universal exemplarity. "What happens," he asks,

> when someone resorts to describing an allegedly uncommon "situation," mine, for example, by testifying to it in terms that go beyond it, in a language whose generality takes on a value that is in some way structural, universal, transcendental, or ontological? When anybody who happens by infers the following: "What holds for me, irreplaceably, also applies to all. Substitution is in progress; it has already taken effect. Everyone can say the same thing for themselves and of themselves. It suffices to hear me; I am the universal hostage."
>
> *(Derrida 1998: 19–20)*

Derrida's answer to the question of exemplarity hinges on the critique of the linguistic sign embodied in his concept of *différance*. If meaning is an effect of relations and differences along a potentially endless chain of signifiers – polysemous, intertextual, subject to infinite linkages – then meaning is always differential and deferred, never present as an original unity, always already a site of proliferating possibilities which can be activated in diverse ways by the receivers of an utterance and which therefore exceed the control of individual users (see especially Derrida 1982a). Language use, despite biological metaphors embedded in expressions like "native language" and "mother tongue," is not natural in its origins, but cultural; not only is it acquired from immersion and education in a culture, but that acquisition so infiltrates individual uses as to make them fundamentally, usually unwittingly, collective. And the relation between the individual and the collective in language is never an equality, but always weighted towards the "other" from which or whom one learns a language. As Derrida remarks,

> We only ever speak one language – and, since it returns to the other, it exists asymmetrically, always for *the other*, from the other, kept by the other. Coming from the other, remaining with the other, and returning to the other.
>
> *(Derrida 1998: 40)*

We only ever speak one language, but it is never our own and never simply one language. The point can be rephrased in more specifically social terms: a language is imposed by the exigencies of a social situation that is structured hierarchically, whether that situation be cultural or political, whether it be a matter of addressing a specialized audience from the margins of an institution or a matter of submitting to the limitations and exclusions of a colonial project.

This resemblance between the cultural and political situations of language can be pursued only so far before it effaces the brutality of a project like colonialism. Still, it is worth pursuing a bit further here for the light it can shed on the marginality of a cultural practice like translation as well as the exemplary status of my own translation of Derrida. Taking his comments as a point of departure, then, we can recognize that the "other" that is a cultural institution or political authority may involve the imposition of a monolingualism, an academic or colonial discourse, that seeks to homogenize and limit language use. By the same token, the monolingualism imposed by the other may endow the specificity of individual use with a collective force and hence a transindividual and possibly universal exemplarity. An individual testimony can incorporate a double structure, "that of exemplarity and that of the host as hostage," because "the structure appears in the experience of the injury, the offense," here a restrictive monolingualism imposed on the group of which the individual is a member (Derrida 1998: 20, 26).

This line of thinking can be illustrated, first, by Derrida's lecture on translation. Entitled "Qu'est-ce qu'une traduction 'relevante'?" (or in my English version "What Is a 'Relevant' Translation?"), the lecture was delivered in 1998 at the annual seminar of the Assises de la Traduction Littéraire à Arles (ATLAS). A French organization with approximately 800 members, ATLAS is dedicated to promoting literary translation and to protecting the status of the literary translator. The prospect of addressing an audience that consisted of professional translators, interested primarily in translation practices rather than theoretical concepts, imposed a certain language and mode of address on Derrida's lecture. Not only does he open with an elaborate apology for speaking about translation to experienced translators, but he also avoids a purely philosophical presentation of his ideas. Instead of resorting to a speculative commentary on a key text, as he has done elsewhere, he addresses one of the most practical themes in the history of translation theory, notably the antithesis between "word-for-word" and "sense-for-sense" translation which occupied such writers as Cicero and Jerome. He also grounds his remarks on an incisive interpretation of the role of translation in Shakespeare's *The Merchant of Venice*. Derrida's effort to give specificity to his ideas, to locate suggestive applications, is most striking in his exploration of particular translation problems, especially those in which we glimpse him as translator. He proposes a French version for a line in Portia's speech on "mercy" and recalls his own French rendering of a central concept in Hegel's dialectics.

These individual cases, furthermore, come to assume an exemplary status in his exposition – exemplary of a universal concept of "relevant" translation and of the cultural and institutional impact that any translation may have. The relevant translation, Derrida writes, is mystifying: it "presents itself as the transfer of an intact signified through the inconsequential vehicle of any signifier whatsoever" (Derrida 2001: 195). Although he questions this mystification, he sees it as inevitable insofar as every translation participates in an "economy of in-betweenness," positioned somewhere between "absolute relevance, the most appropriate, adequate, univocal transparency, and the most aberrant and opaque irrelevance" (ibid.: 179). He then applies this concept to his use of the French word "relève" to render Hegel's term "Aufhebung," a translation that was at first "empirically personal," serving his own interpretive interests, but that ultimately underwent "institutional accreditation and canonization in the public sphere," achieving widespread use as the accepted rendering, becoming "known as the most relevant translation possible" (ibid.: 183).

It is remarkable that Derrida's lecture also *resists* the monolingualism imposed by addressing an audience of French translators. Although written in French, although cultivating a translatorly practicality by discussing specific cases, the text is in fact polylingual, incorporating English and German as well, and the argument takes a philosophical turn at points. Thus Derrida apologizes for choosing a title that is "untranslatable" because the provenance of the word "relevant" remains uncertain: it may be French and therefore translatable into English, or English yet undergoing assimilation into French and therefore resistant to translation. As a result, Derrida argues, the word sheds light on the nature of translation today: because the unity of "relevant" is questionable, because the signifier potentially contains more than one word insofar as it produces a homophonic or homonymic effect, it derails the translation process and makes clear that the so-called relevant translation rests on a particular conception of language, one that assumes "the indivisible unity of an acoustic form incorporating or signifying the indivisible unity of a meaning or concept" (ibid.: 181). Although Derrida tells his audience that he will forego any discussion "on the level of generality, in theoretical or more obviously philosophical or speculative reflections which I have elsewhere ventured on various universal problems of Translation," his specific cases give rise to philosophical reflections and point to universal problems (ibid.: 178). In fact, his lecture answers to a second, more philosophical context: the commentary on Shakespeare's play derives from a seminar on forgiveness and perjury which he taught earlier in 1998.

My translation project, begun in 2000, was likewise situated in two different, even conflicting contexts, straddling two fields, addressing two academic audiences, each of whom imposed a particular conceptual discourse on my work, each of whom demanded a translation that was relevant in their terms. On the one hand was the field known as "cultural studies," a loose amalgam of approaches that was nonetheless dominated by a theoretical orientation, a synthesis of poststructuralism with varieties of Marxism, feminism, and psychoanalysis (see Easthope 1991). This synthesis enabled scholars to range across different historical periods and cultural forms, both elite and mass, and to delimit such areas of research as colonialism, sexual identity, and globalization (see, for example, During 1999). On the other hand was the field known as "translation studies," an equally loose amalgam of approaches that was nonetheless dominated by an empirical orientation, a synthesis of such branches of linguistics as text linguistics, discourse analysis, and pragmatics with "polysystem" theory, wherein culture is viewed as a complicated network of interrelations among diverse forms and practices (see Even-Zohar 1990). This synthesis enabled scholars to study the language of translated texts as well as the norms that constrain translation, in particular cultural polysystems, resulting in research that at its most productive combined linguistic and systemic approaches (see, for example, Hatim and Mason 1997 and Toury 1995).

Cultural studies and translation studies are not necessarily opposed. My own translation research and practice have consistently drawn on work in both fields. Yet as these fields stood at the beginning of the new millennium, they revealed deep conceptual divisions that complicated any project with the goal of addressing scholars in both. The theoretical orientation of cultural studies marginalized research into specific translations and translation practices, whereas the empirical orientation of translation studies marginalized research into issues of philosophy and cultural politics. Because both fields were firmly institutionalized at the time – even if they occupied different institutional sites in different countries – and because they both involved international scholarly communities, they endowed my translation project with a universal significance that exceeded the individual case. If I am inclined to take my own work as exemplary, if I dare to speak for you who share my interest in translation, the reason is that we also share a basic set of institutional conditions. In 2000, those conditions established a double academic marginality: on the one hand, the neglect in cultural studies of the materiality of translation; on the other hand, the neglect in translation studies of the philosophical implications and social effects that accompany every translation practice.

Translation in cultural studies

To understand the peculiar marginality of translation, I want to turn to Pierre Bourdieu's work on academic institutions, where he has located a "special form of anti-intellectualism" (Bourdieu 1988: 94–95). For Bourdieu, academic anti-intellectualism, however oxymoronic the term may seem, consists of a "secret resistance to innovation and to intellectual creativity, [an] aversion to ideas and to a free and critical spirit," which he has linked to "the effect of the recognition granted to an institutionalized thought only on those who implicitly accept the limits assigned by the institution" (ibid.: 95). To work in a field is to accept such institutional limits by maintaining an investment in the materials and practices that define the field, even when a social agent aims to change it in a radical way. As Bourdieu observes, "wanting to undertake a revolution in a field is to accord the essential of what the field tacitly demands, namely that it is important, that the game played is sufficiently important for one to want to undertake a revolution in it" (Bourdieu 1998: 78). Hence attempts to introduce different materials and practices are likely to encounter resistance if they represent a fundamental challenge to the value of institutionalized thought, if they seek to shift the importance invested in it to another kind of thinking. The resistance can take the form of sheer exclusion, such as the refusal of publication by academic journals and presses, the rejection of applications for academic appointments, and the denial of tenure and promotion. The resistance can also take forms that are less drastic, such as negative book reviews, or more revisionary, such as the transformation of marginal materials and practices so that they can be assimilated to the current state of the field. The institutional fate of translation studies in the United States has involved many of these forms of disciplinary resistance.

For the fact is that translation has yet to gain a firm foothold in the American academy. Whereas over the past twenty years European countries have witnessed a substantial growth of translator training faculties as well as graduate degrees in translation research, with some programs dating back to the 1940s, the United States has lagged far behind, so that the translation program, even the odd course or doctoral dissertation in translation studies, remains an exception (for a list of programs periodically updated by Anthony Pym, see http://isg.urv.es/tti/tti.htm).

Translation has encountered the disciplinary resistance that Bourdieu describes, first of all, because it runs counter to institutionalized practices in foreign-language instruction. Since the late 1960s, the most prevalent form of foreign-language pedagogy has been "direct communication" or "total immersion," in which the goal of native proficiency leads to the suppression of any teaching methods that might require the student to rely on the mediation of English. Consequently, translation has been stigmatized and excluded as a method of foreign-language instruction, even though it served precisely this purpose for centuries. Translation has tended to enter the American academy by establishing institutional sites that are relatively autonomous from universities, like the Monterey Institute of International Studies, or cross-disciplinary, like the collaboration between modern foreign languages and applied linguistics that underlies the translation programs at Kent State University. The first decade of the twenty-first century saw more attention paid to translation in departments and programs of comparative literature, partly because of the necessity to teach foreign literatures in English on the undergraduate level and partly because of the return of "world" literature as an area of research (see, for example, Damrosch 2003). Yet translation was "often grudgingly endorsed by comparatists" who continued to assign greater value to original compositions (Saussy 2006: x; cf. Ungar 2006: 127–28). It was not until 2012 that a department of comparative literature in the United States (at the University of Oregon) appointed a tenure-track assistant professor who was qualified specifically to teach and to conduct and supervise research in translation studies.

The sheer practicality of translation – the fact that innovative research can shape practice while innovative practices can stimulate research – has played a part in preventing it from gaining wide acceptance within cultural studies. Here the disciplinary resistance seems to be due to the theoretical orientation that has dominated this field since the 1980s. Because much cultural commentary has taken a highly speculative turn, some of the most distinguished academic journals tend to reject submissions that, in the editors' eyes, lack theoretical sophistication or that focus on particular works and historical periods without raising theoretical issues that are currently under debate. Translation studies can engage with such issues, but insofar as its object is a linguistic practice it will inevitably raise them in specific textual and social terms that qualify theoretical speculation and ultimately expose its limitations in accounting for translated texts. Translation research needs an empirical grounding if it is to affect translation practices as well as translation theory, history, and criticism. Yet this practical dimension has not always been welcomed by journals. *Critical Inquiry*, for example, in nearly four decades, has published only one essay that concentrates on translation practice, the poet-translator Reginald Gibbons's account of his work under the rubric "Artists on Art" (Gibbons 1985). Although this journal has acquired enormous authority as a venue for theoretically based cultural commentary, it did not publish an essay in translation theory until my version of Derrida's lecture appeared in its twenty-seventh volume. Yet much of the theory cited in the journal was first formulated in foreign-language texts that had to be translated into English to exert their influence.

Submissions in translation studies have been made to *Critical Inquiry*, but they were rejected. Of course, they were not made by an author who possesses Derrida's symbolic and cultural capital in American academic institutions. In 1989, for instance, I submitted a manuscript entitled "Simpatico," an early draft of a chapter that would appear in my 1995 book *The Translator's Invisibility*. The manuscript addressed what I believed to be the theoretical issues involved in my translations of a contemporary Italian poet: it explored specific verbal choices by examining their implications for the philosophical themes that the poet had drawn from Nietzsche and Heidegger; and it considered, with the help of such theorists as Gilles Deleuze and Félix Guattari, the larger questions of why and how the translator should signal the linguistic and cultural differences of the source text in a translation. According to the letter of rejection from the managing editor, "there was quite some interest in [my] essay. The general consensus, however, is that it is best suited for a different journal" (letter from James Williams, 5 March 1990). I was recommended to send it to *Translation Review*, the journal of the American Literary Translators Association edited by Rainer Schulte, who was mentioned in the letter. Under Schulte's editorship, this journal has generally avoided scholarly articles, especially those that engage in theoretical commentary, in favor of belletristic essays that address problems of translation practice. Hence it was clear that the editors of *Critical Inquiry* had rejected my manuscript mainly because they did not find it theoretical enough or sufficiently theoretical in their terms.

Those terms have come under scrutiny. *Critical Inquiry*, it has been argued, has not been equally open to every variety of literary and cultural theory that has been imported into the American academy since the 1970s (see Spanos 1993: 182–84 and Cohen 2001). On the contrary, in Sande Cohen's view, the journal "has stressed French theory only when it serves a more rigorous humanism," in fact "the classical subject of liberalism," whereby "the Nietzsche line is all but refused," including not only Nietzsche, but also thinkers he has influenced, such as Heidegger and Deleuze and Guattari (Cohen 2001: 201, 204, 202). This line figured prominently in late twentieth-century Italian poetry, particularly in the tendency of Italian poets to decenter the liberal subject, but it also informed my effort to question the communicative dimension of translation, notably its ability to reproduce a foreign poet's voice. My article ultimately appeared in 1991 in *SubStance*, which bills itself as "a journal of theory and criticism" and has long been receptive, not only to translation studies, but also to the Nietzschean line in European theory.

With the emergence of such areas of research as colonialism, translation has increasingly become a topic of discussion in cultural studies. And rightly so: the colonization of the Americas, Asia, and Africa could not have occurred without inter-preters, both native and colonial, nor without the translation of effective texts, reli-gious, legal, educational. Yet what I shall call the *theoreticism* of some research in this area, the emphasis on the construction of theoretical concepts to the exclusion of textual analysis and empirical research, has limited the attention given to translation.

Homi Bhabha, for instance, one of the most influential theorists of colonial dis-course, opens his essay "Signs Taken for Wonders" by discussing the charismatic quality that the English book acquired in such British colonies as India. As Bhabha notes, it is "a process of displacement that, paradoxically, makes the presence of the book wondrous to the extent to which it is repeated, translated, misread, displaced"; to demonstrate his point, he quotes a lengthy passage in which an Indian catechist describes a huge crowd outside of Delhi reading "the Gospel of our Lord, translated into the Hindoostanee Tongue" (Bhabha 1994: 102–4). Bhabha acknowledges that "in my use of 'English' there is a transparency of reference that registers a certain obvious presence: the Bible translated into Hindi, propagated by Dutch or native catechists, is still the English book" to the colonized (ibid.: 108). And this acknowl-edgment occasions an exploration of colonial authority, in which he relies on a pro-ductive synthesis of such poststructuralist thinkers as Derrida and Foucault. Yet the exposition remains on a very high level of generality, and absolutely no effort is made to consider what implications the translated status of the text might carry for the theory of colonial discourse that Bhabha formulates so powerfully.

An analysis of Hindi translations of the Bible is likely to reveal linguistic and cul-tural differences that support and deepen Bhabha's notion of the inherent ambiva-lence of colonial discourse. Vicente Rafael's work on Spanish colonialism in the Philippines bears out this likelihood: Rafael shows how Tagalog translations of reli-gious texts at once advanced and undermined the Spanish presence (Rafael 1988). In Bhabha's case, however, the theoreticism of the commentary preempts any close textual analysis, whether of literary texts or of translations. Within colonial studies, his work has been criticized for stressing discourse at the cost of neglecting the material conditions of colonialism (see, for example, Loomba 1998: 96, 179–80). The stress on discourse, however, does not include any consideration of the discursive strategies employed in translations.

Even when cultural theorists have themselves produced translations of literary and theoretical texts, their acute awareness that no translation can communicate a source text in an untroubled fashion does not lead them to provide a searching examination of specific translations, whether those made by others or their own. Gayatri Spivak's important essay "The Politics of Translation" (1992) offers an incisive understanding of translation, at once postcolonial and feminist, informed by poststructuralist theories of language and textuality. But her exposition quickly shifts from interlingual to "cultural" translation, from a discussion of the specific linguistic and cultural differences that complicate translating between languages – especially those that are positioned in a hierarchical relation – to a speculative commentary on several literary and theoretical texts. Here she construes translation as adaptation or parody (in *Foe* "Coetzee as white creole translates *Robinson Crusoe* by representing Friday as the agent of a withholding"), as oral transmission ("the change of the mother-tongue from mother to daughter" in Toni Morrison's *Beloved*), and as ideological critique and political appropriation ("to limn the politics of a certain kind of clandestine postcolonial reading" in Peter de Bolla's *The Discourse on the Sublime*) (Spivak 1992: 195, 200). Spivak expresses the hope that this commentary will "pass on a lesson to the translator in the narrow sense," the interlingual translator, but the discussion of the texts under examination, especially de Bolla's, is much more detailed, much more focused on extracts, than the brief comments on actual translation choices in the first part of the essay (ibid.: 197).

Similarly, Spivak's translations from the work of the Bengali fiction writer Mahasweta Devi are accompanied, not by any explanation of her strategies, but by essays that draw on various theoretical concepts to illuminate the political dimensions of Devi's writing. This omission becomes more noticeable when Spivak reports a suggestive criticism of her work. After asserting that the translations are "going to be published in both India and the United States," she mentions that the Indian publisher and translation scholar Sujit Mukherjee criticized their English for not being "sufficiently accessible to readers in this country [India]" (Spivak 1995: xxiii, xxviii). Spivak acknowledges that her English "belongs more to the rootless American-based academic prose than the more subcontinental idiom of [her] youth"; she even admits that whether Indian texts should be translated into Indian English "is an interesting question" (ibid.: xxviii; cf. Devi 1997: 16, where Spivak states that "I have used 'straight English,' whatever that may be"). But, notwithstanding a generally phrased "Translator's Note," she does not address the issue with the sustained attention that she gives to Devi's themes.

What makes the language of Spivak's translations all the more intriguing is the fact that it is richly heterogeneous, far removed from both academic prose and a subcontinental dialect, hardly "straight English." Here are two extracts from her version of Devi's story "Breast-Giver":

> The boy got worried at the improper supply of fish and fries in his dish. He considered that he'd be fucked if the cook gave him away. Therefore on another occasion, driven by the Bagdad djinn, he stole his mother's ring, slipped it into the cook's pillowcase, raised a hue and cry, and got the cook kicked out.
>
> *(Devi 1997: 40)*

> Then Kangali said, "Sir! How shall I work at the sweetshop any longer. I can't stir the vat with my kerutches. You are god. You are feeding so many people in so many ways. I am not begging. Find me a job."
>
> *(Ibid.: 44)*

This mixture of current standard usage with colloquialism and obscenity, of Britishisms with Americanisms, of orthodox with unorthodox spelling to signal differences in pronunciation inevitably raises the question of whether and to what extent Spivak's translating has recreated or transformed Devi's textual effects. To answer this question, the abrupt shifts in dialect, register, and style need to be examined not simply against the Bengali texts but against the translator's interpretation of those texts. How, one wonders, are such verbal choices linked to the cultural values and political agendas that Spivak so ardently espouses in the commentaries that accompany her translations?

Translation in translation studies

During roughly the same period, the 1990s, discursive strategies were paid a great deal of attention within translation studies, but the translated text tended to be treated in such a way as to reveal a different form of academic anti-intellectualism: a focus on the data yielded by close analysis at the expense of the various philosophical, cultural, and political issues raised by translation. Here the disciplinary resistance seems to be due to the empirical orientation that has dominated the field since the 1960s, driven largely by the varieties of linguistics that provided the analytical tools. Thus research that is less empirical and more speculative, or that uses different categories of analysis which are more pertinent to cultural studies, was likely to be not merely misunderstood, but questioned for not providing detail that is sufficient or representative. In a survey of linguistic perspectives on translation, Mona Baker took this position in relation to my work:

> Apart from analysing poetic devices such as metre, rhyme, alliteration, and so on, Venuti draws on categories which a linguistically oriented researcher would consider too broad and too restricted to the traditional levels of vocabulary and syntax: archaisms, dialect, regional choice, syntactic inversions. A linguistically oriented scholar would typically want to provide analyses which offer finer distinctions at the levels of lexis and syntax and which also incorporate other levels of description, such as information flow, cohesion, linguistic mechanisms of expressing politeness, norms of turn-taking in conversation, and so on.
>
> *(Baker 2000: 23)*

Conspicuously absent from Baker's comment is any indication that I was analyzing the literary effects of literary translations, and that the selection of linguistic features was guided by a particular interpretive occasion, an effort to link the effects of specific translation strategies to patterns of reception and to cultural values (she cites Venuti 2008, first published in 1995, and a previously published version of Venuti 1998: chapter 1). Since my analysis used relatively few of the tools that linguists generally bring to translation studies, it implicitly raised the question of whether the "finer distinctions" produced by such tools are necessary for an exploration of literary and cultural issues or even for the development of translation practices. More precisely, the categories that Baker cites make clear that we were relying on *different forms of linguistics*: her comment assumes that translation studies should deploy systemic-functional linguistics ("cohesion") and varieties of pragmatics ("politeness" theory, "turn-taking in conversation"), whereas my analyses are rooted in French discourse analysis and poststructuralist concepts of textuality, particularly the linguistic construction of subjectivity and the remainder that complicates communication (see, for example, Williams 1999 and Lecercle 1990). Ultimately, Baker's comment points to an incommensurability between two current approaches within translation studies, one informed by kinds of linguistics prevalent in anglophone cultures, the other informed by literary and cultural theories imported from the Continent, especially France.

Indeed, from this theoretical standpoint, the results of linguistically oriented approaches can seem trivial, inconsequential not only for translation research but also for translator training. An American linguist, for instance, conducted a study to investigate the connection between "unwarranted transcoding," translating that reproduces the structures of the source text, and the level of translating proficiency that the translator has attained (Colina 1999). The text was the Spanish title of a recipe, "Pastel de queso con grosellas negras y jengibre," with some ineffective renderings taking an ambiguous form, "Cheesecake with black currants and ginger," compared to a clearer version, "Black currant and ginger cheesecake." The study was intended to test a hypothesis formulated by the translation theorist Gideon Toury, namely that "language students would show the most instances of unwarranted transcoding, while professionals would exhibit the fewest cases" because the latter have absorbed professional norms against this kind of translating (ibid.: 382; see Toury 1986; 1995: 275–77). The result – "the number of cases of inappropriate transcoding decreased as experience and/or education in translation increased" – was unremarkable and wholly predictable, so much so as to question the need for an elaborate survey that involved faculty and students at several American universities (Colina 1999: 383).

What is questionable here is not the use of empirical research, which remains valuable to document and explore the factors that figure into the production, circulation, and reception of translations. The problem is rather an *empiricism* that focuses narrowly on minute linguistic materials and practices to the exclusion of such decisive social considerations as the commission that the translator has received and the prospective audience for the translation. As Louis Althusser argued, empiricist epistemologies claim direct or unmediated access to a reality or truth, but this claim mystifies a process of "abstraction" in which essential data are distinguished from inessential on the basis of a privileged theoretical model, and a real object is reduced to an object of a particular kind of knowledge (Althusser and Balibar 1970: 34–43). The empiricism that has long prevailed in translation studies tends to privilege analytical concepts derived from linguistics, regardless of how narrow or limited they may be in their explanatory power. And, from the vantage point of these concepts, the essence of a translation is an abstracted notion of language.

This is most evident in the many university programs that take a linguistics-oriented approach to translation research and translator training. A book that has received many course adoptions in such programs is Basil Hatim and Ian Mason's *The Translator as Communicator* (1997), which brings together an array of linguistic concepts to perform close analyses of translations in different genres and media. For instance, the authors analyze the subtitling in a foreign-language film with the aid of politeness theory, a formalization of speech acts by which a speaker maintains or threatens an addressee's "face," defined as "the basic claim to freedom of action and freedom from imposition" as well as a "positive self-image and the desire that this self-image be appreciated and approved of" (Brown and Levinson 1987: 61). Their analysis of the subtitling demonstrates that the foreign-language dialogue undergoes a "systematic loss" of the linguistic indicators that the characters are satisfying each other's "face-wants" (Hatim and Mason 1997: 84).

The authors, however, go no further than this conclusion. "Far more empirical research would be needed," they state, "to test the generalizability of these limited findings to other films and other languages" (ibid.: 96). Yet one wonders about the implications of their analysis for this particular film. No consideration is given to the impact of translation patterns on characterization, narrative, and theme in the film as a whole or on the audience's potential response to these formal features. Such considerations would require rather different theoretical concepts that take into account but extend beyond the linguistic analysis, a theory of how characters are formed in film narrative, for example, and a theory of audience reception or cultural taste. In Hatim and Mason's analysis, linguistic indicators of politeness function as an empiricist essence abstracted from both the foreign film and the subtitled version.

From the translator's point of view, the empiricism that distinguishes the linguistic approach to translation carries at least two serious limitations. First, because this approach devises and deploys such complex analytical concepts, it always yields much more detail than is necessary to solve a translation problem, threatening to annex translation studies to applied linguistics. Here we can glimpse an instance of what Bourdieu calls "the most serious epistemological mistake in the human sciences," the tendency "to place the models that the scientist must construct to account for practices into the consciousness of agents" who carry out those practices (Bourdieu 1998: 133). In translator training, this mistake transforms translators into linguists by requiring them to learn and apply in their translating a wide range of the analytical concepts that linguists have formulated. In translation research, furthermore, these concepts tend to become standards by which translations are judged. For, despite Hatim and Mason's denial that their "objective had been to criticize subtitlers or subtitling," their analysis lays the groundwork for a judgment that the subtitler who produced their examples failed to establish an equivalence with the foreign-language dialogue: "in sequences such as those analysed," they assert, "it is difficult for the target language auditors to retrieve interpersonal meaning in its entirety. In some cases, they may even derive misleading impressions of characters' directness or indirectness" (Hatim and Mason 1997: 96).

Thus the linguistic analysis of translations is potentially laden with an uncritical prescriptivism, which reveals a second limitation: the translator is given the deceptive idea, not only that such an analysis is impartially descriptive, but also that it will be sufficient for developing, explaining, and evaluating translation decisions. Because such decisions are usually made on the basis of the textual effects, cultural values, and social functions that translations possess in receiving situations, a linguistic analysis that is primarily concerned with equivalence will fail to encompass the factors that are so consequential for translating. Why, we might ask, do the subtitles in Hatim and Mason's examples necessarily give the viewer "misleading impressions" of the characters in the film? Can we not view the impressions as effectively different interpretations, shaped partly by the technical constraints on subtitling (e.g. the limitation on the number of keyboard spaces that can appear in the frame) and partly by the translator's discursive strategies as they are developed for an audience in a different culture? In the long run, the empiricism in translation studies resists the sort of speculative thinking that encourages translators to reflect on the cultural, ethical, and political issues raised by their work.

An interventionist translation

Bourdieu remarks that "the structure of the university field is only, at any moment in time, the state of the power relations between agents," so that "positions held in this structure are what motivate strategies aiming to transform it, or to preserve it by modifying or maintaining the relative forces of the different powers" (Bourdieu 1988: 128). In Bourdieu's account, the power in the university is mediated by the different forms of capital assigned to the fields in which academics work: not only are the fields arranged hierarchically, with some (law, medicine, the sciences) assigned greater economic and cultural capital than others (the arts), but the capital assigned to the materials and practices within particular fields is also distributed unevenly. In American universities, translation undoubtedly occupies a subordinate position, not only in relation to socially powerful fields like law and medicine, but also in relation to fields that are affiliated to translation, such as linguistics, literary criticism, and cultural theory. In my argument thus far, I have tried to be more precise: translation has undergone a double marginalization in which its understanding and development have been limited both by the theoreticism of influential work in cultural studies and by the empiricism of the prevalent linguistic approaches to translation studies.

It was this marginality that motivated my decision to translate Derrida's lecture. I viewed the project as a means of challenging the subordinate position and reductive understanding of translation in the American academy. To intervene effectively, however, my presentation of the lecture – not only my translation strategies, but my very choice of the text – had to answer to the two rather different conceptual discourses that have limited translation, even as I sought to transform them.

Translation has always functioned as a method of introducing innovative materials and practices into academic institutions, but its success has inevitably been constrained by institutionalized values. Foreign scholarship can enter and influence the academy, although only in terms that are recognizable to it – at least initially. These terms include translation strategies that minimize the foreignness of foreign writing by assimilating it to linguistic and discursive structures that are more acceptable to academic institutions. Philip Lewis has shown, for example, that because of structural differences between French and English, along with the translator's announced "aim to anglicize," the first English version of Derrida's essay "La mythologie blanche" suppresses the "special texture and tenor of [his] discourse" by using "an English that shies away from abnormal, odd-sounding constructions" (Lewis 1985: 56). In this domesticated form, the essay significantly influenced the English-language reception of Derrida's thinking, which from the very start had been assimilated to American academic interests (see Comay 1991). The recognizable terms that permit the foreign to enter the academy may also include authors and texts that have already achieved canonical status, as well as issues that are currently under scholarly debate. Hence my choice to translate Derrida's lecture was strategic: it invited recognition but at the same time aimed to precipitate a defamiliarization that might stimulate a rethinking of the institutional status of translation.

Within cultural studies, Derrida has long been a canonical figure, an author of foundational texts in the field. Not only would a previously untranslated work by him be certain to attract a large academic readership, but it would also immediately interest the editors of leading journals. Following Derrida's recommendation, I proposed my translation to the editor of *Critical Inquiry* who quickly accepted it on the strength of a brief summary. The lecture, furthermore, addresses the theme of translation in the context of issues such as racism and political repression, which were then central to debates in cultural studies. Derrida interprets the characters in Shakespeare's *The Merchant of Venice* according to the code of translation, showing how Portia aims to translate Shylock's Judaic discourse of "justice" into the "merciful" discourse that underwrites the "Christian State" (Derrida 2001: 183–94).

This is an unprecedented interpretive move in the critical history of the play, which may now be read differently by Shakespearean scholars who are interested in theoretical approaches. Yet for American readers of Derrida the most unfamiliar move is likely to be his own recourse to translating. He offers not only an exposition of his interpretation, but also an unusual French rendering of Portia's line "when mercy seasons justice," in which the word "seasons" is translated as "relève," the term that he used for the Hegelian "Aufhebung" to highlight the contradictions in the dialectical movement of thinking. In Derrida's philosophical lexicon, "relève" signifies "the double motif of the elevation and the replacement that preserves what it denies or destroys, preserving what it causes to disappear" (ibid.: 196). By rendering Portia's line with a word that has acquired such a conceptual density, Derrida indicates the assimilative force involved in her translation of Shylock's demands for justice into the Christian discourse of mercy. At the same time, he provides a remarkable demonstration that translation too can perform exactly the sort of interrogative interpretation that scholars in cultural studies have come to associate with his work.

Within translation studies, Derrida has carried considerably less weight than a linguist like Halliday or a philosopher of language like Grice. This comes as no surprise: Halliday and Grice have provided the conceptual and analytical tools that have informed the empirical orientation of much translation research, fostering ideas of textual stability and cooperative communication that have in fact been questioned by poststructuralism (see, for example, Baker 1992 and the critique in Arrojo 1998). Nonetheless, even within translation studies, translating Derrida's lecture can be an effective intervention because he addresses relevance, a concept that came to dominate translation theory and practice during the twentieth century. Eugene Nida, for instance, a theorist who has exercised an international influence on translator training for several decades, championed the concept of "dynamic equivalence" in which the translator "aims at complete naturalness of expression, and tries to relate the receptor to modes of behavior relevant within the context of his own culture" (Nida 1964: 159). Subsequently, Ernst-August Gutt developed a cognitive approach to translation based on the branch of pragmatics known as "relevance theory" (Gutt 1991; for the linguistic theory, see Sperber and Wilson 1986). Gutt argues that "faithfulness" in translation depends on communicating an interpretation of the source text through "contextual effects" that are "adequate" because they take into account the receptors' "cognitive environment" and therefore require minimal "processing effort" (Gutt 1991: 101–2). The relevant translation, then, is likely to be "clear and natural in expression in the sense that it should not be unnecessarily difficult to understand" (ibid.: 102).

Derrida's lecture is particularly challenging in this context because, although he admits that relevance is the guiding principle of most translations, he also questions it. He calls attention to its ethnocentric violence, but also to its simultaneous mystification of that violence through language that is seemingly transparent because univocal and idiomatic. The effect of transparency in translation is illusionistic: accessibility or easy readability, what Gutt calls "optimal relevance," leads the reader to believe that the signified has been transferred without any substantial difference. Yet the fact is that any translating replaces the signifiers constituting the source text with another signifying chain, trying to fix a signified that can be no more than an interpretation according to the intelligibilities and interests of the translating language and culture. Derrida goes further than simply demystifying relevant translation: he also exposes its cultural and social implications through his interpretation of Shakespeare's play. Portia's translation of Shylock's demand for justice seeks an optimal relevance to Christian doctrine, which ultimately leads to his total expropriation as well as his forced conversion to Christianity. Derrida thus shows that, when relevant translation occurs within an institution like the state, it can become the instrument of legal interdiction, economic sanction, and political repression, motivated here by racism.

Translating with abusive fidelity

My choice to translate Derrida's lecture aimed to establish a relevance to institutionalized thought which also questioned the subordinate position and limited understanding of translation within academic institutions. Yet my translation strategies risked irrelevance: they were uncompromising in their effort to bring his writing into English so as to demonstrate the power of translation in shaping concepts. More specifically, I sought to implement what Philip Lewis has called "abusive fidelity," a translation practice that "values experimentation, tampers with usage, seeks to match the polyvalencies and plurivocities or expressive stresses of the original by producing its own" (Lewis 1985: 41). Abusive fidelity is demanded by source texts that involve substantial conceptual density or complex literary effects, namely poetry and philosophy, including Derrida's own writing. This kind of translating is abusive in two senses: it resists the structures and discourses of the receiving language and culture, especially the pressure towards the univocal, the idiomatic, the transparent; yet in so doing it also interrogates the structures and discourses of the source text, exposing its often unacknowledged conditions.

In practice, abusive fidelity meant adhering as closely as possible to Derrida's French, trying to mimic his syntax and lexicon by inventing comparable textual effects – even when they threatened to twist English into strange forms. The possibilities are always limited by the structural and discursive differences between the languages and by the need to maintain a level of intelligibility and readability, of relevance, for my English-language readers. I knew that my translation strained the limits of academic English because of the reactions that it received from the editorial staff at *Critical Inquiry*. Thus I wanted to imitate many of Derrida's telegraphic, sometimes elliptical syntactical constructions in English, but the copyeditor tended to recommend insertions that expanded these constructions into grammatically complete units. Here is an example with the copyeditor's insertions in square brackets:

> [It is] As if the subject of the play were, in short, the task of the translator, his impossible task, his duty, his debt, as inflexible as it is unpayable. [This is so] At least for three or four reasons:
>
> *(Derrida 2001: 183)*

Sometimes the copyeditor recommended the insertion of connective words to increase the cohesiveness of the English syntax:

> mercy resembles justice, but it comes from somewhere else, it belongs to a different order, [for] at the same time it modifies justice,
>
> *(Ibid.: 195)*

Derrida's lexicon is even more abusive of academic discourse. Instead of clear, unambiguous terms, he favors complicated wordplay which cannot always be reproduced in translation because of irreducible linguistic differences. Readers of Derrida in English have come to expect a page punctuated by foreign words, so I took advantage of this expectation by inserting Derrida's French within square brackets wherever a particular effect could not be easily achieved in an English rendering. These occasions included his play on "grâce" in the senses of "gratitude," "pardon," and "grace," as well as his play on "le merci," meaning "thanks," and "la merci," meaning "forgiveness" (ibid.: 175, 191). In other instances, however, I was able to imitate the wordplay in English. Thus the French "marche"/"marché" ("step"/"purchase") became the English "tread"/"trade," while in an alliterative series that required an English choice beginning with the consonant cluster "tr" the French "trouvaille" ("windfall," "fortunate discovery," "lucky break") became "treasure trove":

> surenchère infinie, autre marche ou autre marché dans l'escalade infinite
>
> *(Derrida 1999: 35)*

> an infinite extravagance, another tread or trade in an infinite ascent
>
> *(Derrida 2001: 188)*

> une de ces autres choses en *tr.*, une transaction, une transformation, un travail, un *travel* – et une trouvaille
>
> *(Derrida 1999: 46)*

> one of those other things in *tr.*, a transaction, transformation, travail, *travel* – and a treasure trove
>
> *(Derrida 2001: 198)*

The fact that my effort to reproduce Derrida's wordplay tampered with English usage also became apparent in the copyeditor's queries. In one instance, Derrida himself directs the reader's attention to a pun through a parenthetical remark:

> Ceux et celles à qui l'anglais est ici familier l'entendent peut-être déjà comme la domestication, la francisation implicite ou, oserai-je dire, l'affranchissement plus ou moins tacite et clandestin de l'adjectif anglais *relevant*.
>
> *(Derrida 1999: 24)*

> Those of you who are familiar with English perhaps already understand the word as a domestication, an implicit Frenchification or – dare I say? – a more or less tacit and clandestine enfranchisement of the English adjective *relevant*.
>
> *(Derrida 2001: 177)*

To reproduce the pun "francisation"/"l'affranchissement" in English, I chose "Frenchification"/"enfranchisement" and avoided the expected rendering "Gallicization." Yet the copyeditor responded that the pun was more apparent in the French than in the English: "I only found it," she wrote, "after you alerted me to it, and only after rereading the French – and others in the office had the same experience" (email from Kristin Casady, 6 September 2000). She recommended that both French words be included within square brackets after the English ones, and I accepted her recommendation so as to retain a rendering that not only sounded unusual, but also would recreate the pun.

Another of my renderings was sufficiently odd-sounding to draw similar comments from the staff. Here Derrida is interpreting Portia's famous speech on the "quality of mercy":

> Elle sied au monarque sur le trône, dit donc Portia, mais mieux encore que sa couronne. Elle est plus haute que la couronne sur la tête, elle *va* au monarque,

elle lui sied, mais elle *va* plus haut que la tête et le chef, que l'attribut ou que le signe de pouvoir qu'est la couronne royale.

(Derrida 1999: 41)

Mercy becomes the throned monarch, Portia says, but even better than his crown. It is higher than the crown on a head; it *suits* the monarch, it becomes him, but it *suits* him higher than his head and the head [*la tête et le chef*], than the attribute or sign of power that is the royal crown.

(Derrida 2001: 193)

The copyeditor responded that the staff had some difficulty in puzzling through the meaning of this passage. "We're unclear on 'suits higher'," she wrote, while recommending more idiomatic alternatives: "It sits higher than his head? It suits more than his head?" (email from Kristin Casady, 6 October 2000). I explained that the unusual construction results from Derrida's effort to tease out the transcendental logic in Portia's concept of mercy, a logic that is signaled here by her comparative, "becomes [...] better than." Hence "suits higher" means that the monarch's mercy suits the divinity from which monarchy is said to receive its authority. In line with Derrida's interpretation, my rendering of this passage actually creates an instance of wordplay where none exists in the French: the phrase "la tête et le chef" is an idiom which can be translated simply as "the head," yet I saw it as an opportunity to draw the political distinction – to which Derrida refers elsewhere in the lecture – between the king's two bodies, the king as a private person (*his* own head) and as a political figure (*the* head of the state, the crown).

The editorial staff of *Critical Inquiry*, especially the copyeditor Kristin Casady, were very supportive of my translation experimentalism: they appreciated and permitted my abuses of English as well as of the *Chicago Manual of Style*, which is generally applied in copyediting articles for the journal. Among the most important editorial decisions was to retain the polylingualism of Derrida's text, often without bracketed translations and even in places where only a minute difference in spelling indicated a linguistic difference. Not only does Derrida use various languages in the lecture, but he also varies the spelling of "relevant/relevante" to express his uncertainty about its status as an English or French word and thereby to point up the problem that it poses to relevant translation. Retaining the polylingualism of the lecture is essential for the strategic intervention that I had planned: it foregrounds the issue of translation in a most effective way by turning the reader into a translator.

Lewis is careful to note that an abusively faithful translation does not merely force "the linguistic and conceptual system of which it is a dependent," but also directs "a critical thrust back toward the text that it translates and in relation to which it becomes a kind of unsettling aftermath" (Lewis 1985: 43). If my translation abuses the English language and an English style manual, it also has an interrogative impact on Derrida's text. This emerges, for example, in my handling of the key term "relève," which Derrida describes as "untranslatable," and which Alan Bass left untranslated in his English versions of other texts by Derrida (see Bass's discussion in

Derrida 1982: 19–20, n.23). For the most part, I have followed their lead by retaining the French word and thus forcing the reader to perform repeated acts of translation. In some instances, however, I rendered "relève" expansively, making explicit the range of meanings that it accumulates in Derrida's discussion:

> Je tradurai donc *seasons* par "relève": "*when mercy seasons justice*", "quand le pardon relève la justice (ou le droit)".
>
> *(Derrida 1999: 42)*

> I shall therefore translate "seasons" as "relève": "when mercy seasons justice," "quand le pardon relève la justice (ou le droit)" [*when mercy elevates and interiorizes, thereby preserving and negating, justice (or the law)*].
>
> *(Derrida 2001: 195)*

> le pardon *ressemble* à un pouvoir divin au moment où il relève la justice
>
> *(Derrida 1999: 45)*

> mercy *resembles* a divine power at the moment when it elevates, preserves, and negates [*relève*] justice
>
> *(Derrida 2001: 197)*

Such expanded translations interrogate the French text by exposing the conditions of Derrida's interpretation. Because, as he observes, his use of "relève" to render the Hegelian "Aufhebung" became canonical in academic institutions, the retention of the French term throughout my translation would silently participate in this canonization and work to maintain the relevance to Shakespeare's play of what is in fact an irrelevant anachronism, a deconstruction of Hegel. The expanded translations, however, produce a demystifying effect by revealing the interpretive act that is at once embodied and concealed in Derrida's French.

Another abuse in my translation hinges on the recurrent choice of the English word "travail" to render the French noun "travail" and the verb "travailler." At one point, Derrida himself uses the English form "travailing" to pun on the English word "traveling":

> Ce mot ["relevant"] n'est pas seulement *en* traduction, comme on dirait en travail ou en voyage, *traveling, travailing,* dans un labeur, un *labour* d'accouchement.
>
> *(Derrida 1999: 24)*

> The word is not only *in* translation, as one would say in the works or in transit, *traveling, travailing,* on the job, in the *travail* of childbirth.
>
> *(Derrida 2001: 177)*

Following Derrida, I decided to make use of the English word "travail," but my uses far exceeded his: they amount to thirteen instances, which occur at the beginning and the end of the translation and are therefore quite noticeable to the reader. Some were determined by Derrida's characteristic wordplay, such as the alliteration of the consonant cluster "tr":

le motif du *labour*, du *travail* d'accouchement mais aussi du *travail transférentiel* et *transformationnel*

(Derrida 1999: 23)

the motif of *labour*, the *travail* of childbirth, but also the *transferential* and *transformational travail*

(Derrida 2001: 176)

Other uses were solely my decision, such as turning "un travail du negatif" and "un travail du deuil" into "a travail of the negative" and "a travail of mourning" (Derrida 1999: 47), even though in the latter case Derrida's translator Peggy Kamuf might have chosen the more familiar word "work" as she did in her version of his book on Marx (Derrida 1993; 1994). My use of "travails" is abusive in a number of ways. It deviates not only from the practices of a previous translator, but also, more generally, from current standard English, since the word has become a poetical archaism. It also constitutes a deviation from the French text, because the French words "travail" and "travailler" are neither poetic nor archaic, but very much part of current French usage.

My abusive rendering can be seen as consistent with a distinctive feature of Derrida's writing, his tendency to favor literary effects, to blur the line between philosophy and poetry. Yet the recurrence of "travail" is also interrogative of the French text, particularly since it appears in the phrases that Derrida uses to describe relevant translation. Because "travail" has acquired the status of an archaism in English, the word adds a temporal dimension to his critique of relevant translation, situating it in the past, suggesting that it did not originate with him, that in fact it has a long history in translation theory. In 1813, for instance, Friedrich Schleiermacher had in mind relevant translation when he questioned the translator who "leaves the reader in peace as much as possible and moves the writer toward him" (Schleiermacher 1813: 49). For Schleiermacher too, relevance was suspect because it meant assimilation or domestication, an erasure of the linguistic and cultural differences that constitute the source text by rewriting it in the terms of the translating language and culture. In the twentieth century, Henri Meschonnic attacked the prevalence of relevant translation because it masks a process of "annexation" whereby the translated text "transposes the so-called dominant ideology" under the "illusion of transparency" (Meschonnic 1973: 308, my translation). Of course, the theoretical genealogy of Derrida's critique can be no more than vaguely suggested by the recurrent use of an archaism in my translation. It is only when this abusive choice is juxtaposed to my editorial introduction, where Schleiermacher and other theorists are cited, that the historical conditions of Derrida's treatment become clearer.

Translation and the politics of interpretation

As this last point indicates, even if translation is regarded, not simplistically as an untroubled transfer of meaning, but as an act of interpretation in its own right that works on the linguistic and cultural differences of the source text and thereby alters its meaning, a translation requires yet another interpretation to make explicit its own interpretive force. Thus in translating Derrida's lecture I wanted to suggest, on the one hand, that a more materialist approach to translation can contribute to theoretical speculation in cultural studies and, on the other hand, that a more philosophical and socially aware approach can contribute to empirical research in translation studies. But, despite the fact that Derrida's texts, in any language, are generally read with the closeness reserved for literature, my translation itself cannot achieve these goals. I must still rely on a commentary attuned to the issue of translation, whether an editorial introduction or this very essay, risking the cynical charge of self-promotion that a translator always faces when attempting to describe the choices and effects of his or her work. And if this cynicism should be preempted here by a Derridean argument that a unique translation project can nonetheless exemplify the academic marginality of translation today, then my effort to criticize the circumstances of my work, its institutional trials and obstacles, faces another, equally cynical charge: sour grapes. The peculiar marginality of translation is such that not only is invisibility enforced upon it through a widespread preference for fluent discursive strategies that produce the illusion of transparency, the effacement of the second-order status of the translated text, but also the translator is expected to remain silent about the conditions of translation.

As a result, my intervention can have an impact only if others take up the task of commentary, only if my version of Derrida's essay is submitted to the interpretive practices that are performed in academic institutions. It would need, first of all, to be judged worthy of inclusion in the English-language canon of his writing and so worthy of the close attention that canonicity enforces upon texts. It would then need to play a role in cultural studies teaching and research and would need to be included in reading lists and syllabuses for courses in literary and cultural theory and in philosophy. It would also need to be judged worthy of reading within translation studies, to be included among the empiricist theoretical texts that dominate translation research and to find a place in courses devoted to theory in translator training faculties and in translation studies programs. In these institutional contexts, my translation might well bring about changes because there its abusive strategies can solicit interpretation, prompting further discussion that will ultimately encompass the very institutions in which it circulates.

What institutional changes, then, can possibly be expected from translating Derrida's lecture in the way that I have translated it for my projected audiences? Perhaps the first and most crucial change is an increased visibility for the translator and the act of translation. In pursuing a fidelity to the French text that abuses current English usage and an authoritative style manual, in deviating from the choices that previous translators of Derrida's texts have made for his key terms, I have produced a translation that highlights its own discursive strategies and thereby demands to be read as a translation, as a text that is relatively autonomous from the text on which it depends. Within cultural studies, this increased visibility can alter interpretive practices by leading scholars to focus on translations the interrogative forms of reading that are now routinely applied to literary and philosophical texts, among other cultural products. Within translation studies, a more visible discursive strategy can alter translation research and translator training by leading scholars and teachers to be more receptive to innovative translation practices and to question the enormous value that continues to be placed on a rather narrow form of fluency (largely adherence to current standard usage) and on uncritical notions of equivalence.

Yet these changes assume that a very different approach will be taken to the interpretation of theoretical texts in translation. The approach that currently prevails is to read translated theory for meaning by reducing it either to an exposition of argumentative points or to an account of its conceptual aporias or to both in succession. This communicative approach, however necessary in processing any text, assumes the simplistic notion of translation as an untroubled semantic transfer. And indeed such an approach is invited by fluent translating whereby the source text comes to seem unmediated by the translator's labor of rewriting it in a different language for a different culture. Translating that pursues an abusive fidelity resists this illusion by directing the reader's attention to what exceeds the translator's establishment of a semantic correspondence. To be sure, an excess is present in every translation: a semantic correspondence must be established by deploying dialects and registers, styles and discourses that add to and alter the source text because they work only in the translating language and culture, that make the source text intelligible by linking it to language usage and cultural traditions among the receptors and thereby limit and exclude source-language usage and traditions. Yet only a translation of abusive fidelity foregrounds – by challenging – its linguistic and cultural conditions, which include the language of instruction and research in the academic institution where the interpretation occurs. Clearly, this form of reading translated theory requires some knowledge of foreign languages and cultures. But this knowledge is not enough: the reader must use it to interrogate the linguistic and cultural materials on which the translator has drawn to rewrite the source text.

In the United States, a more visible translation practice can point to the global dominance of the language that prevails in teaching and research: English. An English translation that makes readers aware of its abuses, namely its transformation of the current standard dialect in its interrogative work on a particular source text, will expose the limitations and exclusions of the translating language, showing that "English" is an idealist notion which conceals a panoply of Englishes ranged in a hierarchical order of value and power among themselves and over every other language in the world. Thus a translation practice can turn the interpretation of translated texts into an act of geopolitical awareness. In fostering changes in pedagogical techniques and research methods, more visible translating constitutes a concrete means of forcing a critical self-reflection upon both cultural studies and translation studies, opening them to the global asymmetries in which they are situated and with which – in their use of English – they are complicit. A translation practice might not only advance theories of culture and translation, but also join them to a politically oriented understanding that can potentially extend their impact beyond the academic institutions in which these theories are housed. This is not to say that translation, especially the translation of specialized theoretical texts, can change the world in any direct way. Rather, the point is that translation can be practiced, in various genres and text types, so as to make their users aware of the social hierarchies in which languages and cultures are positioned. And with that awareness the different institutions that use and support translation, notably publishers, universities, and government agencies, can better decide how to respond to the cultural and social effects that follow upon the global dominance of English.

[2003]

4

TRANSLATING JACOPONE DA TODI

Archaic poetries and modern audiences

Conceptualizing the problems

I write here as a literary translator, prefacing my own work, but I do not intend to offer yet another belletristic commentary on translation. My aim is also to challenge the prevailing tendency among contemporary translators to make fairly impressionistic remarks on their practice, on its literary and cultural values, on the equivalence they believe to have established between their translations and the source texts. In adopting this approach, translators actually avoid addressing the conceptual problems posed by translation and so inadvertently raise the question of whether any translation practice can ever take into account these problems without a sustained theoretical reflection. Such a reflection, I believe, can enrich practice in ways that have yet to be fully explored.

My starting point is a skepticism as to whether cross-cultural understanding is possible in literary translation, particularly when the source text was produced in a remote historical period. Maintaining a strict semantic correspondence based on dictionary definitions cannot obviate the irreparable loss of the context in which the source text originated. Translation radically decontextualizes that text by uprooting it from the literary traditions and practices that not only give rise to it, but also make it meaningful to readers who have read widely in the source language and literature. This context of production and reception can never be restored so as to provide the reader of the translation with a response that is equivalent to the informed source-language reader's response to the source text (I dissent from the widely held notion of "equivalent effect," particularly as formulated by Nida 1964: 158). For source-language traditions and practices, their cultural meanings and historical weight can rarely (if ever) be signified in the translation itself, at any textual level, whether linguistic or stylistic, discursive or thematic, prosodic or generic.

Of course, a scholarly apparatus might help immensely in compensating for the loss of context. But any such compensation, however much learning it incorporates, can never enable the translation to elicit an equivalent response: the very term "scholarly" means, not only that the audience of the translation has been narrowed to readers seeking specialized knowledge in the form of historical scholarship, but also that the source-language audiences for which the source text was originally written have been displaced. These audiences were never limited to scholars or other professional readers. And historical scholarship, notwithstanding its enormous value in understanding past moments, always asks questions of those moments that they did not ask of themselves, questions that issue from the moment of historical research and the historian's particular methods. This fundamental anachronism in historical scholarship is exacerbated in the translation of archaic literatures. Because translation is decontextualizing, it inevitably opens up a historical difference from the source text through the very linguistic choices that the translator makes to overcome that difference. For these choices expose the translator's address to audiences in another culture at a later moment.

Archaic poetries bring the added difficulty of generic and prosodic features that, even when they have been revived by modern poets, continue to signify a historical remoteness to modern readers. During the twentieth century, the practice that came to dominate English-language poetry translation was to avoid developing comparable prosodic features, especially rhyme schemes and stanzaic structures, and rather assimilate the source text to the forms that dominated English-language poetry: varieties of unrhymed metrical verse and free verse. Indeed, the dominance of these forms has been so decisive that many modern readers take them as the distinguishing feature of "modern" vs. "archaic" poetry. In the case of translation, this dominance has created a set of reader expectations that have undoubtedly limited the translator's choices, but that can be strategically frustrated to produce a range of effects in the translating language and culture. These effects might be designed to evoke the form of a foreign archaic poetry. But insofar as they violate a modern poetic norm, they might also defamiliarize prevailing translation practices.

Archaic poetic forms cannot be easily imitated in English. Prosody, in particular, is a repository of literary traditions and practices, so that the translator's effort to imitate somehow the meter or rhythm of a foreign archaic poem cannot simply restore past sounds and listening experiences for readers who do not have sufficient access to the foreign context. On the contrary, such efforts risk the infiltration of later sounds and listening experiences – which is to say the inevitable problem of anachronism in translation.

The translator, however, might admit this inevitability and turn it to advantage. Ezra Pound's translations and his commentary on them can prove exemplary here. Pound showed how a foreign archaic poem might be rendered through the imitation of an analogous poetry in the translating language or, in other words, through a calculated recontextualization. Nonetheless, he was acutely aware that the analogy was never a perfect stylistic or temporal fit and could not control every reader's response. In "Guido's Relations" (1929), for instance, Pound describes his effort to translate Cavalcanti's poetry by drawing on "pre-Elizabethan English." And he anticipates two

> objections to such a method: the doubt as to whether one has the right to take a serious poem and turn it into a mere exercise in quaintness; the

> "misrepresentation" not of the poem's antiquity, but of the proportionate feel
> of that antiquity, by which I mean that Guido's thirteenth-century language is
> to twentieth-century Italian sense much less archaic than any fourteenth-, fifteenth-,
> or early sixteenth-century English is for us.
>
> *(Anderson 1983: 250)*

By "quaintness," the first objection, Pound seems to be referring to a superficial appearance of historical difference, a pastiche, say, whereby the translation does not offer readers a compelling depth of engagement as a historically situated foreign poem might do. Avoiding this appearance depends much on the translator's skills, not only as a writer of the translating language, but also as a literary imitator with a wide stylistic repertoire. Two kinds of imitation are at stake. In addition to maintaining a semantic correspondence, the translator mimics distinctive features of the foreign poem by mimicking an analogous style drawn from the poetic traditions in the translating language. The stylistic analogue does not supply the loss of the foreign context, nor does it enable an equivalent effect; it rather provides another context in the receiving culture, a context of production and reception in which the translator inscribes the foreign poem with an interpretation that is both illuminating and convincing, that does not seem merely a literary prank.

The second objection to Pound's method is perhaps more consequential: creating an analogue from literary traditions and practices in the translating language can distort the historical difference that a foreign archaic poetry signifies in its own language. Here Pound has run up against the inevitable anachronism in translation, which occurs whether the translator relies on current usage or resorts to the imitation of an archaic poetry. To object that Pound's poetic analogue is historically distorting assumes that a literary translation can establish a relation of historical adequacy to the source text, regardless of the fact that languages and literatures develop disjunctively, at different speeds, establishing different relations to other languages and literatures. The objection, then, does not recognize the radical decontextualization at work in every literary translation.

Yet Pound's response also remains questionable. He does not insist on the inevitable anachronism that accompanies the loss of context in translating, but rather assumes that a degree of historical adequacy is possible between the source and translated texts. Thus he suggests that his pre-Elizabethan English versions of Cavalcanti "can show where the treasure lies" to the modern reader who cannot read the Italian (Anderson 1983: 251). Yet he describes that "treasure" with such terms as "clarity and explicitness" as opposed to "magniloquence and the thundering phrase" and thereby reveals his preference for poetries that reflect his modernist concern for linguistic precision, excluding the work of Marlowe and Milton, among other poets (ibid.: 250). Pound assumes that his reading of foreign archaic poetries is true to the texts themselves, to their essential values, not one possible interpretation determined by his own modernist poetics and underwritten by a modernist canon of English-language poets (see Venuti 2008: 165–78). And he does not admit that he is translating for like-minded readers, modernists, or at least for readers whom the very power of his translating might persuade to accept a modernist aesthetic in a translation.

Despite these problems, Pound's translation method remains an advance over widely adopted approaches (namely, maintaining a semantic correspondence in current standard usage), and it should not be rejected by modern translators of foreign archaic poetries. Yet it does require greater self-consciousness on the translator's part, greater attention, on the one hand, to the relation between the translation and the source text and, on the other, to the relation between the translation and the literary traditions and practices from which an analogue is fashioned in the translating language. These two relations are both interpretations, enacted in the translation process, and so they are provisional, directed to specific audiences, engaged in the reproduction of forms and meanings in a particular cultural situation at a particular historical moment. And because both interpretive relations are culturally and historically variable, neither leaves its object – the source text and the literature in the translating language – unaffected or intact. To a certain extent, both objects are transformed, at once imitated and inscribed with an interpretive difference, trusted as meaningful yet submitted to a revisionary manipulation. As a result, the translator's creation of a stylistic analogue signals the linguistic and literary features of the source text in a disjunctive and indirect manner, through the interpretive differences that transform the source-text forms and themes as well as the receiving literature.

Yet the problem of modern audiences still looms in the background. For which readers will both the source text and receiving literature be transformed? Can a translation of a foreign archaic poem be appreciated by readerships who do not necessarily share the interpretation that the translator has inscribed in the text through a stylistic analogue? Is the translation necessarily directed to a readership that possesses specialized knowledge of literature in the translating language or can it cross the boundaries between readerships, appealing to readers who have limited or no access to that knowledge?

These reflections have increasingly shaped my approach to translating poetry, including a recent project in which I attempted versions of the medieval Italian poet Jacopone da Todi. What follows is a set of introductory comments on the poet and his work, on some previous translations, and on my own versions, two of which are reproduced below. None of this commentary constitutes the contextualization that the materials deserve. I rather present them with two aims: to stimulate further consideration of the problems posed by translating archaic poetries and to encourage experimentation with the methods used in translating them.

A medieval poet in Umbrian

Compared to other European poetries, poetry in Italian languages developed late, not emerging till the twelfth century. At first it was dominated by the chivalric romances of northern France and the love lyrics of the Provençal troubadours, but the Bible was also a strong influence. The *Ritmo Laurenziano* ("Laurentian Verse," named after the Biblioteca Laurenziana in Florence where it was discovered) is the oldest surviving poetic composition in an Italian language. Written between 1150 and 1170 in the Tuscan dialect, it is the work of a troubadour who requests the gift of a horse from a bishop. Between 1224 and 1226, St. Francis of Assisi wrote his hymn *Laudes creaturarum*, "Canticle of the Creatures," in the Umbrian dialect, modeling it on the Psalms and the Book of Daniel.

During the thirteenth century, Italian poetry was a mixture of secular and religious genres in various dialects, northern and southern. Among the most striking of the early poets is Jacopone da Todi, who wrote in Umbrian. Jacopone produced more than a hundred poems in a genre called the *lauda*, a religious song or hymn, designed for a soloist with a chorus and framed in different meters and verse structures. Although Jacopone's themes were fundamentally religious, his poetry was unique in giving them a distinctly personal cast. He used the *lauda* not only to explore theological concepts, but also to express his psychological state during mystical experiences. He also used the form to petition a pope for pardon and even to satirize him and his supporters. Appreciating Jacopone's poetry, then, requires some knowledge of pertinent events in his life, even if the power and popularity of his work soon inspired biographical legends that overlaid the incomplete historical record and complicate any attempts to separate fact from fiction.

Jacopone was born Jacopo dei Benedetti in Todi around 1230, a member of a noble family. He was trained as a *notaio*, an office that combined the functions of a notary and an attorney, and he argued cases in Bologna, amassing great wealth. In 1267, he married a pious noblewoman named Vanna di Bernardino di Guidone, in whose judgment he dwelt too much on earthly things. The following year, she met her death when the platform on which she was standing at a ball suddenly collapsed and crushed her. Stricken with guilt as well as grief, Jacopone noticed that she was wearing a hairshirt. Thus he became painfully aware that she had led a penitent life on his behalf. This sequence of events motivated his abrupt conversion to a rigorous asceticism. He abandoned the legal profession, distributed his wealth and possessions among the poor, and pursued a penitential course of self-denial in poverty. He became a humble Franciscan tertiary. His piety sometimes took the form of mysticism, bouts of ecstatic madness that cast doubt on his mental stability. His poetry suggests that he was familiar with the mystical works of such authors as Hugh of St. Victor and St. Bonaventure.

In 1278, Jacopone attempted to become a Franciscan brother, but was rejected because of rumors concerning his sanity. That same year, however, he was admitted to the Order of Friars Minor on the strength of a poem he had written: it deplored the vanity of worldly values. He gravitated towards a faction known as the *Spirituali*, the Spirituals, who wished to return the order to the extreme poverty espoused by St. Francis. By the end of the thirteenth century, Jacopone assumed a position of leadership in the Spiritual faction, which mired him in the political struggles surrounding the newly elected pope, Boniface VIII. The Spirituals' bid for clerical autonomy had been denied by Boniface, whom Jacopone opposed in 1297 by signing a manifesto that declared the pope's election invalid. In 1298, Boniface retaliated by excommunicating Jacopone and sentencing him to life imprisonment. The pope's death in 1303 brought Jacopone's release, whereupon he retired to the monastery in the Umbrian town of Collazzone and died three years later.

The first printed edition of Jacopone's poetry appeared in 1490, but by that time it had already enjoyed wide circulation. Many manuscript copies were made, stretching into the seventeenth century. Individual texts were enthusiastically sung by confraternities or guilds who performed *laude* in processions and dramatic recitations. The intensity of Jacopone's poems also appealed to heretical sects such as the wandering flagellants who sang them as devotional hymns. These diverse performances show that his writing, although influenced by both religious and secular literature, made an important contribution to popular piety in Umbrian towns.

The poems I have chosen to translate are representative of Jacopone's forms and themes. In "O papa Bonifazio," an epistolary poem evidently written during his imprisonment, he addresses the papal retaliation against the Spirituals by questioning it even as he appeals for Boniface's mercy. The Umbrian text is written in couplets that vary from seven to eight syllables, and the meter is fairly singsong, despite the variations. As scholars have shown (Bettarini 1997: 284–90), the language is extremely heterogeneous: although generally simple, it employs the extended metaphor of the shield for theological concepts and mixes doctrinal and liturgical terms ("scommunicazione," "assoluzione") with a Latin phrase and a vernacular Latinism ("per secula infinita" and "Absolveto," which was a popular form for *absolvetur*).

In "O iubelo del core," Jacopone addresses a recurrent theme in mystical literature, the inexpressibility of the ecstatic experience. Here too the meter is irregular, with lines varying from seven to eight syllables, but the verse structure is much more intricate: the opening couplet (xx) is followed by five six-line strophes with an alternating rhyme scheme (ababbx) and an incremental repetition of the key word "iubelo." The language is also marked by heterogeneity: the simple lexicon contains dialectal forms (the repeated assimilation of -nd- to -nn- in "quanno" for "quando," "granne" for "grande," "pensanno" for "pensando") and vernacular forms of Latin words and phrases ("iubelo" from "iubilo," "'n deriso" from "in derisum"). A couple of words that have since become archaic in Italian point to a French or even Provençal influence ("dolzore" for "dolcezza," "convenente" for "conveniente").

Twentieth-century versions

The formal features of the Umbrian texts, notably their prosody and language, clearly pose difficulties to the modern English-language translator who wishes not only to establish a semantic correspondence, but also to compensate somehow for the loss of the medieval context. Because of this loss, the form cannot be reproduced so as to enable a response that is equivalent to the responses of Jacopone's contemporaries. Consequently, modern translators have been forced to develop strategies that answer primarily to the function that the translations were designed to serve. Two translations produced during the twentieth century are particularly worth examining because they exemplify very different approaches.

The first consists of a selection of Jacopone's poetry included in Evelyn Underhill's 1919 biography. The translator is identified on the title page only as Mrs. Theodore Beck. The function of the translations, as Underhill stated in her preface, was "to illustrate the most important points of his mystical growth and outward career" (Underhill 1919: vi). She viewed the literary dimension of Jacopone's "career" as combining two contemporary influences: "secular poetry" represented by the philosophical love lyrics of the *dolcestilnovisti* and "that popular demand for vernacular moral and devotional songs which the penitential movements of the thirteenth century – especially the Franciscan revival – had created and developed" (ibid.: 212, 217).

Interestingly, Underhill's interpretation of Jacopone's poetry can be glimpsed in Beck's translations, although only very indirectly, through the translator's decision to develop a resonant stylistic analogue. Here are the opening lines from her version of "O iubelo del core":

> Thou, Jubilus, the heart dost move;
> And makst us sing for very love.
>
> The Jubilus in fire awakes,
>   And straight the man must sing and pray,
> His tongue in childish stammering shakes,
>   Nor knows he what his lips may say;
>   He cannot quench nor hide away
>   That Sweetness pure and infinite.
>
> *(Underhill 1919: 279)*

Beck obviously tried to evoke the meter and rhyme scheme of Jacopone's six-line strophes. Yet the fluent regularity of her tetrameter lines, combined with her reliance on standard usage mixed with poetical archaisms, suggests that her model was the eighteenth-century hymn. A similar six-line stanza frequently recurs in John Wesley's collection of Methodist hymns (this analogy was proposed by an anonymous reader who evaluated my essay for the journal *Translation and Literature*, but who cannot be held responsible for what I made of it). The following example is typical:

> Come, Holy Ghost, all-quick'ning fire,
> My consecrated heart inspire,
>   Sprinkled with the atoning blood;
> Still to my soul thyself reveal,
> Thy mighty working may I feel,
>   And know that I am one with God!
>
> *(Wesley 1983: 503)*

In translating Jacopone's poem "O papa Bonifazio," Beck likewise imitated his couplets. Here too the analogue with the hymn can be perceived, along with her use of poetical archaisms. Her version breaks the Umbrian text into four-line stanzas, another form that appears in Wesley's collection. I print one of Beck's stanzas followed by a stanza from another hymn:

Though fierce and sharp be thine attack,
By Love I'll beat thine onslaught back;
I'll speak to thee with right good will,
And gladly shalt thou listen still.

(Underhill 1919: 441)

When rising floods my soul o'erflow,
When sinks my heart in waves of woe,
Jesu, thy timely air impart,
And raise my head, and cheer my heart.

(Wesley 1983: 487)

If Beck's translations are compared only to the Umbrian texts, her work can easily provoke criticisms. It might be objected, not just that she translates too expansively, adding words to fill out her lines, but also that her meters are too regular, her diction too smoothly poetical, to mimic Jacopone's irregular rhythms and heterogeneous language. And indeed a contemporary reviewer complained that Beck's translations are "stilted, artificial, unpleasantly anthropomorphic, and appallingly flat" (Willcox 1920: BR166). Such criticisms, however, ignore the irreparable loss of the medieval context at the level of the poetic line and the interpretive relation that the translator created with English-language poetry to compensate for that loss. At her later moment, Beck does create a convincing stylistic analogue that gives a glimpse of the formal features of the Umbrian texts, and the various archaisms do signal the historical remoteness of the poems. This historicizing effect is produced by the archaic lexical and syntactical items in her English (other examples include "fray," "foeman," and "If thou canst pink me openly"), as well as the use of a medieval Latin word, "Jubilus," signifying an exultant shout.

The analogy with the eighteenth-century hymn, once perceived by the reader, results in a translation that possesses greater historical depth than a quaint pastiche. In effect, Beck's stylistic analogue invests Jacopone's poetry with considerable cultural value in English: it positions him in a popular poetic tradition that has long supported religious worship. At the same time, however, the formal and thematic differences between Jacopone's *laude* and the hymns remain sufficiently clear in the translations to invite the reader to think differently, more searchingly, of both poetries. Because Wesley's hymns contain so many phrases taken from canonical poets such as Milton, Dryden, and Pope, because he expressed his own literary aspirations in claiming that his hymns reveal "the true spirit of poetry" (Wesley 1983: 74), the stylistic analogue can point to the secular influence on Jacopone's poems, the *dolcestilnovisti*, leading the informed reader to ask whether those poems seemed more literary to the uneducated segment of his contemporary readership than they do today. A reader sensitive to the stylistic analogue might also wonder about the extent to which the extreme states depicted in Jacopone's poetry, whether the physical coarseness of his asceticism or the psychological imbalance of his mysticism, overshadow the devotional advance offered by the plain, direct language of Wesley's hymns, while calling attention to the fact that their theological content did not deviate from Anglican doctrine. The interpretation enacted by Beck's translations can be doubly interrogative, posing questions about Jacopone's poems and about the English-language poetry on which she draws to fashion an analogue.

Her work differs markedly from the first complete version of Jacopone's *laude* published in 1982 by Serge and Elizabeth Hughes. Able to benefit from a century of historical scholarship, these translators are more aware of the sheer hybridity of the poetry: in his introduction, Serge Hughes calls it "a rough-textured coat of many colors, with nothing in it of the ideal of seamless beauty" (Hughes and Hughes 1982: 3). Hughes's interpretation, however, foregrounds the religious themes, which he describes as "the mottled word of Jacopone, his multifaceted meanings, the twists and turns of his descent into the self, his wrestling with God," arguing that "the place of music in the *Lauds* as a whole is that of a humble handmaiden" (ibid.: 4, 3). In accordance with this theme-oriented interpretation, the translation makes no attempt to recreate the formal features of the poems. Hughes in fact feels that Jacopone's prosody is not consistently effective:

> The *Lauds* are not well served by making rhyme and meter the primary considerations. Indeed, all too often in the original those considerations become the tail that wags the dog. A translation that concentrates on the strength of Jacopone, by contrast, the mottled word, can bring out the muscular texture of that utterance.
>
> *(Hughes and Hughes 1982: 64)*

The result of this approach is generally a prosaic rendering in current standard usage. Here are the Hughes versions of the opening lines from the two poems we have examined:

> O heart's jubilation, love and song
> Joy and joy unceasing,
> The stuttering of the unutterable –
> How can the heart but sing?
>
> O Pope Boniface, I bear the marks of your preface –
> Anathema, and excommunication.
>
> *(Ibid.: 227, 177)*

These extracts show that the stress on theme does not entirely rule out sound effects, but it does lead the translators to depart from the lineation of the Umbrian texts. It is also clear that they have avoided the creation of a stylistic analogue or any comparable English-language poetry and have chosen an English that is not marked in any distinctive way.

It might be objected, then, that the translation does not imitate the "muscular texture" of Jacopone's Umbrian texts, that the English versions lack the linguistic heterogeneity characteristic of his work. In the second extract, moreover, the weakness of the translation is evident in the misleading literalism "preface" to render "prefazio," an Italian calque for *Praefatio*, a part of the Mass where the celebrant makes a solemn invocation to introduce the Eucharistic prayer. Jacopone's use of the liturgical term initiates the satire of his poem: it ironically refers to Boniface's harsh sentence. The English rendering is obscure and actually exposes rather than compensates for the loss of the medieval context.

Nonetheless, the translators have succeeded in realizing their main intention: to communicate to the late twentieth-century reader the main theme of every poem attributed with certainty to Jacopone. Their imagined reader does not possess any specialized knowledge of Italian medieval literature and culture, nor does he or she wish more than the basic information about Jacopone's life and work. As Serge Hughes states, "since this translation is principally an introduction to the *Lauds*, it has not been weighed down with a detailed commentary" (Hughes and Hughes 1982: 65). The translation presents Jacopone's poetry, not as a body of literature that reflects Italian literary traditions and practices at a particular historical moment, but as a document in the history of Christianity which reveals the author's personal experiences. This presentation was also determined by the conditions under which the translation was published: it was issued by the Paulist Press, an American Catholic publisher operated by an order of missionary priests, and was included in their series the Classics of Western Spirituality, which contains more than 130 works from various religious traditions. In this context, religious theme is assigned much greater value than literary form.

An experimental translation

Today the Beck and Hughes versions, even if effective in their own terms, have come to seem limited, and their very existence has led me to experiment in retranslating Jacopone's poetry for a different audience at a later moment. Like Beck, I tried to cultivate a stylistic analogue, but mine aimed to suggest precisely the heterogeneity of his language while recreating his loose, jogtrot meters and his rhyme schemes. This sort of analogue, attuned to formal features but avoiding the plainness and metrical regularity of the eighteenth-century hymn, was designed to inscribe my interpretation of the Umbrian texts as at once literary and popular.

English-language poetic traditions contain useful models in which Jacopone's work can be recast. I have imagined him partly along the lines of the early Tudor poet John Skelton, who, following medieval literary genres, wrote satires and ballads in language that mixes learned and oral forms. I was particularly attracted to Skelton's remarkable prosody, in which short, irregularly metered lines are joined to rhyme schemes that vary from stanzaic structures to unpatterned repetitions of sounds. Skelton's poetry, like Jacopone's, sometimes adopts a typically medieval attitude of *contemptus mundi*, pointing to the transitory nature of human life. Here is an extract from a poem "uppon a deedmans head" (c. 1498):

It is generall
To be mortall:
I have well espyde
No man may hym hyde
From deth holow-eyed
With synnews wyderyd [withered]
With bonys shyderyd [shattered]
With hys worme-eatyn maw
And hys gastly jaw
Gapyng asyde
Nakyd of hyde,
Neyther flesh nor fell [skin].

(Skelton 1983: 39)

Skelton's satires on Tudor courtiers and statesmen were immediately suggestive of Jacopone's wry epistles to Boniface VIII. Here is an extract from Skelton's attack on Cardinal Wolsey, *Collyn Clout* (1519):

And yf ye stande in doute
Who brought this ryme aboute,
My name is Collyn Cloute.
I purpose to shake oute
All my connynge bagge,
Lyke a clerkely hagge.
For though my ryme be ragged,
Tattered and jagged,
Rudely rayn-beaten,
Rusty and mothe-eaten,
Yf ye take well therwith,
It hath in it some pyth.

(Ibid.: 248)

Skelton's writing is so strongly marked that a limited imitation might be easily noticeable for modern readers who have read widely in English poetic traditions. With other, less informed readers, his early modern English and "ragged" prosody, although useful in creating a stylistic analogue for Jacopone's poems, could not be followed closely without risking unintelligiblity. The effect I wanted, moreover, was not merely an archaism that signaled the historical difference of the Umbrian texts, but a heterogeneity through which their various influences and audiences might be perceived. So not only did I use archaisms ("thy," "fare thee well," "penetrate" as a past participle) and jargon both theological and liturgical ("excommunication," "absolution," "Ego te absolvo"), but I also incorporated current usage, both standard and colloquial forms, including idioms and clichés ("head out," "stick out," "forked tongue," "vale of tears").

Translating archaic poetry, however, is always more complicated than inventing a stylistic analogue because of the inevitable anachronism entailed by the address to a later audience. The task for the translator is perhaps how to control this inevitability, how to turn it to effect in supporting and developing the analogue. Because I am translating Jacopone's poems at the beginning of the twenty-first century, the infiltration of popular music seems pertinent and unavoidable. Indeed, when I read the Umbrian texts, I often hear not only Skelton, but also a rap artist like Eminem, with echoes of his endlessly played hit, "The Real Slim Shady" (2000). Here is an extract:

> We ain't nothing but mammals; well, some of us cannibals
> who cut other people open like cantaloupes.
> But if we can hump dead animals and antelopes
> then there's no reason that a man and another man can't elope.
> But if you feel like I feel I got the antidote.
> Women wave your panty hose, sing the chorus and it goes …
> I'm Slim Shady
> Yes I'm the real Shady

In combining colloquial language with varying rhythms and rhymes, rap music offered another poetic form that can prove helpful in signifying the popular dimension of Jacopone's poetry.

Still, nothing remains unchanged in fashioning a stylistic analogue. The hybrid I sought also redounds upon the various forms that compose it, exposing and interrogating the differences among them and the cultural situations in which they emerged. The extreme individualism of much rap music, the focus on the typically male singer who is given to chest-thumping machismo, can only be questioned by Jacopone's mystical asceticism which extols the virtues of penance and self-denial. Similarly, Jacopone's rejection of the world, his fearless criticisms of a pope, his harsh imprisonment reveal the considerable extent to which Skelton's privileged position allowed him to mount satiric attacks on government officials. Although at Wolsey's order Skelton was once imprisoned for a short time, the poet enjoyed a number of distinguished offices and appointments: after serving as rector of a Norfolk parish church, he became tutor to Henry VIII, Poet Laureate, and King's Orator. Yet Skelton can also come back to worry Jacopone by pointing to his aristocratic status, especially the education and wealth that enabled the Italian poet to write with a knowledge of both secular and religious literary traditions. And when juxtaposed to Jacopone's poetry, rap, performed by so many artists with working-class origins, might pose the question of how many medieval poets were lost to poverty and the absence of patronage.

Of course, these implications can be pursued only by an informed reader who also brings an understanding of the translation method that I have sketched here. This reader was not in the audience for which I first translated Jacopone's poems: a group of American students who were spending a junior year at the Rome campus of

Temple University. This campus attracts a student body from as many as fifty American schools, ranging from elite private institutions to small liberal arts colleges to large public universities. Each semester begins with an outing to Umbria that includes a stop at Todi where students can visit the church of San Fortunato, the site of Jacopone's grave. On one such outing I read my translations, along with a brief sketch of Jacopone's life and my translation method. Very few members of this audience were students of Italian or English literature; none, as I recall, had heard of Jacopone or his poetry. Yet they were all able to grasp the affiliations that the translations tried to construct with rap music.

Will the translations work for an audience of literary historians, translation scholars, and translators who not only have some familiarity with the traditional materials I have used, but also can understand (if not accept) the theoretical rationale for my method? This is precisely the question I wish to pose to you, my informed reader, who alone are in a position to answer it.

[2003]

Two Laude by Jacopone da Todi

Translated from the Umbrian by Lawrence Venuti

Ivi

O papa Bonifazio,
eo porto el tuo prefazio
e la maledezzone
e scommmunicazione.
Co le lengua forcuta
M'hai fatta esta feruta;
che co la lengua ligne
e la plaga ne stigne;
ca questa mia ferita
non pò esser guarita
per altra condezione
senza assoluzïone.
Per grazia te peto
che mi dichi: "Absolveto,"
l'altre pene me lassi
finch'io del mondo passi.
Puoi, se te vol' provare
e meco essercetare,
non de questa materia,
ma d'altro modo prelia.
Si tu sai sì schirmire
che me sacci ferire,
tengote ben esparto,
sì me fieri a scoperto:
c'aio dui scudi a collo,
e s'io no i me ne tollo,
per secula infinita
mai non temo ferita.
El primo scudo, sinistro,
l'altro sede al deritto.
Lo sinistro scudato,
un diamante aprovato:
nullo ferro ci aponta,
tanto c'è dura pronta:
e quest'è l'odïo mio,
ionto a l'onor de Dio.
Lo deritto scudone,
d'una preta en carbone,

O papa Bonifazio

My dear Pope Boniface,
I suffer your disgrace,
the dreaded malediction
of excommunication.
You spoke with forkéd tongue
and deeply I was stung:
it has to lick my sore
to show the plague the door;
because I'm sure my grief
can't find the least relief
without the execution
of your absolution.
Out of grace I beg you,
say, "Ego te absolvo,"
leaving my other fears
till past this vale of tears.
You can test your might
and meet me for a fight –
without the self-same arm
that did me all this harm.
Should you draw the blade
that drove me to this shade,
able I can deem you
but then you must strike true:
the two shields that I bear
will banish every care
if I make them mine
until the end of time.
The shield that's on the left
never will be cleft:
a diamond truly tested,
it never will be bested:
thus is my self-hate,
to God's glory conjugate.
The shield that's on the right,
made of carbuncle bright,
is burning like a flame
of an amorous game:

ignita como foco	the same is love thy neighbor
d'un amoroso ioco:	filled with a kindled ardor.
lo prossimo en amore	If you wish t'advance,
d'uno enfocato ardore.	you're free to take a chance;
Si te vòi fare ennante,	but try howe'er you might,
puo'lo provar 'n estante;	love won't lose the fight.
e quanto vol' t'abrenca,	I'd talk when you have leisure:
ch'e' co l'amar non venca.	I think you'll get some pleasure.
Volentier te parlara:	So, fare thee well, fare well,
credo che te iovara.	may God take all your evil
Vale, vale, vale,	and grant it me for grace,
Deo te tolla onne male	in pain with a smiling face.
e dielome per grazia,	This rhyme I've shaken out
ch'io el porto en leta fazia.	and now I'm heading out.
Finisco la trattato	
En questo loco lassato.	

(Contini 1960: 69–70)

lxxvi

O iubelo de core,
che fai cantar d'amore!

Quanno iubel se scalda,
sì fa l'omo cantare,
e la lengua barbaglia
non sa que se parlare:
dentro non pò celare,
tant'è granne 'l dolzore.

Quanno iubel è acceso,
sì fa l'omo clamare;
lo cor d'amor è appreso,
che nol pò comportare:
stridenno el fa gridare,
e non virgogna allore.

Quanno iubelo ha preso
lo core ennamorato,
la gente l'ha 'n deriso,
pensanno el suo parlato,
parlanno esmesurato
de che sente calore.

O iubelo del core

Heartstruck jubilation,
erotic incantation!

Whenever joy enkindles,
the soul begins to sing,
the tongue is tied in mumbles,
speech doesn't know a thing:
you can't keep on hiding
such immense delectation.

Whenever joy is burning,
the soul begins to shout;
with love your heart is yearning
much more it can't stick out:
you scream, you shriek without
the slightest humiliation.

Whenever joy takes hold
of the heart enamored,
people turn so bold,
mocking how it stammered,
they utter things unmeasured
when it feels the calefaction.

O iubel, dolce gaudio
che dentri ne la mente,
lo cor deventa savior
celar suo convenente:
non pò esser soffrente
che non faccia clamore.

Chi non ha costumanza
te repute 'mpazzito,
vedenno esvalïanza
com'om ch'è desvanito;
dentr'ha lo cor ferito,
non se sente de fore.

(Contini 1960: 105–7)

Joy, sweet blissfulness,
the mind is penetrate,
the heart would be sagacious
to conceal its estate:
you can't hardly obviate
such clamorous exclamation.

Lacking this experience,
people judge you insane,
seeing your divergence
like a man grown vain;
but within your heart is pain,
undetected by observation.

5

RETRANSLATIONS

The creation of value

Inscriptions and institutions

Translation, like every cultural practice, involves the creation of values, linguistic and literary, religious and political, commercial and educational, as the particular case may be. What makes translation unique is that the value-creating process takes the form of an interpretation inscribed in a source text, whose own values inevitably undergo diminution and revision to accommodate those that appeal to cultural constituencies in the receiving situation. Translation is an inscription of the source text with intelligibilities and interests that are specific to the translating language and culture, even when the translator maintains a strict semantic correspondence and incorporates aspects of the cultural context in which the source text originated. Retranslations constitute a special case because the values they create are doubly bound to the receiving situation, determined not only by the receptor values which the translator inscribes in the source text, but also by the values inscribed in a previous version. Of course, retranslations may be inspired primarily by the source text and produced without any awareness of a pre-existing translation. The cases to be considered here, however, possess this crucial awareness and justify themselves by establishing their differences from one or more previous versions.

These differences may first be introduced with the choice of a source text for retranslation, but they subsequently proliferate with the development of discursive strategies to retranslate it. Moreover, both the choice and the strategies are shaped by the retranslator's appeal to the constituencies who will put the retranslation to various uses. A typical case is the choice of a source text that has achieved canonical status in the translating culture. The sheer cultural authority of this text – the Bible, for instance, the Homeric epics, Dante's *Divine Comedy*, Shakespeare's plays, or Cervantes' *Don Quixote* – is likely to solicit retranslation because diverse readerships in the receiving situation will seek to interpret it according to their own values and hence develop different retranslation strategies that inscribe competing interpretations.

Here the choice of the text for retranslation is premised on an interpretation that differs from that inscribed in a previous version, which is shown to be no longer acceptable because it has come to be judged as insufficient in some sense, perhaps erroneous, lacking linguistic correctness. The retranslation may claim to be more adequate to the source text in whole or in part, which is to say more complete or accurate in representing the text or some specific feature of it. Claims of greater adequacy, completeness or accuracy should be viewed critically, however, because they always depend on another category, usually an implicit basis of comparison between the source text and the translation which establishes the insufficiency and therefore serves as a standard of judgment. This standard is a competing interpretation. It is not only inscribed by a translator or an editor; it is also at work when a publisher chooses to invest in a retranslation so as to capitalize on the sheer marketability of the source text, when, in other words, the value created by the retranslation aims to be primarily economic rather than, say, literary or scholarly. In this case, the decisive factor in the inscription is likely to be not a more reliable edition of the source text or more incisive scholarly research or greater stylistic felicity, but rather a bibliographic code that enables the translation to compete strongly on the book market, a code constituted by "ink, typeface, paper, and various other phenomena" like cover art and illustrations, the source author's portrait, and endorsements (McGann 1991: 13).

The issue of readership is especially important with retranslations that are housed in social institutions. Generally, a translation that circulates in such a setting contributes to the identity formation of the agents who function within it, to their acquisition of values that constitute qualifications, and so a translation can affect the operation and reproduction of the institution (see Venuti 1998: 75–81, 103–4). Retranslations are designed deliberately to form particular identities and to have particular institutional effects. In religious institutions, retranslations help to define and inculcate orthodox belief by inscribing canonical texts with interpretations that are compatible with prevailing theological doctrine. In academic institutions, similarly, retranslations help to define and inculcate valid scholarship by inscribing canonical texts with interpretations that currently prevail in scholarly disciplines.

Retranslations can thus maintain and strengthen the authority of a social institution by reaffirming the institutionalized interpretation of a canonical text. Alternatively, retranslations can challenge that interpretation in an effort to change the institution or found a new one. The King James Bible consolidated the authority of the Anglican Church during the early seventeenth century by drawing on the Protestant versions of previous English translators, such as William Tyndale and Richard Taverner (Daniell 2003: 157–58; Westbrook 1997). Yet before the Reformation in England Tyndale's translations were considered heretical and subversive by the Catholic Church because they ran counter to the Vulgate by introducing interpretations grounded in Protestant theology.

Since the 1970s, to cite a scholarly example, the retranslations of Thomas Mann's fiction by the Germanist David Luke have asserted the authority of academic specialists in German literature by locating and correcting linguistic errors in Helen Lowe-Porter's earlier versions (see Luke 1970: xxxv–xxxviii and Buck 1995). Lowe-Porter, despite her errors, had already established Mann as a major twentieth-century fiction writer among British and American readers several decades before Luke's retranslations. The shifts between the German texts and her versions were not always erroneous deviations from a semantic correspondence, but interpretations informed by her cultural situation: she was writing for a general readership in the United States during the early twentieth century. Academics like Luke wished to correct her work so as to bring translations of Mann in line with current scholarly interpretations that situate his fiction in German literary traditions. In the 1990s, much to the dismay of Luke and his colleagues, John Woods successfully brought Mann to a new generation of general readers through retranslations that reflect contemporary English usage. The English retranslations of Mann have become the site where two kinds of institutions, the academic discipline and the commercial publisher, have competed over the interpretation of the German texts (see the exchange in Luke 1995 and Venuti 1995).

A source text that is positioned in the margin of literary canons in the translating language may be retranslated in a bid to achieve canonicity through the inscription of a different interpretation. Although the prolific Italian fiction writer Grazia Deledda won the Nobel Prize for literature in 1926, her work has tended to be regarded merely as a variety of regionalism, a representation of family life in her native Sardinia. Hence relatively few of her many books were translated into English at the beginning of the twentieth century, and she remained marginal in relation to such novelists as the flamboyantly decadent Gabriele D'Annunzio and the sensationalist raconteur of bourgeois decadence Alberto Moravia. In the 1980s and 1990s, however, Deledda's strong female characters attracted feminist-oriented English-language translators who made available several texts, one of which was a retranslation (Deledda 1905; 1984). Similarly, the feminist interest in rediscovering neglected women writers played a role in the retranslation of Sibilla Aleramo's autobiographical text *Una donna* by Rosalind Delmar for the British feminist press Virago (Aleramo 1908; 1979). As these examples suggest, retranslations of marginal texts are likely to be motivated by a cultural political agenda in which a particular ideology guides the choice of an author or text and the development of a retranslation strategy.

Retranslations can help to advance translation studies by illuminating several key issues that bear directly on practice and research, but that can be most productively explored only when a linguistic operation or a textual analysis is linked to the cultural and political factors that invest it with significance and value. Foremost among these issues is the translator's agency, the ensemble of motivations, conditions, and consequences that decisively inform the work of translating and allow it to produce far-reaching social effects. The translator's actions also involve the creation of an intertextual dimension for the translated text, a network of relations, not only to the source text, but also to other texts written in the translating language. And the issues of agency and intertextuality ultimately point to the role of history in translation, not only the influence of the historical moment in which the translator works, but also the literary and cultural histories on which the translator draws to bring the source text into the translating language.

Agency

Any translating is obviously intended action: a translator aims to rewrite a source text in another language, imitating its specificity as much as linguistic and cultural differences permit and audiences require. As Anthony Giddens has argued, furthermore, intended action involves a "reflexive self-monitoring" in which the agent submits his or her behavior to ongoing evaluation according to "rules and resources" that already exist in a social situation (Giddens 1979: chapter 2). The translator's intention, then, is always already collective, determined most decisively by linguistic usage, literary canons, translation traditions, and the institution where a translation is produced and where various other agents have a hand in such procedures as negotiating translation rights and commissioning the translator, editing and printing the translated text, promoting and marketing the printed book.

A comparable line of thinking has been developed specifically for translation by Gideon Toury, who has argued that a translator evaluates his or her decisions according to "norms" or values in the translating culture (Toury 1995: 53–69). Linguistic and cultural norms determine not only the selection of texts for translation, but also the strategies devised to translate them and the relations of equivalence established between the source and translated texts. The norms may be formulated in precise terms by a client or institution who commissions a translation so as to produce a particular effect for a particular audience. This is usually the case with technical or pragmatic documents, as Hans Vermeer (1989) has indicated, since the function of the translation can be defined in a contract and a standardized language may already exist to serve that function. More often, however, translation norms are assimilated through the translator's education and experience working with clients.

Giddens allows us to extend this thinking about the translator's agency by pointing out that intended action occurs amid "unacknowledged conditions" and can cause "unanticipated consequences" which can affect social reproduction, whether by maintaining the status quo or by leading to change. Translators do in fact make many decisions automatically, without any critical reflection on the norms that constrain their work. Even when an experienced translator is capable of articulating these norms wholly or in part, the translating will proceed amid conditions that remain preconscious or subliminal, even entirely unconscious (see chapter 2). These conditions may include pertinent information about the source culture, author, and text, the canon of the source literature in translation, translation practices in the receiving situation, the interpretation that the translator inscribes in the source text, and the ways in which the publisher plans to print, market, and promote the translation. Such unacknowledged conditions subtly overdetermine the translating, which can therefore result in consequences that the translator did not anticipate, especially consequences for reception. A translation may be judged unacceptable by readerships who possess the information that the translator lacked, who value the literary canon or discursive strategy that the translator unwittingly challenged, who interpret the source text differently from the translator, or who are alienated by the publisher's practices. If the translator succeeds in appealing to an intended audience, the translation may nonetheless be read by a different audience who finds it unacceptable. The commissioning institution may engage in practices that remain unknown to the translator, but that enable the translation to produce unforeseen social effects which are ethically and politically questionable. Thus a translation of an instruction manual could conceivably contribute to patterns of exploitation established by a multinational corporation in its treatment of overseas workforces.

In the case of retranslations, the translator's agency is distinguished by a significant increase in self-consciousness that seeks to take into account the manifold conditions and consequences of the translating. Retranslations typically highlight the translator's intentionality because they are designed to make an appreciable difference. The retranslator's intention is to interpret the source text according to a different set of values so as to bring about a new and different reception for that text in the translating culture. The retranslator is likely to be aware, then, not only of the competing interpretations inscribed in the source text by a previous version and by the retranslation, but also of the linguistic and cultural norms that give rise to these interpretations, such as literary canons and dominant discursive strategies. A retranslator may aim to maintain, revise, or displace norms and the institutions in which they are housed.

Retranslations can also call attention to the overdetermining role of a commissioning institution, which may require the translator to work with a particular source text and discursive strategy to enforce a particular ideology. A commercially oriented publisher may decide to issue retranslations of canonical texts that have fallen into the public domain simply because their canonicity ensures a market demand and they are cheaper to publish than copyrighted texts, which require the purchase of translation rights from the source-text author or his assignees. Hence an ideology of commercialism will govern the selection of a source text for retranslation and dictate a discursive strategy that enhances the readability of the translation to ensure sales. Or a publisher driven by a profit motive may wish to save the expense of commissioning a retranslation by reprinting a previous translation that has proven itself in the marketplace, even if in a revised version. In the United States, this has been the practice of a publisher like Random House, who kept reprinting C. K. Scott Moncrieff's version of Proust, *Remembrance of Things Past* (1922–31) until it brought out Terence Kilmartin's 1981 revision, which was itself revised by D. J. Enright in 1992. Yet even small literary publishers may be forced to economize in this way so as to continue issuing translations of canonical texts that might nonetheless interest a limited audience. In 1999, Vermont-based Steerforth Press reissued Angus Davidson's 1951 translation of Moravia's novel *Il conformista*, although in a revised version; in the same year, London-based Prion Books reprinted Davidson's translation without revision.

Of course, a retranslation may be motivated by no more than the retranslator's personal appreciation and understanding of the source text, regardless of transindividual factors. Retranslators of canonical poets like Virgil and Catullus, Baudelaire and Montale routinely justify their projects solely on the basis of the aesthetic values they perceive in the source text. Yet insofar as every translation inscribes the source text with an interpretation informed by the source and translating cultures, insofar as the source author enjoys a canonical status in the translating culture and translations of the author's work continue to interest publishers, transindividual factors inevitably enter into translation projects that seem simply an expression of the translator's literary taste and sensibility. Moreover, even when a retranslator has gained a sophisticated awareness of the conditions and consequences that accompany a complex action like translating, this awareness can never be omniscient, nor can it ever give the retranslator complete control over transindividual factors.

A case in point is Québécois translation after 1968, when the nationalist movement emerged to demand political autonomy for Quebec. As Annie Brisset has shown (1996: 162–94), drama translations were produced to form a national cultural identity. Nationalist writers, poets as well as lexicographers, fashioned Québécois French into a native or mother tongue, a language of community, while translators worked to turn it into the support of a national literature by rendering canonical writers who had entered a world canon of drama, such as Shakespeare, Strindberg, Chekhov, and Brecht. The goal was to endow Québécois French with cultural authority so as to challenge its subordination to two dominant languages, North American English and Parisian French. A key strategy in achieving this goal was the retranslation of canonical drama that had previously been available only in the French of France. The rarely acknowledged conditions of this nationalist project included the linguistic and cultural differences of the source texts, as well as a sizeable immigrant population whose native language was not any dialect of French. Hence in attempting to construct a homogeneous national identity on the basis of Québécois French the retranslations entailed an ethnocentric reduction of other languages and cultures and thereby set up hierarchies that were just as exclusionary as those that had subordinated Quebec.

Intertextuality

The translator's agency centers on the construction of various intertextual relations, starting with the production of a text that relates to a source text (see Venuti 2009). The forms of intertextuality that a translator might construct are always figurative. They never result in an exact or literal reproduction of the source text, but rather establish a ratio of loss and gain through an interpretive inscription that is shaped by different linguistic structures and cultural discourses. In constructing a relation to the source text, a translation is simultaneously linked to other texts written in the translating language.

Perhaps the most prevalent intertextual relation in translating is analogical or metaphoric: for the chain of signifiers that constitutes the source text, the translator substitutes another signifying chain in the translating language on the basis of a semantic similarity that relies upon current definitions for source-language lexical items. This sort of equivalence is properly called lexicographical; the intertext consists of relations to dictionaries. Such metaphoric relations can be misleading, however, by suggesting that a one-to-one correspondence exists between the source and translated texts when in fact the correspondence is limited to a reductive semantic core which does not take into account other linguistic features that significantly affect meaning, such as register and dialect, or that establish more complicated intertextual relations, such as those involving style and genre.

In my English translation of the twentieth-century Italian poet Antonia Pozzi, for instance, I maintained a semantic correspondence that is fairly close to the Italian texts so as to recreate her hermeticism (*ermetismo*), a modernist poetics that combines precise language, dense imagery, and free verse. In the process, I also drew on anglophone poetic traditions that bear some resemblance to hermeticism. Here is Pozzi's poem "Capodanno" ("New year") followed by my English version:

> Se le parole sapessero di neve
> stasera, che canti —
> e le stelle
> che non potrò mai dire …
>
> Volti immoti s'intrecciano fra i rami
> nel mio turchino nero:
> osano ancora,
> morti ai lumi di case lontane,
> l'indistrutto sorriso dei miei anni.

(Pozzi 1998: 304)

> If words might
>   know
>   snow
>   tonight,
>   what songs —
>   & stars
> I couldn't ever
>   utter …
>
> Motionless
>   faces mesh
>   amongst the branches
> in my blue black:
>   dead
> in the lights of distant houses
>   they still dare
>   the undying
>   smile
>   of my years.

(Pozzi 2002: 159)

The clause that begins the Italian text, containing a verb in the imperfect subjunctive, can be translated with clarity and exactness as follows: "If words could give the impression of snow/this evening." The fourth line can similarly be translated: "that I will never be able to express." An English version could also adhere to the distinctive nature of Pozzi's free verse, which parses the lines by breaking them into grammatical units. My choices, however, create a lexicographical equivalence attentive to syntax while producing certain prosodic effects: I resorted to the phrases "might/know/snow/tonight" and "I couldn't ever/utter," cultivating rhyme and assonance in a form of free verse that annotates the syntax by singling out specific words for emphasis (for the distinction between "parsing" and "annotating" free verse, see Longenbach 2008: 50–81). As a result, an intertextual relation is constructed: the translation links Pozzi's poem to modernist poetries in the United States, not only the annotating free verse of William Carlos Williams, but particularly the work of Lorine Niedecker, distinguished by angular rhythms and mellifluous sound effects. Here is an extract from Niedecker's group of poems "Traces of Living Things":

Smile
> to see the lake
>> lay
> the still sky
And
> out for an easy
>> make
> the dragonfly

(Niedecker 2002: 242)

An alternative intertextual relation is metonymic: a translation might focus on re-creating specific parts of the source text which acquire significance and value in relation to literary trends and traditions in the translating culture. In rendering the poetry of the *dolcestilnovisti*, Ezra Pound was occasionally "preserving one value of early Italian work, the cantabile," song-like metrical effects that evoke "the Elizabethan lyric" (Anderson 1983: 246). Pound knew that the establishment of a metonymic relation in a translation never gives the entire source text: in stressing "the cantabile," he observed, "I have let go the fervour and the intensity," sacrificing lexical or stylistic features of the Italian text (ibid.). Yet the sacrifice would be invisible to the reader who cannot read Italian, and so the part can easily pass for the whole. This is what Roland Barthes calls the "metonymic falsehood": "by stating the whole for the part, it induces error or at least masks the truth, hides vacuum under plenitude" (Barthes 1974: 162). Hence Maria Tymoczko's sweeping assertion that translation "is a form of representation in which parts or aspects of the source text come to stand for the whole" not only reduces every intertextual relation constructed by a translation to one figure, metonymy, but also is uncritical in its failure to acknowledge metonymic falsehood (Tymoczko 1999: 55). Moreover, a metonymic translation is not simply an incomplete representation; like every translation, it is also a slanted interpretation, at once fragmentary and biased. Pound's use of the word "preserving," then, like Tymoczko's repeated use of it, is misleading: a translation can never preserve any feature of the source text in the sense of communicating it intact; if a metonymic relation is constructed, as with Pound's "cantabile" value, the part is not only emphasized but actually transformed in the translation, assimilated to the translating culture (see Tymoczko 1999: 50, 52, 55, 56).

Intertextual relations may escape the translator's conscious control because they fall either among the unacknowledged conditions of the translation or among its unanticipated consequences when it is read by different audiences. And in the effort to recreate a stylistic innovation in a source text, the translator may produce a "fidelity" that is, as Philip Lewis (1985) has argued, doubly "abusive": innovative translating may not only challenge the structures and discourses of the translating language and culture, but also criticize the source text by pointing towards interpretations and effects that its author did not anticipate (see chapter 3: 74). My translation of Pozzi's poetry affiliated it with the work of H. D. and Amy Lowell, Mina Loy and Lorine Niedecker, and this affiliation situated the Italian texts in a tradition of women writing in English, displacing the Italian men who influenced her, notably Giuseppe Ungaretti, Eugenio Montale, and Salvatore Quasimodo, while putting anglophone modernist poetries to a different, foreign use. The English versions exposed and at the same time provided what Pozzi lacked in Italian, a feminine poetic tradition.

Because retranslations are designed to challenge a previous version of the source text, they are likely to construct a more dense and complex intertextuality so as to signify and call attention to their competing interpretation. The Québécois retranslations of canonical world drama distinguished themselves from the Parisian French versions by drawing on dialects that were described by Québécois lexicographers, used by Québécois playwrights and poets, and championed by polemical defenders of Québécois French. In other cases, the intertext in a retranslation might not deploy a dialect but a style or discourse. Pound's versions of Guido Cavalcanti's poetry were in some cases retranslations that sampled "pre-Elizabethan" English poets such as Sir Thomas Wyatt to recreate values that Pound found "obfuscated" by the pre-Raphaelite medievalism of Dante Gabriel Rossetti's versions (Anderson 1983: 243, 250). The more dense and complex such intertextual relations, the more a retranslation risks effacing the linguistic and cultural differences of the source text to serve a cultural politic agenda in the receiving situation. Pound was nonetheless able to register these differences through his modernist poetics because his discursive strategy developed an archaism that noticeably deviated from current standard English and dominant poetic styles.

Through links to cultural discourses in the translating language, retranslations may select and narrow their audience to those readers who possess the specialized knowledge to recognize the intertextuality and hence the new interpretation inscribed by the retranslator. Yet because general readers may in fact know a previous version, they may perceive the difference signaled by a retranslation even when they fail to recognize a particular intertextual connection. Richard Pevear and Larissa Volokhonsky retranslated Dostoevsky's novel *The Brothers Karamazov* by adhering closely to the Russian text, reproducing its peculiar stylistic innovations and challenging previous renderings that resorted to freedoms to increase readability, notably the Edwardian version of Constance Garnett (Dostoevsky 1912; 1990; May 1994: 53–55). General readers who know Garnett's version will be immediately struck by what seem to be the peculiarities of the closer retranslation. Pevear and Volokhonsky are writerly translators, not scholars, yet a scholarly reader familiar with twentieth-century literary theory and criticism may notice a striking resemblance between their retranslation and the interpretation of the Russian theorist Mikhail Bakhtin, who viewed Dostoevsky's novels as "dialogic" or "polyphonic," characterized by a heterogeneous, multivocal style (Bakhtin 1984). The intertextual relations established by a retranslation might thus encompass an understanding of the source text that is shared by native readers as well. Or, in the effort to surpass a previous version, the intertext in a retranslation may exceed and even criticize the source culture. Gary Wills suggested that Robert Fagles's 1996 version of the *Odyssey* reflected the questioning of traditional gender roles initiated by American feminist movements, a questioning that is obviously at odds with the gender inequalities of ancient Greece (Wills 1997).

A retranslation is sometimes accompanied by a more immediate form of intertextuality, paratexts, which signal its status as a retranslation and make explicit the competing interpretation that the retranslator has tried to inscribe in the source text. Paratexts are supplementary materials that may include introductions and afterwords, annotations and commentaries, the endorsements of academic specialists and the publisher's advertising copy. Pound's prefaces and notes to his versions of Cavalcanti, along with his separately published essays, rationalized his choice and interpretation of the source text as well as his discursive strategies. Vladimir Nabokov's retranslation of Pushkin's *Onegin* maintained a lexicographical equivalence and added copious annotations to question the accuracy of previous versions that relied on what he called "poetical" strategies, free renderings and rhyme schemes (Nabokov 1955: 512). Nabokov's commentary in annotations as well as in separately published essays sought to reconstruct the literary context of the poem, the intertextual network in which the Russian text was embedded and with which academic specialists are familiar. Paratexts might go some way towards restoring the linguistic and cultural differences that translation necessarily removes from the source text by rewriting it in another language with different cultural traditions. My version of Pozzi's poetry was a retranslation, and in describing it as such in an introductory essay, I was able not only to distinguish my modernist interpretation from the sentimentalizing version of Pozzi's first translator, Nora Wydenbruck, but also to indicate how Wydenbruck, a friend of the family, assisted the poet's father in crafting a respectable image of his daughter by editing her texts (see Pozzi 2002: xii–xiii, xxi). This editorial history was further documented in endnotes to specific poems.

History

Translations are profoundly linked to their historical moment because they always reflect the cultural formation where they are produced, circulating in institutions where values are arranged hierarchically and undergo various developments over time (see Venuti 2005). The cultural formation mediates every stage of the translation process, from the choice of a source text to the invention of discursive strategies to the reception of the translated text by particular audiences. Thus literary translators are often led to favor certain source texts and genres by prevailing literary trends. In eighteenth-century Britain, the dominance of a neoclassical aesthetic was instrumental in the repeated translation of classical epics, whereas during the nineteenth century the rise of romantic expressivism encouraged British translators to render classical lyric poetry that had hitherto been neglected. The canonical status of the source literature remained constant in the translating culture, which, however, underwent a change in aesthetic values that stimulated a later revaluation of that literature.

Discursive strategies reveal the historicity of a translation in the very texture of its language. The translator's invention of a lexicon and syntax for the source text may draw on dialects or styles that prevail during the period when the translation is produced. Wyatt's Petrarch, Florio's Montaigne, Pope's Homer, Rose's *Orlando Furioso*, FitzGerald's *Rubáiyát*, and Pound's *Cathay* exhibit linguistic structures and stylistic features that link them to certain moments in the histories of the English language and English literatures. A translation may be characterized by linguistic variations that are favored by translators at specific historical moments. The pre-Raphaelite medievalism of Rossetti's *dolcestilnovisti* or the Jacobean English in Benjamin Jowett's Plato typify the strain of poetical archaism in Victorian translations, whereas the mixture of archaism with modern colloquialism in Paul Blackburn's versions of Provençal troubadours typifies the modernist experimentalism in translation. The interpretation that a translator inscribes through a discursive strategy also carries a historical significance, since it may mirror or revise values that prevail at particular moments in the translating culture. At the end of the nineteenth century, the Chinese translator Lin Shu sought to strengthen imperial culture by rendering such Western novelists as Dickens into the classical prose instead of the vernacular and by inscribing them with Confucian moral concepts. Ultimately, discursive strategies point to historically specific standards of accuracy, making clear that even definitions of translation vary from period to period. In 1714, Antoine Houdar de la Motte regarded his work on the *Iliad* as stopping short of "losing any important features of the plot," even though he reduced the twenty-four books of the Greek text to twelve in French (Lefevere 1992: 29). Today, we would obviously consider La Motte not simply a translator or adaptor, but an editor as well.

Retranslations deliberately mark the passage of time by aiming to distinguish themselves from a previous version through differences in discursive strategies and interpretations. Since they rely on a more dense and complicated intertextuality to produce these differences, they are likely to defamiliarize the source text as well as forms and traditions in the translating culture. In the 1920s, Martin Buber and Franz Rosenzweig rendered the Hebrew Bible into German so as to evoke the oral quality of the Hebrew, at once inscribing their Jewish interpretation and distinguishing it from Luther's Christian version (see Reichert 1996). They resorted to various departures from standard usage, including Hebraicized syntax, archaisms, and stylistic devices such as Buber's "Leitworte" or leitmotifs, the modernist technique of incorporating recurrent details or images in a work of art. As a result, their translation not only cast the Hebrew Bible in a different light, but also introduced a note of foreignness into the German language. And since Wagner had powerfully developed leitmotifs in his operas, the use of this technique to translate the canonical Hebrew text also unsettled German cultural traditions at a moment when they were increasingly invested with nationalist and racist ideologies.

Retranslations are not merely historical in their affiliations with a specific moment, but also historiographical in their effort to signal and rationalize their differences from previous versions by employing various narrative genres, often a mixture of them. Perhaps the most common genre here is romance, according to Hayden White's classification (see White 1973), where the historical narrative is evolutionary or progressive, culminating in some form of transcendence – here a transcendence, not of the difficulties in translating the source text, but of the defects that are perceived to have marred an earlier rendering. Thus retranslations are often presented as a significant improvement because they rely on a definitive edition of the source text which was not formerly available or because they employ a discursive strategy that maintains a closer semantic correspondence or stylistic analogy. Some retranslations do no more than update the translating language. An editor at the *New York Times* responded favorably to John Woods's 1995 retranslation of Thomas Mann's novel *The Magic Mountain* solely because Helen Lowe-Porter's language has come to seem antiquated and Woods used the current standard dialect of English (Bruckner 1995).

Alternatively, a retranslation may be conservative, premised on a satiric historical narrative. Here the retranslator criticizes a previous version, but casts doubt on the notion of progress in translation and returns to a discursive strategy or interpretation that was developed in the past, while admitting its inadequacy. Nabokov thus justified his close, unrhymed retranslation of *Onegin* by arguing that previous English versions were "grotesque travesties of their model, rendered in dreadful verse, teeming with mistranslations" (Nabokov 1955: 504). Yet he could only hope for a "reasonable accuracy" that relied on annotations (ibid.: 512). A retranslation may also be premised on a comedic narrative of reconciliation, in which a discursive strategy is used to bring the source text to a hitherto excluded readership or to cross the cultural boundaries between readerships. The Penguin Classics originated, in fact, in just such a project of making available to mass audiences classical literature that had previously been accessible to scholars and university-educated readers exclusively.

Retranslations reflect changes in the values and institutions of the translating culture, but they can also produce such changes by inspiring new ways of reading and appreciating the source texts. To study retranslations is to realize that translating cannot be viewed as a simple act of communication because it creates values in social formations at specific historical moments, and these values redefine the source text and culture from moment to moment. To retranslate is to confront anew and more urgently the translator's ethical responsibility to prevent the translating language and culture from effacing the linguistic and cultural differences of the source text, its foreignness. The lesson of retranslation is that this responsibility can be met most effectively by allowing the retranslator's situation, especially the existence of a previous version, to open up new paths of invention so as to inscribe a competing interpretation. It is only through the inscription that a translator can hope to make a linguistic and cultural difference that signals the foreign at home.

[2004]

6

HOW TO READ A TRANSLATION

Among the many pronouncements that have shaped our understanding of literary translation, perhaps none is more often echoed than John Dryden's preface to his version of the *Aeneid* (1697). "I have endeavour'd to make *Virgil* speak such *English*," asserted Dryden, "as he wou'd himself have spoken, if he had been born in England, and in this present Age" (Dryden 1958: 1055). No doubt Dryden's achievement is to have made many of his contemporaries believe that he had impersonated the Latin poet. But this is merely a poetic sleight of hand. Dryden's Virgil abandons the unrhymed verse of the Latin poem for English couplets while cribbing lines from a previous translator, the poet Sir John Denham (see Venuti 2008: 52). A skeptic might well wonder why Virgil should come back as Dryden instead of an epic poet who lived in the same period and wrote his epic without rhyme: John Milton. Should we not expect an English Virgil to be more attracted to the grand style of *Paradise Lost*?

The answer has less to do with a fancied reincarnation than with the fact that literary taste changes. And when it does change, a corresponding style of translation falls into disuse or is preempted, never to be adopted by leading translators (especially when, like Dryden, they happen to be Poet Laureate). By the end of the seventeenth century, the blank verse of Shakespeare and Milton had lost symbolic and cultural capital to the couplet, so that a poet as talented and celebrated as Dryden could make the latter seem to be the most natural vehicle for a Latin poem written in a completely different verse form (for the seeming naturalness of the couplet, see Easthope 1983: 110–12). The translator is no stand-in or ventriloquist for the author of the source text, but a resourceful imitator who rewrites it to appeal to another audience in a different language and culture, often in a different period. This audience ultimately takes priority, insuring that the verbal clothing the translator cuts for the source text never fits exactly.

The most questionable effect of Dryden's assertion, to my mind, is that it winds up collapsing the translator's labor into the source-text author's, giving us no way to understand (let alone judge) how the translator has performed the crucial role of cultural go-between. To read a translation as a translation, as a text in its own right, we need a more practical sense of what a translator does. I would describe it as an attempt to compensate for an irreparable loss by controlling an exorbitant gain.

The source language is the first thing to go, the very sound and order of the words, and along with them all the resonance and allusiveness that they carry for the reader with source-language proficiency who is immersed in the source culture. Simultaneously, merely by choosing words from the translating language, the translator adds an entirely new set of resonances and allusions designed to imitate the source text, while making it comprehensible to a reader who is proficient in the translating language and immersed in the translating culture. These additional meanings may occasionally result from an actual insertion or deletion for clarity. But they in fact inhere in every choice that the translator makes, even when the translation sticks closely to the words in the source text and conforms to their current dictionary definitions. The translator must somehow control the unavoidable release of meanings that work only in the translating language. Apart from threatening to derail the project of imitation, these meanings always risk transforming what is linguistically and culturally different into something too familiar or simply irrelevant. The loss in translation remains invisible to any reader who does not undertake a careful comparison to the source text – i.e., most of us. The gain is everywhere apparent, although only if the reader looks.

But usually we don't look. Publishers, copyeditors, reviewers have trained us, in effect, to prefer translations with an easy readability which enables them to appear untranslated. In practice, this preference tends to be a narrowly defined fluency achieved by adhering to the current standard dialect, the most familiar form of the translating language and hence the most powerful in giving the illusory impression that we are reading the source text (Venuti 2008: 1–5). We typically become aware of the translation only when we run across a bump on its surface, a nonstandard item, an unfamiliar word, an error in usage, a confused meaning that may seem unintentionally comical. Think of the bad English translations you've encountered abroad, the dry cleaner urging potential customers to "Drop your trousers here for best results," the restaurant announcing that "Our wines leave you nothing to hope for," the hotel advising its guests to "Please leave your values at the front desk."

Our laughter at their ineffectiveness betrays a confidence, perhaps a complacence, in our English proficiency. But something more instructive is revealed: we laugh only because we have sorted out the confusions, demonstrating quite clearly that readers of translations can perform several mental tasks at once. In reading to comprehend, we focus on both form and meaning, so that when the meaning turns obscure or ambiguous, we instantly clarify or untangle it by correcting the error in form, in word choice or grammar. Thus the first rule of reading translations: *Don't read just for meaning, but for language too; appreciate the formal features of the translation.*

Savor the translator's diction and phrasing, the distinctiveness of the style, the verbal subtleties that project a tone of voice and sketch the psychological contours of a character. Still – a reader may ask – don't these qualities belong to the source text?

Not at all, certainly not in the sense that the translator just transfers them intact, without variation. They of course result from the translator's imitation of the source text. But the fact remains that the translator has chosen every single word in the translation, whether or not a source-language word lies behind it. And the translator's words, in our case, function only in English, releasing literary effects that may well exceed the language chosen by the author of the source text.

Consider a passage from Margaret Jull Costa's version of *The Man of Feeling* by the Spanish novelist Javier Marías. The narrator, an opera singer, is writing the story of his chance encounter with a woman:

> I knew nothing at all about her history or past or life, apart from the scant information vouchsafed to me in Dato's self-absorbed and fragmentary complaint during the first and only opportunity I had had to talk to him alone (too soon for my curiosity to have learned how to direct its questions) and from the enthusiastic remarks which, rarely and only in passing, she made about her brother, Roberto Monte, that recent émigré to South America.
>
> *(Marías 2003: 75)*

The most striking feature of this sentence is its sheer length: it appears uncommonly long against the backdrop of current English-language fiction. It matches Marías's Spanish, but we don't need to know that to appreciate how effectively Costa constructs the English sentence, allowing it to unfold at a measured pace, embedding self-conscious qualifications at key points. She also chooses language that creates a slightly elevated, even precious tone, including various nonstandard items like poetical archaisms ("scant," "vouchsafed") and a foreign loan-word ("émigré") as well as phrases that display a punctilious care with grammar ("had had," "to have learned"). With all these features, the translator has shrewdly avoided more colloquial English so as to fashion a somewhat affected character. The affectation is actually more pronounced in the English version because the Spanish is fairly common, using, for example, "me había permitido entender" ("had allowed me to understand") instead of an archaic phrase like "vouchsafed to me."

Costa's sentence points to a second rule: *Don't expect translations to be written only in the current standard dialect; be open to linguistic variations.* The translator's hand becomes visible in deviations from the most commonly used forms of the translating language. Social and regional dialects, slang and obscenities, archaisms and neologisms, jargons and foreign borrowings tend to be language-specific, unlikely to travel well, their peculiar force difficult to render into other languages. Thus they show the translator at work, implementing a strategy to bring the source text into a different culture. Matthew Ward's 1988 version of Albert Camus's novel *The Stranger* opens with the surprising line "Maman died today" (Camus 1988: 3). The context makes clear that the French "maman" means "mother." Ward retains Camus's use of the word, yet it means so much more in English: not only does it signal the childlike intimacy of the narrator's relationship, but it also tells us that we are reading a translation, a hybrid, not to be confused with the French text.

The translator's language can also send down deep roots into the receiving culture, establishing suggestive connections to styles, genres, and texts that have already accumulated meaning there. This inevitable result of the translation process underlies a third rule: *Don't overlook connotations and cultural references; read them as another, pertinent layer of significance.* In 1924, Dorothy Bussy published her English version of André Gide's novel *La Porte étroite*, under the inspired title *Strait is the Gate.* Both titles allude to the Gospel of Luke, but the English one elegantly glances at the King James Bible ("Strive to enter in at the strait gate"). Bussy's phrase invests Gide's work with a cultural prestige that could not be achieved by referring to a less authoritative or less influential version of the Bible.

The connections inscribed in a translation are often stylistic, conjuring up literary genres or traditions that enhance and perhaps comment on the source text. In my 2006 translation of Massimo Carlotto's Italian novel *The Goodbye Kiss*, I developed a style that mines a rich vein of colloquialism, slang, and obscenity, including underworld argot, phrases like "slammer" (for "prison"), "bulls" (for "policemen"), "rousted by a stoolie," "a bad egg," "beat the rap," and "tipped me on the heist" (Carlotto 2006: 18, 21, 24, 41, 61, 80). On the one hand, this language fits the narrator, a leftwing terrorist who, after his release from prison, becomes a criminal, involved in drug-trafficking, prostitution, robbery, extortion, and murder; on the other hand, the language fits the genre, a noir fiction in which the narrator's collusion with a police detective and a lawyer turned politician critiques corruption in the Veneto.

My English aims to match the mixture of standard and nonstandard items in Carlotto's Italian, but the translation does not maintain a perfect correspondence. One conversation among the criminals, for instance, contains this line:

"Pensi che voglia fottermi? Perché sai, ci metto un secondo a piantargli una lama in pancia," sibilò in tono bellicoso.

(Carlotto 2000: 95)

"You think he wants to fuck me? Because you know, I'd stick him in a second, right in the belly," he whispered in a punchy tone.

(Carlotto 2006: 80)

Where Carlotto uses the standard dialect, I occasionally shift to colloquial usage: "Pensi" ("Do you think") becomes the clipped form "You think," "piantargli una lama in pancia" ("thrust a blade in his belly") is telescoped to "stick him [...] right in the belly," "bellicoso" ("bellicose" or "belligerent") becomes "punchy."

In linking style to genre, however, even with such departures from the Italian, my translating is far from arbitrary. I decided that I would bring Carlotto into English through the tradition of hardboiled prose in modern American fiction, stretching from Dashiell Hammett and James M. Cain to Raymond Chandler and Jim Thompson to Andrew Vachss and James Ellroy. The reader familiar with this tradition, or at least some of the writers who form it, can detect its presence in my translation as an intertext constructed through a distinctive lexicon, syntax, and rhythm. Here is a characteristic passage:

> I went to a club in Jesolo where I heard a forty-something English entraîneuse was working. She was a letdown. Thin as a rail, flat chest. She had her clientele, but she wasn't my type. I bought her drink. Forced myself to listen to some bullshit stories, then went home.
>
> *(Carlotto 2006: 40)*

The slang and obscenity, the short, abrupt sentences, the fragments, the suppression of subjects – these features I modeled on the style of English-language crime novels like Thompson's *A Hell of a Woman* (1954):

> She was out of this world, that little girl. Not one of those goddamned tramps like I was always latching onto. You could really go places with a kid like that.
>
> Hell, hadn't he done the same thing a hundred times before? Picked at me; tried to rattle me; nosed around like a skunk in a garbage dump.
>
> *(Thompson 1954: 38, 122)*

The hardboiled prose in the translation winds up heightening the Italian cultural markers, likening certain social developments in Italy to a noirish underworld, while pointing to the origins of Carlotto's novel in American crime fiction (which he read in Italian versions: Thompson began to be translated into Italian in the 1960s). At the same time, the stylistic effects are so deeply rooted in English and have achieved such a high degree of conventionality that they can call attention to the translated status of my translation, its relative autonomy from the Italian source text, and perhaps suggest that Carlotto's novel needs to enter English through a recognizable literary tradition to attract a viable readership. Hence the hardboiled prose serves as a reminder of what most readers implicitly know: a translation can never be identical to the source text or communicate it in some direct, untroubled manner, not even if the translator pursues a strict semantic correspondence. But we may be less willing to accept a corollary: a translation is fundamentally incapable of providing its reader with an experience that equals or closely approximates the one that a reader with source-language proficiency can have with the source text. To provide this sort of experience, a translator would have to endow us with a lifelong immersion in the source language, literature, and culture. Only then can we read the translation with anything resembling the informed sensibility that a source-language reader brings to the source text. Although translators are undoubtedly creative, they can't change the linguistic community to which a reader belongs or the cultural identity fostered by a reader's use of a particular language.

What translators can do, however, is write. We should view the translator as a special kind of writer, possessing not an originality that competes against that of the source-text author, but rather an art of mimicry, aided by a stylistic repertoire that taps into the literary resources of the translating language. A translation does not communicate the source text itself but the translator's interpretation of it, and the translator must be sufficiently expert and innovative to interpret the linguistic and cultural differences that constitute that text. When a classic is retranslated, furthermore, we expect the translator to do something new to justify yet another version. And in raising the bar we might also expect the translator to be capable of describing this newness.

Richard Pevear and Larissa Volokhonsky's 1990 version of *The Brothers Karamazov* utterly changed the understanding that many readers of English have long had of Dostoevsky's novel. As Pevear explains in his preface, previous translators "revised, 'corrected,' or smoothed over the Russian writer's idiosyncratic prose, removing much of the humor and distinctive voicing of the novel" (Dostoevsky 1990: xi). Pevear and Volokhonsky sought "a truer rendering" that restored "phrases, mannerisms, verbal tics" (ibid.: xi, xv). Their exemplary translation necessitates a fourth rule: *Don't skip an introductory essay written by a translator; read it first, as a statement of the interpretation that guides the translation and contributes to what is unique about it.*

Nonetheless, the translator's interpretation remains partial, both incomplete in omitting irrecoverable aspects of the source text and slanted towards what is intelligible and interesting in the receiving situation. It also reflects the cultural and financial interests of publishers, the gatekeepers who decisively exercise the power to admit or exclude foreign works. For an entire foreign literature is never translated, most of what has been translated rarely remains in print for very long, and everywhere translations of fiction far outnumber those of poetry, among other genres (hence the emphasis in my examples). Not only can't we read a recently translated novel with a sense of how the source text draws on the source-culture traditions where it emerged, but uneven translation patterns can all too easily harden into misleading cultural stereotypes. Because the rate of translation into English is so low – roughly 2–4% of annual book output in the United States and the United Kingdom, compared to 20–25% in countries like Italy and Spain – a reader may be unable to find a selection of translations from the work of the same foreign author, even from the same language. This situation gives a special urgency to a fifth and final rule: *Don't take one translation as representative of an entire foreign literature; compare it to translations of other works from the same language.*

Some languages and literatures are particularly undertranslated today. Take Arabic. Relatively little Arabic writing is available in English, much less than Hebrew writing, for instance, undermining any effort to gauge the cultural impact of social and political developments in the Middle East. The Egyptian novelist Naguib Mahfouz deserves to be ranked among the most fascinating Arabic writers, but to regard him as the literary spokesman for the Arab world is undoubtedly a mistake. Mahfouz should be read alongside his countryman Abdel Hakim Qasim, whose *Rites of Assent* (translated by Peter Theroux in 1995) combines modernist techniques with Qur'anic allusions to interrogate Islamic fundamentalism, the forced conversion of an Egyptian Copt under the aegis of the Muslim Brotherhood. Qasim might then be juxtaposed to Sayed Kashua, whose Hebrew novel *Dancing Arabs* (in Miriam Shlesinger's 2002 translation) incisively depicts the identity crisis of an Arab Israeli who, although raised in a family of militant anti-Zionists, tries to pass among Jews. Sometimes, to gain a broader view of the cultural situations that translation leaves behind, a reader must venture into neighboring languages and territories.

As these examples suggest, an aesthetic appreciation of translated literatures can powerfully illuminate the cultural differences that have led to political divisions and military conflicts. The fact is, however, that the current predicament of English translation doesn't favor sharp distinctions between the literary and the political, the aesthetic and the sociological. English is the most translated language worldwide, but relatively little translated into, particularly given the size and profitability of the American and British publishing industries. Foreign publishers scramble to issue translations of English-language fiction, but publishers in the United States and the United Kingdom tend not to reinvest their enormous profits from selling translation rights into translating foreign fiction. The figures are staggering, even if we set aside the immediate worldwide translation of bestsellers like Stephen King, Danielle Steel, and Tom Clancy and focus on authors with literary reputations. In France and Germany, for example, Joyce Carol Oates and Philip Roth each have translations of more than twenty works currently in print; in Italy and Germany, more than thirty titles by Charles Bukowski are available in translation (eighteen in France, fifteen in Spain). Rare is the contemporary foreign novelist whose body of work enjoys such representation and availability in English. In these circumstances, even to read a translation purely for its literary qualities can be seen as a political gesture, an act of resistance against long-standing publishing practices that have severely restricted our access to foreign literatures.

A translation ought to be read differently from an original composition precisely because it is not an original, because not only a foreign work, but also a foreign culture is involved. My aim has been to describe ways of reading translations which increase rather than diminish the pleasures that only reading can offer. These pleasures involve primarily the linguistic, literary, and cultural dimensions of translations. But they might also include the devilish thrill that comes from resistance, from challenging the institutionalized power of cultural brokers like publishers, from staging a personal protest against the grossly unequal patterns of cultural exchange in which readers are unwittingly implicated. Read translations, although with an eye out for the translator's work, with the awareness that the most a translation can give you is an insightful and eloquent interpretation of a foreign text, at once limited and enabled by the need to address the receiving culture. Publishers will catch on sooner or later. After all, it's in their interest.

[2004]

7

LOCAL CONTINGENCIES

Translation and national identities

Preliminary distinctions

> When you offer a translation to a nation, that nation will almost always look on the
> translation as an act of violence against itself. Bourgeois taste tends to resist the
> universal spirit.
>
> To translate a foreign writer is to add to your own national poetry; such a widening
> of the horizon does not please those who profit from it, at least not in the beginning.
> The first reaction is one of rebellion.
>
> (Lefevere 1992: 18)

These comments are drawn from Victor Hugo's 1865 preface to his son François-Victor's
version of Shakespeare's works. They are worth examining, not simply because Hugo
uses translation as the basis for a critique of nationalism, but because his critique at
once exposes and is itself riddled with contradictions that have characterized the
relations between translation and national identities, regardless of the language and
culture in which the translating is performed. Formulating the contradictory implications of Hugo's comments, then, will be a useful way to introduce my reflections
on nationalist agendas in translation.

Translation can be described as an act of violence against a nation only because
nationalist thinking tends to be premised on a metaphysical concept of identity as a
homogeneous essence, usually given a biological grounding in an ethnicity or race
and seen as manifested in a particular language and culture. Since translation works
on the linguistic and cultural differences of a source text, it can communicate those
differences and thereby threaten the assumed integrity of the national language and
culture, the essentialist homogeneity of the national identity. As an example, Hugo
cites Voltaire's attack on the Shakespearean translator Pierre Letourneur, who is said
to "sacrifice every French writer without exception to his idol (Shakespeare)" and
"does not deign even to mention Corneille and Racine," an omission deplored as an

"offense that he gives to France" (Hugo 1985: 456). Nationalism, Hugo suggests, goes hand in hand with a literary xenophobia, a fear that foreign literatures might contaminate native traditions, an attitude that he tellingly phrases in biological terms: "Who could ever dare think of infusing the substance of another people into its own very life-blood?" (Lefevere 1992: 18).

This attitude, however, is contradicted by the fact that nations do indeed "profit" from translation. Nationalist movements have frequently enlisted translation in the development of national languages and cultures, especially national literatures. A language, Hugo remarks, "will later be strengthened" by translation, even if "while waiting it is indignant" (Hugo 1985: 455). The forms taken by such translation agendas vary with the social situations in which they are deployed, and their varying approaches to source texts and cultures may be diametrically opposed, seeking either to preserve or to erase linguistic and cultural differences. Yet in both cases the differences of the source texts are exploited to construct a national identity that is assumed to pre-exist the translation process. As Jacques Derrida explains, nationalist thinking rests on a circular logic: the nation, imagined to be a homogeneous essence, must be constructed, but the construction is understood as "a recourse, a re-source, a circular return to the source" (Derrida 1992: 12). Nationalist translation agendas depend on the same circularity: the national status of a language and culture is simultaneously presupposed and created through translation. Insofar as such agendas implicitly reveal the incompleteness of the nation, translation is a scandal to nationalist thinking, providing yet another motive for indignation and offense, for perceiving a translated text as an international act of violence.

The concept of nation, moreover, can be regarded as democratic, at least in principle, subsuming social divisions beneath a collective identity. The term that Hugo uses in his critique is "le peuple" (the people), an undifferentiated population united here in its resistance to a translation. Yet the arbiters of a national culture, even the theorists who articulate the very idea of a nation, may well belong to an elite minority. Hence Hugo implicitly equates the cultural values of one class, "bourgeois taste," with the collective culture that resists translation. Nationalist translation agendas have often been initiated by cultural elites who aim to impose their linguistic and literary values on an entire population. The success of these agendas shows, however, that nationalisms cannot be viewed simply as forms of class dominance: translations must be accepted by a mass audience to be effective in constructing national languages, cultures, identities (cf. Easthope 1999a: 6–8).

Do Hugo's comments, although critical of nationalism, take a clear stand on nationalist translation agendas? Here too contradictions emerge. On the one hand, he acknowledges that translation traffics in linguistic and cultural differences that threaten nationalisms even while enriching national literatures. On the other hand, he suppresses the constructive hybridizing effects of these differences by positing the existence of a "universal spirit," an essentialist concept of humanity that transcends the boundaries of class and nation. In a posthumously published commentary on translation, similarly, he asserts that translators "transfuse the human spirit from one people to another," but when he addresses the languages that mediate this transfusion, his thinking again issues into contradiction: "The human spirit is greater than every idiom. Languages do not all express the same quantity of it" (Hugo 1985: 631). Even though translation is seen as the practice that overcomes the boundaries between national languages and cultures to communicate the universal spirit, we must still ask what linguistic and cultural differences shape the translator's work on another literature and complicate the communicative process. At every turn, Hugo must confront the question of which nation at once gives rise to and is affected by a particular translation practice.

His universalism actually reveals the close relationship between his thinking and nationalism. Derrida points out that "nationalism does not present itself as a retrenchment onto an empirical particularity, but as the assigning to a nation of a universalistic, essentialist representation" (Derrida 1992: 19). Considered from the vantage point of an individual social agent, then, nationalism is not the empirical fact of national citizenship, but an identification with or self-recognition in a particular discourse of nation. Thus, despite the fact that Letourneur was a French citizen, his translation of Shakespeare might still cause offense to Voltaire's nationalistic investment in French literature, might still be perceived as an insult to France. The English playwright seems a "monster" and "a barbarous actor" to Voltaire because he identifies with an essentialist image of French culture which assumes that it is the seat of two universal principles: human nature and civilization (Hugo 1985: 456). Hugo, in effect, attributes to humanity what Voltaire attributes to France. Universalism can be useful in criticizing the exclusionary effects of nationalism, but by suppressing linguistic and cultural differences it preempts the articulation of theoretical concepts to understand how national identities are formed and what role translation might play in their formation.

To work towards such an understanding, I shall set out from Antony Easthope's productive synthesis of poststructuralism and psychoanalysis in which human subjectivity is seen as constructed in language, in the subject's identification with a self-image reflected by an other's language use (see Easthope 1999a: 3–57). This language-based process of identification at once elicits desire and – since that desire originates in an external object – defers its satisfaction, producing an irremediable lack in the subject. A national identity is constructed when the external object is both a particular discourse of nation and a social group, so that a double process of identification is enacted and housed in social institutions designed to reproduce the national culture and the nation-state. Yet neither culture nor state can guarantee the unity of the nation: not only are they disjunctive, characterized by incommensurate institutions and practices that may be in conflict (such as when a national cultural agency exacerbates political divisions), but they are also each in their turn heterogeneous, since citizenship can be granted to foreigners, and foreign values can be assimilated into the domestic culture. These incommensurabilities and heterogeneities, in the presence of such other conditions as the modern displacement of traditionally close-knit communities by impersonal social relations and the domination of a colonial or hegemonic power, evoke within individuals the desire for a national collective and sustain the process of national identity formation. As Easthope observes, "the disjunction in nation between state and culture (as well as the heterogeneity of each) is disavowed through fantasy identification with a unified identity, state and culture together" (ibid.: 46).

Translation can support the formation of national identities through both the selection of source texts and the development of discursive strategies to translate them. A source text may be chosen because the social situation in which it was produced is seen as analogous to that of the translating culture and thus illuminating of the problems that a nation must confront in its emergence. A source text may also be chosen because its form and theme contribute to the creation of a specific discourse of nation in the translating culture. Similarly, a source text may be translated with a discursive strategy that has come to be regarded as a distinguishing characteristic of the nation because that strategy has long dominated translation traditions and practices in the translating culture. A translation strategy may also be affiliated with a national discourse because it employs a dialect that has gained acceptance as the standard dialect or the national language. Such translation practices form national identities through a specular process in which the subject identifies with cultural materials that are defined as national and thereby enable a self-recognition in a national collective. The fact that the materials at issue may include forms and themes, texts and cultures that are irreducibly foreign is repressed in a fantastic identification with an apparently homogeneous national identity. The irreducible foreignness of these materials may actually result in an intensification of national desire: in this instance, whatever linguistic and cultural differences may be communicated by a translation elicit a desire for a unified nation that the translation cannot fulfill by virtue of those very differences.

Intentionality and the translator's unconscious

Although translation nationalisms are usually deliberate, driven by specific cultural and political goals, neither translators nor their audiences need be aware of the social effects produced by translated texts. The formation of national identities can remain unconscious because it occurs in language that originates elsewhere, in the subject's relations to others, but that the subject perceives as his or her own self-expression. In Easthope's words, nation is "an identity that can speak us even when we may think we are speaking for ourselves" (Easthope 1999a: 5). A translation, then, might serve a nationalist agenda without the translator's conscious intention. Hugo remarks that "Letourneur did not translate Shakespeare; he parodied him, ingenuously, without wishing it, unknowingly obedient to the hostile taste of his epoch" (Hugo 1985: 457). Letourneur's decision to translate Shakespeare deviated from contemporary French literary canons, but his discursive strategy unconsciously conformed to them. This conformity could only highlight Shakespeare's deviation, simultaneously intensifying and offending Voltaire's nationalistic investment in French literature.

The translator's unconscious formation of national identities can be developed further if we examine a specific case more closely. Consider the American translator William Weaver's 1968 version of Italo Calvino's scientific fantasies, *Cosmicomics*. On

a few occasions, Calvino uses "ricotta" as an analogy to describe imaginary features of
the moon and interstellar matter. The word refers to a soft, mild Italian cheese made
from the whey of cow's or sheep's milk. Weaver repeatedly replaces it with English
words that do not maintain a semantic equivalence with the Italian:

Il latte lunare era molto denso, come una specie di ricotta.
Moon-milk was very thick, like a kind of cream cheese.

La ricotta volava
The cheese flew

adesso s'erano trovati prigionieri d'una specie di ricotta spugnosa
now they were imprisoned in a kind of spongy cream
(Calvino 1965: 6, 7, 27; 1968: 5, 6, 24)

In each instance, Weaver suppresses the cultural specificity of "ricotta" by using
words that are more familiar to English-language readers. His choices include
"cheese," which generalizes the Italian word; "cream," which diverges from the very
notion of cheese; and "cream cheese," which for many readers would refer to a distinctively American cheese made from cream and milk, sometimes associated with a
brand name, "Philadelphia Cream Cheese," but in any case very different from Italian
ricotta. These renderings constitute lexical shifts that assimilate the Italian text to
English-language cultural terms, a tendency that recurs in the translation:

La Galassia si voltava come una frittata nella sua padella infuocata, essa stessa
padella friggente e dorato pesceduovo
The Galaxy turned like an omelet in its heated pan, itself both frying pan and
golden egg

cosa volete che ce ne facessimo, del tempo, stando lì pigiati come acciughe?
what use did we have for time, packed in there like sardines?

Attraversai una metropoli nuragica tutta torri di pietra
I crossed a piled-up metropolis of stones

—Ragazzi, avessi un po' di spazio, come mi piacerebbe farvi le tagliatelle! –
"Oh, if I only had some room, how I'd like to make some noodles for you
boys!"
(Calvino 1965: 41, 45, 49, 57; 1968: 38, 43, 46, 56)

In each case, the translation adheres closely to the Italian passages until a culturally
specific term appears, at which point a lexical choice reveals a discursive strategy that
can be called Anglocentric. The word "pesceduovo," or "fish [made] of egg," refers
to an omelet that has been folded to form an elongated, fish-shaped roll. Weaver not

only simplifies the word for English-language readers, but actually strips it of its peculiarly Italian significance. With the Italian phrase "pigiati come acciughe," or "pressed like anchovies," he removes "anchovies," a staple of Italian rather than British or American cuisine, and reverts to an analogy that has long been a cliché in English: "packed like sardines." The Italian word "nuragica," a technical term that refers to the prehistoric conical monuments found in Sardinia, is similarly replaced by a simpler yet somewhat unclear rendering, "piled-up." And the Italian word "tagliatelle," referring to a long, ribbon-like pasta, gives way to the generic "noodles."

These Anglocentric renderings belong to an overall strategy in which the translator's choices are evidently made to enhance intelligibility for a broad English-language readership. The translation is primarily written in the current standard dialect of English, devoid of any typically British or American markings. It also draws on fairly common colloquialisms. Thus "Ignoranti ... Ignorantoni" ("Ignoramuses ... The big ignoramuses") is translated as "Bunch of ignorant louts ... Know-nothings"; "la forte miscela" ("the strong mixture") becomes "the heady blend"; "la partita è nulla" ("the game is invalid") becomes "the game's null and void"; "poteva avere torto marcio" ("he could be totally wrong") becomes "he could be dead wrong"; "l'avreste capita" ("you would have understood") becomes "to catch on"; "non mi sarei cambiato" ("I would not have changed") becomes "I wouldn't have traded places"; "sbranarla" ("tear her to pieces") becomes "tear her from limb to limb" (Calvino 1965: 30, 58, 67, 74, 83, 99; 1968: 27, 57, 66, 73, 82, 98). These examples show that Weaver consistently favors the colloquial word or phrase, the cliché-like idiom, the informal contraction, even where Calvino uses standard Italian. As a result, the translation is extremely fluent, immediately recognizable to English-language readers and therefore easily readable.

This discursive strategy allows the translation to produce several potentially nationalistic effects. The easy readability fosters an illusion of transparency whereby the second-order status of the translation is effaced and the reader comes to feel as if he or she were reading, not a translation, but the source text, Calvino's Italian. Through this illusionism, the translation validates the most widely used forms of English by seemingly demonstrating their power to express the truth of Calvino's writing. Here the experience of reading Weaver's translation coincides with the formation of a national identity. Whether the nationality is British or American (or linked to some other English-speaking country) depends on the reader to a significant extent because Weaver's English is not regional, not geographically marked. Yet the identity should be considered national because it is grounded in a validation of a national language, the standard dialect and the most familiar colloquialisms, and reinforced through Anglocentric cultural terms. The very illusion of transparency, furthermore, is characteristic of British and American cultural traditions: not only has it dominated English-language translation at least since the seventeenth century, but, in implying that language use can give unmediated access to truth or reality, it is also closely linked to the empiricist epistemologies that have long distinguished British and American philosophies (Venuti 2008; Easthope 1999a). The transparency of Weaver's translation invites a British or American reader to identify with a particular discourse of nation, a British or American national culture, defined as empirical, commonsensical, and pragmatic insofar as the translator's work was governed by an Anglocentric norm of acceptability. The fact that Weaver's version of *Cosmicomics* might effectively form a national identity was confirmed in 1969, a year after publication, when it won the National Book Award for translation, a prize given by a consortium of American publishers who judged it, not according to standards of accuracy or adequacy to the Italian text, but according to literary standards that they also applied to contemporary American writing.

Nonetheless, the translator remained entirely unaware of the potential cultural and political effects of his translation. In a 1980 interview, Weaver's response to the question "Should translations sound foreign?" contradicted the Anglocentric strategy he employed with Calvino's *Cosmicomics*:

> Yes, I think sometimes they should. I don't think they should sound American. I don't think Italian characters should say "gee whiz" to each other or "gosh" or whatever, and I don't think if they're eating pizza you should translate it into peanut butter sandwiches or anything like that. And I think occasionally you can leave a word in Italian [...] because it can't otherwise be translated. Or sometimes I leave it in Italian and add a very tiny apposition, explaining what it is.
>
> *(Venuti 1982: 19)*

Calvino's text is fantasy, of course, and the characters are not presented as specifically Italian, but rather as personifications of scientific concepts and phenomena. Still, Calvino was undoubtedly writing in Italian for an Italian audience, and the retention of such words as "ricotta" and "tagliatelle" would help to signal the Italian origin of the text to English-language readers. Yet they are replaced by words such as "cream cheese" and "noodles" which do indeed "sound American." In a later interview, when asked why he avoided the word "ricotta," Weaver explained that it fit the context of a cheese-coated moon: "I used 'cheese' because we used to say, 'the moon is made of green cheese.' But also thirty years ago nobody in the US knew what ricotta was" (phone conversation: 10 November 2001). This comment reveals the translator's Anglocentric strategy, his effort to bring English-language cultural traditions to bear on his translating (the comparison between the moon and green cheese actually dates back to the sixteenth century) and to avoid communicating any sense of Italianness to the English-language reader by, for instance, retaining the Italian word and adding an explanatory phrase in apposition. In fact, when asked why he rendered "tagliatelle" as "noodles," Weaver responded, "Well, they *are* noodles," demonstrating that his investment in transparent translating continued to be so deep as to suppress the linguistic and cultural differences of the source text. A translator too can identify unconsciously with a national cultural discourse, here with the empiricist privileging of transparency that has long prevailed in British and American thinking about language.

A translation intended to serve a nationalist agenda might similarly have unanticipated effects that conflict with the translator's intention, whether in serving the
interests of one social group instead of a national collective or even in undermining
those group interests. Consider Sir Thomas Hoby's 1561 translation of Baldassare
Castiglione's courtesy book *The Courtyer*. Hoby, like other Elizabethan translators,
presents his work as a contribution to an English national culture (see Ebel 1969).
"Englishemen," he argues in his dedicatory preface, "are muche inferiour to well
most all other Nations" in their unwillingness to translate foreign literary, philosophical
and scientific texts, and so they fail to render "a commune benefite to profite others
as well as themselves" (Hoby 1900: 8). Hoby wishes to reverse this tendency, not
only because Castiglione's work possesses such moral value that it ought "to be in
estimation with all degrees of men" in England, but also because the practice of
translation can develop the English language:

> As I therefore have to my smal skil bestowed some labour about this piece of
> woorke, even so coulde I wishe with al my hart, profounde learned men in
> the Greeke and Latin shoulde make the lyke proofe, and everye manne store
> the tunge according to hys knowledge and delite above other men, in some
> piece of learnynge, that we alone of the worlde maye not bee styll counted
> barbarous in oure tunge, as in time out of minde we have bene in our manners.
>
> *(Ibid.: 9)*

Yet, despite Hoby's repeated insistence that his work aims to benefit the nation, his
very decision to translate a courtly text makes clear that his primary concern is the
aristocracy. Thus in dedicating the translation to Lord Henry Hastings Hoby asserts
that "none, but a noble yonge Gentleman, and trayned up all his life time in Court, and
of worthie qualities, is meete to receive and enterteine so worthy a Courtier" as
Castiglione describes in his book; and when Hoby turns to list the "degrees" or social
classes that he imagines as his readership, he includes only "Princes and Greate men,"
"yonge Gentlemen," and "Ladyes and Gentlewomen" (ibid.: 6–7). Such remarks
assume an ideological representation of absolute monarchy wherein the royal court
governs the nation, not merely through its political authority, but also through
its exemplary morality. Within absolutist ideology, Hoby's address to the aristocracy is
consistent with his nationalist agenda, so that his nationalism takes the form of class
dominance. The wide circulation of his translation suggests that it was instrumental in
forming courtly identities, regardless of the social position occupied by his readers. During
the Elizabethan period alone, it was reprinted three times, in 1577, 1588, and 1603.

Hoby's discursive strategy, even though it can be considered Anglocentric in sixteenth-
century terms, further complicates his nationalist agenda. He follows the example set
by the humanist Sir John Cheke who in a prefatory letter to the translation urges
English writers to avoid foreign borrowings and use primarily Anglo-Saxon words:

> our own tung shold be written cleane and pure, unmixt and unmangeled with
> borowing of other tunges, wherin if we take not heed by tijm, ever borowing

and never payeng, she shall be fain to keep her house as bankrupt. For then
doth our tung naturallie and praisablie utter her meaning, when she bouroweth
no counterfeitness of other tunges to attire her self withall, but useth plainlie
her own, with such shift, as nature, craft, experiens and folowing of other
excellent doth lead her unto […]

(Hoby 1900: 12)

Cheke's purist recommendation constitutes a vernacular nationalism in which words
derived from Anglo-Saxon are assumed to express an essential Englishness, the truth
of an English "self" that would be obscured by the "counterfeitness" of foreign
borrowings. In Hoby's translation, this Anglo-Saxonism leads to a remarkable rendering of the key Italian term "sprezzatura":

vendo io già più volte pensato meco onde nasca questa grazia, lasciando quelli
che dalle stelle l'hanno, trovo una regula universalissima, la qual mi par valer
circa questo in tutte le cose umane che si facciano o dicano più che alcuna
altra, e ciò è fuggir quanto più si po, e come un asperissimo e pericoloso sco-
glio, la affettazione; e, per dir forse una nova parola, usar in ogni cosa una certa
sprezzatura, che nasconda l'arte e dimostri ciò che si fa e dice venir fatto senza
fatica e quasi senza pensarvi.

(Castiglione 1972: 61–62)

I, imagynyng with my self oftentymes how this grace commeth, leaving a part
such as have it from above, fynd one rule that is most general whych in thys
part (me thynk) taketh place in al thynges belongyng to man in worde and
deede above all other. And that is to eschew as much as a man may, and as a sharp
and daungerous rock, Affectation or curiosity and (to speak a new word) to use
in every thyng a certain Recklesnes, to cover art withall, and seeme whatsoever
he doth and sayeth to do it wythout pain, and (as it were) not myndyng it.

(Hoby 1900: 59)

The Italian "sprezzatura" is a neologism which Castiglione devises to signify the
effortless grace that distinguishes the ideal courtier's actions. Hoby, who knew
French, might have used a French loan word, namely "nonchalance," but in his adherence
to Cheke's vernacular nationalism he instead chose "Recklesness," a word derived
from the Anglo-Saxon *recceléas*. Hoby clearly intended the word to communicate a
sense of natural, spontaneous action, seemingly without thought or deliberation,
without "reck" or care. Yet in the sixteenth century, as today, "Recklesness" denoted
neglect, carelessness, irresponsibility, meanings that worry Hoby's etymological rendering and transform it into a moral criticism of courtly behavior which subverts the
nationalist agenda he imagined for his translation. A similar effect occurs in his rendering of Castiglione's assertion that the courtier can acquire his skills from "ottimi
maestri" or "bon maestri" ("excellent teachers," "good teachers"): in both instances,
Hoby uses "cunning men," another Anglo-Saxonism that carries negative

connotations in Elizabethan English, since "cunning" might signify not only skillful, expert, learned, but also crafty, guileful, sly (Castiglione 1972: 60–61; Hoby 1900: 57–58). At such points, the different national discourses that inform Hoby's translation, absolutist as well as humanist, issue into contradictions of which he was obviously unaware.

Although ethnocentric discursive strategies may endow a translation with a nationalistic effect, they can never entirely remove the foreignness of a source text. Cultural differences will still be communicated on other textual levels, both formal and thematic, insofar as they deviate noticeably from texts and traditions in the translating language. Any such differences, in conjunction with the translator's strongly assimilative work on the language of the source text, can acquire a nationalistic value in reception. More precisely, they can intensify a reader's sense of belonging to a national collective and may even elicit an unconscious desire for a unified nation distinct from the source culture which the text is taken to represent, usually a foreign nation. These possibilities are suggested by D. J. Enright's admiring response to Weaver's version of Calvino's *Cosmicomics* in the *New York Review of Books*:

> The opening story, which makes the film *2001* look about as imaginative as a spilled bucket of distemper, tells of the time when the moon was so close to the earth that Qfwfq and his companions could row out in a boat and scramble up on it to collect Moon-milk, which was "very thick, like a kind of cream cheese."
>
> *(Enright 1968: 23)*

Here not only is Calvino's story treated as uniquely "imaginative," but it also serves to remind this British reviewer of an Anglo-American work that he had found disappointing, Stanley Kubrick's recently released film *2001: A Space Odyssey*. The contrast in aesthetic value tacitly rests on a national distinction that involves Enright's own culture, the Italian writer vs. the American director resident in England. And Calvino's narrative premise of a moon coated with "cream cheese" is cited to illustrate the imagination that determines the cultural difference of his story. Nonetheless, Weaver's Anglocentric rendering, "cream cheese," is evidently as transparent to Enright as the Britishism "distemper" (where an American writer might use "whitewash"), demonstrating that his own identity as a reader is inextricably bound to a national language, the British dialect of English – which he assumes will be immediately intelligible to the predominantly American audience of a New York-based periodical. When confronted with an Italian work of fiction, Enright seems to feel all the more strongly his investment in English linguistic and cultural forms, notwithstanding – or because of – the hybridity of the language and the imaginative weakness he perceives in the film.

Translation and nationalist cultural politics

Nationalist translation agendas have been devised to intervene into specific social situations, but they do possess a number of common features. While taking into account significant historical differences, I want now to present a critical taxonomy of these features, considering how translation theories and practices have been used to shape a concept of nation and what cultural and social effects have resulted from this use. I will focus on two especially revealing cases: Prussia during the Napoleonic Wars and China under the late Qing dynasty.

In both of these cases, translation was enlisted in a defensive nationalist movement which was designed to build a national culture so as to counter foreign aggression. During the eighteenth century, the Prussian aristocracy had fallen under French cultural domination so that, as Friedrich Schleiermacher complained, even King Frederick II "could not possibly have written in German the philosophy and poetry he set down in French" (Schleiermacher 1813: 57). After 1806, when Napoleon defeated Prussia, Schleiermacher's sermons not only called on congregations to resist the French occupation, but also articulated a concept of the German nation. With a victory, he told them, "we shall be able to preserve for ourselves our own distinctive character, our laws, our constitution and our culture" (Schleiermacher 1890: 73). A key factor in this nationalist agenda was the German language, which Schleiermacher felt might be best improved through translation: "our language," he argued in a lecture delivered in 1813, "can most vigorously flourish and develop its own strength only through extensive contacts with the foreign" (Schleiermacher 1813: 62).

Later in the nineteenth century, China faced a somewhat different adversarial situation, characterized by foreign commercial and military invasion. Defeated in the war against Britain over the opium trade (1839–42), China was forced to grant economic and political concessions to several Western nations who established colonies in various ports and, after the Chinese lost the first Sino-Japanese War (1894–95), divided the country into spheres of interest. Just as the Boxer Uprising against the foreign presence was repressed by an international force (1898–1900), translators such as Lin Shu and Yan Fu began introducing Western ideas to reform the Chinese nation and enable it to struggle against the invaders. Lin Shu's preface to his version of Rider Haggard's novel *The Spirit of Bambatse* suggested that such Western literary texts were valuable because "they encourage the white man's spirit of exploration" and can instill a similar "spirit" in his Chinese readers:

> The blueprint has already been drawn by Columbus and Robinson Crusoe. In order to seek almost unobtainable material interests in the barbarian regions, white men are willing to brave a hundred deaths. But our nation, on the contrary, disregards its own interests and yields them to foreigners.
>
> *(Lee 1973: 54)*

Similarly Yan Fu, who had studied in England during the 1870s, rendered works on evolutionary theory by T. H. Huxley and Herbert Spencer precisely because he believed them to be useful to the "self-strengthening and the preservation of the race" (Schwartz 1964: 100).

As the translators' comments indicate, they intended their translations to form national identities by soliciting their readers' identification with a particular national discourse that was articulated in relation to the hegemonic foreign nations. This relational identity, always fundamentally differential, shaped through a distinction from the other on which the identity is nonetheless based, might be either exclusionary or receptive. German translators defined the German nation as incorporating a respect for the foreign which led them to reject French cultural practices that did not show this respect. They valued a foreignizing method of translation, described by Schleiermacher as one in which "the translator leaves the writer in peace as much as possible and moves the reader toward him," a literalism imprinted with the foreignness of the source text, whereas the French were seen as advocating a domesticating method, in which the translator "leaves the reader in peace as much as possible and moves the writer toward him," a much freer rewriting of the source text according to the intelligibilities and interests of the receiving culture (Schleiermacher 1813: 49). French translation, from the German point of view, even went to the extremes of paraphrase and adaptation, both of which were to be lamented. In a satiric dialogue from 1798, August Wilhelm Schlegel, whose own versions of Shakespeare's plays exemplified the foreignizing method, demonstrated how different translation practices might be taken as representative of opposed national identities:

> Frenchman: The Germans translate every literary Tom, Dick, and Harry. We either do not translate at all, or else we translate according to our own taste.
> German: Which is to say, you paraphrase and you disguise.
> Frenchman: We look on a foreign author as a stranger in our company, who has to dress and behave according to our customs, if he desires to please.
> German: How narrow-minded of you to be pleased only by what is native.
> Frenchman: Such is our nature and our education. Did the Greeks not hellenize everything?
> German: In your case it goes back to a narrow-minded nature and a conventional education. In ours education is our nature.
>
> *(Lefevere 1977: 50)*

Chinese translators, in contrast, sought to form a national identity by accepting Western values. They particularly prized the individualism and aggressiveness that seemed to them so important in motivating Western imperialism in China. For Lin Shu, the emulation of these values required that they be assimilated to Chinese cultural traditions which were consequently revised or in certain instances abandoned. Hence his criticism of the Confucian virtue of "yielding" or deference:

> The Westerners' consciousness of shame and advocacy of force do not stem entirely from their own nature but are also an accumulated custom. [...] In China, this is not so. Suffering humiliation is regarded as yielding; saving one's own life is called wisdom. Thus after thousands of years of encroachments by foreign races, we still do not feel ashamed. Could it also be called our national character?
>
> *(Lee 1973: 54)*

Chinese notions of deference and self-preservation ran counter to the collective "consciousness of shame" that might accompany the recognition of one's self as belonging to a nation under siege. Lin Shu's reference to a Chinese "national character" was itself a cultural import from the West.

In using translation to form national identities, the translators expose the contradictory conditions of their nationalist agendas. Terms such as "nature" and "race" point to a concept of nation as an unchanging biological essence which pre-exists the translation process and so reveals the circular logic of nationalism: the translating can only return to the identity that it is said to create. Yet terms such as "education" and "custom," along with the very use of a cultural practice like translation, imply that identity is constructed in a discursive formation and therefore can be changed and developed, precisely to intervene against the embattled social situations where the German and Chinese translators were working. The essentialistic strain in their thinking, furthermore, coincides with a universalism. The national identity that translation is summoned to form in each case embodies universalistic traits. For Schleiermacher, what distinguishes the German nation is its capacity to mediate all other national cultures, making it the historical culmination of "translation as a whole":

> our people, because of its esteem for the foreign and its own mediating nature, may be destined to unite all the jewels of foreign science and art together with our own in our own tongue, forming, as it were, a great historical whole that will be preserved at the center and heart of Europe, so that now, with the help of our language, everyone will be able to enjoy all the beautiful things that the most different ages have given us as purely and perfectly as possible for one who is foreign to them. Indeed, this seems to be the true historical goal of translation as a whole, as it is now native to us.
>
> *(Schleiermacher 1813: 62)*

Here German culture, created through translation, achieves global domination, and the "esteem for the foreign" that is characteristic of the German "nature" ultimately suppresses the cultural differences of other nations by forcing them to appreciate the canon of world literature in German. A. W. Schlegel similarly argued that the practice of translation is synonymous with German culture: because "poetic translation is a difficult art," he asserted, "its invention was reserved for German fidelity and perseverance" (Lefevere 1992: 78–79). In Lin Shu's thinking, the universalism took the form of assuming the global validity of Chinese cultural traditions, notably Confucianism. Thus he read the most diverse British novels as exempla of the Confucian reverence for filial piety, an interpretation that he made explicit in his habit of retitling the English texts. His version of Dickens's *The Old Curiosity Shop* became *The Story of the Filial Daughter Nell* (Lee 1973: 47).

Nationalist agendas in translation involve the conceptual violence that occurs whenever the unity of a nation is proclaimed, whether at its founding moment or subsequently in its cultural and political institutions. An assertion of national unity fictively creates that unity in the very process of asserting it by repressing the differences among the heterogeneous groupings and interests that comprise any social collective. As Derrida remarks, "the properly *performative* act must produce (proclaim) what in the form of a *constative* act it merely claims, declares, assures it is describing" (Derrida 1987: 18). Translation nationalisms are based on performative acts of this sort because they assert a homogeneous language, culture, or identity where none is shared by the diverse population that constitutes the nation. Such agendas in translation necessarily entail various exclusions, not only in drawing distinctions between the nation and its foreign others, but also in privileging certain cultural forms, practices, and constituencies within the supposedly unified nation. Source texts are chosen because they fall into particular genres and address particular themes while excluding other genres and themes that are seen as unimportant for the formation of a national identity; translation strategies draw on particular dialects, registers, and styles while excluding others that are also in use; and translators target particular audiences with their work, excluding other constituencies.

Thus the German translators at the turn of the nineteenth century aimed to build a national language and culture, but they actually belonged to an elite bourgeois minority whose taste dictated both the selection of source texts and the development of discursive strategies. The translators focused on canonical works of European literature and philosophy. Johann Heinrich Voss rendered Homer, Schleiermacher Plato, and A. W. Schlegel Shakespeare, to cite a few representative examples, whereas the great majority of German-language readers preferred translations of French and English novels by such authors as Choderlos de Laclos and Samuel Richardson (see Ward 1974). The foreignizing method of translation, although relying on the standard dialect (High German), avoided familiar, conversational forms: "an indispensable requirement for this method," in Schleiermacher's words, "is a disposition of the language that not only departs from the quotidian but also lets one perceive that it was not left to develop freely but rather was bent to a foreign likeness" (Schleiermacher 1813: 53). And although the German translators wished their translations to be read by every member of the German nation, the foreignizing method was guided by an appeal to an elite segment of the national audience, "the well educated man," states Schleiermacher, "whom we are in the habit of calling, in the best sense of the word, an amateur and connoisseur" (ibid.: 51). The identity formed by the resulting translations was less national than learned and bourgeois.

The Chinese translators, in rendering Western literary, philosophical, and scientific texts, unavoidably displaced native cultural traditions, but they also tended to neglect foreign texts that in their view were not conducive to the creation of a resistant national identity. Because their political goal was reformist, intended to strengthen an imperial culture that had lost authority amid foreign invasion, they adopted a domesticating method of translation that resulted in diverse forms of cultural and social exclusion. Thus Lin Shu and Yan Fu not only translated into the classical literary language (*wenyan*) to appeal to an academic and official elite, but in some cases they also revised Western texts so as to assimilate them to Chinese values and make their nationalist agenda more acceptable to their readers. Lin Shu's 1899 version of Alexandre Dumas fils's *La Dame aux camélias* renders the French "ange" ("angel") with the Chinese "xian" ("fairy maiden") which evokes ancient Chinese mythology in place of the Judeo-Christian tradition (Wong 1998: 213). Similarly, when in the novel a man greets a woman by kissing her hand, Lin Shu inserted an explanatory note to anticipate the Chinese reader's surprise at this Western practice. The identity formed by such translations could only be hybrid, not simply national, but imperial, not simply classical Chinese, but also modern and Western to some extent.

To produce significant cultural and political effects, however, nationalist movements must win the spontaneous support of a broad cross-section of the population, even if this very breadth simultaneously puts into question the notion of a unified nation. Translation nationalisms likewise cannot be restricted to the cultural elite who is most likely to devise and execute them; the translations that are designed to form a national identity must circulate widely among the diverse constituencies that comprise the nation so as to produce a nationalistic effect that might result in social change. From this point of view, the German translators' impact was inevitably limited. Although they initiated a translation tradition that stretched into the twentieth century, inspiring such theorists as Nietzsche and Walter Benjamin, in their own historical moment their foreignizing translations of canonical texts were most powerful in forming a national identity among readers who, like them, were not just scholarly in their interests, but also acquainted with previous German translations as well as German literary developments. Thus in 1814 Goethe argued for the usefulness of a prose translation of Homer "in the first stages of education," observing that "If you want to influence the masses a simple translation is always best. Critical translations vying with the original really are of use only for conversations the learned conduct among themselves" (Lefevere 1992: 75).

Wilhelm von Humboldt's preface to his 1816 version of Aeschylus' *Agamemnon* took an opposing view, although the nationalistic tenor of his remarks shows that he was engaging in precisely the sort of learned conversation that Goethe had in mind:

> What strides has the German language not made, to give but one example, since it began to imitate the meters of Greek, and what developments have not taken place in the nation, not just among the learned, but also among the masses, even down to women and children since the Greeks really did become the nation's reading matter in their true and unadulterated shape? Words fail to express how much the German nation owes to Klopstock with his first successful treatment of antique meters, and how much more it owes to Voss, who may be said to have introduced classical antiquity into the German language. A more powerful and beneficial influence on a national culture can hardly be imagined in an already highly sophisticated time, and that influence is his alone.
>
> *(Ibid.: 137)*

Given the fact that in successive editions Voss brought the German of his Homeric translations closer to the Greek and so increased the difficulty of reading them, one must doubt Humboldt's enthusiastic assessment of their mass readership. Schleiermacher, in fact, seems to have felt that Voss's foreignizing version was too extreme to be pleasurably readable (see Bernofsky 1997). In Humboldt's case, the linguistic differences of the Greek poems intensified his own national identity even as they deepened his appreciation for Voss's translation, as well as the dramatist Friedrich Klopstock's imitation of classical prosody.

The social impact of the Chinese translators' work was much more consequential because it was extremely popular, extending beyond the academic and official elite that was their immediate audience to encompass independent intellectuals and both secondary-school and university students. Among this wide readership, to be sure, Lin Shu's version of Dumas fils's sentimental novel did not consistently elicit the same patriotic response that he voiced in drawing an analogy between the courtesan Marguerite and two Chinese ministers renowned for their devotion to the emperor. Here the cultural differences of *La Dame aux camélias* strengthened his nationalistic identification with imperial culture:

> Strong are the women of this world, more so than our scholar-officials, among whom only the extremely loyal ones such as Long Jiang and Bi Gan could compare with Marguerite, those who would die a hundred deaths rather than deviate from their devotion. Because the way Marguerite served Armant is the same way Long and Bi served their emperors Jie and Zhou.
>
> *(Hu Ying 2000: 83)*

Nonetheless, the nationalist agenda of the late Qing translators established a model for a later, more radical generation. Lu Xun, the modernist innovator in Chinese fiction, read their versions of Haggard and Huxley and decided to translate science fiction because he believed that Western popularizations of science might "move the Chinese masses forward" (Semanov 1967: 14). By 1909, however, he had rejected the strongly Sinicizing approach of his predecessors while retaining their project of building a national identity so as to alter China's subordinate position in geopolitical relations. He wrote foreignizing translations of fiction from Russia and Eastern European countries that occupied a similar position, but whose literatures subsequently gained international recognition (for a detailed account, see Venuti 1998: 183–86). Yan Fu's translations, especially his version of Huxley's *Evolution and Ethics*, had a much more direct influence on Chinese identity. A contemporary observer noted that "after China's frequent military reversals, particularly after the humiliation of the Boxer years, the slogan 'Survival of the Fittest' (lit., 'superior victorious, inferior defeated, the fit survive') became a kind of clarion call" (Schwartz 1964: 259, n.14).

Translation nationalisms in time: Catalonia

Although translation nationalisms turn to essentialistic concepts to articulate a discourse of nation, such agendas are fundamentally determined by the local contingencies into which they intervene. The communicative effectiveness of any translation in fact depends on its capacity to engage with the intelligibilities and interests that define the social situation where the translator is working. Nationalist agendas that seek, not just to communicate the meanings of source texts, but to use those texts in constructing national identities must tactically take into account the linguistic forms, cultural values, and social groups that are arrayed, always hierarchically, in their historical moment. And this accounting inevitably shapes the translating as well as the kind of national identity which the translator aims to establish, challenging any essentialism. I want to develop these points further by considering translation nationalisms within the same culture at two different moments. My site is Catalonia during the twentieth century; my cases are two influential Catalan translators, Josep Carner (1884–1970) and Joan Sales (1912–83).

Catalan nationalism emerged during the nineteenth century with the recovery of Catalan as a literary language in opposition to Castilian, the language of the hegemonic Spanish state. By the turn of the century, the formation of a language-based Catalan identity stimulated the pursuit of political autonomy from Madrid, resulting in the establishment of a regional commonwealth or Mancommunitat in 1914 (Balcells 1996: 25–27, 67–72). Enric Prat de la Riba, the elected president, had previously addressed the issue of Catalan "nationality" in a work that relied heavily on Johann Gottfried Herder's notion of *Volksgeist* or the spirit of a people, revealing the contradictions typical of nationalist thinking:

> La societat que dóna als homes tots aquests elements de cultura, que els lliga, i forma de tots una unitat superior, un ésser col·lectiu informat per un mateix esperit, aquesta societat natural és la *nacionalitat*. Resultat de tot això és que la nacionalitat és una unitat de cultura o de civilització; tots els elements d'aquesta mena, l'art, la ciència, els costums, el Dret ... tenen llurs arrels en la nacionalitat.

> *(Prat de la Riba 1906: 66)*

> (The society that gives to men all these elements of culture, that binds them together, and forms from them all a higher unity, a collective being informed by a selfsame spirit, this natural society is *nationality*. The result of all this is that nationality is a unity of culture or of civilization; all the elements of this kind, art, science, customs, Law ... have their roots in nationality.)

On the one hand, nationality is a socially determined form of "collective being" that is manifested in diverse cultural practices; on the other hand, it is the "natural" form of a homogeneous "spirit" that transcends social determinations (cf. Llobera 1983: 345–46). The passage shifts seamlessly between these contradictory concepts, the first materialist, the second idealist, finally treating national identity as a biological essence indistinguishable from the soil in which the national culture is said to take root.

The questionable logic of Prat de la Riba's thinking did not discredit it as an intellectual force in the defensive nationalism that drove the Catalan bid for self-government. On the contrary, the very contradictions were more likely to have stimulated the desire for a unified nation by putting into question its possibility. And in fact his work was extremely effective in rationalizing the cultural and social projects that were initiated during the Mancommunitat, including the standardization of the Catalan language. "La llengua," he wrote,

> és la manifestació més perfecta de l'esperit nacional i l'instrument més poderós de la nacionalitizació i, per tant, de la conservació i la vida de la nactionalitat.
>
> *(Ibid.: 84)*

(Language is the most perfect manifestation of the national spirit and the most powerful instrument of nationalization and therefore of the preservation and life of nationality.)

Although in 1923 the Spanish state intervened to impose an anti-Catalan dictatorship on Catalonia, the elections of 1931 resulted in the establishment of a Catalan republic or Generalitat that broadened the range of cultural and social initiatives. Under the Generalitat, Catalan joined Castilian in becoming an official language in political institutions, the educational system was reorganized to prepare for the introduction of Catalan, and both the Catalan periodical press and book industry underwent a significant expansion (Balcells 1996: 96–100).

These historical developments motivated Josep Carner's work as a translator even as he contributed to them. A prolific prose writer as well as a poet, he belonged to the modernist literary movement known as Noucentisme, which collaborated closely with the Manicommunitat in promoting a standardized language. In his 1913 article "La dignitat literària," he echoed Prat de la Riba in asserting that "la paraula és la pàtria. La seva dignitat és una dignitat nacional" (the word is the fatherland. Its dignity is a national dignity; Carner 1986: 132). Carner, like other Noucentist writers, considered the translation of canonical literary works as a means of developing the Catalan language and literature so as to construct a national identity. In 1907, at the start of his career as a translator, he sketched this project in an article that celebrates the translation of Shakespeare's plays into Catalan:

> Perquè el català esdevingui abundós, complexe, elàstic, elegant, és necessari que els mestres de totes les èpoques i tots els països siguin honorats amb versions a la nostra llengua i, agraïts, la dotin de totes les qualitats d'expressió i diferenciació que li calen. Perqué la literatura catalana es faci completa, essencial, illustre, cal que el nostre esperit s'enriqueixi amb totes les creacions fonamentals. Com podria ésser sumptuós un palau, sense els hostes!
>
> *(Carner 1986: 56)*

(In order for Catalan to become abundant, complex, flexible, elegant, it is necessary that the masters of every period and every country be honored with versions in our language and, in gratitude, endow it with every quality of expression and differentiation that it needs. In order to make Catalan literature

complete, essential, illustrious, our spirit must be enriched with every
fundamental creation. How could a palace be sumptuous without guests
[hostes]!)

Here too Carner adopted Prat de la Riba's essentialistic lexicon in referring to the
Catalan "spirit." Yet, unlike the Catalanist ideologue, Carner took a more materialist
approach. Neither the language nor its literature is adequate or self-sufficient in its
expressive power, and neither can be developed solely on the basis of the
Catalan "spirit," which itself "must be enriched" through literary translation. For
Prat de la Riba, Catalan identity, the "Iberian ethnos," transcends its linguistic and
cultural conditions, predating and persisting through the Roman conquest of the
peninsula:

> Aqueix fet, aqueixa transformació de la civilització llatina en civilització cata-
> lana, és un fet que per ell sol, sense necessitat de cap altre, demostra l'existència
> de l'esperit nacional català. Encara que després d'engendrar la llengua catalana
> no hagués produït res més, l'ànima del nostre poble ens hauria ja revelat les
> ratlles fonamentals de la seva fesomia, estampades en la fesomia de la seva
> llengua.
>
> *(Prat de la Riba 1906: 89)*

> (This fact, this transformation of Latin civilization into Catalan civilization, is a
> fact that by itself, without any need for others, demonstrates the existence of
> the Catalan national spirit. Even if after the Catalan language was begotten it
> had not produced anything more, the soul of our people would have already
> revealed to us the basic lines of its physiognomy, engraved in the physiognomy
> of its language.)

Whereas in Prat de la Riba's thinking Catalan identity pre-exists the language that
constitutes its transparent expression, in Carner's this identity is largely a linguistic
construction that requires translation to be viable, the importation of foreign cultural
materials that complicate any such notion of transparency. Indeed, because the
Catalan word "hostes" is ambiguous, capable of signifying both "guests" and "hosts,"
Carner's metaphor of the palace suggests that Catalan literature lacks not only the
productive influence of foreign writing, but also more sophisticated Catalan writers.
The palace of Catalan literature can be sumptuous only if it is inhabited by hosts who
are imaginatively enriched by translation.

Carner's cultural politics was not simply nationalist, but also implicitly critical of
Catalan traditions and practices that did not seem consistent with his agenda. Hence
his nationalism involved a utopian projection grounded on an estimation of Catalan
deficiencies. In his 1908 article "De l'acció dels poetes a Catalunya," where the word
"acció" signifies not so much action as military or political engagement, he again
resorted to a telling architectural metaphor to describe the work that Catalan poets
must perform on their language and literature:

Nosaltres els poetes som els constructors dels pobles, i avui que tenim encara tanta feina a fer en el casal projectat de la civilització catalana, no sentim, en amidar tot ço que encara ens manca, en veure aqueixos forats per on entra el sol, una impressió de descoratjament i de pessimisme, sinó una ànsia de creació que és benaventurada perquè ha de ser fecunda.

(Carner 1986: 95)

(We poets are constructors of peoples, and now that we still have so much work to do in the house planned for Catalan civilization, we do not feel, in surveying all that we still lack, in seeing those holes through which the sunlight enters, any sense of discouragement and pessimism, but a yearning for creation that is fortunate because it must be fertile.)

Carner seems to have been aware that the "yearning" or desire for a national literature was based on a lack which, however, could never be eradicated because it was supplied through the translation of foreign literatures, through the introduction of linguistic and cultural differences that sustained creativity.

His translating aimed to form a national identity that was based on two exclusions: hegemonic Spanish culture, or in his words "el monopoli castellà dels destins d'Espanya" (the Castilian monopoly on the destinies of Spain; Carner 1986: 77), and limited Catalan literary traditions. This relational identity is evident, first, in his selection of foreign texts for translation. Although, as was typical of twentieth-century Catalan writers, he possessed a native proficiency in both Spanish and Catalan, he avoided Spanish literature and placed the greatest emphasis on French and English traditions. Moreover, he chose to translate texts that were distinguished by fantasy and ironic humor and therefore ran counter to the realism that dominated nineteenth-century Catalan fiction, what Marcel Ortín has described as "the naturalists' limitation to the documentable real" (Ortín 1996: 112). Between 1908 and 1934, Carner published 33 translations, including one or more texts by such writers as Shakespeare and Molière, La Fontaine and Hans Christian Andersen, Dickens and Lewis Carroll, Twain and Robert Louis Stevenson, Erckmann-Chatrian and Villiers de l'Isle-Adam (ibid.: 105–7). Carner was particularly interested in the identity-forming power of children's literature because, as he prefaced his 1918 version of Andersen's tales, "el gradual reviscolament de la imaginació catalana és el primer fonament per a fer pròsperes i invencibles les empreses de l'art i la política, de la cultura i el diner" (the gradual revival of the Catalan imagination is the first foundation for insuring that the enterprises of art and politics, culture and money prosper and become invincible; quoted in ibid.: 43).

To advance his nationalist agenda, Carner wrote translations that were enjoyably readable, but that contained noticeable departures from current usage. Although at the beginning of his translating career the process of linguistic standardization had not yet begun and Catalan usage displayed variations at every level, it is still possible to see that he devised innovative strategies which resulted in a richly heterogeneous Catalan. His lexicon deliberately mixed archaisms, learned diction, dialectalisms, and neologisms, at times deviating from the registers and styles of the source texts, at others resorting to literalisms or calques of foreign words and phrases (Busquets 1977; Sellent Arús 1998: 25; Pericay and Toutain 1996: 266–67; cf. Ortín 2001). Thus in his preface to his 1908 version of Shakespeare's *A Midsummer Night's Dream* he noted his decision to assign "neologismes i arcaismes a personatges qui són en l'espai i el temps tan allunyats de nosaltres" (neologisms and archaisms to characters who are so remote from us in time and space; Carner 1986: 102). Carner's agenda might also lead to more aggressive translation moves, such as the insertion of allusions to the Catalan cultural and political situation. In his version of *Alice in Wonderland*, published in 1927 during the Madrid-imposed dictatorship, the Cheshire cat became "el gat castellà" (the Castilian cat), and the King and Queen of Hearts became "el Rei i la Reina d'Espases" (the King and Queen of Swords), referring not just to the Spanish deck of playing cards, but also to the military repression enacted by the Spanish state, a monarchy (Carroll 1927: 93, 88).

The identity formed by such translations could only be hybrid, cast in the Catalan language yet an amalgam of linguistic and cultural differences that did not conform to the homogeneous essence imagined by Prat de la Riba. Nonetheless, Carner's translations undoubtedly enabled his readers to recognize themselves as Catalans. This becomes clear in a 1921 review in which the Barcelona-based poet and translator Carles Riba admired how Carner handled La Fontaine's fables in a very different cultural situation. The French writer's irony, Riba argued, combines

> una malícia xampanyesa i una restricció mundana, sovint amb llurs formularis mateixos. Les condicions socials de Catalunya, del català per tant, havien for-çosament d'afeblir la mundanitat i engruixudir la plasticitat camperola. Però la meravella de la traducció de Josep Carner consisteix a fondre l'una i l'altra en una bonhomia burgesa, tota barcelonina, amb la seva fraseologia feta i tot.
>
> *(Riba 1979: 170–71)*

> (a wickedness characteristic of Champagne and a worldly restraint, often taking the same form. The social conditions of Catalonia, and therefore of Catalan, inevitably had to weaken the worldliness and thicken the rural plasticity. Yet the wonder of Josep Carner's translation consists in joining both in a bourgeois bonhomie that is entirely Barcelonian, complete with its own phraseology.)

For Riba, Carner's translation communicates the distinctiveness of the French text in a compelling way that reinvents a familiar Catalan identity – although obviously that identity was strongly inflected by bourgeois values.

The Spanish Civil War abruptly suspended the nationalistic effects produced by the work of Noucentist translators like Carner. During the war, the authority of the Generalitat was increasingly weakened both by internal political divisions and by the beleaguered Spanish state, and after 1939 many Catalan politicians and intellectuals went into exile. Franco's regime enforced a harsh repression of Catalan identity which lasted for more than two decades (Balcells 1996: 127, 143–44). Public use of

the Catalan language was prohibited, as was publication of Catalan books and periodicals; teachers suspected of being Catalanist sympathizers were dismissed or transferred to other Spanish regions; and Catalan culture and history were excluded from
curricula. Near the end of the 1950s, however, the Francoist repression began to ease.
Catalan publishing, which had continued outside of Catalonia, witnessed an increase
despite the continuing threat of censorship, and the ban that had been specifically
placed on translations into Catalan was lifted (ibid.: 147–48). Whereas in 1960 Catalan publishers issued 193 books, 10 of which were translations, 1966 saw the publication of 655 books including 207 translations, figures that represent a return to
book-output levels during the 1920s and 1930s (Vallverdú 1968: 102–3).

Joan Sales's work as a publisher, novelist, and translator constituted an important
intervention into this cultural and political situation. During the 1940s, he joined a
group of Catalan writers in Mexico where he published the journal *Quaderns de
l'Exili* (Notebooks from Exile). Their nationalism was based on Prat de la Riba's
essentialist notion of an "Iberian ethnos," which they joined to Catholicism and to
the patriotic romanticism of the nineteenth-century Catalan movement known as the
Renaixença, producing an ensemble of ideological concepts that were militant in
opposing Franco's repressive dictatorship, populist in promoting the egalitarian view
that "La Nació és el Poble" (The Nation is the People), and anti-intellectual in
rejecting Noucentisme (Casacuberta 1989). The first issue in 1943 ran a policy
statement that made clear the editors' approach to culture:

> Defensem la cultura basada en els caràcters nacionals i posada al servei de
> l'home. Rebutgem l'intellectualisme, la deshumanitizació i la supèrbia de tota
> manifestació que s'anomeni cultural a si mateixa, però que pretengui sobre-
> passar o menystenir l'Home. Rebutgem una cultura sense contingut i que es
> nodria infinitament dels seu propis residus. Entenem que l'home val més que el
> seu rostre, el contingut més que la continent, el pensament més que la forma.
> Ambicionem un estil directe, senzill i digne, subordinat a l'obra.
>
> *(Quoted in ibid.: 99–100)*

> (We uphold culture grounded in national characters and put in the service of
> man. We reject intellectualism, dehumanization and the arrogance of every
> expression that calls itself cultural, but that seeks to go beyond or undervalue
> Man. We reject a culture without content which is infinitely nourished by its
> own residue. We take man to be worth more than his face, the content more
> than the container, the thought more than the form. We aspire to a style that is
> direct, natural and appropriate, subordinated to the work.)

In their frank humanism, in their idealist assumption that "Man" exists apart from and
is transparently expressed in language, these values are opposed to the materialist
position of a writer like Carner for whom stylistic innovation was necessary to construct human identity. It was in fact these values that informed Sales's editorial
activities upon his return to Catalonia in 1947: despite the prohibitions of Franco's

regime, Sales sought to popularize canonical works of Catalan literature in adaptations that were cast in current usage and designed especially for young readers (Bacardí 1998: 27–28).

Sales's most consequential work as a publisher and translator began after 1959, when he assumed the directorship of the Catalan press El Club dels Novel·listes. His editorial policy was decidedly nationalist, but also populist. He focused on one literary genre, the novel, as he later said, "perquè precisament els franquistes ho volien impedir i perquè era l'unica manera de fer una literatura contemporània nacional" (because precisely the Franquistas wished to stop it and because the novel was the only way to create a contemporary national literature; Ibarz 1984: 15). Since he aimed to expand the Catalan readership, he published only accessible realistic narratives, rejecting those that were difficult to read because they lacked a coherent plot or required a specialized knowledge of literature. Thus he published Catalan versions of such novels as Giuseppe Tomasi de Lampedusa's *The Leopard* (1962), Alan Paton's *Cry the Beloved Country* (1964) and J. D. Salinger's *The Catcher in the Rye* (1965). Sales himself translated three novels for the press, including Kazantzakis's *The Last Temptation of Christ* (1959) and Dostoevsky's *The Brothers Karamazov* (1961). To insure that the translations effectively produced the realist illusion, Sales insisted that the language closely follow current usage with an emphasis on oral forms, what he called the "llenguatge vivent" (living language) in the preface to his own novel, *Incerta glòria* (1956). This discursive strategy enhanced verisimilitude, but it also effaced the translated status of the texts. As Sales explained in introducing his version of Dostoevsky's novel,

> El Club dels Novel·listes cregué que el que importava per damunt de tot era que el traductor s'identifiqués amb l'esperit i l'estil de l'obra, que se la fes seva, que sabés posar en boca dels seus personatges un català tan viu com ho és el rus de l'original, fins al punt que el lector, llegint-la, arribés a oblidar que llegia una traducció.
>
> *(Sales 1961: 8–9)*

> (El Club dels Novel·listes believed that above all it was important that the translator identify with the spirit and style of the work, that he make it his, that he know how to put in his characters' mouths a Catalan as alive as the Russian of the original, to such an extent that the reader, while reading it, might come to forget that he is reading a translation.)

In the sheer invisibility of Sales's translating, Catalan readers might also overlook the deep contradictions in his nationalist agenda. He wished to create a national identity based on two exclusions: on the one hand, a resistance against the Franquista pressure that Catalans abandon their language and speak Castilian and, on the other, a refusal of the standardized Catalan supported by Noucentist intellectuals, the "exercicis de gramàtica" (grammatical exercise) which he saw opposed to the "living language" (Sales 1956: 10). Yet not only did he translate Flaubert's *Madame Bovary* and *Salammbô* into Castilian, but his reliance on current usage in his Catalan translations as well as his novel resulted in a style filled with Castilianisms (Bacardí 1998: 30–31; Vallverdú 1968: 142–46). Sales questioned the Noucentist emphasis on French literary texts and rather chose to work with foreign literatures that were associated with relatively minor cultures whose subordinate position resembled that of Catalonia: Lampedusa's Sicily, Paton's South Africa, or the Provence of Loís Delluc whose Provençal novel *El garrell* he translated into Catalan in 1963 (Bacardí 1998: 32–33, 36–37). Yet in advocating a discursive strategy that produced the illusion of transparency, Sales was soliciting his reader's identification with the religious values that he himself perceived in the source texts, even *The Brothers Karamazov*, which he described as "l'obra màxima de la novel·la cristiana universal" (the greatest work of the universal Christian novel; Sales 1961: 7–8). There is, finally, the question of the "spirit and style" with which he and his readers identified in his translations of the Kazantzakis and the Dostoevsky: since he knew no Greek or Russian, he queried specialists and based his Catalan text on several other versions of the novels, including Castilian and French (Sales 1961: 9). The linguistic and cultural differences that constituted Sales's translations might do no more than create a hybrid Catalan identity, stimulating the reader's desire for a unified nation which they simultaneously withheld.

Carner and Sales represent two nationalist agendas in translation driven by different theories and practices and reflecting different historical moments. In both cases, their defensive nationalisms sought to construct collective identities based on Catalan, and their translations can be seen as a linguistic ecology, a means of protecting and developing a language that was not simply marginal in relation to the dominant Spanish culture, but threatened with suppression. Yet important distinctions can be drawn between their work. Carner cultivated an experimentalism that took advantage of the variations in Catalan before standardization and challenged prevalent Catalan narrative forms. His translations registered the linguistic and cultural differences of the source texts even as they formed a recognizably Catalan identity. Thus they can be described as foreignizing, employing a strategy that, as Schleiermacher observed, "cannot flourish equally well in all tongues, but rather only in those that are not confined within the narrow bounds of a classical style beyond which all else is deemed reprehensible" (Schleiermacher 1813: 54). Sales's translating, in contrast, was much more conservative, at once consolidating current usage and validating its expressive possibilities during a period when the very viability of Catalan had been weakened by Franco's regime, when "diglossia had established a foothold even in the educated classes and the quality of the spoken language was steadily deteriorating" (Balcells 1996: 144). Sales's translations were thus domesticating, written in the most familiar forms of Catalan, imprinted with religious values that were dominant in Franco's Spain, creating an image in which the reader could experience self-recognition as a Catalan, however much hybridized by the diversity of the language and the source texts.

Carner and Sales also wrote translations that mystified – in their respective ways – the contradictions in their nationalist agendas. Both announced their intentions to translate for a national collective, but both belonged to elite literary groups who comprised their primary readerships. Carles Riba's review is a reminder that Carner's cosmopolitanism was closely linked to the taste of the Barcelona bourgeoisie. And, despite Sales's adherence to popular taste, his directorship of El Club dels Novel·listes made it truly a literary "club" or circle, as Montserrat Bacardí has indicated, by creating "an authentic forum that would permit Catalan writers to comment on and discuss their works, given the absence of communicative media that addressed Catalan literature" (Bacardí 1998: 31).

Perhaps the most instructive distinction between these two translators is the place of essentialism in their nationalistic thinking. Although both were influenced by Prat de la Riba's notion of a transcendental Catalan identity, Carner's openness to linguistic and cultural differences, partly because of his modernist inclination towards stylistic innovation and partly because of the variations in Catalan usage, led him to adopt a materialist approach to translation which assumed that human identity was constructed in discursive formations. The sheer repressiveness of Sales's later period, however, encouraged the adoption of various conceptual defenses, all essentialistic, whether the universalist humanism of *Quaderns de l'Exili* or the egalitarian populism of the "living language."

These cases show that it would be reductive to attempt any ethical or political evaluation of translation nationalisms without considering the historical moments in which they emerged. Translation can be motivated by an essentialism that conceals the constitutive differences of the cultural identity it is deployed to form. But such an essentialism may be strategic, as Gayatri Spivak has noted, used "in a scrupulously visible political interest" (Spivak 1985: 214), with the self-critical awareness that in different historical circumstances it might harden into a conceptual repression just as strong as the political force it is intended to combat. Neither Carner nor Sales could develop this awareness in their defensive cultural situations. But in studying their examples later Catalan translators might, admitting variations in current usage that deviate from standardized forms so as to signal the foreignness of the source texts – and make a productive difference in Catalan identities.

[2005]

8

TRANSLATION, SIMULACRA, RESISTANCE

My point of departure is the following question: To what extent can translation be seen as an intervention into the postmodern culture that has been fostered by the current geopolitical economy? It seems clear that this economy could not survive without translation in many forms, ranging from contracts and patents, instruction manuals and software packages, to advertisements and brand names, film and video soundtracks, bestsellers and children's literature. If translation contributes so materially to economic exchange, whether through business practices or through print and electronic media, if it plays such an important role in commodity production and consumption and therefore in social reproduction, it also raises the question of whether and how it might constitute a cultural means of resistance that challenges multinational capitalism and the political institutions to which the global economy is allied. To what extent, then, might translation transform this political economy through its impact on contemporary cultural forms and practices?

Postmodern culture and multinational capital

My questions assume a certain theoretical concept of postmodernity, and this concept is already a political critique. The global reach of capital, supported by the time-space compression that David Harvey (1989: esp. 293–96) has noted as a distinctive feature of the postmodern situation, has led to the development and exploitation of overseas workforces and markets, so that economic practices have been decentralized to a significant extent. Consider the shoe manufacturer Nike. Although a corporation based in the United States, Nike relies on factories in Latin America and Asia as well as sales outlets worldwide, whereby it profits from cheap foreign labor and the international strength of the dollar, however variable, and thus exemplifies the asymmetrical economic relations that have long existed between hegemonic countries like the United States and such developing countries as Mexico, Indonesia, and

China. In 1998, when United States labor groups determined that a subsistence wage for a Chinese assembly-line worker was $.87 per hour, Nike was paying $.16 to $.19 and forcing its employees to work twelve-hour shifts seven days a week without overtime pay (Klein 2000: 212, 474).

Along with the decentralization of production, communications networks assume greater importance as corporations work to extend the distribution and consumption of commodities into new areas. The global capitalist economy is maintained by what Jean Baudrillard has called the "precession of simulacra," an effect of mass print and electronic media which do not so much reflect as construct reality through encoded forms and images that are determined by various ideologies and elicit, in Baudrillard's words, "a fascination for the medium" over "the critical exigencies of the message" (Baudrillard 1983: 35; cf. Harvey 1989: 288–92). Here advertisements, in their direct support of commodity circulation, come readily to mind: they function as branding, establishing trademarks through images that are charged with a charismatic solicitation of the consumer.

Translation plays a crucial role in insuring that brand names travel into foreign markets. Shi Zhang, assistant professor of Marketing at UCLA (University of California at Los Angeles), and Bernd Schmitt, professor of Business and executive director of the Center on Global Brand Leadership at the Columbia University Business School, have recently formulated strategies for effective translations so that corporations can "safeguard themselves against failures in foreign markets" (Zhang and Schmitt 2001: 313). They offer a Chinese example: "Coca-Cola's Chinese name, 'Ke-kou-ke-le,'" they point out, "sounds like Coca-Cola and means 'tastes good and makes you happy'" (ibid.: 315). This rendering exemplifies their "phonosemantic" strategy, but clearly it signifies beyond a simple semantic correspondence. The exorbitant gain produced by every translation, the release of effects that work only in the translating language, insures that the Chinese translation enacts a branding process which would ordinarily require an elaborate and costly advertising campaign.

In the current stage of globalization, the asymmetry of economic relations is further underwritten by a branding of particular states and cultures. Manufactured images of states and cultures are mutually supportive, carrying economic implications that far exceed government efforts to bolster local tourist industries. "Most states," notes Peter van Ham, "see branding as a long-term cumulative effort that will influence foreign investment decisions and the state's market capitalization" (Van Ham 2001: 4). In Europe, such states are also likely to use branding as a means of strengthening their application for entry into NATO and the European Union. Ultimately, they are competing against the decades-long economic and political hegemony of the United States which coincides with the domination of United States cultural forms and themes on the international market.

Translation is instrumental in maintaining this domination. According to UNESCO statistics, films produced in Hollywood constitute 85 percent of the films shown worldwide, whether in dubbed or subtitled versions, so that in many countries Hollywood productions command a larger share of the box office than locally produced films. Novels written by United States authors and published by presses that belong to European-based conglomerates are also marketed worldwide, achieving commercial success in many languages and cultures. Some of Tom Clancy's political thrillers, for instance, are published by Berkley, a division of the Penguin Group owned by the United Kingdom-based media corporation Pearson, and they usually achieve bestseller status in translation, easily selling more copies than most works originally written in the translating languages. In the case of the United States, the connections between economic, political, and cultural practices remain so strong as to withstand negative commentary on United States foreign policy.

If "brands and states often merge in the minds of the global consumer," as van Ham observes, such that "Microsoft and McDonald's are among the most visible US diplomats" (Van Ham 2001: 2), then languages must also be figured into the branding process. The most powerful Western languages command not only curricula and publication, but also translation. English, not surprisingly, remains the most translated language worldwide. Between 1979 and 2011, according to UNESCO's *Index Translationum*, some 1,216,600 books were translated from English into other languages, an average of roughly 36,800 books per year. French ranked a distant second with some 214,500 books or about 6,500 per year. Five of the top-ten English authors in translation were United States authors, including bestsellers like Danielle Steel, Stephen King, and Nora Roberts, as well as classics like Mark Twain and Jack London, showing that the world canon of United States literature rests on quintessential myths and ideologies such as the frontier and individualism.

For many years, Walt Disney Productions occupied the first place in the list, and it continues to be named as author for an astronomical number of records in the UNESCO database (11,507) as compared to the record for the highest-ranking person named as an author, Agatha Christie (7,279). This fact bears witness to a form of corporate authorship, supported by the electronic media, which could only be possible in the postmodern culture of the simulacra, "a state of such near perfect replication," as Harvey has described it, "that the difference between original and copy becomes almost impossible to spot" (Harvey 1989: 289). In the case of Walt Disney Productions, the author is no longer the producer of an original form, but the licenser of copies that are virtually indistinguishable from the original form. Similarly, the simulacral quality of postmodern culture can be said to encourage not just a particular notion of translation as a replacement that produces the same effect as the source text, a notion that prevails among professional and popular readers alike, but also a particular practice of translating, the creation of an illusory effect of transparency whereby the translation is taken as the source text regardless of the translating language (cf. Venuti 2008: chapter 1).

My critical concept of postmodernity follows Fredric Jameson's (1991: chapter 1) in adopting the Marxist periodization of capitalism at different stages of development set forth by Ernest Mandel (1975), moving from mercantilism in the early modern period to monopoly capital in modernity and the rise of multinationalism after the Second World War. Jameson sees these stages as projecting homologous cultural formations distinguished by a dominant logic or set of characteristic features, namely the series of realism, modernism, and postmodernism. But in considering the possibilities of resistance available in the postmodern situation, I depart from Jameson by abandoning the concept of a homology between socioeconomic and cultural practices and instead imagine a disjunctive or contradictory relation between them, a level of disorganization, wherein capital can be variously reproduced or frustrated by the cultural products to which it gives rise. In Scott Lash and John Urry's account, the disorganization of contemporary capitalism means that "the flows of subjects and objects are progressively less synchronized within national boundaries" (Lash and Urry 1994: 10). As a result, multinational conglomerates cannot exert complete control over the production and consumption of their products. The media corporation CBS owns a variety of radio, television, and cable networks as well as the publisher Simon and Schuster, which has published such critiques of the global economy as William Greider's 1997 book *One World, Ready or Not* (Klein 2000: 187).

To conceptualize this sort of disjunction or contradiction, it is necessary to rely on the very kind of thinking that has been stimulated by the postmodern situation, poststructuralism, notably the work of theorists like Baudrillard and Jean-François Lyotard (1984). The abandonment of what Lyotard would call an economic "meta-narrative" to explain social relations and developments coincides with the recognition not only that class position cannot determine cultural consumption with any finality, but also that a cultural product can support many different meanings and uses which may be conflicting among themselves and inconsistent with the aims, whether cultural, economic or political, that motivated its production. The mass communications industries that are so important for economic exchange and social reproduction in fact abet the disjunctive, contradictory nature of cultural reception through the increasing diversity and speed of the information and cultural products they circulate.

In Baudrillard's view, the circulation of simulacra leads to a dystopia in which both human subjectivity and reality are replaced by the serial repetition of objects and images, so that the very possibility of social critique and political action is preempted by the loss of differences that create meaning. Instead of this loss, however, Lash and Urry argue for a proliferation and intensification of differences that are fundamentally aesthetic: in their more nuanced and more politically productive thinking, the mass communication industries enable social agents to develop an "aesthetic or hermeneutic reflexivity," a self-consciousness that is manifested in more discriminating acts of interpretation which may reinforce or interrogate prevailing social conditions (Lash and Urry 1994: 6). In forming subjectivity, the globalized flow of simulacra can promote "individuation in the sense of the atomization of normalized, 'niche-marketed' consumers" or "aesthetic-expressive individualization" that takes into account a range of cultural, historical, and geographical information, even when this information is shot through with stereotypes and ideologies (ibid.: 113). The postmodern subject may be an obsessively brand-conscious consumer or a cynical social critic or a variable combination of both roles inflected by such other factors as taste and education. This subject may even be compelled by the sheer ephemerality of the simulacra to posit more stable values, beliefs, and representations, however contingent they are on changing social situations, and any such ideological stability will constitute a basis for social critique (Harvey 1989: 292).

Translation, then, might intervene into the postmodern situation by tampering with the simulacra that drive the global economy. A translator might use the images on which capital relies to short-circuit or jam its circulation by translating so as to question those images and the practices of consumption that they solicit. This sort of intervention is distinctly postmodern because it contends with the globalized flow of simulacra that is a hallmark of multinational capitalism and that permeates cultural and social institutions. It also embodies the paradox that Linda Hutcheon has observed in postmodernism, the uneasy combination of "complicity and critique, of reflexivity and historicity, that at once inscribes and subverts the conventions and ideologies of the dominant cultural and social forces" (Hutcheon 1989: 11). Hence insofar as translating establishes a meaning or function that is analogous to that of the source text, a relation of equivalence that is often stipulated in commissions even if constructed with such latitude as to constitute what today is recognized as adaptation, the resulting translation is complicit with the very image that it seeks to question in that text. Yet insofar as the analogical relation is interpretive, requiring the translator to draw on the linguistic and cultural resources of the receiving situation, the translation leaves intact neither that situation nor the source text but rather troubles them both in potentially interrogative ways (see Venuti 2009).

The critical force of this translating necessarily depends on reception, on the audience's ability to perceive and comprehend the cultural political gesture that the translator aims to make. And in the postmodern situation where metanarratives that build totalizing explanations of social forces have lost their epistemological power and in some quarters their cultural authority, the translator cannot assume that an audience will interpret a translated text according to a specific philosophical or political discourse, such as Enlightenment humanism or Marxist historicism. On the contrary, the reception of a translation, as of any cultural product, cannot be completely controlled, if only because the audience is likely to be fragmented into diverse cultural constituencies characterized by different, even conflicting values.

In our current predicament, consequently, the notion that "to be effective for political engagement, a text and a group that uses that text must have widespread and general appeal" (Tymoczko 2000: 41) is conceptually naive. Not only does the insistence on "widespread and general appeal" ignore the audience fragmentation that distinguishes the postmodern cultural situation, but it also assumes an explanation of social forces that is both totalizing and anachronistic insofar as it is predicated on the rise of a mass movement to combat a single dominant political and military force. This notion of political engagement is in fact derived from the Irish nationalist movement instituted at the beginning of the twentieth century by literary elites who translated early Irish texts in their struggle against British colonialism (see Tymoczko 1999). To take such a historically specific movement as an exemplary model, valid for any social formation at any historical moment, risks both anti-intellectualism in oversimplifying the study of cultural practices and defeatism in discouraging other forms of political action.

The political intervention performed by translation in postmodern culture may be more usefully imagined as a local, small-scale activity of resistance against dominant discourses and institutions. Michel de Certeau has described such activities as "tactics of consumption, the ingenious ways in which the weak make use of the strong," tactics that often take the form of analogical or metaphorical procedures "which are transgressions of the symbolic order and the limits it sets" (de Certeau 1984: xvii, 54). The translator who would play havoc with the global cultural economy can stage a transgression on the basis of a source text, possibly violating the business ethics that entails the production of a commodity in favor of a politically oriented ethics of cultural and social change. In engaging with the simulacra circulated by the mass communication industries, the images that not only form subjects but can also nurture an aesthetic reflexivity, the translator constructs a position of potential resistance that remains open to interpretation, always dependent on a particular reader's breadth of cultural discrimination and depth of investment in the simulacra under interrogation.

Political strategies of translation

To develop some of the implications of these ideas for translation practices, I will consider several cases from roughly the past decade. In 2001, Jonah Peretti, a graduate student at MIT (Massachusetts Institute of Technology), challenged Nike through its offer to personalize sneakers by allowing the purchaser to choose a word or phrase to be stitched beneath the manufacturer's trade mark, the swoosh symbol. This offer was obviously a marketing ploy, a shrewdly inventive one, whereby a proper name or nickname could, through mere juxtaposition, partake of the cultural charisma that has accrued to the trade mark. Peretti, however, submitted the word "sweatshop," and when his request was predictably denied, he explained to Nike that he chose this "ID because I wanted to remember the toil and labor of the children that made my shoes" (http://www.shey.net/niked.html).

I read this request as an attempt to perform what Roman Jakobson called an intersemiotic translation, a translation between different sign systems, here between a visual symbol and a verbal sign. Jakobson imagined intersemiotic translation as working only in the reverse direction, as "an interpretation of verbal signs by means of signs of nonverbal sign systems" (Jakobson 1959: 233). But he did not anticipate how the ubiquity and speed of the electronic media could assign a primacy to the visual and link a visual symbol to strings of verbal signs. Through advertising campaigns, Nike itself had translated its trade mark into the slogan "Just Do It," linking a visual image of speed with a notion of performance that is mere physical action, unreflective and unverbalized; Peretti was in turn translating the Nike trade mark into the word "sweatshop," thereby calling attention to Nike's exploitative labor practices and showing how the swoosh symbol in effect conceals them. Although Nike denied Peretti's request, the political intervention he sought to perform was widely publicized by print and electronic media in the United States, including coverage in such newspapers as the *Wall Street Journal* and the *Village Voice* and his personal appearance on the nationally televised program *The Today Show*. He had definitely scored a hit in the very marketing terms that Nike was itself deploying (Peretti 2001).

More precisely, Peretti's intervention bears all the marks of a postmodern translation practice that draws on the simulacra driving capital to expose their socioeconomic conditions. Yet his very choice of the word "sweatshop" should make us
wary of attributing an objective, disinterested truth to his translation. Like the swoosh
symbol, "sweatshop" is simulacral, at once decontextualized, removed from the different economic and political situations where Nike sets up shop, and coded by a
leftwing ideology linked to the history of labor movements. In assuming this ideological standpoint, Peretti projected an audience who would be prompted to read the
translation as he did by the mere juxtaposition of word and visual image.

Once an act of translation enters into the circulation of simulacra, however, its
consequences are difficult to control. The institution that a translation is designed to
challenge may be so powerful as to suppress that translation and its economic and
political effects. Appearing with Peretti on *The Today Show* was a spokesman for Nike
who acknowledged the negative publicity, even the complaints received on the Nike
webpage. But neither the attempted translation nor its aftermath affected Nike's labor
practices or sales in any significant way. Consumers, even when they might have
sufficient information to translate the swoosh symbol into "sweatshop," still buy
Nike. Peretti's intervention, moreover, was itself questioned in the deluge of email
correspondence that he received: some correspondents felt that, simply by buying a
pair of Nike sneakers, he was complicit with the company's labor practices, that the
best course would have been a general boycott. Peretti's translation, as he explained
in an essay published on the web, was an act of "cultural jamming," a subversive
effort to turn a company's practices against itself. Yet the ambiguity of the term
"jamming" points to the political risks of this practice: it can mean not merely
"obstruction" or "stoppage," but "an improvised performance by a group of musicians,"
a fruitful collaboration.

Would the risk of complicity decrease or become more manageable if the translator's intervention were an interlingual translation, focusing on one sign system, language? Consider Victor Pozanco's 1999 Spanish version of Tom Clancy and Steve
Pieczenik's novel *Tom Clancy's Op-Center: Balance of Power* (1998). The plot hinges
on the possibility of another Spanish civil war in which Catalan and Basque insur-
gents join to overthrow the central government in Madrid – only to see their con-
spiracy derailed by a Castilian nationalist who aims to return Spain to a rightwing
dictatorship. To remove this threat to liberal democracy, United States undercover
operatives intervene. Sound familiar? Over the past forty or so years, the precession of
simulacra has been so effective that it is no longer possible to distinguish between
United States foreign policy and the plots of political thrillers, and a recognizable
model has emerged in presidential administrations as well as bestsellers, exercising its
fascination among voters and readers alike.

Nonetheless, bestselling authors, like intelligence agencies and cabinet officers, can
make telling mistakes. Clancy and Pieczenik's novel is filled with misrepresentations
of Spanish history and culture, not simply factual errors, but exaggerations and dis-
paragements that construct negative stereotypes. Alberto Bosch Navarro, for instance,
professor of microbiology at the University of Barcelona, posted a review on

Barnes&Noble.com in which he complained that "Catalonian people are depicted in the book as greedy, racist and assassins." The Spanish version took another path by combining translation with adaptation to alter these misrepresentations: Pozanco corrected errors and revised the images of Spain, Spanish ethnic groups, and other Hispanic cultures. Since his translation renders a text riddled with simulacra, he inevitably substituted or created additional ideology-coded representations that cannot be taken at face value as the truth of Spain or any social situation. Far from it: both the image of Spain and Clancy's Spanish reputation are refurbished.

For example, when a United States operative in the English text asserts, "Madrid is not the underbelly of Mexico City," the Spanish version reads, "Madrid no es el Tercer Mundo" (Madrid is not the Third World) (Clancy and Pieczenik 1998: 8; 1999: 14). Here Pozanco has removed not only the sensationalistic slang of the English ("underbelly"), but also the pejorative reference to another Hispanic culture, which, however, has been applied to developing nations as a group. He also worked to improve the historical accuracy of the English text, as in this passage concerning a United States operative named Aideen:

> Spain's strife had been mostly internal in this century, and the nation had remained neutral during World War II. As a result, the world had paid relatively little attention to its problems and politics. But when Aideen was studying languages in college her Spanish professor, Señor Armesto, had told her that Spain was a nation on the verge of disaster.
>
> *(Clancy and Pieczenik 1998: 14)*

> A lo largo del siglo XX, casi todos los conflictos en los que se había visto envuelta España eran de orden interno. España fue neutral en las dos guerras mundiales y, como consecuencia de ello, el mundo había prestado escasa atención a sus problemas políticos, salvo durante la guerra civil. Pero cuando Aideen estudiaba lenguas en la facultad, su professor de español, el doctor Armesto, le había dicho que España era un país dado a los conflictos internos.
>
> *(Clancy and Pieczenik 1999: 18)*

Next to the sweeping statement that "the world had paid relatively little attention to [Spanish] problems and politics," Pozanco added the qualification "salvo durante la guerra civil" (except during the civil war). And at the end of the passage he replaced the exaggeration in the English text, the phrase "a nation on the verge of disaster," with the more restrained phrase "un país dado a los conflictos internos" (a country given to internal conflicts). Yet this choice can be regarded as a euphemism that minimizes such serious problems as the terrorism of the Basque separatist group Euskadi Ta Askatasuna, known as ETA. At other points, Pozanco's translation sought to bring greater precision to social categories: a reference to "the impoverished Andalusians in the south" – which is not only a gross generalization but also a redundancy that assumes the anglophone reader's geographical ignorance (Andalusia *is* southern Spain) – is rendered as "los campesinos de las zonas más pobres de

Andalucía" (the farm workers of the poorest areas in Andalusia), where the effects of the poverty are depersonalized, questionably displaced from the workers themselves onto a region (Clancy and Pieczenik 1998: 7; 1999: 13). Pozanco also deleted Clancy and Pieczenik's misleadingly reductive account of the Republican side in the civil war – "insurgent Communists and other anarchic forces" (ibid.) – in which an anti-Communism indicative of the Cold War era not only eliminates the heterogeneity of the Republicans' political ideals (which encompassed nationalism and liberalism as well as various leftwing ideologies) but also excludes the idea that they had in common a struggle for democracy. The translation, however, does not supply these historical facts.

In a prefatory note to the Spanish version, the publisher, Barcelona-based Planeta, offered an account of the translator's work, indicating that Pozanco corrected errors and avoided cultural and political stereotypes that were not only offensive to Spanish readers, but also potentially damaging to cross-cultural relations insofar as Clancy's novels are so widely circulated as to shape readers' attitudes towards the United States as well as foreign cultures like Spain. After interviewing Pozanco in April of 2002, I can report that the decision to make the changes originated with the translator himself, and the publisher supported it. In our exchange, Pozanco referred to his effort to recreate the generic features of the English text, but he characterized his translation primarily in cultural political terms, revealing the ideological basis of his choices. The translator of seven novels by Clancy, as well as approximately one hundred English-language literary texts by such authors as Dickens, Rider Haggard, Joyce, Nadine Gordimer, and Margaret Atwood, Pozanco remarked that

> I approached the English text with the aim of preserving the adventure, leaving in a second place any other considerations. Personally I am convinced that to treat the book otherwise would have destroyed the good image of Mr. Clancy that I believe I contributed to create with *Debt of Honor* and the rest of the books I have translated. I never had a bad image of Mr. Clancy, basically because he always fought terrorism, all kinds of terrorism, and I think this is good. I just see him as a very conservative man, defending democracy in the American way and, above all, fighting terrorism.

Pozanco's remarks testify to the changes in meaning and ideology that a literary text can undergo in translation. Whereas in the United States Clancy's novels are read according to popular taste as suspenseful technothrillers with patriotic overtones or according to elite taste as simplistic narrative forms larded with reactionary political themes, abroad they might support diverse, even conflicting responses, depending on attitudes towards United States culture and foreign policy. For Pozanco, Clancy's novels reflect democratic values, conservative, to be sure, but admirable in their opposition to terrorism. And Pozanco distinguished this view from that of other Spanish readers who, in his words, see the United States author as a "rightist too prone to military methods."

In Spain, although such newspapers as *El País* and *La Vanguardia* criticized Pozanco's changes, as well as Clancy's novel, the Spanish version seems to have reinforced Clancy's marketability. Neither *Debt of Honor* nor *Balance of Power* appeared on any bestseller lists when they were published in Spanish, but Pozanco's five other Clancy translations did. In aiming to preserve the "good image" conveyed by his previous translations, Pozanco's latest remained complicit with, even while explicitly questioning, Clancy's symbolic and economic capital as a United States author in Spain. This case also makes clear that a postmodern translation practice with a political agenda may require a redefinition of translating to extend beyond the fairly close adherence to the source text that is customarily regarded as inter-lingual translation today so as to include more revisionary forms of rewriting like adaptation.

Can more extensive rewriting give the translator sufficient control over the reception of the translation to insure that its political force is not compromised? Consider the Italian version of Martin Dunford and Jack Holland's *New York City: The Rough Guide*, both published in 2000. The translation, produced by a group of writers, is remarkable for exaggerating Dunford and Holland's mythologizing portrait of New York and simultaneously questioning the sanitized image of the city manu-factured for tourist consumption by the municipal government. These complicated effects are achieved through revisions. Whereas the English text illustrates Manhattan's "massive romance" by referring to "the 4am half-life Downtown, or just wasting the morning on the Staten Island ferry," the Italian version resorts to a lexicon that is both melodramatic and lyrical: "il Greenwich Village, dove la vita *ferve ancora* alle 4 del mattino, il traghetto di Staten Island in un mattino *luminoso*" (Greenwich Village, where life *still rages* at four in the morning, the Staten Island ferry on a *luminous* morning) (Dunford and Holland 2000a: ix; 2000b: 7, my emphasis). At the same time, whereas the English text reports that the crime rate has dropped significantly, "especially in the Mayor Giuliani years," the Italian version deletes any specific reference to the mayor and adds a critical commentary that includes some cynical satire, noting that in the wake of the lower crime figures "le autorità di Manhattan recentemente si sono lasciate andare a avventate manifestazioni di autocongratulazioni e pacche sulle spalle" (the Manhattan authorities have recently allowed themselves to sink to the level of rash expressions of self-congratulation and pats on the back: (ibid.). The translators resisted the publicity generated by Rudolph Giuliani's admin-istration (1994–2001) and offered the Italian tourist a more incisive representation of the city that is nonetheless encoded by the simulacra of Hollywood films and television programs.

It must be noted that the Rough Guides permit this form of rewriting. When in May of 2001 I brought the Italian commentary on Giuliani to the attention of Richard Trillo, director of marketing, publicity, and rights at Rough Guides in London, he responded that "Our partners are allowed some freedom to add new material into the Rough Guide text." Thus although the adaptive Italian translation is complicit with the romantic simulacra that the municipal government has used to sell New York to tourists worldwide, it still carries out a form of resistance that de

Certeau would have appreciated: a local revolt that encourages skepticism towards official representations.

When a travel guidebook is translated, however, the interrogative effect of the translation does not stop at the simulacra from which a foreign place may be indistinguishable in the minds of tourists. The guidebook itself may be submitted to questioning since it too purveys images laden with ideologies. The Italian version of *New York City: The Rough Guide* substantially revises Dunford and Holland's social diagnosis, implicitly treating it as superficial, imprecise, and too tolerant. In commenting on the enormous socioeconomic differences between Manhattan neighborhoods, for example, the British authors assert that "The city is constantly like this, with glaring, in-your-face wealth juxtaposed with urban problems – poverty, the drug trade, homelessness – that have a predictably high profile" (Dunford and Holland 2000a: ix). But the Italian translators present a more penetrating and harsher account:

> Tutta la città è così: in nessun altro luogo del mundo occidentale ci sono tanti derelitti vicino a un lusso così sfacciato, e tanti problemi (razzismo, droga, senzatetto) ancora irrisolti.
>
> *(Dunford and Holland 2000b: 7)*

> (The entire city is like this: in no other place in the western world are there so many derelict [buildings] next to a luxury so shameless, as well as so many problems (racism, drugs, homelessness) still unsolved.)

Not only do the translators create an international context ("the western world") in which to describe and evaluate the city, but they also delete Dunford and Holland's mitigating remark that the "problems [...] have a predictably high profile" and instead assert that solutions are lacking. In citing "racism," furthermore, the translators point to an ideological determinant that may well underlie the more familiar and therefore more easily dismissed catalogue of urban problems in the English text. The Italian version is creating a different kind of tourist, certainly attracted by the simulacra that unavoidably mediate a visit to New York, but acutely aware that at least some of those images can mystify the social conditions of any such encounter. Of course, an awareness that these conditions exist is not the same as a transparent representation of them, and readers must be inclined to assume the skeptical attitude of the Italian version in order to treat its interpolations as demystifying. For the fact remains that even the reference to "racism, drugs, homelessness" possesses a simulacral quality, having figured prominently in media images of New York for decades.

Not every translation of a travel guidebook encourages the tactics of consumption that de Certeau imagines as acts of resistance. A translation may so rewrite the representation of a foreign place as to reinforce the precession of simulacra and disarm criticism of them. The Dutch version of Dunford and Holland's *New York City: The Rough Guide*, a group production like the Italian, shows some effort to tone down their hyperbole, but it recreates their mythologizing image. Whereas the English text observes that after a week in the "admittedly mad" city "the shock gives way to myth," the Dutch version omits any mention of "shock" and "myth" and indicates a very different reaction: "voorbij is het aanvankelijke wantrouwen" (the initial suspicion is past) (Dunford and Holland 2000a: ix; 1998: 9). The notion of suspicion is telling, suggestive of an image informed by crime reports as well as the many police procedurals set in New York, whether novels, films, or television programs. This suggestion is borne out by the translators' handling of the chapter entitled "Police and trouble." Dunford and Holland state – in all seriousness, apparently, although nonetheless with comical exaggeration – that "the atmosphere of impending violence is sometimes sniffable," but the translators endow the "atmosphere" with the force of a threat, appropriately couched in the clichéd language of crime fiction: "De dreiging van geweld die in de lucht hangt, is soms haast voelbaar" (the threat of violence that hangs in the air is sometimes palpable) (Dunford and Holland 2000a: 41; 1998: 46). The Dutch version, like the English text, seems to be anticipating the media-coded preconceptions that tourists are likely to bring to New York, but it confirms rather than challenges them. It even projects a stereotypical Dutch tourist obsessed with the cost of things, inclined to spend as little as possible. "For the *avid consumer*," assert the British authors in their typically hyperbolic style, "the choice of shops is vast, almost numbingly exhaustive," whereas the Dutch translators write that "Wat de koopjes-jager betreft, de keus aan winkels is enorm" (as far as the *bargain-hunter* is concerned, the choice of shops is enormous) (Dunford and Holland 2000a: xi; 1998: 11, my emphasis). The Dutch version of *New York City: The Rough Guide* is creating a tourist who is fascinated by the romantic simulacra of the city (if less enthusiastic than British and Italian counterparts), but likely to be closed off from – and therefore deeply unsettled by – the cultural differences that they conceal.

Local contingencies

Yet even if such quiescent translations are set aside as conservative, involved in maintaining the integrity of the simulacra that are affiliated with dominant cultural and social institutions (including the travel guidebook industry), we might still question the extent of the social impact produced by any translation project that aims to be transgressive. Is de Certeau's local intervention the only form of resistance that a translator can hope to achieve? If so, the narrative underpinning my essay might be classified as ironic – cultural politics uncontrollably contained by the powers-that-be – rather than romantic – political resistance that issues into a social transcendence which can potentially transform geopolitical relations. I am not certain that translation can do any such thing on an international or global scale – short of translators collectively organizing a work stoppage that removes translations from the market and from business practices. All those translations of contracts and patents, instruction manuals and software packages are too busy extending the economic network without any room for the sort of rewriting performed with the Clancy novel and the Rough Guide. And what of politically engaged translators who are contractually bound to produce a precisely accurate version, particularly in the case of academic research? How can they balance their business ethics, fulfilling the demands of their contract, with their ethical politics, taking a stand against ideologies to which they are opposed?

Consider Herminia Bevia and Antonio Resines's 2002 Spanish version of Richard Falk's *Predatory Globalization: A Critique* (1999). The decision to translate this work must first be figured into any assessment of the translators' intervention since, as Falk's title makes clear, his aim is to present a frankly political analysis: he argues that in deferring to the global economy states have compromised their obligation to preserve the rights and welfare of their citizens by exacerbating social and environmental problems. Yet Bevia and Resines did not accept the project for ideological reasons. The translators of over one hundred English-language texts, ranging from novels, poetry, and film soundtracks to scholarly works in the natural and social sciences, they depend on translation for their livelihood. During an interview in July of 2005 when we discussed their work on Falk's book, they remarked that "we couldn't decline this job. We needed the money." All the same, this translation has contributed to debates on globalization in the Spanish-speaking world, receiving citations in the press as well as in academic research. A translation of a text with a political theme can thus produce an ideological effect, can influence political discourse in the receiving culture, even when the translator's decision to undertake the project is not a deliberate political act.

Although Bevia and Resines's primary motive was subsistence rather than politics, their translation does involve an intriguing choice that carries geopolitical implications and was made precisely for this reason. For the tendentious term "rogue states," which has appeared in United States foreign policy statements since the 1980s and was used in 2003 to justify the George W. Bush administration's military aggression in Iraq, the translators substituted "Estados díscolos," or "disobedient states." Here, for example, is their version of a sentence in which Falk cites Michael Klare's 1995 book *Rogue States and Nuclear Outlaws*:

> Michael Klare has persuasively argued that US non-proliferation efforts in recent years have been mainly directed against the so-called rogue states, a shifting classification currently consisting of Iraq, Iran, Libya, Syria, and North Korea.
>
> *(Falk 1999: 84)*

> Michael Klare ha argumentado de manera persuasiva que los esfuerzos en favor de la no proliferación de Estados Unidos durante los últimos años han estado principalmente dirigidos contra los considerados Estados díscolos, una mutable clasificación que hoy engloba a Irak, Irán, Libia, Siria y Corea del Norte.
>
> *(Falk 2002: 120)*

Bevia and Resines's version adheres closely to Falk's lexicon and syntax, maintaining a close semantic correspondence – with the exception of their choice for "rogue states." Because Spanish has no exact equivalent for "rogue," the translators considered various alternative renderings, including "gamberro," meaning "trouble-maker" or "hooligan." They excluded this possibility, as they explained in our interview, because

> "gamberro" connotes a certain vileness of character which "díscolo" lacks. The difference is not really very important, but the use of "díscolo," we felt, did take the propaganda iron out of the expression in a situation where judge, jury and executioner are one and the same.

Although Bevia and Resines felt that "the difference [in verbal choices] is not really very important," they do give a political rationale for their rendering. In choosing "díscolo," they sought to produce an approximate translation which removes the stigma of criminality that the propagandistic term "rogue" attaches to certain nation-states in United States foreign policy. The notion of criminality remains with such other renderings as "Estados delincuentes," or "delinquent states," the choice made by Juan Gabriel Lopez Guix in a number of articles that he translated for *La Vanguardia* (see, for instance, Polk 2004). In an interview during June of 2005, Guix explained that his use of "delincuente" was designed to emphasize the concept of legality:

> "Delincuente" had the contravening-of-law nuances I wanted to transmit (in Spanish "delincuente" is the transgressor of law, and the word is not particu-larly linked as in English to "juvenile"). And it also seemed to fit better in stylistic terms, since the oxymoron was more fully visible (the State, law-giver, as wrong-doer).

Guix's use of "delincuente" applies a particular concept of equivalence, an adequacy to "rogue" that adheres – as Gideon Toury (1995: 56–57) might point out – to "source norms," which here do not enforce a simple linguistic choice or establish a close semantic correspondence, especially in the absence of a ready equivalent for the English word, but rather involve a precise political significance: "delincuente" com-municates the Bush administration's definition of "rogue states" as "outlaw regimes," the term that Bush himself used in his speech announcing the start of the Iraq war in March of 2003. This political adequacy, along with the intelligibility of the word in Spanish, insures that "delincuentes" would also be acceptable in Toury's sense of subscribing to norms in the receiving culture (see Toury 1995: 57), which are again political, since the then Spanish President José Maria Aznar strongly supported United States foreign policy from 2001 onwards. Bevia and Resines's use of "díscolo," in contrast, tampers with the Bush administration's definition of "rogue states" by eliminating any explicit reference to the law. Although "díscolo" is sufficiently intelligible to be accepted as rendering "rogue" according to linguistic norms in Spain, it ran counter to dominant political values, "dominant" insofar as they were held by the current government.

"Díscolo" continues to resonate, however, releasing other meanings that effectively question United States foreign policy. Because the Spanish word is most often used to describe disobedient children, it replaces the propagandistic stigma of criminality with a generalized notion of disobedience towards a higher authority or sovereign power, implying that the so-called rogue states disregard the policies of an international body like the United Nations or refuse the demands of hegemonic nations like the United States. "Díscolo" can thus be read so as to turn the tables on the Bush administration: it glances at the supremacy that the United Nations Charter assigns to the United States as a permanent member of the Security Council, and it suggests that the United States makes demands for obedience which it does not itself fulfill by violating the autonomy of other nation-states. For in violating this autonomy the United States exercises a sovereign power that disallows the element of participation or sharing central to democracy and thereby fits its own definition of a "rogue state." In his speech at the start of the Iraq war, in fact, Bush asserted that "We have no ambition in Iraq, except to remove a threat and restore control of that country to its own people." Jacques Derrida has explained the contradictory dependence of democracy on sovereignty:

> For democracy to be effective, for it to give rise to a system of law that can carry the day, which is to say, for it to give rise to an effective power, the *cracy* of the *dēmos* – of the world *dēmos* in this case – is required. What is required is thus a sovereignty, a force that is stronger than all the other forces in the world. But if the constitution of this force is, in principle, supposed to represent and protect this world democracy, it in fact betrays and threatens it from the very outset, in autoimmune fashion […] As soon as there is sovereignty, there is abuse of power and a rogue state.
>
> *(Derrida 2005: 100, 102)*

By introducing the notion of obedience, "Estados díscolos" can expose the questionable political conditions of the United States's sovereignty, which underlies any recourse to such institutions as the United Nations.

Of course, to articulate the ideological critique at work in Bevia and Resines's translation, their inventive challenge to the political simulacra of both the Bush and Aznar administrations, is not to gauge the accessibility of that critique to their readers or to assess its political impact. Their Spanish version, like Falk's English text, was directed primarily to an intellectual elite that included an academic or professional audience, even if it exceeded that audience to some degree. For such works to receive notice in widely circulated periodicals is hardly to extend their reach to popular readers. Still, the elite readership that was drawn to Bevia and Resines's translation would be capable of noticing and analyzing subtle differences in the rendering of an ideologically loaded phrase like "rogue states," even when that phrase was used a handful of times in an academic text.

Their translation, more importantly, was affiliated with a significant development in Spanish political opinion. Since it was published in 2002, after the State of the Union Address in which Bush joined the rhetoric of "rogue states" to the equally propagandistic phrase "axis of evil," the choice of "díscolo" to render an incisively critical text like Falk's can be seen as reflecting the rising tide of Spanish opposition, not merely to United States foreign policy, but also to President Aznar's unflinching support of the invasion of Iraq. In March of 2004, furthermore, Aznar's political party, the Partido Popular, lost the general elections that brought to power another party, the Partido Socialista Obrero Español, which not only was critical of the United States, but also engineered the withdrawal of Spanish military forces from Iraq. This sequence of events certainly cannot be attributed to Bevia and Resines's translation in any direct way, especially since the elections took place soon after the terrorist train bombing in Madrid and the confused reaction that caused Aznar's government to suffer a loss of political capital. We can infer, however, that Bevia and Resines's rendering of a key term contributed to political debates, not only because their choice was interrogative, but also because it increased the range of possible translations and therefore the possibility of conflicting Spanish interpretations of United States foreign policy. The political efficacy of an ideologically coded translation, such as the different versions of "rogue," need not depend on the precise reading that the translator may have intended or that another politically sympathetic reader may give to it. The very differences among the simulacra can metamorphose into the cultural conditions that make possible a critique, can stimulate a critical reflexivity among readerships in specific social situations, particularly those situations that are characterized by divided opinion and controversy.

Because translation is always constrained by cultural and social factors in the receiving situation, notably values, beliefs, and representations that are arrayed in a hierarchical order of power and prestige, the selection of source texts for translation and the development of discursive strategies to translate them inevitably involve taking sides to a certain extent, aligning with some constituencies and institutions more than others. The reception of translated texts, although it cannot be strictly controlled by the translator's choices, is not so much unpredictable as informed by the cultural and social divisions that constitute any receiving situation. For these reasons, a translation can acquire political force, even if the ideological valence of translator's choices as well as their social effects may take varying and sometimes conflicting forms, always subject to the local contingencies that inform a particular audience's reception of the translation. In the postmodern culture of the simulacra, where the most heterogeneous images circulate rapidly and networks of production can increase the disjunctive, contradictory nature of cultural forms and practices, audiences are fragmented into overlapping constituencies, elite and popular, and the possibilities for political intervention become localized, circumscribed by medium and audience but still possessing the potentiality for affiliations with broader developments that can result in cultural and social change.

These conclusions, however tentative in view of the limited number of cases I have examined, suggest some directions for translation studies. To advance thinking about forms of resistance based on translation, we must study what it does – in every genre or text type, whether humanistic, pragmatic, or technical – and then explore what it might do – whether at the local, national or international level – to make a difference in people's lives. This sort of research involves studying how readers process and use translated texts. But insofar as the aim is to treat translation as a cultural practice that somehow intervenes into the current geopolitical economy, we must also consider how we might teach readers to read translations *as translations*, relatively autonomous from the foreign texts they translate, how to draw distinctions between different discursive strategies, whether translative or adaptive, whether intralingual, interlingual, or intersemiotic, and how to assess the potential impact of translations against the hierarchy of values, beliefs, and representations in any culture. Not only must translation research develop a truly global sense of its intellectual project, but to treat translation as a political intervention it must also set out from the assumption that cultural practices are both ideological resolutions of real social problems and expressions of utopian aspirations for social life (see Jameson 1981: 291). Only then can translation studies formulate a concept of its own social responsibility that does not acquiesce before the status quo but rather submits it to a searching critique.

[2008]

9

TRANSLATIONS ON THE BOOK MARKET

At the Frankfurt Book Fair, where thousands of publishers from around the world annually squeeze inside huge exhibition halls to buy and sell foreign rights, a typical booth contains several tiny tables at which agents and editors cut their deals. Stopping to peruse what books are on offer, you wouldn't have to strain to get wind of potential translations into some language or other. I recently attended the event and overheard a conversation that was startling and not a little worrying.

At the booth of an Italian trade publisher, a British representative was handed a new publication and, smiling, said, "The cover looks smart." The Italian rights manager asked, "Do you mean 'clever'?" Her prospective client paused, a quizzical expression on his face, before responding, "Sure," as if to quash any doubt that they were on the same ... page? I myself wasn't sure they were speaking the same language, even though it was English. "Smart" can mean "clever" and more, of course, but in this context the British speaker was probably referring to appearance, not intelligence. What would happen, I wondered, when these two started discussing the book's actual content? Could it be the same book in their words? Their minds? Given the substantial amounts of money that normally change hands in Frankfurt, you might expect a greater sense of mutual understanding to accompany any financial dealings. The conversation hardly inspired confidence about the current state of literary translation.

As an English-language translator who has worked with a wide range of publishers for some three decades, but who is also inclined to take a theoretical approach to his work, I have become a critical observer of the ways in which foreign texts are chosen for translation. Publishing practices that date back to the beginning of the twentieth century have decisively shaped our intercultural exchanges and have contributed, I believe, to the appallingly low volume of anglophone translations since the Second World War, now just over 2% of total annual book output according to industry statistics (Venuti 2008: 11). These practices are questionable not merely because they have admitted relatively few foreign texts from a narrow range of foreign cultures, but also because they have formed aggressively monolingual readerships in the United Kingdom and the United States, generally uninterested in translations. Ironically, then, publishers seem not to have acted in their own best interests, whether those interests are cultural or commercial or both.

The main problem is that long-standing practices reveal a conceptual naïveté, a limited understanding of translation, of the cultural issues that any translation project must confront and somehow resolve if it is to be successful both critically and commercially. Hence I want to suggest that, where translation is concerned, these practices need to be rethought, if not simply abandoned, and replaced by a more savvy approach that is truly concerned with cultural as well as commercial factors. Otherwise anglophone publishers, and no doubt publishers in other languages as well, will remain complicit in our present predicament: the absence of what I shall call a translation culture, that is to say, a culture that can sustain the study and practice of translation, that can foster a sophisticated and appreciative discourse about translation in its many aspects, and that can create an informed readership to support and encourage the publication of translated texts (for an extended consideration of this point, see chapter 14).

Early in the twentieth century, a largely unwritten policy came to prevail among anglophone publishers. Buy the translation rights to a single book by a foreign author. If soon after publication the translation suffers a substantial loss or fails to earn back its production costs or to realize a modest profit, then stop publishing translations of the author's books. If, however, the first translation manages to break even or to approach a break-even point, then continue to publish translations of that particular author in the hope that more will create a readership and add profitable titles to the backlist, which itself might begin to turn a profit.

What I am describing as a prevalent policy dictated a print run that turned into an industry standard by the 1940s. In 1949, the translator F. H. Lyon proposed that Stanley Unwin publish an English version of Finnish writer Jarl Hemmer's novel *A Fool of Faith*, but Unwin declined on the basis of a sales projection. "We need to be sure of selling the greater part of 5,000 copies," Unwin wrote back, "if we are not to lose money on a novel today, and we have no confidence that we could achieve this result with Hemmer's work" (Allen and Unwin Archive, University of Reading: 17 November 1949). Sales in the range of 5,000 copies became a benchmark for a successful translation of a novel. Yet the figure also came to reflect the sad reality of publishing translations in English. After directing the Harvill Press from 1978 to 1999 and creating a list that included a significant number of translations, Christopher MacLehose observed that "for the most part now the majority of even the finest books that are translated find their way to sales between 1,500 and 6,000" (MacLehose 2004–05: 113).

Since the beginning of the twentieth century, few English-language translations have managed to reach that upper limit. As a result, most foreign authors who have had a book translated into English have not been translated again, either by the initial publisher or by others, who were scared off by the poor market performance of the first translation. A case in point is the Italian writer Paola Capriolo, who since 1988 has published over twenty books, including novels, short-story collections, and children's literature. Although her inventive narratives have been translated into some twelve languages, British and American publishers have avoided her work because the first translations did not sell well. Serpent's Tail brought three of her novels into English: *Floria Tosca* (1997), *The Woman Watching* (1998), and *A Man of Character* (2000). But diminishing sales led publisher Pete Ayrton to abandon her. She has yet to find another trade publisher in English.

Ayrton, to his credit, was willing to support Capriolo's work through three translations. Although he was then running a mid-sized press, small compared to the multinational conglomerates, like them he was implementing a practice that is more than a century old. Focusing on a single book by a foreign author or on a single author from a foreign language forces publishers to decide whether to continue translating that author in order to build a readership – which is only a readership for that author and may carry no implications for other books translated from that foreign language or others. Given this practice, it is more than probable that a publisher, whether large or small, will abandon an author that has done poorly on the book market.

The exceptional cases are remarkable because they involve the great works of modern literature. In translation, these works were commercial failures initially, according to the standards in place then and now, and it is only because some of the publishers involved were willing to add the titles to their backlists or to sell off reprint rights that the translations achieved canonical status in the United Kingdom and the United States (the sales figures reported below come from the Archive of British Publishing and Printing at the University of Reading). In 1922, Chatto and Windus published C. K. Scott Moncrieff's version of Proust's *Swann's Way* in two volumes, and within a year 3,000 copies were in print. Yet five years later volume one had sold only 1,773 copies and volume two only 1,663. In 1928, Martin Secker published his first translation of a novel by Thomas Mann, Helen Lowe-Porter's version of *The Magic Mountain*, but it took seven years to sell 4,641 copies, helped no doubt by the translations of seven other books by Mann that Secker had issued in the interval. In 1929, the Hogarth Press published Beryl de Zoete's version of Italo Svevo's novella *The Hoax*, but after selling 500 copies in the first year the book showed a loss, and publisher Leonard Woolf was soon looking to remainder 300 copies. In 1930, Woolf also published Svevo's collection of stories, *The Nice Old Man and the Pretty Girl*, which met the same fate. He attempted to sell the translation of the stories to Alfred Knopf, who had published Svevo's *Confessions of Zeno* in 1930. The editor at Knopf, R. W. Postgate, declined. "I am afraid there is no question," he replied, "but that he has been a failure, although we made immense efforts to put him across" (Hogarth Press Archive, University of Reading: Postgate to Woolf, 12 January 1931).

I take these "immense efforts" to be promotion and marketing schemes like running advertisements, sending out review copies to newspapers and magazines, and contacting editors and reviewers in order to generate some favorable publicity. But any such efforts cannot address a crucial fact about the translation process: it so radically decontextualizes the source text that a translation can be hard for a reader to appreciate on its own, even a group of translations from the work of the same author.

Translation detaches a source text from everything that makes it uniquely meaningful in the culture where it originated: patterns of linguistic usage, literary traditions, conventions, and practices, a spectrum of cultural values, and forms of reception in print and electronic media and in social institutions. Consequently, a translation makes possible a reading experience that differs markedly from the experience of a reader with access to the source text, especially since the source-language reader may well possess a broad and deep familiarity with the source culture. This disjunction is increased by the limited availability of works in translation. Entire literary traditions, even entire literary canons, are never translated into a particular language, certainly not into English. And rarely is a substantial and diverse selection of contemporary works in print at any one time, regardless of how many publishers invest in translations from a globally dominant language like English. No wonder, then, that when confronted with a translation readers automatically fall back on what they do know and prefer: they read and evaluate the translation mainly against linguistic patterns, literary traditions, and cultural values in the receiving situation, which is usually their own culture.

Yet this sort of reception is risky. It can invite a dismissal of a foreign literary work that may not be recognizable or intelligible in relation to texts and traditions in the translating language. It can invite a complacent reaffirmation of the reader's cultural values and an ethnocentric rejection of a foreign culture merely because the foreign text cannot be understood in its own terms.

This can happen even with elite readerships who are capable of dealing with challenging texts. While Proust and Svevo initially failed to appeal to English-language readers, Virginia Woolf did appeal and in spades: most of her books met with immediate success upon publication. In 1925, the Hogarth Press published *Mrs. Dalloway*, and it sold 2,136 copies in its first year alone, earning a profit of £150, which is quite impressive for a modernist experiment that attracted a fairly specialized audience. (The profit may seem small today, but it needs to be situated in its moment: in 1932, the Kafka translators Willa and Edwin Muir rented a house in the trendy London neighborhood of Hampstead for an annual cost of £120 (Muir 1968: 158).) *Mrs. Dalloway* was so successful, I suggest, because enough readers could understand and appreciate its experimental narrative. By 1923, Dorothy Richardson had published seven novels distinguished by a similar stream-of-consciousness technique. In 1919, excerpts from James Joyce's *Ulysses* had appeared in the magazine *The Egoist,* with the full text published in Paris three years later. English-language readers keen on modernist fiction had a cultural context in which to read Virginia Woolf's novels, as well as those of Richardson and Joyce. But these readers weren't crossing over to foreign modernisms.

What context could have enabled the first English translations of Svevo's writing to find an audience? Joyce's admiration of it obviously did little to improve sales. The Italian fiction then available in English was dominated by varieties of naturalism, most of which were worlds apart from Svevo's wry, psychoanalytically inflected tales of anti-heroes. The most popular Italian writer was Matilde Serao, who explored themes like illicit romance among aristocratic and middle-class women, the uneven cultural and economic development between North and South, and the provinciality and poverty of her native Naples. In 1901, Henry James wrote admiringly about the "remarkable spontaneity" of her early fiction, particularly *La conquista di Roma* (1885), in which a Neapolitan deputy takes up his seat in parliament only to fall helplessly in love with a sophisticated Roman woman and ultimately lose his office (James 1901: 372). A succession of translations followed James's article, so that, by 1928, ten of Serao's books had been Englished, even though her writing grew increasingly melo-dramatic. Lacy Collison-Morely, the literary critic and historian who translated Svevo's collection of stories for the Hogarth Press, reviewed an English version of Serao's 1914 novel *Ella non rispose* (She does not respond), describing it as "a positive orgy of feeling" (Collison-Morely 1919: 689).

Nonetheless, Serao had captured the imaginations of anglophone readers. Would British and American publishers have challenged the taste for her fiction if they had paid greater attention to her contemporaries who had revised or abandoned nat-uralism, writers like Luigi Pirandello and Federigo Tozzi? Both wrote realistic narra-tives but devised innovative strategies to probe character psychology, Pirandello resorting to moments of epiphany and irony, Tozzi crafting discontinuous plots shot through with ominous tension. Readers immersed in the work of these writers might well have gravitated to Svevo's experiments too. They would at least have been given the opportunity to experience different kinds of Italian fiction, glimpsing what the Italian reader had to hand. Yet neither Pirandello's nor Tozzi's stories had yet been translated, although it was in their stories that they developed their most intriguing innovations. Several of Pirandello's novels were available in translation, but they received mixed and in some cases dismissive reviews. Tozzi's novel *Three Crosses* appeared in English in 1921, but it was assimilated to the prevailing taste for nat-uralism. Thus although Collison-Morely called it "powerful" in his review, he finally complained that "it is hardly a great novel" while constructing an unfavorable comparison with Giovanni Verga:

> For one thing, we do not spontaneously identify ourselves with the characters, as we must even in Verga. We watch them with curiosity, with profound interest; but we can look on even at Giulio's suicide without being moved to exclaim that there, but for the grace of God, go ourselves.
>
> *(Collison-Morely 1921: 903)*

The appeal of naturalism proved to be too strong even for a translator of Svevo, who was unable to grasp that Tozzi and Verga were engaged in different narrative projects, one estranging, the other illusionistic.

To be sure, various factors play into the reception of any book, in addition to imponderables which guarantee that any prediction of success or failure can never be certain. In the case of translations, however, past practices show quite clearly that publishers have not sufficiently taken into account the decontextualizing process of translating and its adverse impact on the reception of foreign texts. Focusing on a single text or a single author winds up exacerbating this process: it mystifies the loss or sheer destruction of the linguistic and cultural contexts in which the source text emerged and therefore gives the false and misleading impression that any literary work can be understood on its own. This encourages an essentially romantic notion of original genius as transcending the material conditions of reception. Most importantly, it militates against the contextualized reading, the implicit comparisons among texts, which informed readers always do. To enable English-language readers to understand and appreciate a translation, publishers must restore in English at least part of what constituted the originary context for the source text. With individual publishers each pursuing their own single-minded focus, this context is unlikely to materialize.

Hence, where translations are concerned, publishers must rethink their identities as publishers. "Book publishing," Stanley Unwin wrote, "is a very personal business" in the sense that "a publisher's own inclinations determine the selection of the manuscripts chosen for publication" (Unwin 1960: 325). He admitted that these inclinations could be cultural or commercial, but he nonetheless considered them personal. I am suggesting that with translations publishers must take an approach that is not just less personal, but also more critically detached and more theoretically astute, as well as aesthetically sensitive. They must publish not only translations of foreign texts and authors that conform to their own tastes, but more than one text and more than one author from the same language, and they must make choices so as to sketch the cultural situations and traditions that allow a particular text to be significant in its own culture. Translators too need to participate in these choices, since their expertise is invaluable in assessing the losses and gains in the translation process. But they must regard translation in more self-critical ways than is generally the rule today, when translators tend to take a belletristic approach to their work, making impressionistic comments which show that they, like publishers, find writing to be primarily personal, a form of self-expression or a testimony of their aesthetic kinship to the foreign author (see below: 176–78, 235–40). Publishers and translators alike need to depersonalize translation and to become aware of the ethical responsibility involved in representing foreign texts and cultures. What a sad time it is for intercultural exchange when publishers and translators look abroad and see mainly opportunities to imprint their own values.

The decision to publish a translation should be viewed as strategic, changing over time, never definitive, because it is, in fact, an interpretation, a changing assessment of what sort of context might be created in the receiving situation to help readers appreciate translated literatures more deeply. In their interpretations, publishers must rely – as they have always done – on what they know and what they can come to know by consulting others: writers and translators, critics and scholars, booksellers and readers, as well as their colleagues, other publishers. Yet any interpretation must be seen not as based on some value inherent in the source text, but as contingent on the gathered information and the changing situation in the receiving culture, the changes in knowledge and taste that always affect the reception of books, whether original compositions or translations, and decisively determine their value.

The interpretations that drive publishing decisions depend, of course, on the particular foreign language, literature, and texts under consideration. But any such decisions never occur in a vacuum. Publishers should make their choices in relation to previously published translations, not as one-off deals but as contributions to the context that those translations have worked to create, whether by conforming to or by diverging from translation patterns. Publishers should be prepared to translate several texts from the same foreign literature and to sample past and contemporary texts as well as texts that appeal to both elite and popular tastes. Different source texts require different contexts in order to be understood. The aim, however, is not to translate a representative selection of texts from a foreign literature: a selection can never be truly representative, not only because costs dictate that the number of texts chosen for translation will always be limited, but also because literatures develop in complex, heterogeneous ways in different languages and cultures. The aim is rather to choose texts for translation that respond to two questions, one pertaining to the source culture, the other to the receiving culture. How can a translation achieve a degree of intelligibility and interest for readers in terms that are specific to the culture where the source text originated? And how can that same translation prompt readers to rethink the canons of the source literature that always take shape in the receiving situation? For since translation patterns are inevitably selective, excluding many more texts than are translated, those patterns wind up constructing an increasingly familiar image that can too easily harden into a stereotype of a foreign literature, even a foreign culture (see Venuti 1998: chapter 4).

The initiative I am recommending cannot be pursued by one publisher alone without a significant outlay of capital and probably not without the funding and advice of a cultural ministry or institute in a foreign country. But publishers can coordinate their efforts, regarding their colleagues not as competitors but as collaborators, banding together to select a range of texts from a foreign culture and to publish translations of them so as to build a receiving cultural context in which those translations can thrive. This sort of investment cannot insure critical and commercial success. But in the long run chances are that it will pay off handsomely by laying the foundations for an informed readership that will not feel inadequate before translations from a particular foreign language and will actually be eager to experience new texts from it. Readers as well as publishers have much to gain from a translation policy that is based on an incisive understanding of the translation process.

[2008]

10

TEACHING IN TRANSLATION

Whatever theoretical or critical significance is attached to the term "world literature," it will be applied to courses that gather texts originally written in various foreign languages, archaic and modern. And when teachers in the Americas (as elsewhere) undertake these courses, they will rely on translations out of sheer necessity. The factors that prevent us from assigning foreign texts start with the limits of our own educations. But even if we've been fortunate enough to master several languages and literatures, we must still confront the unevenness of foreign-language preparation in any given class and the improbability that many undergraduates will have attained advanced reading proficiency in more difficult languages like Arabic, Chinese, and Russian. The possibility of a bilingual student body in places like Canada and Puerto Rico may lead teachers to expect a class to read French, Spanish, or English texts in the original languages. But here too the difficulty of assuming a uniform level of linguistic and analytical skills, particularly among undergraduates, militates against any such expectation. Teaching world literature means teaching most, if not all, required texts in translation. Yet this inevitability need not be lamented as a distortion or dilution of foreign literatures. It can rather be seen as enriching literary study in unexpected ways. Translation broadens the range of questions that students might ask of languages and texts, traditions and cultures, as well as the relations among them.

Nonetheless, teaching in translation is not the same as raising the issue of translation in the classroom, which must be done in a systematic way to be productive and therefore requires a rationale and a methodology. Perhaps the first reason to introduce this issue is to deepen students' knowledge of languages, native as well as foreign, while improving their skills in linguistic and literary analysis. A detailed comparison between a translation and the source text it translates can work towards these goals by focusing attention not only on lexicon and syntax, but also on patterns of meaning, and not only on denotation and connotation, but also on dialect and register, style and genre, intertextuality and intercultural relations. To conduct this sort of analysis, the instructor needs to present translated passages that are central to the form and theme of the source text. Supplementary materials can be useful here, starting with the most basic: dictionaries. I sometimes bring in entries from various dictionaries in the foreign and translating languages, monolingual and bilingual, including historical dictionaries like the *Oxford English Dictionary* (*OED*) and more specialized ones like the *Dictionary of American Slang*. When dictionaries are used to analyze a translated passage against the corresponding passage in the source text, students can see how the author and the translator each make verbal choices that produce literary effects, although always with suggestive differences. At the same time, students can learn a great deal about the interpretive dimension of translation as well as literary interpretation in general.

To develop and illustrate these points, I shall explore a particularly rich case that might well appear on the syllabus of a course in world literature: the Argentine writer Julio Cortázar's short story "Las babas del diablo" ("The Devil's Drool," in a close rendering), and Paul Blackburn's English version "Blow-Up." Cortázar's text is narrated by a translator, interestingly enough, who is also an amateur photographer. One day, he comes upon a couple that piques his curiosity, an older woman and a teen-aged boy, and he decides to photograph them while speculating about their relationship in a most self-conscious way, treating it as sexual, while remaining aware that he is "guilty of making literature, of indulging in fabricated unrealities" (Cortázar 1967: 124). Cortázar's text is relentlessly self-reflexive: it problematizes the representation of reality in literature through various linguistic and stylistic devices that put into question the narrator's reliability. These devices include constant shifting between first- and third-person points of view, the use of the conditional tense for the narrator's speculative comments, and explicit criticisms of the accuracy of his descriptions.

Suddenly the narrator notices a man sitting in a nearby car, and he revises the sexual scenario he initially saw unfolding between the woman and the boy:

> Y lo que entonces había imaginado era mucho menos horrible que la realidad, esa mujer que no estaba ahí por ella misma, no acariciaba ni proponía ni alentaba para su placer, para llevarse al ángel despeinado y jugar con su terror y su gracia deseosa. El verdadero amo esperaba, sonriendo petulante, seguro ya de la obra; no era el primero que mandaba a una mujer a la vanguardia, a traerle los prisioneros maniatados con flores. El resto sería tan simple, el auto, una casa cualquiera, las bebidas, las láminas excitantes, las lágrimas demasiado tarde, el despertar en el infierno.
>
> *(Cortázar 1959: 69)*

> And what I had imagined earlier was much less horrible than the reality, that woman, who was not there by herself, she was not caressing or propositioning or encouraging for her own pleasure, to lead the angel away with his tousled hair and play the tease with his terror and his eager grace. The real boss was waiting there, smiling petulantly, already certain of the business; he was not the

first to send a woman in the vanguard, to bring him the prisoners manacled with flowers. The rest of it would be so simple, the car, some house or another, drinks, stimulating engravings, tardy tears, the awakening in hell.

(*Cortázar 1967: 129*)

A classroom analysis of Blackburn's translation might begin with this key passage, scrutinizing his use of English dialects and styles that occasionally deviate from the Spanish text. The English version is cast mostly in the current standard dialect, but some choices are distinctly colloquial, whereas the Spanish is consistently written in the standard. Thus Blackburn pointedly renders "el verdadero amo" as "the real boss" and "la obra" as "the business." A Spanish–English lexicon like *Simon and Schuster's International Dictionary* edited by Tana de Gámez or María Moliner's *Diccionario de uso del español* shows Blackburn's hand by indicating a wide spectrum of possible meanings for "amo": they include "master (of the house); head (of the family); owner, proprietor; boss, foreman, overseer." With "obra," a word that can signify such meanings as "work" or "product" and "act" or "deed," Blackburn's use of "business" is more free, but not so much as to constitute a wholesale revision of the Spanish text. Both of his choices reveal an effort to cultivate a strain of colloquialism, and this is confirmed in yet another shift from the Spanish, his insertion of the slangy "tease," which has no corresponding word in Cortázar's text. The word "tease" may not need any lexicographical analysis for anglophone students, but a consultation of the *OED*, especially an entry like "cock-tease," can easily document its sexual resonance. Even with this rapid and selective analysis, it becomes evident that Blackburn's English is doing things that Cortázar's Spanish doesn't do. The shift to a colloquial register introduces what amounts to underworld argot, edging the translated passage towards a noir style. Blackburn's choices exaggerate, even sensationalize the suggestion of a sex crime in the Spanish text, where the boy is assumed to be fifteen years old.

In an undergraduate class that contains students proficient in Spanish, this analysis can be turned into a collaborative activity and extended. Once the instructor has pointed out a few shifts between the Spanish and English, students can locate others on their own and consider the stylistic implications. Colloquialisms occur throughout the translation. Cortázar refers to the teenager variously as "el chico," "el muchacho," "el muchachito," and "el adolescente," whereas Blackburn not only resorts to standard English equivalents like "the boy" and "the young boy," but actually lowers the register by using "the kid" repeatedly (Cortázar 1967: 124, 126, 127). The phrase "el pobre" (the poor [boy]) becomes "the poor kid" (Cortázar 1959: 65; 1967: 125). For "la mujer rubia" (the blond woman), Blackburn similarly substitutes "the blond." The colloquializing tendency sometimes results in free renderings that are tailored to the immediate context, but still maintain a noir style: "resumiendo" (in a word) is turned into "to cut it short," "a disimularlo" (to dissimulate it) into "to play it cool," "para acertar con la verdad" (to guess the truth) into "to hit the bullseye," "socarronamente" (craftily) into "on the sly," "la salida" (the exit) into "the way out" (Cortázar 1959: 62, 64, 65, 66; 1967: 121, 123, 124,

126). At one point, Cortázar's text seems to invite this colloquializing with an image drawn from a sport long associated with the criminal underworld: boxing. The sentence – "el chico había agachado la cabeza, como los boxeadores cuando no pueden más y esperan el golpe de desgracia" (Cortázar 1959: 68) – might be translated closely as "the boy had lowered his head, like boxers when they can do no more and wait for the coup de disgrace." Blackburn's version sacrifices Cortázar's witty play on "coup de grâce" for a more hardboiled lexicon and syntax: "the kid had ducked his head like boxers do when they've done all they can and are waiting for the final blow to fall" (Cortázar 1967: 128). Words like "kid" and "ducked," the use of "like" for "as," and the contraction are noticeably nonstandard usages.

When students are shown how to perform this sort of translation analysis, they will quickly see that Blackburn's style is actually more heterogeneous – even without comparisons to the Spanish text. In the passage I quoted above, the narrator's language turns poetical as he speculates about the man's sexual designs upon the boy. Blackburn's choice of "tardy tears" seems to be partly a literalism for "las lágrimas demasiado tarde" (the too late tears). But with the aid of the *OED* an instructor can demonstrate that "tardy" is one of several poetical archaisms that include "tousled hair" (for "despeinado," "uncombed" or "mussed"), "manacled" (for "maniatados," "hands bound or restrained"), and "stimulating engravings," where "stimulating" is a rather genteel choice for "excitantes," as compared to an alternative like "arousing," which carries a stronger sexual connotation. The deliberateness of Blackburn's choices here, as well as their stylistic significance, can be underscored by referring to earlier passages where he renders two of these same words with colloquialisms: "despeinarlo" is turned into "muss his hair" and "maniatar" into "handcuffing" (Cortázar 1959: 62, 63; 1967: 121, 123). The poeticizing tendency might be described as a Victorian lyricism that works to euphemize what the narrator imagines to be the reality he is witnessing: the woman's seduction of the boy to serve as the object of the man's pederasty.

This analysis rests on several theoretical assumptions which are worth formulating in the classroom as methodological principles. The aim is to read translations as texts in their own right, which are obviously imitative of the source texts they translate but relatively autonomous from those texts because of differences that are both linguistic and literary, structural and cultural. Hence we must abandon notions of equivalence as a one-to-one correspondence, in which a translation is judged acceptable when it apparently reproduces a univocal meaning assumed to be inherent in the foreign text. Several possibilities can be proposed for most words and phrases in any source text. Phrases like "the real boss" and "the business," furthermore, do, in fact, establish a semantic correspondence to the Spanish text based on current dictionary definitions, or in other words a lexicographical equivalence. To dismiss Blackburn's choices as incorrect or inaccurate is not only to ignore this fact, but also to substitute another, unstated criterion of equivalence, perhaps one that gives preference to the current standard dialect of English or to a particular shade of meaning. Blackburn, however, was undoubtedly applying his own criterion, as translators typically do, and it involved the creation of analogues with English-language literary

styles. Translations, even those that adhere closely to the lexical and syntactical features of the source text, produce effects that exceed a lexicographical equivalence and
work only in the translating language and culture. It won't do, then, to insist that
Blackburn's English should match the Spanish in every respect, barring the structural
differences between the languages. The English "tardy" is a calque for the Spanish
"tarde." Not only do they echo each other, but they also share a basic meaning as
well as an etymology. Yet "tardy" has become a poetical archaism, while "tarde"
remains a current standard usage. This effect of the English word is part of the gain
that a translation always inscribes in the source text while losing or deviating from
textual features specific to the source language.

If a world literature course includes a theoretical component, another kind of
supplementary material might be introduced at this point to increase students' critical
sophistication in reading translations: essays in translation studies that take up the topic
of equivalence. To theorize the ratio of loss and gain in Blackburn's translation,
Eugene Nida's concept of "dynamic" equivalence can be fruitfully juxtaposed to
Jacques Derrida's concept of "iterability." Nida argues for an "equivalent effect,"
wherein the translator "is not so concerned with matching the receptor-language
message with the source-language message, but with the dynamic relationship, that
the relationship between receptor and message should be substantially the same as
that which existed between the original receptors and the message" (Nida 1964: 159).
To achieve a dynamic equivalence, the translator "tries to relate the receptor to
modes of behavior within the context of his own culture" (ibid.).

Yet how can an equivalence be achieved, we might ask, if the translating is so
ethnocentric? Won't the equivalence be compromised by the replacement of the
source cultural context with the receiving culture? Blackburn's stylistic analogues are
not present in Cortázar's text, and because they are specific to English-language literary traditions, they insure that the anglophone reader's response to the translation
will differ from the response that the hispanophone reader has to the Spanish text.
We can better understand Blackburn's work by turning to Derridean "iterability," the
idea that the meaning of any sign can change because a sign "can break with every
given context and engender infinitely new contexts in an absolutely nonsaturable
fashion" (Derrida 1982b: 320). Translation partakes of iterability: it is a recontextualizing process that can never produce an equivalent effect because it transforms the
form and theme of the source text, although any transformation is guided fundamentally by structural differences between languages as well as cultural differences
between literary traditions. It is these differences that any translation analysis must
describe and examine insofar as they endow a translated text with significance.

As a result, we must qualify – if not jettison – the instrumental model of translation
that is still widely held by readers, whether professional or popular, scholarly or student. According to this model, translation is the reproduction or transfer of an
invariant contained in or caused by the source text, whether its form, its meaning, or
its effect. To read a translation instrumentally collapses it into the source text and
conceals the translator's labor of transformation. A translation does not reproduce the
source text but rather inscribes an interpretation that varies it according to the

translating language and culture. This interpretation should be articulated for students, not dismissed as arbitrary or irrelevant or displaced by a competing interpretation that the instructor has constructed or culled from specialists in the source-language literature. Blackburn's translation provides ample evidence that he applied what is effectively an interpretant to guide his verbal choices, a stylistic analogue that signifies beyond the Spanish text but is designed to interpret its form and theme. If we treat Blackburn's verbal choices as interpretive moves, if his lexicon and syntax are seen as varying the Spanish text according to forms and meanings that are relevant to that text but related to linguistic usage and literary practices in English, his translation does reflect a careful reading. The mixture of noir and poeticism shapes the characterization of the narrator, indicating his preference for a particular image of what he sees, at once salacious and sensationalizing, threatening and repressively euphemistic.

Here a more general point about literary interpretation might be made for students, namely the idea that interpretation, like translation, is essentially a recontextualizing process, an application of an interpretant to fix the form and meaning of a text that can vary with different interpretants, whether formal (e.g., a theory of interpretation or a concept of equivalence) or thematic (e.g., a code or ideology). To make this point, an instructor might note the similarities and differences between the acts of translation performed by Blackburn and by the translator-photographer who is the narrator. For the narrator also applies an interpretant in his speculations, turning the visual images into a narrative on the basis of a psychoanalytic concept. The Oedipus complex is the *combinatoire* or underlying structure that generates his two conflicting explanations of the interactions between the other characters. He moves from a heterosexual to a homosexual version of what is basically the oedipal triangle, made explicit by the references to the woman and boy as "mother and son" (Cortázar 1967: 118, 123). In effect, the narrator invents scenarios in which he identifies with the emotions that he imputes to the boy, first a masculinist desire for the maternal woman, then a homophobic fear of the paternal man (it is important to keep in mind that he fantasizes the man's homosexuality). The stylistic mix of Blackburn's translation, the combination of hardboiled noir and Victorian poeticism, might therefore be seen as an interrogation of the narrator's unconscious, perhaps his Latin American machismo: the translation highlights his transgressive excitement and his sexual anxiety, his sense that the boy would feel "his manhood diminished" if he fled from the woman, and that the man is trying to commit an "abusive act" beneath a quaintly seductive cover (ibid.: 127, 129).

Thus far, the analysis has been a close reading of translation strategies, assessing their significance in relation to the form and theme of the source text. In the classroom, the analysis might be deepened by situating it in a broader context, the translator's other projects, for instance, or the translation tradition in which those projects emerge. Translation strategies can form fairly continuous traditions with translators adopting similar verbal choices and interpretive moves over long stretches of time or introducing variants and innovations. Blackburn's strategies reflect the modernist experimentalism that characterizes his other projects, including the Provençal troubadours, and these strategies were influenced by Ezra Pound (see Venuti 2008: 194–232).

In his essay "Guido's Relations" (1929), Pound advocates a translating style derived from English-language poetic traditions so as to recreate effects that he perceives in the source text. To render Guido Cavalcanti's thirteenth-century Italian verse, Pound recommends the use of "pre-Elizabethan English," the language of early sixteenth-century poets such as the Tudor courtier Sir Thomas Wyatt and the Scottish cleric Gavin Douglas; and to explain his choice he asserts that these "writers were still intent on clarity and explicitness" (Anderson 1983: 250). Yet Pound underestimates the interpretive dimension of his translating. He believes that the effects he seeks through an early sixteenth-century language are comparable to effects inherent in the Italian texts when, in fact, he is inscribing those texts with his own modernist poetics, applying a formal interpretant that consists of linguistic precision (see Venuti 2008: 166–67; cf. chapter 4: 82). Pound's stylistic analogue recontextualizes both the Italian and the English poetries with a modernist difference, laying the groundwork for their reinterpretation and revaluation.

A similar point can be made of Blackburn's analogues, but because he is translating a contemporary foreign literature, the question of international literary relations comes into play. Here too supplementary materials can be useful to create an interpretive context for the translation. Consider Franco Moretti's controversial effort to reconceptualize comparative literature on the model of world-system theory. He hypothesizes asymmetrical patterns of influence between a "core" represented by the literatures of France, the United Kingdom, and the United States and a "periphery" consisting of other literatures worldwide (Moretti 2000: 56). And from this hypothesis a "law of literary evolution" follows: in the periphery, the modern prose narrative (the novel, for Moretti) "first arises not as an autonomous development but as a compromise between a western formal influence (usually French or English) and local materials," which he ultimately specifies as "*foreign plot*; local *characters*; and then, local *narrative voice*" (ibid.: 58, 65, his emphases). This theory might provoke various questions during a translation analysis, although perhaps the case of Blackburn's Cortázar gives special urgency to one in particular: What happens when a narrative from the global periphery is translated into a core language like English with an English-language stylistic analogue?

Cortázar's text does indeed seem to exemplify the often unstable "structural compromise" at the heart of Moretti's theory, which, however, might need to be qualified because of the textual effects of Blackburn's translation (Moretti 2000: 62). The narrator, one Roberto Michel, is identified as French-Chilean, and the plot that structures his speculations about the woman, man, and boy, insofar as it involves an element of suspense and criminality, derives from the British and American detective stories that began to circulate in Argentina in the late nineteenth century and were also used in innovative ways by Cortázar's countryman Jorge Luis Borges. The noir style in Blackburn's translation, then, exposes the hybrid literary conditions of Cortázar's text, its anglophone formal roots made more self-conscious by Borges's experiments. Yet Cortázar's text comes back to worry Blackburn's stylistic analogue by defamiliarizing it: the psychoanalytic representation of gender and sexual roles interrogates the masculinism typical of noir, exposing its psychological conditions.

A translation strategy, especially if it inscribes a rich intertextual network, can be seen as initiating a critical dialectic between the source and translated texts, a mutual interrogation, whose significance can be articulated by reconstructing the literary traditions, cultural situations, and historical moments in which those texts are produced and circulate. Blackburn's translation belongs to the so-called "boom" in Latin American literature during the 1960s and 1970s, the wave of translations that formed a new canon of foreign literature in English and altered contemporary fiction in the United States, encouraging writers like John Barth to develop related narrative experiments (see Payne 1993: chapter 1). Translation complicates Moretti's theory by opening up another level of potentially unstable structural compromise, one that can enable literary texts from the periphery to destabilize a core literature.

I have tried to sketch a pedagogy of translated literature on the basis of a single translation, but other approaches are possible, perhaps desirable in some cases. Archaic texts that are repeatedly retranslated offer an opportunity to juxtapose different versions of the same passage, revealing different strategies and interpretations (see Venuti 1998: 99–102). The notion of translation might be construed with latitude to include various second-order forms and practices, so that interlingual translations are studied alongside imitations and adaptations in different media. Cortázar's text also became the basis of an intersemiotic translation, *Blowup*, Michelangelo Antonioni's 1966 film adaptation. Whatever the media, however, the pedagogy must include a detailed comparison of the source material and the second-order work so as to locate shifts or variations, the significant differences from which strategies, interpretations, and values can be inferred and subsequently contextualized in cultural and social terms. What may most recommend raising the issue of translation in the classroom is the renewed emphasis it places on reading closely and carefully.

[2009]

11

THE POET'S VERSION; OR, AN ETHICS OF TRANSLATION

Why poetry?

Today poetry may well be the least translated literary genre, no matter where the translating literature ranks in the global hierarchy of symbolic capital that is so unevenly distributed among national literary traditions (see Casanova 2004). Because the hegemonic anglophone cultures have long translated less, their figures for poetry offer no surprise (Venuti 2008: 11–12). Every spring, Poets House in New York City showcases most books of poetry published in the United States during the previous year, building an online bibliography that enables a comprehensive view of the contemporary scene. Translations comprise a tiny fraction of total annual output, hovering at 5–8%. In 2009, United States publishers brought out approximately 2,200 books of poetry, but only about 115 were translations (just over 5.2%). Much lower in the global cultural hierarchy, in Slovenia, for instance, the situation is not much better, even if the considerably lower figures reflect the smaller size of the publishing industry. In 2009, Slovenian publishers brought out approximately 300 books of poetry, including 33 translations (11%) (Kastelic 2010). In a culture like Italy, where since the 1980s translations have constituted 20–26% of new titles each year, more poetry is translated, but again the percentage is small compared to native production: in 2009, Italian publishers brought out 3,769 books of poetry, which included 520 translations (13.77%) (Peresson and Mussinelli 2009; Mondadori's publicity department provided the 2009 data). If in sheer quantitative terms poetry translation appears to be such a marginal genre in the West (and no doubt in other locations as well), why should we devote our attention to the study of it?

The marginality is, in fact, the first reason to move poetry closer to the center of translation studies. Poetry translation attracts a narrow audience and therefore occupies a tenuous position in the process of commodification that allows other literary genres, notably the novel, to become lucrative investments on the foreign rights market. In the United States, most poetry translations are issued by small and university presses, limiting their print run and distribution and making many of them ephemeral publications. These factors, as Pierre Bourdieu observes of poetry in general, turn its translation into "the disinterested activity *par excellence*," determining that it will invite not only "charismatic legitimation" but also "a succession of successful or abortive revolutions" as translators seek to garner "poetic legitimacy" by distinguishing their work (Bourdieu 1993: 51). Released from the constraint to turn a profit, poetry translation is more likely to encourage experimental strategies that can reveal what is unique about translation as a linguistic and cultural practice.

It is the uniqueness of poetry as a form of language use that occasions any such revelations. "The poem," argues Alain Badiou, "does not consist in communication" because it performs two operations: a "subtraction" from "objective reality," whereby the poem "declares its own universe" and "utters being, or the idea, at the very point where the object has vanished," and a "dissemination" which "aims to dissolve the object through an infinite metaphorical distribution," so that "no sooner is it mentioned than the object migrates elsewhere within meaning" through "an excessive equivalence to other objects" (Badiou 2004: 233, 236–37). To translate a poem, then, regardless of the language, culture, or historical moment, has often meant to create a poem in the receiving situation, to cultivate poetic effects that may seek to maintain an equivalence to the source text but that fall short of and exceed it because the translation is written in a different language for a different culture. The source-language poem "migrates" in the sense that it inevitably vanishes during the translation process, replaced by a network of signification – intertextual, interdiscursive, intersemiotic – that is rooted mainly in the receiving situation. As a result, poetry translation tends to release language from the narrowly defined communicative function that most translations are assumed to serve, whether the genre of their source texts is technical, pragmatic, or humanistic – namely, the communication of a formal or semantic invariant contained in the source text. Poetry translation casts doubt on this assumption: in the fact that the same source-language poem can support multiple translations which are extremely different yet equally acceptable as poems or translations, we glimpse the possibility that no invariant exists, that the practice of translation is fundamentally variation.

The emergence of the version

I want to pursue this point by considering a development in the history of translation. The past century witnessed the creation and conceptualization of an unprecedented form of translating poetry and poetic drama practiced mostly by poets. Variously called a "translation" or "adaptation," an "imitation" or "version," the resulting text derives from a specified source, but it may depart so widely from that source as to constitute a wholesale revision that answers primarily to the poet-translator's literary interests. Or it may involve a source language of which the poet has limited knowledge or is completely ignorant, therefore requiring the use of a close rendering prepared by a native informant, an academic specialist, or a professional translator. Such translating can be found in many modern literatures, whether written in hegemonic or in minor languages, whether invested with considerable or with little symbolic capital. Notable instances include such European poets as Paul Celan and Boris Pasternak, but also the Brazilian Haroldo de Campos and the Syrian Adonis. I shall base my discussion primarily on anglophone cases, however, focusing on the work of poets in the United Kingdom where this form of translating has provoked controversy.

Not only has it been viewed as ethically questionable, but also the poets who have practiced it have not always been forthright about what exactly they have done. In 2007, for instance, the year after Robin Robertson published his "versions" of Tomas Tranströmer's poems, they were roundly criticized by Robin Fulton, the Swedish poet's main English translator. Fulton insinuated that Robertson had committed plagiarism ("An excessively large number of Robertson's lines are identical to mine in my Tranströmer translations"), and he claimed that because Robertson did not know the Swedish language he had done violence to the poems ("His versions are neither dependable translations nor independent imitations: they show a cavalier disregard for Tranströmer's texts") (Fulton 2007: 17). Fulton's use of the phrase "independent imitations" suggests that perhaps we should consider the poet's version a *dependent* imitation: it is dependent on the poet-translator's own work or on the work of other translators or on both, but while following the source text in varying degrees, it allows for departures that are not found in "dependable translations." Fulton's distinction implicitly defines a translation as a close rendering.

Such a distinction between translation and imitation differs from the application of these terms in the early modern period, so that the poet's version is not to be confused with the form of translating that John Dryden called "imitation." In the preface to his anthology *Ovid's Epistles* (1680), Dryden put imitation under the rubric of translation, even if he entertained some doubt about this classification because the poet-translator

> assumes the liberty not only to vary from the words and sence, but to forsake them both as he sees occasion: and taking only some general hints from the Original, to run division on the ground-work, as he pleases.
>
> *(Dryden 1956: 114–15)*

Here the departures are deliberate, reflecting not ignorance of the source language but knowledge of it. Hence the imitator is said "to run division on the ground-work," a musical metaphor in which imitation is compared to executing a variation on a theme. Not only must the imitator be capable of comprehending the musical theme or source text, but also the imitation aims to establish a certain kind of equivalence to it. Dryden's example was Abraham Cowley's *Pindarique Odes* (1656), where, he pointed out, "the Customs and Ceremonies of Ancient *Greece* are still preserv'd," and Cowley "alone was able to make him [Pindar] amends, by giving him better of his own, when ever he refus'd his Authours thoughts" (Dryden 1956: 117). In Dryden's view, Cowley's imitation of Pindar produced a stylistic equivalence, regardless of his lexical and syntactical departures, which are seen not as corruptions but as improvements of the Greek texts. Imitation is not, moreover, a form of translating that is suitable for every foreign poet. Pindar's obscurity, Dryden argued, demands imitation because "So wild and ungovernable a Poet cannot be Translated literally," whereas "if *Virgil* or *Ovid*, or any regular intelligible Authours be us'd thus, 'tis no longer to be call'd their work" (ibid.). Although Dryden clearly assumed a contemporary consensus regarding the interpretation of these classical poets, namely, a general agreement about the nature of their distinctive styles, his thinking consistently emphasized the importance of maintaining a relation of equivalence to the source language and text. The equivalence was grounded on that very interpretation.

In the twentieth century, in contrast, the poet's version routinely involved departures from the source text that were motivated by the imposition of a different poetics or by mere ignorance of the source language, although in some cases both factors were operating. This form of translating was decisively influenced by Ezra Pound, if it did not simply originate with him. His 1912 version of "The Seafarer" tampers with the extant Anglo-Saxon text by secularizing it: he not only omitted the Christian references but also deleted the homiletic conclusion of more than twenty lines. Because Pound knew little Chinese, he relied mainly on the Sinologist Ernest Fenollosa's notes when he drafted the free renderings of classical Chinese poems gathered in his 1915 book *Cathay*.

Pound's collected translations were published in 1954, and partly as a result, but also partly because of a more general tendency of modernist poets to make translation a stage in the compositional process (see Hooley 1988; Yao 2002), similar forms of translating began to appear more frequently. Robert Lowell's 1961 volume *Imitations* contained his versions of classical and modern poems in which he admitted to being so "reckless with literal meaning" as to "have dropped lines, moved lines, moved stanzas, changed images and altered meter and intent" (Lowell 1961: xi, xii). Although Lowell included a significant number of Russian poems, he confessed that "I know no Russian," adding that "I have rashly tried to improve on other translations, and have been helped by exact prose versions given me by Russian readers" (ibid.: xii). Christopher Logue's Homeric adaptations, starting with *Patrocleia* in 1962, were not made with any knowledge of Greek. Instead, Logue relied on the classicist Donald Carne-Ross, who "provided translations retaining Greek word order," and he consulted five previous renderings of the *Iliad* that included George Chapman's and Alexander Pope's as well as those in the Loeb Classical Library and Penguin Classics (Logue 2001: vii).

By the end of the twentieth century, the poet's version had become a veritable genre of literary translation. Don Paterson's 1999 volume *The Eyes: A version of Antonio Machado* was drawn not so much from the Spaniard's poetry as from the Hispanist Alan Trueblood's 1982 bilingual selection. Paterson described Trueblood's renderings as "solid literal translations," admitting that he had, "without acknowledgement, stolen lines of his because they seemed pretty much unimprovable" (Paterson 1999: 60). As if anticipating the ethical question raised by his admission of plagiarism, Paterson's afterword offered a frank account of his work that demonstrated the precision and sophistication then possible in explaining what a version is, along with the utter familiarity of the practice. "In writing these versions," he stated,

> I initially tried to be true to a poem's argument and to its vision – if not its individual images – and to the poetic conventions of the language in which I was writing, rather than to its lexis. […] This quickly became the more familiar project of trying to make a musical and argumentative unity of the material at hand, and this consideration, in overriding all others, led to mangling, shifts of emphasis, omission, deliberate mistranslation, the conflation of different poems, the insertion of whole new lines and on a few occasions the writing of entirely new poems.
>
> *(Paterson 1999: 56)*

Paterson has not completely abandoned the notion of equivalence, although his thinking is very far from Dryden's view of imitation as maintaining a stylistic resemblance. As Paterson explained, "the only defensible fidelity is to the entirely subjective quality of 'spirit' or 'vision,' rather than to literal meaning" (ibid.: 58). The version would thus seem to assume an ethics of sheer self-interest, where poetic license has been redefined as the privileging of the poet's interpretation according to the strength of its originality autonomous from the source text – an originality that can only remain dubious, however, insofar as it rests on the use of previous translations and deploys the poetic conventions of the language in which the poet is writing. In Paterson's words, "There are several Antonio Machados, but I've tried to write the poem Machado is for me" (ibid.: 55). Whereas Dryden assumed that the interpretation of a foreign poet enjoyed a consensus in the receiving culture, an agreement among informed readers that validated the translation or imitation, Paterson assumes that the source text is the site of competing interpretations, and the versioning poet selects or constructs the one that answers to a personal preference.

What remained constant in the development of the version during the twentieth century was not only the poet's admittedly self-serving manipulation of the source text and limited-to-no knowledge of the source language, but also the rationale that a version aimed at producing an original composition. What changed in most cases was the resulting text, the nature and effect of the poet's verbal choices. Thus Pound concluded his 1929 essay "Guido's Relations" by distinguishing sharply between the "interpretative" translation, prepared as an "accompaniment" to the source text and usually printed *en face*, and "the other sort of translation," what we recognize today as the version, which, as he described it, "falls simply in the domain of original writing, or if it does not it must be censured according to equal standards" (Anderson 1983: 251). For Pound, however, the "standards" used to judge a translation as an original composition included a discursive heterogeneity that was both an innovation of modernist poetics and a deviation from the linguistic and literary values that currently prevailed. Hence the archaizing strategy of "The Seafarer" and the precise yet discontinuous style of poems in *Cathay* like "The River Merchant's Wife: A Letter." As the century unfolded, Pound's translation experimentalism was avoided more often than not, so that poets' versions, like most translations, tended to be modern but not modernist, cultivating a fluent discourse that adhered to the current standard dialect of English.

This trend can be perceived in Paterson's effort to distinguish between a translation and a version in *Orpheus*, his 2006 rendering of Rilke's *Sonnets to Orpheus*. "A translation," Paterson explained,

> tries to remain true to the original words and their relations, and its primary aim is usually one of stylistic elegance (meaning, essentially, the smooth elimination of syntactic and idiomatic artefacts from the original tongue: a far more subtle project than it sounds) – of which lyric unity is only one of several competing considerations. [...] Versions, however, are trying to be poems in their own right; while they have the original to serve as detailed ground-plan and elevation, they are trying to build themselves a robust home in a new country, in its vernacular architecture, with local words for its brick and local music for its mortar.
>
> *(Paterson 2006: 73)*

Paterson's reference to "stylistic elegance" as the aim for translations glances at the narrowly defined fluency that came to dominate literary translation in the twentieth century, a "smooth" or easy readability (Venuti 2008: chapter 1). Yet his architectural metaphor for versions turns out to be vague and ultimately evasive, for even a cursory reading of his Machado and Rilke reveals that they are characterized by the same stylistic elegance: they are remarkably fluent in assimilating to current standard English the source texts as well as the translations on which he relied, so much so that nonstandard forms have been excluded, both "vernacular" or colloquial items and "local words" in the sense of regional or social dialects. Paterson's versions lack the lexical and syntactical peculiarities that recur in his own poetry, notably the use of slang and Scottish dialect. Thus he has effectively discarded Pound's concept of the translation as original composition by producing versions according to the same standards that he questions in translations.

A hermeneutic model

The poet's version, clearly an amalgam of what we understand today as translation and adaptation, close rendering and free rewriting, raises a range of questions about language, literature, and ethics. To explore these questions further, however, we must abandon the instrumental model of translation, the notion that a translation reproduces or transfers an invariant that is contained in or caused by the source text, whether its form, its meaning, or its effect. This widely held model not only locks translation studies and practices into a limiting and obfuscating comparison between the source text and the translation, but also conceals both the translator's interpretive labor and its linguistic and cultural conditions. As this point suggests, I regard as misleading Pound's distinction between the "interpretative" translation and the translation that is "original writing," as I do Paterson's assertion that "interpretation must precede the acts of both versioning and translation" (Paterson 2006: 78). Every second-order creation, I argue, in any medium regardless of its material basis, is an interpretation enacted during the production process and subject to further inter-pretation by the gamut of receptors who use it, whether the work in question is a translation or an imitation, a textual edition or an anthology, a dramatic or film adaptation, even a museum exhibition.

To be more precise, although in the field of literature translation can certainly be distinguished from adaptation (even if that distinction is historically variable, drawn differently in different periods), both second-order practices are more helpfully understood on the basis of a hermeneutic model. Here they are treated as an inter-pretation of the source text, one among differing and potentially conflicting possibi-lities, which vary the form, meaning, and effect of that text. In advancing this hermeneutic model, I am not suggesting that no formal or semantic correspondences can exist between the source text, on the one hand, and the translation or adaptation, on the other, but rather that any such correspondences are shaped by the exigencies of an interpretive act that is decisively determined by the translating language and culture. The translation or adaptation inscribes its interpretation at every stage in the writing process, starting from the very choice of the source text and including every verbal choice.

Consider the case of a poet-translator from antiquity, perhaps the first poet-translator in the West to conceive of translation as literary, as a process of producing a relatively autonomous literary work (Conte 1999: 40). In the third century BCE, Livius Andronicus, thought to be a Greek born at Tarentum in what is now Apulia in southern Italy, worked as a grammarian teaching Greek and Latin, wrote plays and poems in Latin, and produced a Latin version of the *Odyssey* which today survives only in fragments, as many as forty-five or so phrases and lines, some of doubtful authorship (ibid.: 39–40). Andronicus chose the Latin word *dacrimas* to render the Greek *dakru* (δάκρυ) in his version of a passage where Ulysses wipes away his tears while listening to a singer at the palace of Alcinous (*Odyssey* 8.88; Warmington 1936: 32). *Dacrima* is the archaic Latin form of *lacrima*, or "tear," so for Andronicus' first readers, many of whom were most likely familiar with the Greek text, his verbal choice was seen as an interpretive move, producing an archaizing effect that can signal the historical remoteness of the Homeric epic while creating an elevated tone distinct from ordinary usage and thus suitable to the seriousness of the genre (Lewis and Short 1879, s.v. "lacrima"; Conte 1999, 40–41). In fact, it would have caused this effect whether or not the Roman reader had read the Greek text insofar as Andronicus chose an archaism that could be perceived as such. The example demonstrates that even translations that adhere closely to the source text – so closely as to be calques that echo the very sound of its words – release resonances that exceed a formal and semantic correspondence and ultimately have more to do with the translating language. I would go further: because translation performs an interpretation, it can never be literal, only figurative, or more precisely inscriptive of effects that work only in the translating language and culture.

Translation should be seen as interpretation because it is radically decontextualizing. The structural differences between languages, even between languages that bear significant lexical and syntactical resemblances based on shared etymologies or a history of mutual borrowing or analogous formal features like inflections, require the translator variously to dismantle, rearrange, and finally displace the chain of signifiers that make up the source text. Three source-language contexts are lost. The first is intratextual and therefore constitutive of the source text, of its linguistic patterns and discursive structures, its verbal texture. The second is intertextual (in the sense of relations to pre-existing texts) and interdiscursive (in the sense of relations to pre-existing forms and themes) yet equally constitutive, since it comprises the network of linguistic relations that endows the source text with significance for readers who have read widely in the source language. The third, which is also constitutive but at once intertextual, interdiscursive, and intersemiotic, is the context of reception, the various media through which the source text continues to accrue significance when it begins to circulate in its originary culture, ranging from editorial decisions like typography, trim size, and binding to jacket blurbs, author photos, and advertisements to periodical reviews, academic criticism, and internet blogs to different editions, anthology extracts, and adaptations of various kinds (dramatic, film, comic strip). By "constitutive," I mean that this triple context comprises the signifying process of the source text, allowing it to support meanings, values, and functions which therefore never survive intact the transition to a different language and culture.

As a result, a reader of a translation can never experience it with a response that is equivalent or even comparable to the response with which the source-language reader experiences the source text, that is to say a reader who has read widely in the source language and is immersed in the source culture. Not even a bilingual reader familiar with both the source and the translating cultures will experience the two texts in the same or a similar way. The strategies that Andronicus implemented in his *Odyssey* included a Latinization of the Greek names for mythological and heroic figures. *Kronos* became *Saturnus*, *Musa* became *Camena* ("Song-Goddess"), *Moira* ("Fate") became *Morta* ("Death"), *Odysseus* became *Ulixes*, *Hermes* became *Mercurius*, and the muse Mnemosyne was called *Moneta* (*Odyssey* 1.1, 1.45, 2.99, 8.322–23, 8.480–81; Warmington 1936: 24, 28, 32, 34). These choices entailed the loss of Greek cultural references. The bilingual Roman reader schooled in Greek literature could no doubt have supplied the loss of context, but that reader would have simultaneously perceived the disjunction created by Andronicus' interpretive moves. A reader of the Greek text, whether that reader was Roman or Greek, would have perceived no such disjunction.

As the case of Andronicus makes clear, the interpretive force of translation means that the source text is not only decontextualized, but also *recontextualized* insofar as translating rewrites it in terms that are intelligible and interesting to receptors, situating it in different patterns of language use, in different cultural values, in different literary traditions, and in different social institutions. The recontextualizing process involves the creation of another set of intertextual and interdiscursive relations established by and within the translation, a receiving intertext. When translated, then, the source text undergoes not only a formal and semantic loss, but also an exorbitant gain: in an effort to fix the form and meaning of that text, the translator develops an interpretation in the translating language that ultimately proliferates cultural differences. The extant lines of Andronicus' *Odyssey* indicate that his version may well have been not only Latinized, but also more explicitly detailed than the Greek text. In the passage where Alcinous' daughter Nausicaä invites Ulysses to visit her, Andronicus inserted the phrase *me carpento vehentem* ("driving in my carriage") which has no Greek counterpart in the Homeric poem (*Odyssey* 6.295; Warmington 1936: 22). The Latin version thus supplied a Roman context: Andronicus added a reference to the *carpentum*, a two-wheeled carriage that was used by Roman matrons in processions during public festivities (Lewis and Short 1879, s.v. "carpentum").

Such verbal choices are not simply linguistic, but also cultural. They do not simply render words and phrases, but also establish culturally specific meanings. The translator inscribes an interpretation by applying a category that mediates between the source language and culture, on the one hand, and the translating language and culture, on the other, a method of transforming the source text into the translation. This category consists of *interpretants*, which may be either formal or thematic. Formal interpretants may include a concept of equivalence, such as a semantic correspondence based on philological research or dictionaries, or a concept of style, a distinctive lexicon and syntax related to a genre or discourse. Thematic interpretants are codes: values, beliefs, and representations that may be affiliated to specific social groups and institutions; a discourse in the sense of a relatively coherent body of concepts, problems, and arguments; or a particular interpretation of the source text that has been articulated independently in commentary. The modern poet's version, for example, often begins with a specific formal interpretant, a distinctive poetics or a pre-existing translation by another hand, both of which are simultaneously thematic, encoded by the repertoire of topics that the versioning poet has treated in his or her poetry or by the previous translator's interpretation which undergoes revision according to a different set of interpretants applied by the poet. Interpretants are fundamentally intertextual and interdiscursive, based primarily in the receiving situation even if in some cases they may incorporate materials specific to the source culture. It is the translator's application of interpretants that recontextualizes the source text, replacing relations to the source culture with a receiving intertext, with relations to the translating language and culture which are built into the translation.

The concept of the interpretant helps to clarify Andronicus' handling of the *Odyssey*. He applied several formal interpretants: they included an archaizing style that drew on lexical and syntactical items from Old Latin, but also a certain poetic form, the Saturnian meter, which is thought to have been native to Latin poetic traditions, reserved for genres like epitaphs and triumphal commemorations which match the solemnity of epic. He chose not to develop a prosody based on the Greek hexameter, a practice that distinguished the work of later poets like Ennius. Andronicus also adopted a concept of equivalence, whereby, for the most part, he maintained a semantic correspondence to the Greek text. Unlike such later Roman writers as Plautus, Horace, and Catullus, he seems not to have relied wholly on adaptation, even if his translating included departures and interpolations. In these instances, he applied a thematic interpretant, evident both in his Latinization of Greek cultural references and in his insertion of Latin terms like *carpentum*: he encoded his translation with distinctively Roman values. Another example of this encoding occurs with an epithet used to describe Patroclus, *theophin mestor atalantos* (θεόφιν μήστωρ ἀτάλαντος; 3.110), which can be rendered as "the peer of the gods in counsel." Andronicus, however, substituted *vir summus adprimus*, "the very first of men," expressing an early Roman reticence towards any erasure of the metaphysical distinction between human and divine, a reticence that did not survive the Republic (Warmington 1936: 26). "In Rome," Denis Feeney has observed, "no human was the object of a [divinizing] cult between Romulus/Quirinus and Julius Caesar" (Feeney 1998: 110).

The translator's interpretation is always performed in and influenced by a cultural situation where values, beliefs, and representations as well as the social groups to which they are affiliated are arrayed in a hierarchical order of power and prestige. And the intertextual and interdiscursive relations established by the interpretation affect both the source text and texts in the translating culture. These relations are created by reproducing a pre-existing word, phrase, or passage in the translating language, whether specifically through quotation or more generally through imitation of graphemes and sound, lexicon and syntax, style and discourse. In a translation, as in an original composition, quotation and imitation do not produce sameness or a simple repetition of the pre-existing text. As soon as the reader recognizes the intertextuality, a difference also becomes apparent because of what Jacques Derrida has called the "iterability" of language, the change in meaning that can occur with a change in context (Derrida 1982b: 320). A translation, then, recontextualizes both the source text that it translates and the translating-language text that it quotes or imitates, submitting them to a transformation that changes their significance. Hence the intertextual and interdiscursive relations that a translation establishes are not merely interpretive, but also potentially interrogative: they inscribe forms and meanings that invite a critical understanding of the quoted or imitated texts – even the cultural traditions and social institutions in which those texts are positioned – while simultaneously inviting the reader to understand the source text on the basis of texts, traditions, and institutions specific to the translating culture.

Andronicus is thought to have been a freed slave, and so his Latinized translation may actually reflect both his deep investment in his Greek cultural origins and his strong attachment to the dominant Roman culture of which he was a contributing member. Later Roman writers such as Cicero and Horace considered him to be the initiator of Latin literature, and his version of the *Odyssey* was adopted as a school textbook for the next two centuries, probably used to teach Greek (Conte 1999: 40). Whether or not Andronicus' hybridity is taken as complicating his intentions as a translator, whether, in other words, his agency as a colonial subject is conflicted in some decisive way, we can nonetheless see that his reference to the Roman *carpentum* constitutes a node of proliferating meanings in his translation. On the one hand, the specialized and privileged nature of this carriage – linked to Roman matrons, used most frequently on festive occasions, otherwise banned from the city during the entire era of the Republic – makes it an appropriate vehicle for a king's daughter like Nausicaä and simultaneously points to the limited circumstances of the Homeric poem, the product of an oral archaic culture at a rudimentary stage of literary and social development (Smith 1875: 242–43). On the other hand, the Greek text comes back to worry Roman culture through the very word *carpentum*, creating a context that not only highlights the very sophistication of that culture but also exposes the class and gender ideologies that informed it, even in such mundane objects as a carriage. This reading would have been available to Andronicus' first audience, I suggest, again whether Latin or bilingual, because they would have been sensitive to such cultural and historical distinctions. Today only an elite reader, a reader with the specialized knowledge of a classicist, might entertain it.

Yet who would read the fragments of Andronicus' translation in the way that I have? It would have to be a reader who shares my assumption of the hermeneutic model in analyzing those fragments as an interpretive inscription that rests on intertextual and interdiscursive relations in the receiving culture. The reader must further put the translator's inscription to a thoroughgoing historical contextualization, treating it as operating in a specific cultural situation where values and practices are arranged hierarchically, where hierarchical relations likewise characterize intercultural relations, and where practices like translation are active both in the formation of cultural identities for social agents and in the functioning of the social institutions where those agents work. The reader would also have to deploy ideas about language and translation that have been formulated by poststructuralist thinkers like Derrida, restricting the plurality of possible interpretations supported by the fragments while emphasizing the most interrogative among them. The reader I am describing, in other words, must apply a specific set of *critical* interpretants so as to infer and formulate the interpretation inscribed by a translation. Critical interpretants may also be formal or thematic, including, for instance, a methodological assumption like the hermeneutic model or a philosophical discourse that encompasses a theory of value.

Every interpretation is fundamentally evaluative insofar as it rests on the implicit judgment that a text is worth interpreting, not only in commentary but also through translation or adaptation (Smith 1988: 10–11). Andronicus' decision to render the *Odyssey* initiated what would subsequently become the routine practice of Roman writers, the exploitation of the cultural prestige of Greece by translating Greek models to develop a competing Latin literature. Interpretants, moreover, are always already implicated in the hierarchies of value that structure the receiving culture at a particular historical moment, its centers and peripheries, its canons and margins. Andronicus' decision to Latinize Greek mythology deferred to linguistic and cultural norms in Rome. Yet because a translation or adaptation necessarily transforms the source text by detaching it from its originary context and simultaneously recontextualizing it, neither can be evaluated merely through a comparison to that text without taking into account the cultural and social conditions of their interpretation.

The evaluation must be shifted to a different level that seems to me properly ethical: in inscribing an interpretation in the source text, a translation or adaptation can stake out an ethical position and thereby serve an ideological function in relation to competing interpretations. Although Andronicus applied interpretants that reinforced dominant cultural forms and practices in the Roman Republic, he brought into Latin what did not exist there before, the poetic genre known as the epic. He thus performed a creative act that could not be judged by current literary norms, creating a generic subset within which the translating subject was marked as neither specifically Greek nor Latin, and that, in putting to new uses archaic linguistic and literary forms, Old Latin and the Saturnian meter, left open the possibility of other versions enabled by different interpretants, formal and thematic, and different combinations thereof, whether residual, dominant, or emergent.

An ethics of translation

Here I am drawing on Alain Badiou's thinking, specifically his concept of a truth-based ethics. For Badiou, truth is not adequacy to reality or illumination; it is rather an investigative process set going by an "event, which brings to pass 'something other' than the situation" defined by "opinions" and "instituted knowledges" (Badiou 2001: 67). The event simultaneously locates and supplements a "void" or lack in that situation, creating a subject who committedly maintains a "break" with it by articulating and investigating the consequences of the event, the ramifications of the idea, form, or practice that acquires such value as to be called a "truth." "It is by violating established and circulating knowledges," remarks Badiou, "that a truth returns to the immediacy of the situation, or reworks that sort of portable encyclopedia from which opinions, communications and sociality draw their meaning" (ibid.: 70). A truth is specific to the situation from which it arises, yet its address is universal, equally applicable to every individual who becomes a subject committed to the truth process, who works within the universe constructed by that process. A truth, however, stops short of asserting a totalizing power that is exclusionary or repressive because it is grounded on an "unnameable," an element that lies outside its conceptual grasp. "Unnameable," Badiou points out, "should be understood not in terms of the available resources of knowledge and encyclopedia, but in the precise sense in which it remains out of reach for the veridical anticipations founded on truth" (Badiou 2004: 130). To acknowledge the existence of an unnameable, a point of indiscernment that escapes the truth process, is to refuse to impose the truth as definitive.

   This process represents what is good. It becomes bad when inverted in a pseudo-event that locates not a void in the situation but a "plenitude" or "substance" and thus results in a "simulacrum of truth" (Badiou 2001: 72–73). Far from being universally addressed, the simulacrum is affiliated with "the absolute particularity of a community" that admits or excludes individuals (ibid.: 73–74). To be committed to a simulacrum is to seek to totalize its power by incorporating every element within its interested knowledge, thereby affixing a name to the unnameable (ibid.: 85–87). In

Badiou's thinking, the ethics of truth promotes innovation and equality, serving a "disinterested interest" that is shared universally, whereas the unethical simulacrum enforces conformity and domination, serving the interest of a particular community (ibid.: 49, 74).

Badiou's ethics raises a number of questions, not the least of which is the nature of his antipathy towards the communitarian (ibid.: 73–74), as if every social grouping were exclusionary or repressive, as if it were possible to imagine a social formation or perform a political action without such groupings and their hierarchical relations. His answer is that a collective emerges when subjects are formed in their commitment to an event that changes the situation and establishes their equality in the investigative process of a truth (Badiou 2008: 163). I want to question this point in his thinking insofar as no truth process can occur apart from an institutional site: Badiou's very definition of an event assumes a break from yet within an institution precisely because every institution encompasses competing ideas, forms, and practices, which, upon their emergence, always take up a position in hierarchies. The unethical should be seen not as knowledge that serves any communitarian interest whatsoever, but only as knowledge affiliated with a group that has achieved such dominance in an institution as to exclude or marginalize the competing knowledges of other groups.

A translation, then, might be evaluated according to its impact, potential or real, on cultural and social institutions in the receiving situation, according to whether it challenges the styles, genres, and discourses that have gained institutional authority, according to whether it stimulates innovative thinking, research, and writing. The bad in translation is "the desire to name *at any price*" (Badiou 2008: 127), imposing cultural norms that seek to master cognitively and thereby deny the singularity that stands beyond them, excluding the alternative set of interpretants that enable a different translation, a different interpretation. Hence a translation, including a poet's version, should not be faulted merely for exhibiting features that are commonly called unethical: wholesale manipulation of the source text, ignorance of the source language, even plagiarism of other translations. We should instead examine the cultural and social conditions of the translation, considering whether its interpretants initiate an event, creating new knowledges and values by supplying a lack that they indicate in those that are currently dominant in the receiving situation. The lack may be an interpretant that a poet's version can or cannot supply, for instance, a concept of equivalence that involves a semantic correspondence or even close adherence to the source text. The most authoritative and widely circulated translations may themselves not apply such an interpretant, or, if they do, a new edition of the source text or a new, independently articulated interpretation of it may require that the concept of equivalence applied in previous translations be revised in a retranslation (cf. chapter 5). Nonetheless, no interpretant can be regarded as inherently valuable, apart from its situation in a specific culture at a specific historical moment.

The ethics of translation I am outlining here also follows Badiou in avoiding any treatment of the bad as "the non-respect of the name of the Other" (Badiou

2008: 127). This move is made by a theorist such as Antoine Berman, who in *La traduction et la lettre* (*Translation and the letter* [1985]) argues that translation can and ought to respect the differences of foreign texts and cultures through discursive strategies designed to show or make manifest ("révéler, manifester") those differences, while resisting any ethnocentric reduction or removal of them (Berman 1999: 76). In characterizing translation as a "manifestation," Berman draws on Heidegger's concept of truth as disclosure. "To say that an assertion '*is true*' signifies that it uncovers the entity as it is in itself," argues Heidegger in *Being and Time* (1927), where "the *Being-true* (*truth*) of the assertion must be understood as *Being-uncovering*," or allowing the entity to be seen "in its uncoveredness" (Heidegger 1962: 261; cf. Massardier-Kenney 2010, 266). In the "Letter on Humanism" (1947), Heidegger explicitly makes language the site where "being" is disclosed:

> Language is the house of being. In its home human beings dwell. Those who think and those who create with words are the guardians of this home. Their guardianship accomplishes the manifestation [*Offenbarkeit*] of being insofar as they bring this manifestation to language and preserve it in language through their saying.
>
> *(Heidegger 1947: 193)*

We can grasp the Heideggerian assumptions in Berman's thinking by substituting, in this passage, "the foreignness of the foreign text" for "being," "translators" for "human beings," and "translations" for "saying." Thus in Berman's formulation the ethical dimension of translation is "the desire to disclose the Foreign as Foreign in its own linguistic space" ("désir d'ouvrir l'Étranger en tant qu'Étranger à son proper espace de langue"; Berman 1999: 75, where this statement is italicized). To achieve this Heideggerian manifestation of the foreign, Berman recommends a particular formal interpretant, "fidelity" to the "letter," to the linguistic features and signifying structures of the source text, or what is in effect a literalizing strategy ("fidélité [...] à la lettre"; ibid.: 77). He finds Hölderlin's versions of Sophocles exemplary precisely because the German poet's strategies include "etymologizing literalism" ("littéralisme étymologisant"), whereby "Greek invests the German" ("le grec investit l'allemand"; ibid.: 88, 91).

During the translation process, however, the source text is never available in some unmediated form. Ethnocentrism inevitably enters because that text is recontextualized in the translating language and culture, and so its foreignness can never be disclosed "in itself" through and in a translation. Berman himself describes a "system" of ethnocentric "forces" or "tendencies" in translation that "deform" or "destroy" the source text, and he goes so far as to assert that these strategies, normative since classical antiquity, "operate in every translation" ("opérant dans toute traduction"; Berman 1999: 49). In this instance, Berman seems to acknowledge that translation is transformation, implicitly contradicting his Heideggerian assumption that the "Foreign as Foreign" can be manifested in a translated text. Moreover, Hölderlin's interpretants include the use of a regional dialect, Swabian, and archaism, leading

Berman to consider textual effects that actually depart from the Greek text and work only in the receiving situation:

> La traduction du poète […] ressuscite l'archaïque de l'allemand pour accueillir l'archaïque du grec, et cela est lié à l'intensification, car tous ces mots – dialectaux ou anciens – tiré du "fond" de la langue sont plus forts, contribuent à edifier la grande langue sauvage qui, par-delà le classicisme, doit parler dans la tragédie. […] la traduction hölderlinienne tente délibérément de détruire la vision "classique" du l'art grec[.]
>
> *(Berman 1999: 94)*

> (The poet's translation […] revives the German archaic to welcome the Greek archaic, and that is linked to intensification, for all these words – whether dialectal or ancient – drawn from the "bedrock" of the language are stronger, contribute to the construction of the great brutal language that, beyond classicism, must speak in tragedy. […] the Hölderlinian translation deliberately tries to destroy the "classical" vision of Greek art[.])

Berman assigns a metaphoric "accueillir" ("welcome") to the resemblance he perceives between Hölderlin's German archaism and classical Greek, and since the French word can signify not only "to welcome" but also "to host" or "to lodge," it recalls Heidegger's concept of language as the "home" of "being." Yet Berman's point is questionable: Sophocles' Greek was *not* archaic to him or to his Hellenic audiences; the historical remoteness of the source language is perceptible only from the translator's moment, so that any attempt to create an analogy with German archaism would be fundamentally ethnocentric. Far from disclosing the foreignness of the Sophoclean text, Hölderlin's translation deviates from it by using a heterogeneous German language, which, because it is "brutal" ("sauvage"), challenges a view of ancient Greek literature prevalent in the late eighteenth century: classical antiquity as embodying order, balance, and restraint. Berman's analysis rests on shifting and contradictory assumptions: on the one hand, an essentialism that projects translation as a direct manifestation of linguistic and cultural differences, through literalism, a metaphysics of the foreign, and, on the other hand, a materialism that projects translation as an innovative practice which signals differences indirectly by deviating from dominant linguistic forms and institutionalized knowledge, a contingent foreignness that undergoes cultural and historical variation. In the end, and not entirely conforming to his intention, Berman's analysis demonstrates that Hölderlin's translations exemplify an ethics of difference, but only because they run athwart the hierarchy of values, beliefs, and representations in the receiving situation (see Venuti 1998: 82).

An academic translation vs. a poet's version

We can develop this ethics further by considering another ancient text, Seneca's drama *Oedipus*, and two renderings written in virtually the same historical moment by two British translators, the classicist E. F. Watling's 1966 translation for Penguin Classics and the poet Ted Hughes's 1969 adaptation for the director Peter Brook. Watling applied several formal interpretants endowed with considerable cultural authority at the time: he adhered fairly closely to the Latin, thereby implementing a prevalent concept of equivalence in translating classical literature; he resorted not only to iambic pentameter but also to blank verse, the prosodic form that has accrued the most value in anglophone poetic traditions; and he combined the current standard dialect of English with early modern lexical and syntactical items, a range of poetical archaisms that included some inverted word order (e.g. "accursed," "craven," "noisome," "slain," "thou shalt," "the curse my own unhappy coming brought"). The intertext of Watling's translation is Elizabethan drama, a point that is never stated explicitly in his introduction but is rather implied in his lengthy and favorable account of the Elizabethans' enthusiasm for the Latin author (Watling 1966: 9–11, 26–38). A critical effect of this interpretant is to interrogate the modern reception of Seneca's tragedies by suggesting that, if the plays continue to hold any interest, it derives from the fact that they significantly influenced the Elizabethan dramatists.

Watling wrote a magniloquent verse evocative of Marlowe and Shakespeare. Here is his version of a speech assigned to Oedipus near the beginning of the text:

> No man can brand me with the name of coward.
> My heart is innocent of craven fears.
> Against drawn swords, against the might of Giants,
> Against the fiercest rage of Mars himself
> I would march boldly forward. Did I run
> From the enchantment of the riddling Sphinx?
> I faced the damned witch, though her jaws dripped blood
> And all the ground beneath was white with bones.
> There, as she sat upon her rocky seat,
> Waiting to seize her prey, with wings outspread
> And lashing tail, a lion in her wrath,
> I asked "What is your riddle?" She replied,
> Shrieking above me with a voice of doom,
> Snapping her jaws and clawing at the stones,
> Impatient to tear out my living heart.
> Then came the cryptic words, the baited trap;
> The monstrous bird had asked her fated riddle,
> And I had answered it! ... Fool that I am,
> Why should I now be praying for my death? ...
> You could have had it then!
>
> *(Watling 1966: 212)*

In such passages, Watling's blank verse is remarkable for its ability to create a coherent speaking voice. The syntactic continuity compels the reader to read for meaning over the line breaks, and the metrical variations give rise to conversational rhythms, so that the speech produces an illusion of transparency, Oedipus comes before us as a redoutable presence, and the psychological contours of a character are sketched. (I am relying on the account of iambic pentameter in Easthope 1983.) These effects indicate yet another interpretant at work in Watling's translation: T. S. Eliot's criticism of Elizabethan drama. In his 1927 essay "Shakespeare and the Stoicism of Seneca," Eliot pointed out that "What influence the work of Seneca and Machiavelli and Montaigne seems to me to exert in common on that time, and most conspicuously through Shakespeare, is an influence toward a kind of self-consciousness that is new; the self-consciousness and self-dramatization of the Shakespearean hero, of whom Hamlet is only one" (Eliot 1950: 119). Eliot's impact can be glimpsed in Watling's introduction where, on the one hand, he acknowledges "the bombastic extravagance, the passionate yet artificial rhetoric, of the tragedies" while, on the other hand, he finds an "attitude of introspection" in them, asserting that "what really interests him [Seneca], and what brings life to his otherwise frigid reproductions of Greek masterpieces, is the exploration of the human conscience, of man's need to know and justify his motives" (Watling 1966: 7, 36–37). By creating a blank verse evocative of a speaking voice, Watling inscribed Eliot's notion of Elizabethan "self-consciousness" in his rendering of a Latin verse drama whose emphasis on rhetoric over psychology, on melodramatic display to the exclusion of subtle introspection, comes back to worry his inscription.

Ted Hughes's approach was very different. He noted in his preface to his published text that, in contrast to Sophocles' "fully civilized" play, Seneca's "figures" are "more primitive than aboriginals" (Hughes 1969: 8). This interpretation suited Peter Brook's stylized production which, in Hughes's words, involved a "heightened and to some extent depersonalized manner of speaking" (ibid.). In a later edition, Brook himself explained that "this text demands a lost art – the art of impersonal acting," which Hughes's poetry supported "by his rigorous eliminating of all unnecessary decoration, all useless expressions of personality" (Brook 1972: 6, 8). Here is Hughes's version of the same Latin passage I reproduced from Watling:

```
have I turned back        whatever there is that frightens
men in this world        whatever shape terror pain and
death can come in        it cannot turn me back        not
even Fate frightens me        not even the sphinx
twisting me up in her twisted words she did not
frighten me        she straddled her rock        her nest of
smashed skulls and bones        her face was a gulf her
gaze paralysed her victims        she jerked her wings up
that tail whipping and writhing        she lashed herself
bunched herself        convulsed        started to tremble
jaws clashing together biting the air        yet I stood
there        and I asked for the riddle        I was calm
her talons gouged splinters up off the rock        saliva
poured from her fangs        she screamed        her whole
```

body shuddering   the words came slowly   the
riddle   that monster's justice   which was a death
sentence   a trap of forked meanings a noose of
knotted words   yet I took it   I undid it   I
solved it

that was the time to die   all this frenzy now   this
praying for death it's too late   Oedipus

(Hughes 1969: 18–19)

Working directly from the Latin, as he explained, "with the help of a Victorian crib," Hughes maintained a certain semantic correspondence, even if not as close and precise as Watling's (ibid.: 8). But he avoided any sort of canonizing interpretation such as Eliot's notion of Elizabethan self-consciousness. Hughes, in fact, undermined the evocation of a voice by applying two formal interpretants: he developed a poetic style that is repetitive to the point of incantation, and he borrowed the discontinuous prosody known as "projective verse" from contemporary United States poets like Charles Olson and Paul Blackburn who used unconventional spacing to create a text that was also a score for performance (Feinstein 2001: 179). Olson, seeking to abandon the romantic poetics of self-expression, turned to a "machine," the typewriter, to continue the modernist break with the iambic pentameter tradition: "It is time we picked the fruits of the experiments of Cummings, Pound, and Williams," he wrote, "each of whom has, after his way, already used the machine as a scoring to his composing, as a script to its vocalization" (Olson 1960: 393).

In addition to a particular style and prosody, Hughes also assimilated the Latin text to his own poetic experiments at the time. He was simultaneously writing the poems that would appear in his 1970 collection *Crow*, where he was effectively reinventing British poetry, using a prosaic free verse with an extremely heterogeneous lexicon and syntax, at once archaic and current, mixing standard and nonstandard forms, drawing on ancient mythology and literature, creating a philosophically incisive yet unremittingly bleak view of human and natural violence. His mythic persona Crow impersonates Oedipus in a few poems, and Hughes later acknowledged that "I did that [the adaptation of Seneca's play] in the middle of writing those Crow pieces. And that turned out to be useful" (Faas 1980: 212). The intertext in his version thus consists not only of a contemporary poetic experimentalism from the United States, but also the experimental poetry that he himself was writing to challenge the British poetic mainstream, the post-Second World War trends dominated by the restrained, introspective formality of John Betjeman and Philip Larkin, where the construction of a distinctive voice taken as expressive of the poet's personality remained central to their projects (cf. the dissenting view of Hughes's poetry in Easthope 1999a: 192). The interpretants that Hughes applied in adapting Seneca's play stage an interrogation of it by avoiding Watling's psychologism and rather locating a primitivism in the rhetorical display of the Latin text. Yet that primitivism in turn troubles Hughes's version by calling attention to the sheer literary sophistication of the intertext he constructs.

How do we weigh the different ethical significance of Watling's translation and Hughes's adaptation? In both cases, the very decision to translate Seneca's *Oedipus* constitutes an event that supplies a lack in British cultural institutions in the mid-1960s, specifically in the academy and the theatre. By that time, Seneca's plays had long been marginalized in the canon of classical drama. In the 1957 edition of the *Encyclopedia Britannica*, Alexander Mair, a classicist at the University of Edinburgh, articulated the reigning assessment in his entry on Seneca's life and work. "Nine tragedies," Mair wrote, "modelled on Greek exemplars, show the rhetorical characteristics of his prose and are of small poetic merit" (Mair 1957: XX, 323). Not unexpectedly, then, between the close prose rendering published in the Loeb Classical Library in 1917 and Watling's verse translation for Penguin Classics in 1966, no other English translation of the play had appeared. Twentieth-century translators clearly favored the Greek tragedians, Aeschylus, Sophocles, and Euripides. In reviving Seneca's drama, both Watling and Hughes were engaged in acts of canon reformation, questioning the marginality of this Roman writer's work and asserting its poetic value through their translations.

But here the similarity ends. Watling's translation was a pseudo-event that disclosed a plenitude in contemporary academic institutions: the canonical status of modernist critical discourses whose formidable explanatory force could master any literary text, regardless of the historical period. The authority of Eliot's judgments had become so unimpeachable as to influence not only scholarship on classical and early modern drama, but even a classicist translating for a widely circulated series of course textbooks. Watling's translation presented a simulacrum of truth, affiliated to an academic elite, in which Seneca's text was rewritten as an Elizabethan drama according to the dominant discourse. Hughes's version, however, set going a truth process that created a new interpretation of Seneca beyond this authoritative reading, that drew its most decisive interpretants from largely marginal poetic materials, the avant-garde United States movement called Black Mountain as well as Hughes's own experiments, creating a generic subset outside of British literary norms that did not mark the translating subject as specifically British or American. These interpretants did not exert the totalizing power of Watling's modernist discourse: their marginality implicitly acknowledges the possibility of multiple interpretations that are likewise located in the margins of cultural institutions, whether academic, theatrical, or literary, and that might enable translations or adaptations different from that of Hughes's. I am assuming that only one interpretation or set of related interpretations can achieve institutional dominance at any specific historical moment, and with that dominance multiplicities are excluded or repressed.

In approaching a literary translation from an ethical perspective, whether a close rendering or a version that makes use of adaptation, the question should never be whether it successfully captures the features of the source text or whether it contributes to a comprehensive understanding of the source literature. Both questions already assume – but simultaneously mystify – notions of what is successful in a translation and comprehensive in understanding a literature, and those notions are based in turn on essentialist concepts of equivalence and representation wherein the source text and literature are held to contain invariant features that can be reproduced or transferred in a translation or body of translations. The process of translating shows that invariants do not exist, that the features of the source text must be fixed in an interpretive act, and that any such fixing can only be provisional. A translation can only communicate an interpretation, never the source text itself or some form or meaning believed to be inherent in it. The interpretation that a translation inscribes, furthermore, is partial and contingent: partial because it is incomplete in recreating the source text and slanted towards the receiving culture; contingent because it is fixed by a set of interpretants that vary among receiving cultural constituencies, social situations, and historical moments. As students of translation, therefore, we should concentrate on those interpretants, especially the relations that the translation constructs to traditions and conventions, styles and genres, discourses and canons, so as to consider whether it inscribes an interpretation that is new vis-à-vis whatever interpretation has achieved authority in the receiving culture. This is also, of course, a call to action for translators, a call to an ethical action that is neither arbitrary nor anarchically subversive, but rather determined to take responsibility for bringing a foreign text into a different situation by acknowledging that its very foreignness demands cultural innovation.

Translation can occasion a searching investigation of language, literature, culture and their interrelations as we try to increase our knowledge of translation practices. My choice of a genre like poetry to stage this investigation, a genre that retains a certain prestige despite its marginality in publishing and in translation studies, was strategic. Perhaps that prestige can help to stimulate new research in translation along similar lines, particularly the translation of text types that are more central than poetry to intercultural exchange. We know more about the translation of technical and pragmatic texts, where the interpretants tend to be relatively limited to idiomatic usage, standardized terminologies, and precisely defined functions, than we do about the history and current state of humanistic translation, translation in the full gamut of the arts and human sciences, in such areas as anthropology, art history, film, philosophy, political history, and religion. Here too, as with poetry, interpretants are constantly developing to reflect changing cultural and social conditions. In the end, the question I want to pose is much broader than the focus on poetry might suggest. I would phrase it as follows: What might the hermeneutic model bring to light about the translation of the forms and practices by which most of us are likely to encounter other cultures?

[2011]

12

TRANSLATION STUDIES AND WORLD LITERATURE

Defining world literature through translation

World literature cannot be conceptualized apart from translation. In most historical periods as well as in most geographical areas, only a small minority of readers can comprehend more than one or two languages, so that, considered from the reader's point of view, world literature consists not so much of original compositions as of translations – that is to say, foreign-language texts translated into the language of the particular community to which the reader belongs, usually the standard dialect or a dominant language in multilingual situations. Translation thus enables the international reception of literary texts, underwriting the idea that "world literature is not an infinite, ungraspable canon of works but rather a mode of circulation and of reading" (Damrosch 2003: 5).

At the same time, translation is fundamentally a localizing practice. Every step in the translation process, starting with the selection of a source text, including the development of a discursive strategy to translate it, and continuing with its circulation in a different language and culture, is mediated by values, beliefs, and representations in the receiving situation. Far from reproducing the source text, a translation rather transforms it by inscribing an interpretation that reflects what is intelligible and interesting to receptors. The transformation occurs even when the translator tries to maintain a fairly strict formal and semantic correspondence. The complex of meanings, values, and functions that the source text comes to support in its originary culture insures that any translation will at once fall short of and exceed whatever correspondence a translator hopes to establish by supporting different meanings, values, and functions for its receptors. This ratio of loss and gain allows a translation to be constructed as an object of study that is relatively autonomous from the source text but always tied indissolubly to the receiving situation.

As a result, translation deepens current definitions of world literature. If world literature is "characterized by the opposition between the great national spaces, which are also the oldest – and, accordingly, the best endowed – and those literary spaces that have more recently appeared and that are poor by comparison" (Casanova 2004: 83), then the intercultural relations in which translation figures are in any historical moment not just asymmetrical but also hierarchical. Major literatures achieve dominance or centrality because their extensive traditions have accrued cultural prestige, whereas minor literatures occupy a dominated or peripheral position because their development has been limited in comparison. A minority status often drives a literature to increase its resources by translating texts from its major counterparts, importing forms and practices that its writers had not previously used and transferring the prestige that accompanies texts in major traditions. By the same token, a majority status leads a literature to translate less because its broad range of forms and practices can sustain independent development. When a major literature does translate, it invests source texts with its cultural prestige, performing an act of "consecration," especially when those texts originate in a literary minority (Casanova 2004: 135; see also Casanova 2010).

Still, translation patterns may not be as straightforward as terms like "importing" and "transferring" might suggest. Intermediary forms and practices can decisively intervene between a source text and a translation. Early twentieth-century Catalan writers such as Josep Carner not only sought to modernize Catalan literature by translating British novels of the Victorian and Edwardian periods, but they also looked to France for guidance as to which novels to translate, adopting French critical categories and even French translation strategies (Coll-Vinent 1998). Alfred Gallard's 1930 Catalan version of Joseph Conrad's novel, *Typhoon* (1903), imitates the lexical and syntactical features of André Gide's 1923 French version (ibid.: 219–23). Where translation is concerned, major literatures might manifest similar dependencies. Publishers in the United States rejected proposals to translate the Argentine Jorge Luis Borges's innovative fiction – until French translations had appeared during the 1950s from a distinguished press, Gallimard, and Borges had been awarded the Formentor Prize by an international group of publishers based in Western metropolitan centers (Levine 2005: 310).

Because translation always answers to contingencies in the receiving situation, the intercultural hierarchies in which it is implicated turn out to be more complex than the simple binary opposition between major and minor literatures. Lu Xun, the early twentieth-century Chinese writer, also looked to France for source texts that could be useful in modernizing Chinese culture, but in 1903 he chose to translate Jules Verne's science fiction novel *De la terre à la lune* (1865; *From Earth to the Moon*) because it contained popularizations of science in an entertaining form that could appeal to a wide readership (Semanov 1967: 14). In bypassing canonical Western novels for an author and a genre that were marginal in the contemporary canon of French literature, Lu Xun exposed a hierarchy *within* French literary culture (Evans 2000). Minor literatures might thus interrogate their major counterparts by translating so as to raise issues such as canon formation. They might also translate among themselves so as to explore the possibilities for cultural change offered by their shared minority status. In 1909, Lu Xun and his brother Zhou Zouren collaborated on an anthology of translated fiction, and since they sought to use literary translation as a means of altering China's subordinate position in global political relations, they drew on minor literatures that had achieved international recognition (Eber 1980: 10; Lee 1987: 22–23). Their anthology presented the work of such authors as the Russian symbolist Leonid Andreyev and the Polish historical novelist Henryk Sienkiewicz.

Translation likewise complicates the effort to conceive of world literature as a special kind of textuality that combines foreign and local materials. This definition – developed to explain the transmission of a Western genre like the novel to other, usually minor literatures in the Eastern and Southern hemispheres – has been refined to encompass "a triangle: foreign form, local material – *and local form*. Simplifying somewhat: foreign *plot*, local *characters* and then local *narrative voice*," where the local narrator's commentary can become "unstable" in negotiating foreign formal features (Moretti 2000: 65; Moretti's emphases). This account aims to describe original compositions whose constitutive materials are assumed to be readily identifiable as foreign or local in origin – an assumption that may not, in fact, be upheld by analysis because literary texts tend to be heterogeneous cultural artifacts. Translation increases the heterogeneity because the translator's verbal choices amount to interpretive moves that vary the source text. The variations may be determined not simply by the receiving language and culture but also by a reading of the source text that incorporates knowledge of the source culture as well. The localizing drive of translation can therefore change the very nature of the categories "foreign" and "local" as they are understood by readerships in the receiving situation.

Translation and the world literary text

Consider the British writer Ian McEwan's novel *The Comfort of Strangers* (1981), an illuminating case for considering the notion of world literary textuality because within roughly a decade of publication it was translated into some fifteen languages, not only major European (French, German, Italian, Russian, Spanish) but also Near and Far Eastern (Chinese, Hebrew, Japanese, Turkish) and minor European (Catalan, Czech, Dutch, Finnish, Polish, Romanian). Because this text consists of literary and cultural forms that are recognizably British, it might be considered local in origin to a large extent. It exemplifies the classic realism that dominated the development of the British novel from the eighteenth century onwards, creating an illusion of reality not just by accumulating verisimilar detail but also by establishing for the anglophone reader a position from which the narrative becomes intelligible and thus plausible, a position of identification that can move between an authorial voice and points of view linked to specific characters (see Belsey 1980: 64–77). McEwan's characters are also local. The narrative follows a British couple, Colin and Mary, who describe themselves as "on holiday" in Venice where they meet another couple, an Italian named Robert and his Canadian wife Caroline (McEwan 1981: 12). The foreign setting and the presence of foreign characters actually indicate that the origins of the text are local, even though including localized foreign elements. British travelers in Italy became a veritable convention of British prose fiction between the sixteenth and the twentieth centuries, from Thomas Nashe's *The Unfortunate Traveller* (1594) to E. M. Forster's *A Room with a View* (1908) and beyond.

The jolting climax of McEwan's novel, in which Robert and Caroline are revealed to be sadomasochistic murderers who kill Colin for their pleasure, similarly derives from British literary traditions that often intersect in specific texts: the thriller genre and the stereotype of Italians as immoral, inclined to deceit, lasciviousness, and violence. Italophobia in British literature dates back at least to the Elizabethan period, present in a treatise like Roger Ascham's *The Scholemaster* (1570), where the Englishman under Italian influence is called a devil incarnate. Yet the same sort of ethnic stereotype subsequently recurs in suspenseful plots that anticipate McEwan's, stretching from Ann Radcliffe's Gothic romance *The Mysteries of Udolpho* (1794), which features several Italian villains, to Daphne du Maurier's mystery of clairvoyance *Don't Look Now* (1971), in which a serial murderer terrorizes Venice. Behind McEwan's treatment of the city as a stage where tragic desire is enacted lie not only these British traditions and conventions, but also the German writer Thomas Mann's *Der Tod in Venedig* (1912; *Death in Venice*), so that the British novelist can be seen as revising and updating a foreign plot as well, recasting it in British terms (Von der Lippe 1999).

Some of the identifiably British materials can be noticed in Colin and Mary's first encounter with Robert near the very beginning of the novel. The couple gets lost while searching for a restaurant late at night, and, as Mary tries to find their bearings, they suddenly come upon Robert:

> She pointed at a doorway several yards ahead and, as if summoned, a squat figure stepped out of the dark into a pool of street light and stood blocking their path.
>
> "Now look what you've done," Colin joked, and Mary laughed.
>
> The man laughed too and extended his hand. "Are you tourists?" he asked in self-consciously precise English and, beaming, answered himself. "Yes, of course you are."
>
> *(McEwan 1981: 25)*

The passage exhibits the hallmarks of classic realism. Through the pronoun "she," the reader is positioned in Mary's point of view, which is initially spatial: she indicates a spot where she and Colin had passed a few days before, the reader looks in that direction with her, and the fictive world is made plausible. Insofar as she is uncertain about how the man came to be there – he seems to be magically "summoned" by her gesture, as if he were a spirit in a Gothic romance – the spatial point of view becomes cognitive and then psychological: the reader is positioned to share her laughter at Colin's joke that her pointing inadvertently did something wrong. The joke and the laughter show Colin and Mary's lack of fear and suggest their familiarity with the space: the man blocks their path, but not deliberately, only because they are standing in a narrow Venetian street which is the width of an alley. Robert's question might be considered intimidating because it quite baldly exposes their vulnerability as tourists: they are in fact lost. Yet any possibility of intimidation is preempted by the man's participation in Mary's laughter, by his effort to greet them, and by the signs of his own vulnerability: he gestures to shake hands, seems insecure about speaking their language (his English is "self-consciously precise"), and takes boyish pride (he is "beaming") both in his correct pronunciation and in his certainty that they are tourists. Hence his answer to his own question effectively removes any hint of intimidation, as well as any physical danger, by implying his sympathetic awareness of their situation. No appreciable distinction appears between the characters and the authorial voice that has represented the encounter from Mary's point of view. In terms of British literary traditions, the exchange adheres to a familiar convention, the meeting between British travelers and a native Italian in an Italian locale where every character speaks English.

The Italian translation of McEwan's novel maintains the realism of the narrative, but since Italian literature has a strong realist tradition that extends from the nineteenth century to the present, the Italian reader is unlikely to regard the form as foreign rather than local (see Carsaniga 1974). The English passage where Colin and Mary meet Robert, moreover, undergoes a significant transformation in Italian, starting with the substitution of an Italian measurement ("qualche metro"/several meters) for an English one (McEwan's "yards"):

> Indicò una porta qualche metro piú avanti e, come evocata, una figura tozza emerse dal buio entrando nel raggio di un lampione e si fermò in modo da bloccare la strada.
> – Guarda cosa hai fatto, – scherzò Colin, e Mary rise.
> Rise anche l'uomo, porgendo la mano. – Siete turisti? – chiese in un inglese deliberatamente preciso e, sorridendo, rispose per loro. – Certo, naturalmente.
> *(McEwan 1983a: 21)*

Here too Mary establishes the point of view, yet the characterization of Robert displays several striking shifts. He is portrayed as *intentionally* blocking Colin and Mary: "si fermò in modo da bloccare la strada" (he stopped in order to block the path). Although the passage indicates that he speaks in English, the Italian grammar introduces a perceptible change in his tone: he is meeting the British couple for the first time, but he boldly uses the familiar second-person form of the verb "to be" ("siete"/ you are) instead of showing respect with the polite third-person form, so that calling them tourists seems confrontational, an insistence on their vulnerability. His English is described as "deliberatamente preciso" (deliberately precise), as if he wished to make clear that he knows just how vulnerable they are. The boyishness of "beaming" in the English text here becomes the more ambiguous "sorridendo" (smiling), and he responds to his question "per loro" (for them), tacitly taking control of the situation. His response, "Certo, naturalmente," suggests that their vulnerability as tourists is inevitable: in a close back translation, "Of course, naturally."

Through such shifts, the Italian version suffuses the entire scene with an ominous atmosphere that is absent from the English passage. Robert is depicted as aggressive, even menacing. This change in his characterization weakens Mary's reliability as the position from which the scene becomes intelligible to the italophone reader: although at first her point of view makes spatial sense of the action, her laughter at Colin's joke implies that, like him, she is unaware of Robert's potential danger, and so another, more reliable point of view is created, that of the implied author, with whom the reader shares the ironic knowledge that Robert's threatening appearance is no joking matter. Suspense is generated, consequently, an uncertainty about what will happen to Colin and Mary.

The translation thus inscribes an interpretation that is rather different from the meaning that can be perceived in the English passage. The verbal choices evidently rewrite Robert's entrance in light of the murder he will commit much later, altering the subtle positioning by which the reader shares Colin and Mary's initially unsuspecting attitude towards him. The difference in point of view and characterization is also a difference in genre. The English text presents a conventional realistic narrative virtually until the violent climax, whereas in this early scene the Italian version suddenly transforms the narrative into a thriller with decidedly Gothic overtones. The Italian word that describes Robert's abrupt appearance, "evocata," although it accurately renders "summoned," differs from the English word in being primarily occult in significance, as in "to conjure up" a spirit or demon.

Nonetheless, any precise identification of foreign and local elements in the Italian version remains difficult, if not impossible. A translation recontextualizes the source text by creating a receiving intertext that replaces relations to the source literature with relations to literary traditions in the receiving culture, so that a reader of the translation must possess the literary and cultural knowledge to perceive the intertext as well as the critical competence to formulate its significance for both the source and the translated texts (see Venuti 2009). An italophone reader familiar with British literature could certainly read the ironic point of view and the negative portrayal of Robert as establishing a correspondence to the English text, where these features derive from the Italophobic stereotypes of Italian characters in British genres such as the Gothic romance and the thriller. Yet the same features could be read as the inscription of foreign form and characterization, an Italian interpretation of the English text, since the genres also exist in Italian literary traditions (see Billiani and Sulis 2007; Carloni 1994). This indeterminacy in potential Italian responses might be attributed to the uncertain status of Italian literature today when seen in a global framework, not quite minor, endowed with rich literary traditions, but not quite major, lacking the cultural prestige possessed by English or French.

The interpretation inscribed by the Italian version, furthermore, cannot be regarded as distinctively Italian: it also appears in translations of the novel into other languages, major and minor. In the Spanish version, the man, whose mysteriousness is made explicit with the term "el desconocido" (the stranger), "permaneció en pie sin moverse, cortándoles el paso" (remained standing without moving, cutting off their path) (McEwan 1982: 26). In the French version, the man suddenly "jaillait" (sprang out), "alla se planter au milieu d'une flaque de lumière et leur barra le passage" (went and planted himself in the center of a pool of light and blocked their path) (McEwan 1983b: 34). In the Catalan version, the man "va col·locar-se sota un raig de llum, barrant-los el pas" (positioned himself under a ray of light, barring their way) (McEwan 1997: 33). These translations, like the Italian version, transform the scene into a threatening encounter so as to foreshadow the climactic murder. Perhaps they should all be read as interpretations that question the source text, challenging the apparently innocent presentation of Robert in the English passage, calling the author's bluff, in a sense, by suggesting what is to come later, a confirmation of . British traditions, conventions, and stereotypes. In this respect, the interpretations inscribed by the translations might well signal a resistance towards the majority of the English literary text, which in turn uncovers an aggressiveness, even an antipathy engendered by their minority status in relation to English.

Clearly, the formal and semantic gain that enables translation to define world literature cannot be perceived without close reading, without a detailed analysis that examines shifts between the source and translated texts. "Distant" reading, where emphasis is placed on either "smaller" textual features like "devices, themes, tropes" or "larger" structures like "genres," traditions, and cultural "systems," is essential to understanding world literature as an intricate, historically developing ensemble of cross-cultural relations among major and minor traditions (Moretti 2000: 57). Yet allowing the text to disappear as a unit of analysis between these two extremes would be counterproductive: the text not only links the small feature and the large structure, showing how they depend on one another for their literary and cultural significance, but it also makes visible the role of translation in the construction of world literature. The idea that close reading "necessarily depends on an extremely small canon" (ibid.) is false; the problem is rather that close reading continues to be performed on a limited canon of original compositions, betraying, I would argue, an unexamined investment in a romantic concept of authorial originality that marginalizes a second-order practice like translation. Corpora of translations can be analyzed at a distance, so as to consider how patterns of exchange influence receiving literary traditions. But individual translations can also be submitted to close reading, so as to consider how specific interpretations of the source texts shape that influence. This methodological point may become more persuasive when we recognize that not every text can be classified as world literature simply because not every text reveals the impact of a foreign tradition and, perhaps most importantly, not every text is translated.

Canons of foreign literatures in translation

We can exemplify an approach to world literature that combines distant and close reading of translations by developing first a systemic view. The theorist Gideon Toury offers a basic account that can serve as a point of departure:

> Translation is a kind of activity which inevitably involves at least two languages and two cultural traditions, i.e., at least two sets of norm-systems on each level. Thus, the "value" behind it may be described as consisting of two major elements:
>
> (1) being a text in a certain language, and hence occupying a position, or filling in a slot, in the appropriate culture, or in a certain section thereof;

(2) constituting a representation in that language/culture of another, pre-existing text in some other language, belonging to some other culture and occupying a definite position within it.

(Toury 1995: 56)

Toury's distinctions make clear that a translation never gives back the source text itself, only a mediated form of it, a "representation," and that the mediation registers "norms" or values in the receiving culture. More precisely, the source text and its translational representation are situated in a "norm-system" or hierarchy of values in their respective cultures, where the "position" or "slot" occupied by each might be central or peripheral, canonical or marginal. The position that the translation occupies in the receiving culture can determine its representation of the source text: an emergent, avant-garde practice in the periphery is likely to produce a translation that differs markedly from a dominant practice that controls the center, the former inclined towards radical experimentation, the latter towards conservative maintenance of canons.

Toury observes that receiving cultural values are also instrumental in motivating the very choice of a source text for translation, and a "translation policy" can be inferred from a corpus of translations insofar as a succession of choices establishes patterns (Toury 1995: 58). Yet translation patterns are also partial in two senses: they are incomplete in their representation of a source literature, since a literature is never translated in its entirety, always selectively, and they are slanted towards the receiving culture in the choice of source texts, since the decision to translate is usually made by receptors, and only texts that are acceptable to receiving cultural values tend to be chosen. As a result, canons of foreign literatures are formed in and through translation, and these canons can become stereotypical representations that diverge to varying degrees from literary canons that have been constructed in the foreign culture.

This point can be illustrated by examining a culture where a significant amount of translated literature is regularly published. I shall choose Italy to continue developing the case considered in the previous section. After the Second World War, the Italian publishing industry grew increasingly dependent on translations, so that at the beginning of the 1950s 16 percent of total annual book output consisted of translations, a figure that rose to 20 percent during the 1980s and finally peaked at approximately 25 percent during the 1990s (Turi 1997: 408, 444; Peresson and Mussinelli 2009: 255). In 2008, the number of adult titles published in Italy reached 49,767 (excluding children's books and school textbooks), 10,046 of which were translations (20.1 percent) (Peresson 2010: 62–63). For the past sixty years, 50–60 percent of Italian translations issued annually have taken English as their source language. Given the high volume of translations from English, we might ask: What is the current canon of contemporary United States fiction in Italian translation and what values have given rise to it?

Drawn primarily from a printed edition of the *Catalogo dei libri in commercio* (2006), the list of Italian books in print, the data I will present are sufficient to sketch the main tendencies in the selection of United States texts for translation and thereby the broad outlines of the Italian canon, even if the figures cannot be taken as a precisely accurate count. The availability of the translations suggests not only that they continue to be commercially viable, capable of selling on the Italian book market, but also that they have been invested with various kinds of value by Italian readers, whether judged according to elite or popular taste. This investment is perhaps most clear in the case of texts that were translated several decades ago but remain in print.

Translations of United States bestsellers have consistently thrived on the Italian market. Currently available in Italian are fifty-seven titles by Danielle Steel, fifty-five by Stephen King, twenty-eight by Tom Clancy, twenty by John Grisham, and fifteen by Anne Rice, some of which were first published during the 1970s. The genres of the novels – romance, horror, thriller – explain in part the success of the translations: they appeal to popular taste, enabling the pleasures of vicarious participation grounded on a sympathetic identification with characters (see Bourdieu 1984: 32). Yet because the authors also address material that is specific to the United States, whether settings or themes, some of a historical or topical nature, their appeal is inseparable from the symbolic capital that United States culture acquired in Italy during the latter half of the twentieth century. This capital can also explain in part the interest of Italian readers in elite novels which contain realistic depictions of United States cultural and social issues, although here a detached appreciation of literary form comes into play, at least with some segments of the audience. Thus, currently available in Italian are twenty-two titles by Joyce Carol Oates, eighteen by Philip Roth, and fourteen each by Raymond Carver and Anne Tyler. Not unexpectedly, given these translation patterns, experimental narratives by United States writers are marginal in Italy. The difference in the figures is striking: Italian booksellers are likely to stock only three titles by Donald Barthelme, two by Robert Coover, two by William Gaddis, one by William Gass, one by Kathy Acker, and none by David Markson.

The canon of contemporary United States fiction in Italian translation, then, is composed mostly of various forms of realism and culture-specific themes. It can be described as overlapping to some extent with the canon of this fiction in United States culture, especially as defined in the academy, but the exclusions are conspicuous, notably the marginal position assigned to experimentalism. At the center of the Italian canon, however, outstripping the elite novels and rivaling the bestsellers in sheer market presence lies a substantial body of work that is affiliated with the Beat Generation, or that explores nonconformist lives on the fringes of United States society, or that falls into the category of hardboiled crime fiction. Currently available in Italian are thirty-nine titles by Charles Bukowski, thirty-three by Jack Kerouac, twenty-two by William S. Burroughs, twenty by James Ellroy, eighteen by Ed McBain, seventeen by John Fante, and all eight books written by Edward Bunker. Kerouac and Fante have been singled out for special treatment: both have volumes devoted to their work in "I Meridiani" (the highpoints), the series of classics created by the trade publisher Mondadori, where they are positioned among figures in the Western canon like Homer and Dante, Shakespeare and Goethe, Baudelaire and

Joyce, on the one hand, and canonical United States authors like Hemingway and Fitzgerald, Pound and Faulkner, on the other.

The values underlying the Italian canonization of such authors include, of course, the profit motive that drives commercial publishing in Italy as elsewhere, along with the prestige that United States culture has accrued among Italian audiences and the appeal to popular taste present in realistic narratives. Yet more is clearly at stake because of the genres and themes specific to the writing: the center of the Italian canon ultimately rests on a valorization of a particular brand of romantic individualism, which prizes not only outspoken self-expression but also freedom from social constraints to the point of flouting bourgeois respectability by cultivating nonstandard language and unconventional, even illicit behavior.

These values can be glimpsed in the Italian reception of Edward Bunker's novel *No Beast So Fierce* (1973), which was reviewed by Carlo Lucarelli in 2001 when the 1996 Italian translation was reprinted. Lucarelli, a prolific author of crime fiction who has published twenty novels among other works, remarks that what "gli scrittori di genere come me" (genre writers like me) find worthy of "invidiare" (envy) in Bunker's writing is not his life as a career criminal and prison convict, but a style that Bunker shares with such other United States novelists as Hemingway, Dashiell Hammett, and James Ellroy, namely

> la capacità di raccontarla, questa vita, di fartela vedere, con lo stile oggettivo ma intenso di osservatore. [...] Ed Bunker ha questo stile incredibilmente oggettivo e secco, spietato e durissimo, un dialogo, un'azione e un commento, uno accanto all'altro, senza spazio per niente che non sia essenziale, e tantomeno per la retorica. È il modo di parlare di chi è stato in galera, fatto di frasi significative, di fatti, e anche di silenzi molto eloquenti. La cosa sconvolgente è quello che questo stile racconta, la violenza delle cose che accadono, la rassegnazione senza scampo delle persone che le vivono, i colpi drammatici di un destino feroce, anche lo squallore e la disperazione.
>
> *(Lucarelli 2001: 8)*

(the ability to narrate this life, to make you see it, with the objective yet intense style of an observer. [...] Ed Bunker has this incredibly objective and abrupt style, ruthless and very hard – dialogue, action, commentary, one after the other, with no room for anything that isn't essential, least of all rhetoric. It's the speech of someone who's been in jail, composed of loaded words, deeds, and the most eloquent silences. The shocking thing is what this style tells, the violence of the things that happen, the hopeless resignation of the people who experience them, the dramatic blows of a savage fate, as well as the squalor and desperation.)

Lucarelli's account finally does not distinguish between the author's life and his writing. On the contrary, his comments indicate that he has somewhat naively succumbed to the illusionism of Bunker's realistic narrative: although Lucarelli cites comparable stylists, he seems unaware that the tradition of hardboiled prose in

United States fiction, extending from Hammett and James M. Cain to Raymond Chandler and Jim Thompson to Andrew Vachss and James Ellroy, is very much a "rhetoric," a stylization that is immediately recognizable as such, and that has developed autonomously without any necessary connection to a particular author's life. Lucarelli's enthusiastic appreciation of Bunker's novel depends on a deep investment in the romantic notion that the United States author is writing directly from his experience, expressing his criminal personality.

This appreciation, so typical of Italian fiction writers in Lucarelli's generation, crosses the boundaries between Italian cultural constituencies, elite as well as popular. Lucarelli, who was born in 1960, possesses a taste for contemporary United States fiction that is clearly popular, given to an imaginary involvement in the plot and characters, erasing the boundary between art and life. Yet his account of Bunker's writing closely resembles that of an elite novelist like Niccolò Ammaniti, who was born in 1966. Ammaniti has received the prestigious Viareggio and Strega prizes for compelling novels that draw on the conventions of crime fiction to probe Italian social issues, *Io non ho paura* (2001; *I'm Not Scared*) and *Come Dio commanda* (2006; *As God Commands*). In a brief introduction to the translation of *No Beast So Fierce* that Lucarelli reviewed, Ammaniti at first remarks that Bunker "costruisce un carattere indimenticabile, dostoevskiano, un personaggio lacerato tra la consapevolezza di essere un reietto e il desiderio impossibile di tornare a essere considerato un uomo normale" (constructs an unforgettable Dostoevskian character, a figure torn between the consciousness of being an outcast and the impossible desire to be considered a normal man again) (Bunker 2001: x). Here Ammaniti displays a detached critical appreciation of Bunker's character based on a familiarity with a highbrow novel, Dostoevsky's *Pryestupleniye i nakazaniye* (1866; *Crime and Punishment*). But no sooner does he formulate this response than he leaves it behind and adopts Lucarelli's reduction of the writing to the author's life: "Bunker scrive la sua storia con la conoscenza di chi ha vissuto sulla propria pelle le cose che racconta, senza retorica e senza la mitizzazione del mondo criminale cara a gran parte degli scrittori di *crime-stories*" (Bunker writes his story with the knowledge of someone who has experienced in his own skin the things he tells, without rhetoric and without the mythicizing of the criminal world dear to most writers of crime fiction) (ibid.). The literary sensibilities of Lucarelli and Ammaniti have been formed by an immersion in United States culture, especially popular genres like crime fiction, although not so much that fiction itself or its reception in the United States as the canon of translated fiction built by Italian publishers. Their participatory response to this canon has evidently prevented them from recognizing the conventionality of the genre, its "rhetoric," while suppressing any awareness that in treating the writing as a transparent representation of the author's life they have romanticized the criminality he has depicted – even when they protest to the contrary.

Translated canons and translation strategies

Although neither Lucarelli nor Ammaniti refers to reading Bunker's novel in English, and although neither comments on the features of the Italian version, they are novelists who write in a national language, not multilingual literary scholars, and so their acquaintance with the canon of United States fiction, like that of their Italian readers, would have inevitably been mediated by translations. This seems to have been the case with *No Beast So Fierce*, since both authors express interest in reading the Italian version of Bunker's memoir *Education of a Felon*, which was not translated until 2002, although it was available in English a couple of years earlier. To what extent, then, does the Italian version of Bunker's novel, *Come una bestia feroce* (Like a ferocious beast), support the sort of romanticizing response recorded in their remarks? More generally, what can a close reading of this translation disclose about the relations between translated literary canons and the individual translations that comprise them?

In the following passage, the narrator and main character of Bunker's novel, Max Dembo, who is about to be released from prison after serving an eight-year sentence, searches for an inmate he had befriended during his incarceration:

> Aaron Billings, the person I really wanted to see, failed to appear. He was black and would avoid a group of whites, just as I would avoid a group of blacks. The races had become totally polarized during recent years. Because of this I'd talked with Aaron less and less, but our friendship remained. He'd stopped me at the dentist's office yesterday (he worked there) and mentioned that he might be transferred to camp and wanted me to help him escape. There'd been no time to talk, and he was going to meet me this morning.
>
> *(Bunker 1998: 14)*

The Italian version, although it maintains a core semantic correspondence to the English text and even adheres to the English syntax, contains some intriguing shifts, indicated below in bold:

> Aaron Billings, l'uomo che volevo vedere **piú di tutti**, non era fra loro. Era un nero e avrebbe evitato **un drappello** di bianchi esattamente come io avrei evitato un gruppo di neri. Nel corso degli ultimi anni le razze si erano **violentemente divise all'interno della prigione**. A causa di ciò con Aaron parlavo sempre meno, ma la nostra amicizia restava **viva**. **Il giorno precedente** mi aveva fermato nella studio del dentista dove lavorava e mi aveva accennato che forse l'avrebbe trasferito in **un campo di lavoro**. Voleva che lo aiutassi a fuggire. **Al momento** non avevamo potuto parlarne, ma **mi avrebbe spiegato tutto** il mattino del**la mia liberazione**.
>
> *(Bunker 2001: 14)*

Two marked tendencies can be detected here. One involves a higher register and more explicit language than the English. The passage is cast in the current standard dialect of Italian, which deviates from Bunker's conversational use of contractions and at points reverts to greater formality: "yesterday" becomes "il giorno precedente" (the preceding day), "there'd been no time" becomes "al momento" (at the moment), and the omission of the relative pronoun, "that" or "who," in the clause "the person I really wanted to see," is supplied by "che" (unavoidably, due to structural differences between the languages, since the absence of "che" would be regarded as an error). The Italian inserts phrases to signify meanings that are left implied in the English. These additions include the location, "all'interno della prigione" (inside the prison), the nature of the "camp," specified as "un campo di lavoro" (a work camp), and the key event of "this morning," namely "la mia liberazione" (my release). Similarly, the English assumes that Billings "was going to meet" Dembo to discuss his "escape," but the Italian spells out the purpose of the meeting: "mi avrebbe spiegato tutto" (he would have explained everything to me).

The other tendency involves a degree of exaggeration that moves the Italian towards melodrama. The simple emphasis in "really," a conversational usage that singles out Billings among the other inmates to whom Dembo says goodbye, is replaced by the intensified "piú di tutti" (more than anyone), a phrase that again makes explicit what is implied in the English. The rather detached reference to the "races" as "totally polarized" is transformed into a suggestion of physical aggression, "violentemente divise" (violently divided), while the loose "group" of white prisoners becomes a more organized "drappello," a military term that is also used for athletic teams: "a squad." And where the English merely states that Dembo's "friendship" with Billings "remained," the Italian adds "viva," which can carry the force of "alive," but also "intense."

The two tendencies in the translated passage, one formalizing and explicitating, the other intensifying and melodramatizing, join to form a distinct interpretation of the English. The first shows an effort to create an Italian text that is immediately intelligible by filling in gaps in the reader's knowledge and thereby compensating for cultural differences. This tendency apparently contradicts Lucarelli's notion that Bunker writes with "the most eloquent silences," but it is offset by the adherence to the English syntax, which creates a series of relatively short sentences that imitate Bunker's "abrupt style," while reflecting the movement in contemporary Italian prose away from the traditional periodic constructions towards greater simplicity (see Mengaldo 1991 and Testa 1997). This Italian intertext prevents the translation from recreating the polysyndeton in Bunker's penultimate sentence, the repetition of "and" so characteristic of Hemingway's prose, which, as Lucarelli recognizes, constitutes part of the English intertext. Yet the clarity and precision of the translation works to enhance the tendency towards melodrama, fashioning an image of prison life as extreme. Other examples include the rendering of "racial climate" as "tensioni razziali" (racial tensions) and of "there were murderous skirmishes" as "gli omicidi si susseguivano incessanti" (the murders followed each other non-stop) (Bunker 1998: 16, 17; 2001: 16, 17). The Italian does not reproduce every stylistic feature of the English text, but it can nonetheless support the fascination with nonconformist and criminal experience found in the Italian canon of United States fiction.

Bunker's copious lexicon of slang and obscenity proves to be particularly challenging to match in Italian. Some of his slang is dated, specific to the 1960s, or affiliated with African-American usage. Dembo's conversations with Billings, for instance, contain phrases like "up tight," rendered as "teso" (tense), and "right on," rendered as "giusto" (right) (Bunker 1998: 16, 231; 2001: 16, 277). In each case, the translation establishes a semantic correspondence but raises the register and loses the ethnic affiliation. Similar shifts occur with underworld and prison argot. A "hit man" becomes a "sicario" (assassin), "the big yard" becomes "i cortili delle prigioni" (prison courtyards), and "fingered" becomes "tradito" (betrayed) (Bunker 1998: 68, 194, 269; 2001: 79, 232, 322). The recurrent obscenities receive Italian counterparts, although the sheer brutality of the English is not always possible to recreate. Verbal abuse like "motherfucker" and "fuck your mother" is rendered as "figlio di puttana" (son of [a] whore) and "fottiti" (fuck you), but the ejaculation, "Fuck no!" becomes "No, cazzo!" (no, cock), and "bullshitter" becomes "ballista" (liar) (Bunker 1998: 28, 110, 145; 2001: 31, 132, 174). Still, the translation assembles a broad variety of nonstandard Italian forms to signify an analogous violation of linguistic taboos, not only substantiating Lucarelli's view that Bunker's language is "ruthless and very hard," but assimilating the English text to the increasing orality of Italian literary prose (Spunta 2004). These forms include "stronzo" (turd, shithead) for "asshole," "non bidonarmi" (don't swindle me) for "don't hang me up," pivello (inexperienced boy) for "squarejohn," as well as the retention of English words that have entered current Italian usage, such as "putting green," "freezer," and "whiskey" (Bunker 2001: 25, 31, 109, 146, 170; 1998: 23, 28, 92). The Italian syntax also turns conversational in passages of dialogue: "better than a cell" is closely translated as "sempre meglio di una cella" (still better than a cell), and the standard construction "the bottom of a burnt spoon left this" is clipped to "lasciata dal fondo di un cucchiaino bruciato" (left by the bottom of a burnt spoon) (Bunker 1998: 101; 2001: 120).

By far the most suggestive shifts carry implications for Dembo's values. When a robbery turns him into a hunted fugitive and he decides to murder the friend who betrayed him to the police, he considers the people who would be hurt by his action, concluding that "They would never understand the law of my world, which was all I had to live by" (Bunker 1998: 270). The Italian version alters the last clause to "l'unica che io potessi seguire per sopravvivere" (the only [law] I could follow in order to survive), reducing a code of criminal conduct to mere animal instinct, characterizing Dembo as desperate, whereas in the English he is more detached and calculating (Bunker 2001: 323). At another point, he settles into a satisfying relationship with a woman, but his criminality leads him to question it: "When I thought of how fragile this interlude was, how doomed (I was still a wanted man, still committed to further crimes), it hurt" (Bunker 1998: 207). The Italian again treats Dembo as a less reflective character:

> Se mi ritrovavo a pensare a quanto fosse fragile quell'interludio, a come fossi condannato a una condizione di ricercato e criminale, soffrivo.
>
> *(Bunker 2001: 248–49)*

(If I found myself thinking of how fragile that interlude was, of how I was condemned to the status of a wanted criminal, I suffered.)

"If I found myself thinking" suggests, of course, that Dembo is not constantly scrutinizing his relationships, that he privileges action over contemplation. Similarly, the substitution of the word "condannato" (condemned) for the phrase "still committed" removes the idea that he has, in fact, chosen to violate his parole and to embark on a crime spree. In such passages, the Italian version inscribes the English text with the strongly deterministic notion of human action that characterizes naturalism in the international history of the novel, including the subgenre of hardboiled crime fiction. That notion also supports Lucarelli's sense of the "hopeless resignation" experienced by the criminals depicted in Bunker's narrative.

It is extremely important that the shifts in the translation not be regarded dismissively as errors in need of correction. They rather show that the translator has applied his own interpretants in translating the novel, a concept of equivalence (the degree of formal and semantic correspondence permitted by linguistic differences) and a fictional discourse (a naturalism that befits criminality), and these choices (among the others I have indicated) constitute a strategy that inscribes a nuanced interpretation. To treat a specific verbal choice as incorrect without careful examination of the context risks the unwitting assumption of a different interpretation as a standard of evaluation. This move is questionable because no translation can reproduce a source text with completeness and precision or without a gain of translating-language form and meaning. Worse, it deprives the translator of the right to interpret the source text for audiences in the receiving situation.

In the case of Bunker's novel, we should think twice about depriving the translator of this right because he is so highly accomplished. Stefano Bortolussi, born in 1959, is an experienced professional who over the past two decades has translated more than sixty contemporary anglophone novels into Italian. His authors include many who write genre fiction, including hardboiled crime novels. Among them are James Lee Burke, James Ellroy, Carl Hiaasen, Stephen King, Val McDermid, Richard Price, and John Godey, the author of *The Taking of Pelham 123*. Bortolussi's Italian version has produced an interpretation that creates analogous effects against the backdrop of current Italian literature. His work seems to have been powerful enough to contribute to that literature by helping to inspire, along with various foreign and Italian traditions, a new generation of writers to deploy crime fiction in representing Italian society. Canons of foreign literatures in translation, although undoubtedly exclusionary to some extent and even stereotypical in the images they create of those literatures, rest on relatively coherent translation strategies that can exert a decisive influence on literary traditions in the receiving situation.

To focus on translation is to redefine the study of literature in the most material ways. The production, circulation, and reception of translations does not simply involve crossing national boundaries, but also requires inserting texts into global networks that are inflected by national literary traditions, to be sure, but that reveal the national as constructed by international affiliations. These networks change from one historical period to another, and, as we move further into the twenty-first century, enable modes of reception to multiply and overlap. The same source text may be translated into many languages, assimilated in varying degrees to receiving cultural values. To understand the impact of translation in the creation of world literature, we need to examine the canons developed by translation patterns within receiving situations as well as the interpretations that translations inscribe in the source texts. To be productive, to yield the most incisive findings, this sort of examination must combine distant and close reading of translations to explore the relations between canons and interpretations. For most readers, translated texts constitute world literature, even if we are still in the process of learning how to read translations as translations, as texts in their own right, which are significantly independent of the source texts they translate.

[2012]

13

TRANSLATION TREBLED

Ernest Farrés's *Edward Hopper* in English

Theory and serendipity

As a reader, I have long been intrigued by ekphrasis, the verbal representation of visual art, and so it was inevitable that, as a translator, I would long to translate an ekphrastic text. I imagined the project as a translation of a translation or, with the precision that Roman Jakobson's terms can give, as an interlingual translation of an intersemiotic adaptation, which transforms visual into verbal signs but nonetheless resembles a translation since both are second-order creations that operate on prior materials (Jakobson 1959: 233). Such a project, I believed, requires the translator to pay attention not only to the source text and its place in the source language and literature, but also to the art work and its place in art historical traditions, not only to the linguistic patterns and literary traditions of the receiving culture, but also to the critical reception of the artist among both academic and general readers, the potential audiences of the ekphrasis as well as of the translation.

At this point, you may feel that my interest in translating an ekphrastic text issues merely from the fascination of what's difficult. But I say, no, it is translation that's difficult, and in fastening on ekphrasis I am seeking an understanding of what is translation, although in a novel way. Whatever I might learn would depend on the heightened self-consciousness that comes from juxtaposing two instances, which are connected, to be sure, but relatively autonomous, working between different media and languages.

If the approach I am sketching provokes any resistance, the reason is likely to be not so much its difficulty as the implications it carries for the understanding of translation that prevails today. To figure a wide range of factors into the translation process is to move beyond the commonsensical dichotomy between the source and the translated texts. My approach insists that common sense is nonsense: the dichotomy is not only reductive but also mystifying of the translator's work because it is grounded on an instrumental model of second-order creation. This model treats practices like ekphrasis and translation as reproducing an invariant contained in or caused by the source material, whether formal, semantic, or effective. To attend to the cultural and social conditions of a second-order creation is rather to adopt a hermeneutic model (this concept of the "hermeneutic" differs from the German tradition and from translation theories informed by that tradition: see Venuti 2012: 495–99; and above: 4, 185–87). Here ekphrasis and translation are seen as interpretive acts which vary the form, meaning, and effect of their respective source materials according to the conditions selected by the writer or translator to frame an interpretation. The source material never remains intact because its originary contexts are displaced by those of the second-order creation, contexts that are constitutive, comprised of a specific medium or language and overdetermined by divergent cultural practices and social developments, modes of reception in institutional sites.

This fact makes the interpretation an inscription that is always already at work, starting with the very choice of source material, including every act of viewing or reading it, and encompassing the verbal choices that constitute the ekphrasis and the translation. The source material is continually processed, never available in some unmediated state, so that the inscription is partly deliberate but also partly unconscious, the effect of intended actions situated in conditions that cannot be completely grasped or controlled and causing consequences that are in part unanticipated. As a result, the relation between a second-order creation and its source material might be intended as a straightforward interpretation, but it can become interrogative, especially among more suspicious readers, taking the form of a critical dialectic in which each work questions the other (for a fuller exposition of this approach, see Venuti 2010).

In 2006, I finally got an opportunity to translate an ekphrastic text. I was invited to contribute to an unusual book for young readers, an anthology of foreign poems inspired by art work (Greenberg 2008). My first impulse was to search for examples in Italian, the source language for most of my translations. Yet, despite a Roman colleague's help, I was not turning up many texts, and the few I located, although engaging enough for me to translate, were rejected. The editor judged them inappropriate for the projected readership because they were either conceptually dense (Valerio Magrelli's experiment with a symbolic image by the Futurist Carlo Carrà) or potentially prurient (Anna Cascella's evocation of a nude by Amedeo Modigliani).

In those years, I was spending summers in Barcelona, and while browsing in a bookshop there I happened upon a remarkable collection of Catalan poems based on paintings by a United States artist: Ernest Farrés's *Edward Hopper* (2006). I immediately abandoned my search for ekphrastic poetry in Italian, which has ranked fairly high among the languages most translated into English since the Second World War, and I embarked on a book-length translation from Catalan, which has ranked among the most neglected. The anthology editor finally accepted a translation from this project, delighted as much by its accessibility and seeming innocuousness as by Hopper's fame.

Hopper's paintings had mesmerized me ever since 1980, when I took in the huge retrospective of his work at the Whitney Museum of American Art. By that time, I

had become a New Yorker, and his urban scenes, his images of anonymity and soli-
tude, his obscure yet atmospheric narratives made uncanny sense to me, even though
many were more reminiscent of film noir than my everyday encounters. But now
I grew obsessed with Farrés's poetic take on Hopper's art. I wondered what sort of
poetry a canonical painter in a hegemonic culture might elicit from a writer in a
minor language and literature, a writer who had yet to gain much recognition in his
own culture – despite the fact that his Hopper book had won the Englantina d'Or of
the Jocs Florals, a prestigious Catalonian poetry prize that dates back at least to the
nineteenth century. How, I asked myself, would the hierarchy that underlies the
cross-cultural relation affect the interpretation inscribed by the ekphrasis? And how
would my own interpretation be affected by the minority status of the poetry when
I translated it into English, the language that enjoys global dominance?

Life stories aslant

Farrés's *Edward Hopper* comes before the reader as a typical book of ekphrastic poems:
the table of contents indicates that each poem takes as its title the title and date of a
painting by Hopper. But the collection is not a stroll through a museum: the poems
are not arranged in the chronological sequence of a retrospective exhibition. They
rather sketch a biographical narrative, following a male persona as he moves from a
small town to a big city, from the search for a job to the daily grind of a career, from
being single to having a female partner, from youthfulness to old age, with occasional
sojourns in coastal areas. The biography belongs to Hopper, who was raised in Nyack
and later settled in Manhattan, working as an illustrator until his paintings attracted
collectors and critics, spending summers in the Massachusetts town of Gloucester and
in Maine before building a house on Cape Cod. Yet the biography also belongs to
Farrés, who grew up in the industrial town of Igualada and later moved to Barcelona,
a city on the Mediterranean coast, to study at the university and to work as a journalist, eventually assuming his current position as an editor for the cultural supplement
of the newspaper *La Vanguardia*.

The lives overlap only in the most general outlines, however, and in some
poems Farrés insinuates as much by inserting details that are out of place. The setting
in "The City, 1927" is indicative of New York, referring to "altes arquitectures
futurists i blocs/de pisos sense personalitat" ("towering futuristic architecture/and
characterless apartment blocks"). But then the reader encounters a quintessentially
Mediterranean sight:

> oliveres de rabassudes soques
> que fructifiquen a les acaballes
> de la tardor

> olive groves cleared of stumps
> yielding a crop in the last days
> of fall

(Farrés 2009: 22, 23)

In such instances, Farrés's ekphrasis goes beyond description to appropriate Hopper's painting, using it not just to relate a Catalan life, but also to expose the limit of the image: it is so localized, so recognizably American, that it can be made more encompassing only through a surreal juxtaposition – which immediately reveals Farrés's poem to be an appropriation.

Thus the poet is and is not the painter. In the opening poem, based on Hopper's *Self Portrait* (1925–30), Farrés explains the skewed positioning of his biographical approach. The self-portrait is called "un mirall" ("a mirror") that reflects not so much Hopper's image as Farrés's, "com li agradaria al fantasista Borges" ("as would bring delight to Borges the fantasist"), and the reader is invited to accept the Borgesian premise: "Podem ben creure-ho:/Hopper i jo formem una sola persona" ("Make no bones about it:/Hopper and I form one single person") (Farrés 2009: 2, 3). The phrase "formem una sola persona" is a Catalan approximation of the sentence that concludes Borges's story "Los teólogos" (1947; "The Theologians") in which two invented church doctors, Aurelian of Aquileia and John of Pannonia, are locked in a competition to refute heresies: "formaban una sola persona" (Borges 1949: 43). Aurelian brings about John's conviction as a heretic, and the story ends "in Paradise," as James E. Irby's version reads, where "Aurelian learned that, for the unfathomable divinity, he and John of Pannonia (the orthodox believer and the heretic, the abhorrer and the abhorred, the accuser and the accused) formed one single person" (Borges 1964: 126). Hopper and Farrés, it is implied, quite like Aurelian and John, comprise an identity in difference, complementary yet opposite. The reader of Farrés's poem who becomes aware of the Borgesian intertext assumes a point of view that, hardly divine, is all too human in its wariness, ready to question the identities of both painter and poet, unable to tell which is the believer and which the heretic yet in the end suspecting the poet for his sly invocation of Borges.

Farrés subsequently formulates this suspicion in terms that are even more explicit and more precisely literary. Another intertext in the poem is Harold Bloom's notion that Kafka represents the culmination of German cultural traditions in which Goethe is a dominant influence. "Kafka," as Bloom puts it, "is a highly original crossbreed of an aphorist and a teller of parables, oddly akin to Wittgenstein as well as to Schopenhauer. Behind all of them is Goethe in his role as wisdom writer" (Bloom 1994: 454). Farrés strips away the generic determinations in this account so as to transform it into a fantastic analogy:

> Si Goethe es reencarnà en Kafka,
> Hopper en una transmigració
> plena d'encert ho féu en mi

> If Goethe was reincarnated in Kafka,
> Hopper in a transmigration most apt
> pulled it off in me

(Farrés 2009: 2, 3)

The poet continues to wink at us: he wryly attributes the "transmigration" to Hopper, who "pulled it off," when obviously it is due not to the painter but to

Farrés's own poetic sleight of hand. If Goethe, at once classical and romantic, meta-
morphosed into the absurdist Kafka, we should expect Farrés to interpret Hopper's
realism with an irony that is fundamentally indeterminate. "In his kind of irony,"
Bloom writes of Kafka, "every figure he gives us is and is not what it might seem to
be" (Bloom 1994: 451).

In this respect, the programmatic poem on the self-portrait does not disappoint. It
keeps indicating what the painting does *not* represent:

> L'home del quadre ja no és
> aquell pintor prim com un tel de ceba
> que va venir de jove a Europa a trencar el glaç,
> sinó el pintor casat, de vida estable,
> que mostrarà el seu món personal reflectint
> profusament ciutats, paisatges, dones.
> ("No faig," va dir, "sinó pintar-me a mi mateix.")
> Erra qui veu representacions
> d'Amèrica del Nord on de debò bateguen
> els tràfecs de la solitud humana,
> on intuïm les pors, obsessions, neguits,
> dilemes o estats d'ànim de l'artista
> i hi apareix la Jo, l'omnipresent esposa.
> Com la pintura emmarcada, també
> les abundants finestres i portes són miralls.

> The man in the picture no longer is
> that painter thin as a sliver of onion
> who came to Europe young to break the ice,
> but the married painter, his life settled,
> who will exhibit his personal world profusely
> reflecting cities, landscapes, women.
> ("I'm just trying to paint myself," he said.)
> You're off the track to see representations
> of North America where what really stirs
> is the agitation of human solitude,
> where we intuit the fears, obsessions, anxieties,
> dilemmas or states of mind of the artist
> and Jo appears, the omnipresent wife.
> Like the framed painting, the scads
> of windows and doors are mirrors too.

(Farrés 2009: 2, 3)

The parenthetical line quotes an interview with the American curator Katharine Kuh
in which Hopper denied that his subject is "the American scene" and claimed only to
be expressing his personality: "The man's the work," he told her, "I'm trying to paint

myself" (Kuh 1962: 131, 135). Yet in Farrés's account the matter is more compli-cated: the self-portrait shows Hopper to be "settled," "his pose relaxed and sober" ("el seu posat tranquil i seriós"), not racked by whatever "fears, obsessions, anxie-ties,/dilemmas" surface in his other works. And his wife, the painter Josephine Nivison, does not appear at all in the self-portrait, so that the epithet "omnipresent" comes off as ironic, a reminder that, although she frequently posed for the female figures in Hopper's paintings, he rarely made portraits of her, only one in oil (Levin 2007: 284).

In effect, Farrés suggests that the self-portrait is a second-order creation, a transla-tion of Hopper's experience, complete with its own peculiar ratio of loss and gain. Hopper had himself used the metaphor of translation to describe his work in the interview with Kuh. The painting *Early Sunday Morning* (1930), he said,

> was almost a literal translation of Seventh Avenue. Those houses are gone now. But most of my paintings are composites – not taken from any one scene. There was a canvas, though, I did on the Cape called *Cape Cod Afternoon* – just a house and shed done directly from nature. There have been a few others which were direct translations – but earlier.
>
> *(Kuh 1962: 131)*

If, for Hopper, a painting translates the figures, objects, and settings that it represents, it does not reproduce an invariant contained in them for several reasons: the settings can change, the image is a composite of different scenes, and, most importantly, since "The man's the work," the translations can never be "direct" because they are always mediated decisively by Hopper's psychological state. Like the Freudian dreamwork, the creative process that produces the composite image simultaneously involves a condensation of certain details and a displacement of others. The self-portrait repressed various facts of Hopper's life, and the doorframe glimpsed at the right edge of the canvas can be taken as a mirror of his very repression, insofar as what he cannot psychologically manage has been shut out, the door leading to a hidden life. The role played by Farrés's ekphrasis, I am arguing, is to open that door, to articulate the unrepresented conditions of the painting, even if in a telegraphic or oblique manner. As he observes in the poem entitled "Stairway, 1949," he seeks a poetry "Que, com una clau al pany, obri les portes/a l'aire vivificant i al safareig" ("That like a key in a lock can open doors/to a quickening wind as well as the laundry room"), glancing at the Catalan expression "treure els draps bruts," or what in English we call "airing dirty laundry," personal information that if made public might cause embarrassment or scandal (Farrés 2009: 6, 7).

Hence the conundrum that the poet is and is not the painter persists to trouble the close of the poem on the self-portrait:

> els seus neguits o estats d'ànim són meus
> i a la vegada els meus de tots a la llum
> d'una mateixa lluna arreu del món.

his anxieties and states of mind are mine
and mine, in the same breath, belong to everybody
in the light of the same moon all over the world.

(Farrés 2009: 4, 5)

After pointing to the differences between painter and poet as well as between the
self-portrait and the painter's life, Farrés seeks to resolve them through a universaliz-
ing gesture: he fashions himself as an everyman. Yet his ability to represent humanity,
his claim that everybody's psychology is identical to his, is undercut not only by the
very language in which he writes, Catalan, but also by the minority status of that
language. On the one hand, the poet's effort to identify with Hopper expresses
deference and dependence, both of which are commanded by the prestige and power
of an American cultural icon. The opening lines of the poem present the ekphrasis as
a ventriloquist act in which Hopper speaks through his dummy-poet Farrés:

On escric tot aquest assortiment de versos
    hi ha de fet l'Edward Hopper que els engendra
    i que, bo i transcendint l'espai-temps, ve a donar-me
    les consignes.

On the spot where I write all this hodgepodge of verses
    stands Edward Hopper, in fact, who engenders them
    and who, neatly transcending space-time, sends me
    the signals.

(Farrés 2009: 2, 3)

On the other hand, the poet's effort to interrogate his identification with Hopper as
well as the paintings expresses irreverence and independence which derive from the
marginality and exclusion of Catalan literature, especially in the United States. Thus
Farrés marshals a range of destabilizing intertexts, including Borges on heresies,
Bloom on Kafka, and Hopper himself rejecting the Americanness of his paintings in
his interview with Kuh. To identify with Hopper is to become universal only
because during the twentieth century his influence became international as the
United States achieved global cultural dominance. Just as a minor language acquires
symbolic capital by translating literary works from a major language or by being
translated into one (Casanova 2002), so Farrés aims to translate himself into Hopper,
while translating Hopper's paintings into Catalan poetry. The poet's universalism is
thus sheer utopianism, an imaginary resolution of a hierarchical relation. His translating
is designed to level that relation, but actually instantiates and uncovers it.

The empire stricken

As the translator of Farrés's book, I wanted my translation to perform a function that
was not imaginary but real in its cultural effects. Given the minority of Catalan in

anglophone cultures, the mere decision to English Farrés would invest his poetry with literary capital by testifying that it is valuable enough to translate into the dominant language. Yet the nature of his project promised even more: because the poems not only take Hopper's life as their subject matter but also carry the potential to interrogate his images, a translation might defamiliarize a canonical United States painter by locating new and different meanings in his work. In the process, Farrés's project would in turn undergo interrogation. After all, I was involved in a triple translation: I was interpreting Farrés's ekphrasis as his interpretation of how Hopper's paintings interpret various American scenes through his psychology. Because each translation in this sequence is an interpretive act, each can set going a critical dialectic with its source material, a reciprocal interrogation, provided that it found a suitably suspicious audience. How, you might wonder, did this sense of the translator's task inform my English versions of the Catalan poems? By what means, whether textual or paratextual or both, did I inscribe my interpretation?

Farrés's biographical narrative, particularly in its Borgesian ramifications, became a crucial point of departure. I took it literally, thinking that, since I was translating into English, my lexicon and syntax might well borrow from the language spoken and written by Hopper (1882–1967) and Nivison (1883–1968). Their language was a rich form of American English that was prevalent from the late nineteenth to the mid-twentieth centuries. They routinely mixed registers and styles, formal and colloquial, poetically archaic and street-wise slangy, evoking a wide variety of cultural discourses. Hopper might use a phrase redolent of the King James Bible, such as when he replied to an inquiry about a watercolor by writing, "I am sure I do not know when such a one will come to pass" (quoted in Levin 2007: 505). Or he might comment on his work with scholarly abstraction: "The attempt to give concrete expression to a very amorphous impression," he wrote to a collector, "is the insurmountable difficulty in painting" (ibid.: 408–9). Yet his speech might also revert to underworld argot, such as when he called Madison Avenue "the gip St.," or to a down-home usage like "aw shucks" (ibid.: 453, 545). To learn about Hopper's and Nivison's language, I immersed myself in the painters' biographies and gathered extracts from the documents that survived them – diaries, letters, record books, interviews. I collected representative words and phrases and used them in the translations where I could create a semantic correspondence with the Catalan texts. To make the reader aware of my strategy, I described it in my introduction and put the words and phrases I selected in a section of endnotes where I also included the sentence or passage that contained the item along with a brief reference to the occasion or context. But I did not stop here: I viewed Farrés's biographical narrative as license to cultivate *throughout the translation* a linguistic heterogeneity comparable to the painters' speech and writing. Hence I incorporated diction that did not actually appear in their documents, but that they might have used, in my view, considering their habitual forms of expression.

Nonetheless, I consider my work to be not an adaptation, not a free rewriting of the Catalan texts, but a translation as the term is commonly defined today, governed by an equivalence in meaning according to current dictionary definitions and generally respectful of sentence construction, line length, and enjambment as far as structural differences between Catalan and English allow. The translation also adheres quite closely to the form of Farrés's Catalan, which is itself heterogeneous, combining the current standard dialect with colloquialisms and slang, academic and technical jargons, foreign loan words, and neologisms. Some examples: "plegar de la feina" ("to knock off work"), "cama-segada" ("leg-weary" or, in my version, "bone-tired"), "fer castells a l'aire" ("to build castles in the air"), "testimoni" ("deposition"), "temps anticiclònic" ("anticyclonic weather"), "Bildungsroman," "vulgus," "tantsemenfo-tismes" ("couldn'tgiveadamnism") (Farrés 2009: 24–25, 46–47, 88–89, 6–7, 18–19, 20, 36, 8–9).

On more than one occasion, Farrés's frequent use of idioms forced me to depart from close renderings and settle for approximations. "És com caure del candeler o com treure'ls/un pes de sobre," two common expressions that can be translated into standard English as "It is like losing influence or like removing/a weight from themselves," became "It's like losing clout or taking/a load off their minds," while the equally common expression "perdo l'esma," which can be translated as "I lose my orientation," became "I lose my north" (ibid.: 10–11, 50–51). As these examples indicate, my choices tended to exceed the Catalan because I searched for marked nonstandard items to match Hopper's and Nivison's American vernacular. I even chose nonstandard alternatives at points where the Catalan was in the standard dialect. Thus "tot" ("everybody") became "all and sundry," "una gran mentida" ("a big lie") became "a cock-and-bull story," "planys" ("complaints") became "bellyaching," the sentence, "El cas és que transmits tensió i malestar" ("The fact is that you transmit tension and uneasiness") became "Fact is, you seem jumpy, in a stew," and "portentosa" ("portentous") became "wondrous strange" (ibid.: 4–5, 52–53, 58–59, 54–55, 66–67).

Developing a style that samples or is analogous to the painters' language enables a range of potential effects. It challenges the strategy that has long dominated literary translation in English among many other languages, fluency or easy readability in the current standard dialect, whereby the translator's interpretive labor is made invisible (Venuti 2008: 1–5). Securing fluency by relying on a restricted form of the translating language, the most familiar and most homogeneous dialect, produces an illusion of transparency, the sense that the translation is not a translation but the source text, whereas variations on the standard can shatter that illusion and call attention to the second-order status of the translation, enriching the receptive reader's response in a way that can increase rather than diminish pleasure. In my versions of Farrés's poems, this effect is supported by the bilingual format of the book, so that an anglophone reader expecting fluency in the standard dialect might encounter a nonstandard item in the English text and be driven to glance across the page at the Catalan, suddenly confronted with the awareness that an original composition lies behind the transla-tion, and even that in this particular project they might be seen as working together. Thus a reviewer for the foreign-literature weblog *Three Percent* experienced a certain estrangement at coming across the word "bellyaching" in the translation of "Summer in the City, 1949." She described it as the surprise of "bellyaching" which glides smoothly in the voice of Hopper, until the startling realization occurs that this is Hopper speaking Catalan and so "bellyaching" is a moment of linguistic impossibility that prevents the reader from becoming too comfortable with the language.

(Mena 2010)

Although the reviewer was clearly open to my strategy, willing to think through its implications, the very notion of "impossibility" might be further unpacked: it can be taken as the first stage in constructing a critical dialectic between the Catalan and English texts. Farrés's choice of "planys," a current standard usage in Catalan that can easily be translated into standard English with "complaints," exposes the shift in register involved in the slang term "bellyaching," thereby worrying the equivalence in my choice and revealing my appropriation of the Catalan text to serve my cultural political agenda (namely, to challenge current translation practices and to increase the translator's visibility by broadening the conditions of readability). Yet "bellyaching," noticeable precisely because it deviates not only from the narrowly defined fluency that dominates anglophone translation but also from the rather homogeneous context I created in my version, can also call into question Farrés's project, the authenticity or plausibility of his ventriloquist act, simply because he wrote his poems in Catalan and I chose to translate them into an English woven with Hopper's and Nivison's language. "Bellyaching" is a point where the ventriloquism breaks down because of linguistic differences.

The strategy I adopted can also release meanings that are specific to the poem in which the nonstandard items occur. The Catalan text of "Self Portrait, 1925–30," in its ironic mention of biographical details that are not represented in the painting, refers to Nivison as "l'omnipresent esposa" ("the omnipresent wife"). But it is in the translation that the reader can glimpse Nivison's presence, not merely through the retention of her name but also through her language. In a letter from 1943, Nivison invited an art critic to view her work, but she apparently lacked confidence and vacillated, writing, "Of course there are skads of reasons why this could never be" (quoted in Levin 2007: 361). I used "scads" (a variant spelling to signal a different context) to render the Catalan "abundants," maintaining a semantic correspondence since both words signify "large quantities": "Like the framed painting, the scads/of windows and doors are mirrors too." The source of my choice is identified in an endnote, making possible a critique of Hopper's image as well as Farrés's ventriloquism: the word can encourage the reader both to interpret the closed door in the self-portrait as Hopper's repression of his marriage to a painter (who is working in the next room) and to acknowledge that in the translations the voice heard might be hybrid, both Hopper's and Nivison's. That the mirror-like door resembles a framed painting is a reminder that Hopper's self-image might even be taken as a portrait of Nivison, who tirelessly supported his career: she inspired him to experiment with watercolor, depicted in her paintings architectural structures that reappeared in his, kept careful records of the work he sold, and tempered her own painterly ambitions (Levin 2007: 168–69, 199). Hopper was, in fact, uncomfortable with Nivison's work as a painter: when she once asked him, "Isn't it nice to have a wife who paints?" he replied, "It stinks" (her diary entry from 10 September 1941, quoted in Levin 2007: 343). My choice of "scads" again shifts from standard Catalan to colloquial English, putting into question the equivalence established by the translation, while revealing my appropriation of the source text to serve a gender politics (namely, to question the asymmetry in the painters' careers). The word is a node of interrogative meanings, awaiting a suspicious reader to gauge their effects in relation to Farrés's poem and Hopper's image.

Farrés could not have anticipated that his ekphrastic poetry would be translated into a dominant language like English, let alone by a theoretically oriented translator who aims to challenge that language as well as the practices that continue to dominate anglophone translation. But the poet's own playful inclination towards irony, at times of a Kafkaesque sort, can go some way towards justifying a translation that favors a hermeneutics of suspicion, as Paul Ricoeur called it (Ricoeur 1970: chapter 1), discounting the seemingly coherent surface of a work so as to probe for latent meanings through omissions, additions, or discrepancies.

Male(s) gazing

This approach is especially illuminating with distinctive aspects of Hopper's paintings, such as their voyeurism. Consider Farrés's poem on Hopper's painting, *Compartment C, Car 293* (1938):

> Rostre sever, cabells
> més o menys rossos, ulls
> amb una espurna d'introversió,
> cutis al pic de la vida, posat
> de vés-guipant-me-fins-que-t'avorreixis,
> vestit negre que li estrenyia els pits
> i un joc de cames llargues i en plenes facultats,
> era, i fa de bon dir, una dona atractiva
> i, en el sentit modern del mot, "independent."
>
> Aquelles hores mortes del tren eren propícies
> per llançar-li mirades furtives a la dona
> que seia a l'altra banda del passadís. Llegia,
> la pobra, amb tanta concentració
> que a l'horabaixa li passà per alt
> que els últims raigs del sol s'adherien encesos
> per l'oest a la volta sense límits del cel.

> Face stern, hair
> more or less blonde, eyes

with an inward-looking glint,
skin in the pink, wearing
a stare-till-you're-bored attitude
in a black dress that hugged her breasts
and a pair of long legs, in good working order,
she looked real swell, sure enough,
and "independent," as the saying goes.

The down time on the train was just
the ticket for stealing looks at her
as she sat across the aisle, reading –
poor kid – with such concentration
that at dusk she completely missed
the sun's last rays burning in the west,
stuck to the limitless vault of the sky.

(*Farrés 2009: 17, 18*)

The most remarkable feature of Farrés's ekphrasis is the addition of a character who does not appear in the painting, the speaker of the poem, who, because of the overarching biographical narrative, can be identified as male. This addition is transformative: the focus of the painting is the solitary woman, whereas the focus of the poem is a man whose erotic attraction to the woman moves him to watch, describe, and comment on her.

To a large extent, Farrés's poem interprets the painting in accordance with the art historical reception of Hopper's work. Gail Levin formulates the prevalent view by observing that the "works of his maturity" issue from "his experience" in representing "the loneliness of recurrent tense interiors, the sexual undercurrent, and the perspective of the voyeur" (Levin 2007: 81). *Compartment C, Car 293* possesses a more precise biographical connection. In the weeks immediately before Hopper began the painting, he had traveled by train to serve on juries at art museums and institutes in Philadelphia, Richmond, and Indianapolis. Because Hopper's trip constituted the longest period he was apart from Nivison since their marriage more than a decade before (ibid.: 300), the painting might be taken as a complicated expression of his desire for his wife, although filtered through other women he may have encountered while traveling. It was Nivison who posed for the figure, a woman reading in a train car.

The voyeuristic quality of the image represents the woman as an object of desire. Yet the desire must be inferred since it is no sooner registered than repressed, a contradictory effect made possible by divergent pictorial features. These features begin with the size of the canvas itself, which at $20'' \times 18''$ is significantly smaller than most of Hopper's oil paintings, including two that he completed in the following year: *Cape Cod Evening* ($30 \frac{1}{4}'' \times 40 \frac{1}{4}''$) and *New York Movie* ($32 \frac{1}{4}'' \times 40 \frac{1}{8}''$). Not only is the voyeurism implicit, then, but it is also contained within the narrow confines of the pictorial space. The figure is eroticized by her positioning: her downward look, with her face partially concealed by her hat, directs the viewer's eye to what can be seen of her body – her blonde hair and red lipstick, already linked to sexual appeal in the 1930s, the contour of her breasts, her crossed legs bared to the knee and offering a glimpse of one thigh. Still, any titillation is preempted: the woman's legs are cropped by the edge of the canvas, and the long-sleeved dress is buttoned to her neck. Other signs of repression include not only the constricted quality of the space but also the curved panel over the window, which Nivison identified in the record book as "the upper berth," a bed that is stored out of sight (Levin 1995: 258).

The green that dominates Hopper's painting adds to the sense of repressed desire, although through an intervisual connection. Levin describes the unsettling effect produced by the coloring: "The overall green tonality and the harsh glare of electric bulbs cast a light that disturbs an otherwise calm and quiet mood" (ibid.). To my mind, this effect evokes Van Gogh's *The Night Café* (1888), which had been bought in 1933 by Hopper's patron, Stephen Clark, and exhibited with the painter's works on two occasions (Vincent and Lees 2006: 156; Levin 2007: 310). Van Gogh's green, covering the ceiling and the billiard table, is garish, mixed with yellow, so that it contributes to the lurid atmosphere of the scene, whereas Hopper's green is relatively restrained because it is softer, more pale, but it is nonetheless disturbing in that it is much more extensive, covering walls, windows, blinds, and seats. "Everything about the car green," wrote Nivison, "from spot of strong reflected light high on wall at R. – to deep shadow over upper berth" (Levin 1995: 258). Van Gogh described the aim of his painting to his brother Theo: "I have tried to express the terrible passions of humanity by means of red and green" (Van Gogh 1888). In Hopper's painting, the passion is not terrible but tempered, perhaps somewhat guilt-ridden, since his sexual relationship with Nivison was troubled by his selfish demands and her inexperience (Levin 2007: 178–83).

Farrés's poem detaches the painting from Hopper's biography so as to inscribe a related but rather different significance, thereby establishing the basis for a critical dialectic between image and text. In an interview during January of 2009, I asked Farrés to explain his representation of modern life in the poem, and he referred to a generalized voyeurism as well as the biographical narrative:

> La presència de la dona m'ajudava a introduir el tema del voyeurisme (un voyeurisme quotidià que experimenta qualsevol persona diàriament) i la fascinació no corresposta del "jo" poètic (Hopper i jo alhora) per les dones (atractives).

> (The presence of the woman helped me to introduce the theme of voyeurism (a quotidian voyeurism that any person experiences daily) and the unreciprocated fascination of the poetic "I" (Hopper and me at the same time) for (attractive) women.)

Yet the poem is the seventh in the sequence, a position that places it in the section that portrays the poetic "I" as a young man, while Hopper was fifty-five when he painted *Compartment C, Car 293*. This discrepancy became more apparent in the interview:

> El poema el vaig col·locar en la part inicial del llibre perquè em servia per explicar els inicis de Hopper i el pas a la gran ciutat (Nova York): es troba entremig d'altres poemes/quadres amb referències ferroviàries, la majoria d'exteriors (vies, estacions, trens, túnels) excepte aquest, que és un interior, per tant era l'únic que em permetia parlar del "viatge" des de dins, des del punt de vista del viatger.

> (I put the poem in the initial part of the book so that it would serve as an explanation of Hopper's beginnings and the move to the big city (New York): it is positioned among the other poems/paintings with railroad references, the majority of exteriors (streets, stations, trains, tunnels), except that this painting, which is an interior, is therefore the only one that allowed me to speak of the journey from the inside, from the point of view of the traveler.)

Farrés seems to have intended a simple correspondence between his poem and the painting, but the painting does not represent "Hopper's beginnings." The chronological discrepancy exposes the poet's departure from the painter's life to represent "the point of view of the traveler," which can only be that of the poet himself: he was thirty-nine when he published his book of ekphrastic poems and much younger when he first traveled to Barcelona. Farrés's poem does not so much present a twinned biography, that of painter and poet, as hijack the painting to depict a moment in his own life.

At the same time, Farrés's addition of the male speaker sends us back to the image to recognize its different spatial perspective. The reader of the poem assumes the speaker's position, sitting across the aisle from the woman, level with her, while the viewer of the painting is positioned at an acute angle slightly above the female figure, precisely as if we were with Hopper at his easel, standing at his full height (six feet, five inches) and looking down at his model who is also his wife. In severing the image from Hopper's biography, Farrés removes the sense of repressed desire. But his poem also foregrounds the voyeurism and emphasizes that it is gender-specific. By situating the image in a narrative and assigning the description to a narrator, Farrés's poem reveals exactly how the male gaze turns the female figure into an object of desire.

On this score, too, the differences between painting and poem tell more than the similarities. Hopper's impressionistic brushwork leaves indistinct the woman's physical appearance and facial expression and thereby highlights the rhetoric of Farrés's description, which is quite detailed. The poem moves from head to toe in imitation of a conventional blazon, evoking the compliment of the lady's beauty in the Petrarchan tradition and leading the informed reader to recognize the resemblance between the two-part structure of Farrés's sixteen-line poem and a typical sonnet, fourteen lines that might be divided into an octave and sestet. In the Petrarchan tradition, as Nancy Vickers has argued, the blazon is a form of mastery exerted through the fragmentation and reification of the woman's body: "to describe is," she observes, "to control, to possess, and ultimately to use to one's own ends" (Vickers 1986: 219). The Petrarchan lover maintains his psychological coherence when confronted with the lady's unwillingness to reciprocate his love by rhetorically dismembering her in his compliment (Vickers 1981). Similarly, Farrés's male speaker constructs his blazon of the solitary woman while "llançar-li mirades furtives" ("hurling furtive glances at her") – an aggressive gesture, to be sure, that ignores her "stern" look and is apparently designed to combat her "vés-guipant-me-fins-que-t'avorreixis" ("peek-till-you're-bored") defiance and to break her silent "concentració" ("concentration"). His blazon can be seen as a means of mastering or overcoming her attitude, which, if we judge by the image, is simply introspective and oblivious to the presence of any viewer. A similar effect is produced by the condescension in his use of "la pobra" ("the poor woman"), a tone that aims to give him the upper hand in asserting his knowledge of what is best for her.

The Petrarchan intertext enables a critique of the masculinist ideology that informs Farrés's treatment of the speaker. It is only near the end that the poem seems momentarily to escape this critique, in the self-consciousness signaled in the penultimate line by the word "s'adherien," from "adherer," a verb meaning "to adhere" or "to stick." The idea that "the last rays of the sun" are "stuck" to the sky can imply that the sunset is an image or representation, affixed, possibly painted, but in any case not real. As a result, a poem that depends throughout on creating the illusion of reality suddenly tips into artifice, and the reader is potentially distanced from any identification with the speaker whose values appear as cultural constructions attributed to Hopper's painting by Farrés, but evidently belong to the poet.

Translating voices

The translation inscribes yet another interpretation, reflecting my analysis of both painting and poem. I sought to work Hopper's biography back into the English version by following the strategy of drawing on his lexicon. I translated the eighth line, "era […] una dona atractiva" ("she was […] an attractive woman"), as "she looked real swell" because in 1931 Hopper had used the word "swell" in a letter to the author of the first monograph on his work: "I think you did a swell job on me as a Puritan in the Whitney Museum book" (Levin 2007: 239). The quotation was placed in an endnote so that the reader might not only learn the source of "swell" but also be made aware of the theme of repression through the reference to Hopper as "a Puritan." In the translation, the word joins a string of similar colloquialisms which were current during Hopper's lifetime. Thus "cutis al pic de la vida" ("skin at the peak of life") became "skin in the pink," "fa de bon dir" ("it is easy to say," "it goes without saying") became "sure enough," and "propícies" ("favorable") became "just the ticket." Similarly, I increased the sexual resonance of the Catalan text so as to pick up the repressed desire in the painting. The line "vestit negre que li estrenyia els pits" became "in a black dress that hugged her breasts," avoiding simple, descriptive choices for "estrenyia" ("pressed," "tightened around") in favor of a suggestive personification ("hugged"). The phrase used to describe her legs, "en plenes facultats" ("fully functional"), became "in good working order," which in the voyeuristic context might acquire a salacious undertone. The more pronounced colloquialism of the translation at once discloses and compensates for Hopper's diminished presence in the Catalan text.

It also winds up deepening the characterization of the male speaker. The register of the English is lower than that of the Catalan, which is predominantly in the current standard dialect. In the translation, as a result, the speaker is endowed with a colorful directness or frankness, but he is also positioned in a lower social class and so becomes representative of the milieu where Farrés himself was born and raised as the child of textile workers (Hopper, in contrast, was born into a middle-class family: his father owned a dry-goods store). The working-class affiliation hints that the speaker's education is limited, an implication that is consistent with the Catalan text insofar as the speaker feels sorry for the woman because she is reading rather than gazing out of the window. This point is reinforced by a discrepancy between Hopper's painting and Farrés's poem: the woman in the painting is reading magazines, identified by Nivison as *The New Yorker* and *Reader's Digest,* and since this material does not require intense concentration, it would seem that the speaker is questioning the mere act of reading (Levin 1995: 258). Hence I translated "la pobra," not as "the poor woman" or "the poor girl," both renderings in the standard dialect, but as "poor kid," a slangy expression that communicates much greater condescension. The choice might be seen as more evocative of Farrés as a young man, the first in his family to attend university, and therefore supports his explanation of the poem as recording the speaker's "beginnings."

The colloquialism serves to heighten the social difference between the woman and the speaker, a difference of which he himself seems to be very much aware in calling her "independent." Along with the phrase "en el sentit modern del mot" ("in the modern sense of the word"), "independent" alludes to women's changing status during the early twentieth century when through education and a significant presence in the work force they achieved an economic and social autonomy that was accompanied by greater control over their sexuality. This development occurred in both the United States and Catalonia, although for American women it was somewhat derailed by the Depression while for their Spanish contemporaries it suffered a serious setback under Franco's repressive dictatorship (Kleinberg 1999: 207–12, 217–20, 234–36, 242–44; Nash 1983: 24–25, 49–52). The historical allusion identifies the speaker with Hopper, whose wife epitomized the social changes (both were in their forties when they married) but who was uncomfortable with them since "all his life [he] felt acutely the conflicts between traditional and modern" (Levin 2007: 111, 206–8). Thus he disapproved not only of Nivison's painterly ambitions but also of her interest in driving their car. In the poem, similarly, the woman's independence is simultaneously attractive and off-putting to the speaker. Yet Hopper was an avid reader of English and French, art criticism as well as literature, whereas for the speaker reading is questionable, particularly if it is being done by a woman who appeals to him. The formulaic phrase "en el sentit modern del mot," by indicating a knowledge of language change, undermines the verisimilitude of the Catalan text since it does not plausibly fit a character who expresses an antipathy towards reading. The rather academic formula is more appropriate for the university-educated Farrés, living in post-Franco Catalonia where women have not only regained but also improved upon the emancipatory developments that preceded the Civil War (Jones 1997: chapters 1–3).

No translation can be expected to put into play this dense network of meanings. Furthermore, a close rendering of the phrase "in the modern sense of the word" would involve the use of standard English. Instead, I translated freely: "as the saying goes." This choice keeps to the colloquial register, strengthening the speaker's working-class affiliation. It might even acquire an ironic note, if it is taken as a knowing wink at the reader, turning "independent" into a euphemism for sexual freedom. Yet the bilingual format of the book can also reveal that here the English rendering significantly departs from the Catalan text, prompting a closer examination of Farrés's formulaic phrase. The suspicious reader might then perceive that in the Catalan it is a point of implausibility where the identity between the university-educated poet and the speaker comes apart, and what becomes discernible is not only the pressure to make Hopper's painting represent a moment in the history of Catalan women, but also Farrés's effort to voice his own desire through the American painter.

The concluding phrase "vault of the sky" adds another facet to the speaker: pretentious romanticism. The Catalan "la volta [...] del cel" is current usage, rather ordinary, whereas the English "vault" is a poetical archaism, less likely to be encountered in modern American English than in Shakespeare or Alexander Pope. The "vault of the sky" might have been written by Hopper, given his occasional use of language that was both formal and literary. It can also be taken as highfalutin speech, suggesting how the speaker might try to impress an educated woman, or at least a woman who reads. Yet how would he have come to be acquainted with such a poeticism? By reading the King James Bible, of course: "He spreadeth out the heavens like a vault" (2 Esdras 16:59).

Letting the reader out of the bottle?

Initially, the reception of my translation was mixed. In an effort to create an audience for the project, I tried to place some of the English versions in magazines in both the United States and the United Kingdom. Over a two-year period (2007–09), sixteen magazines rejected my submissions, with some editors turning down several different groups of poems (namely *Poetry*, *The New Yorker*, and the *Times Literary Supplement*), while another fifteen magazines accepted them. In the meantime, I was approaching publishers but having no success in finding one who might publish the complete manuscript. I had thought that Hopper's popularity would attract attention, but, paired with an unknown Catalan poet, that wasn't exactly opening doors. By 2009, eight publishers had declined to bring out the translation for reasons that were literary or financial or both.

Apart from the reiterated view that the book was unmarketable, I learned that the translations did not appeal to a prevailing taste for poetry that was intensely emotional and thereby invited the reader's vicarious participation. Alane Salierno Mason, senior editor at W. W. Norton and co-founder of the online literary magazine *Words without Borders*, felt that the poems were "a little boxy and cerebral," although she remarked that her preference for more "lyric" writing was "no doubt a sign of middlebrow-ness" (email: 13 May 2008). Jill Schoolman, the publisher of Archipelago Books, has focused her list almost exclusively on translations of elite literature since she founded the press in 2003. But her response was similar to Mason's: "I don't respond in a visceral way to his poetic voice" (email: 14 May 2008). Much to my disappointment, Farrés's ekphrastic project was not finding favor for precisely the reason that it fascinated me: it demands a more insistently interpretive approach that brings to the fore the issue of translation, even if the heterogeneity of the English in my versions might be appreciated on its own terms. Or so I learned in 2009, when by some miracle the poet-translator Richard Howard chose the manuscript as the winner of the Robert Fagles Prize for a translation of a contemporary poet. Howard's citation praised the translation for "its resourceful eloquence, its persistent vitality." The prize included publication, which was handled by Graywolf in the United States, and this development led to Carcanet's decision to publish the book in the United Kingdom.

And so *Edward Hopper: Poems* was published in two anglophone cultures that translate relatively little foreign-language literature (Venuti 2008: 11–12; for statistics on poetry translations, see chapter 11: 171). Despite the dismal market prospects for a poetry translation, the book sold reasonably well, just over 600 copies within the first year. It received only a handful of reviews, five to my knowledge, but they were appreciative, and a few recognized the interpretive challenge posed by ekphrastic poems, if not the task of translating them. Erica Mena's review for *Three Percent* was the most discerning, willing to examine the translations against the Catalan texts and to remark on the defamiliarizing effects of my strategy. Natalie Whittle, the reviewer for the *Financial Times*, noticed the suggestive disjunction between the poems and the paintings, although the limitations imposed by a brief notice in a newspaper did not allow for any elaboration:

> poet and painter seem to operate in opposite vernaculars: where Hopper excludes all vitality, Farrés fills it back in, almost as if gossiping about Hopper's subjects. In "Hotel Room, 1931", Farrés writes, "She'll start to pace around the room/leaving a fruity fragrance in the air/that reeks of mustiness," playfully adding smell to art. For Hopper's famous "Nighthawks", Farrés writes a snarky dialogue for the man and the woman in the painting who sit deadpan at the bar.
>
> *(Whittle 2010: 16)*

Whittle read the poems closely. What translator, you might ask, could quarrel with that? The fact remains that her account is misleading: the dialogue happens to be considerably more snarky in the English version than in the Catalan because of the American vernacular, its tendency towards the hardboiled and the noirish. For

Whittle, however, although she called the translation "wonderful," the textual effects must all be attributed to Farrés as if the English were a transparent window onto the Catalan. In pointing to Farrés's "vitality," she may well have been pointing to what Howard saw as the "persistent vitality" of the translation, but without any awareness that she was doing so.

The habit of commenting on the translation as if it were the source text has long plagued the reception of translations, and it is still widespread among reviewers as well as readers, even among publishers and translators themselves. It shows that the most positive response can involve an utter misunderstanding of translation and a wholesale suppression of the translator's writerly interpretation. In 2010, Karen Rigby, a poet who also co-edits an online literary magazine that is hospitable to translations, *The Cerise Press*, praised Farrés's book without qualification in her review for *Words without Borders*. Her article was judged exemplary by the National Book Critics Circle, which posted it as a "featured review" on the Board of Directors' blog, *Critical Mass*. Like other reviewers of *Edward Hopper: Poems*, she astutely observed that it "demonstrates the possibilities of the ekphrastic, and the importance of moving beyond the transcriptive and towards the transformative," and she noted the twinned biography in Farrés's narrative, treating "the artist and the poet [as] two personas who are fused" (Rigby 2010). But when she discussed Farrés's droll invocation of the Muses, her comments assumed that translation is merely transcriptive:

> In "Stairway, 1949" we find the *ars poetica* of this new poetic character:
>
> > … inspire in me a poetry that doesn't concede
> > the benefit of the doubt, that scrapes together
> > profound thoughts and enables [this] our world,
> > so inscrutable, to seem transparent.
> > That like a key in a lock can open doors
> > to a quickening wind as well as the laundry room.
>
> We are reminded that patience is required to produce, regardless of the medium. These "profound thoughts" do not arrive as lightning. They must be scraped with an effort that recalls Hopper's own response when asked about the origins of his paintings: "It's very hard to define how they come about but it's a long process of gestation, in the mind and a rising emotion … " The poet's sensibility, that "scrapes together" words, is like that of the artist, who is bound by vagaries of weather and light, and who must similarly wait for ideas to come.
>
> *(Rigby 2010)*

Rigby did her homework: to support her idea that Hopper and Farrés are fused into one poetic character, she quoted from the art historian Brian O'Doherty's interview with the painter (O'Doherty 1973: 22). Yet her reading rests on the misapprehension that the key phrase "scrapes together" simply reproduces or transfers Farrés's Catalan. It doesn't. I chose that phrase to render the Catalan "reculli," which is usually translated into standard English with such words as "collects" or "gathers." Thus although the choice maintains a core semantic correspondence, it hardly signals the meaning of the Catalan word without transformation: it rather reflects my colloquializing strategy, while hinting at the sort of creative effort that Rigby sought to document with the quotation – except that the effort has been made not only by Hopper and Farrés but by me too. That hint is an interpretation that I inscribed through my translation; it does not exist in the Catalan text. Rigby thought otherwise: for her, the speaker encompassed only Hopper and Farrés, whereby she suppressed the translator's intervention because she assumed a model of translation that is instrumental, not hermeneutic.

You may feel inclined to argue – in the reviewer's defense – that only a knowledge of Catalan and an ability to compare the English to the Catalan text can support the kind of response I am advocating. But this argument isn't persuasive: the reviewer's ignorance can't justify the failure to take into account the translated status of the book under review. Translations can begin to be read as translations only when the reader assumes that translating is interpretive and therefore transformative of the source text, even when a semantic correspondence is constructed. The translator picks every word in the translation, regardless of whether a word in the source text lies behind it, and since for many decades now translations have submitted to a discursive regime that privileges a variety of fluency restricted to current standard usage, nonstandard items can be taken as sites where the translator's interpretive labor becomes visible. Rigby clearly latched onto an English colloquialism that noticeably deviates from the standard dialect and so prompts commentary. The pressing question then becomes: Why read the deviation as if it occurred in the Catalan text and not in the English translation, as if the poet were completely responsible for it (he wrote only in Catalan!) and not the translator? This reading of the deviation occurs because a translation is expected to be a transparent reproduction of a semantic invariant which the source text is imagined to contain. Interestingly, the word "this" was deleted from the translation extract quoted in Rigby's review – the third line should end with the phrase "this our world" – although whether the deletion was made by her or by the magazine's editors is not clear. An archaic construction classifiable as early modern English, the phrase might conjure up John Milton or William Blake: it glances at Hopper's occasional use of poetical language as well as the traditional form that Farrés adopts in the poem, the invocation of the Muses typical of epic. But it has no counterpart in his Catalan text. In omitting a striking deviation from current standard English, someone has removed yet another sign of the translator's presence.

If the study and practice of translation are to advance, translations must be read as texts in their own right. This is not to say that only my understanding of my Farrés translation is the right understanding, that only the reading that interprets the paintings, poems, and translations as I have interpreted them can be seen as acceptable. No, the point is not to valorize a specific interpretation, but rather to set out from the assumption that translation, like any second-order creation, performs an

interpretive act or a set of multiple interpretations which make it relatively autonomous from the source materials that it interprets. In this way, a second-order creation
can support varying interpretations, depending on the interpretants (ideas, discourses)
that the reader or viewer brings to it. Insofar as this assumption constitutes a theory, I
am arguing that the more theoretical sophistication a reader can bring to a response to
a translation, the better equipped that reader will be to understand it as a translation
without collapsing it into the source text.

This position risks the charge of elitism, I realize, by emphasizing the need for
specialized knowledge in approaching translations. But under examination any such
charge turns out to be naïve political posturing that encourages anti-intellectualism
and threatens to reinforce the cultural marginality from which translation continues
to suffer today, especially in anglophone cultures like the United States and the
United Kingdom. For readers must be taught to read translations just as literacy must
be taught – is the very act of reading therefore undemocratic or exclusionary? – and
the academy is the most appropriate place to teach translation-oriented reading, since
it is colleges and universities that produce the readers who are most likely to be
interested in translations, not only of literary works but also of texts in the arts and
human sciences generally. To insist that today literacy is essential to a viable social life
whereas reading a translation is a luxury begs the question of what constitutes contemporary citizenship. The cultural and political asymmetries that characterize our
globalized world and reach deeply into local situations have brought a new urgency
to the recognition of different languages and cultures, so that translation remains a
central practice in encouraging an ethical cosmopolitanism (see Cronin 2003: 6;
2006: chapter 1). Globalization has brought a dependence on translation, despite
widespread multilingualism, and this development points to the necessity to produce
and appreciate translated texts in the most sophisticated ways. Perhaps most importantly, no reading can occur except on the basis of theoretical concepts that at once
enable and constrain the understanding of texts, so that theory in some form, whether
unconsciously applied or inchoate or formulated with abstract precision, cannot be
separated from reading. Translation has largely been excluded from the theoretical
self-consciousness that has grown among university-educated readers over the past
half-century because an instrumental model remains entrenched even in academic
institutions.

I conceive of the value of theory rather differently from Wittgenstein's famous
assertion in his *Philosophical Investigations* that his "aim in philosophy" is "To show the
fly the way out of the fly-bottle" (Wittgenstein 2009: 110). This metaphor has been
understood as expressing his therapeutic conception of philosophy: the aim is to
release humans from cognitive traps by rejecting the obfuscating questions that academic philosophers raise and by removing the fallacies that are embedded in everyday
language (Schroeder 2006: 125; Hallett 1971). In Garth Hallett's view, "The source
of our difficulties is the whole conceptual system in which we live and move and
have our being from the moment we are born," and this system is coterminous with
"language, the invisible force which, both for better and for worse, shapes all our
thinking and our world" (Hallett 1971: 85, 104). Yet if "language is the bottle," in

Hallett's words, we cannot get out of it: that would lead to silence, and confusion would reign. The metaphor is useful in thinking about the relation between theory and translation insofar as translation has long been trapped by an instrumentalism that fosters the illusion of transparency through fluent translating narrowly defined. As a result, the translator is made invisible, and the study and practice of translation continue to be marginal in many if not most academic institutions as well as in the culture at large, not only in the anglophone world but also worldwide. The solution, however, is not to be released from the bottle – the source text is never accessible without mediation – but to replace instrumentalism with a hermeneutic model that can disclose the interpretation inscribed by translation. This bottle, we might say, is not clear and smooth but tinted and textured.

Or perhaps now is the time to abandon entirely the recurrent tendency to formulate metaphors for translation. The word "translation" itself is metaphorical, derived from the Latin *transferre*, to carry across, so that it contains an etymological insistence on the instrumental model, an assumption of a source invariant that might be transferred from one space to another (Hermans 1999: 51–52). Instead of developing analogies for translation, especially those rooted in instrumentalism, we should rather study its materiality, the changing linguistic and cultural conditions in which translated texts are produced and circulated. Only in this way can we learn how the translator's verbal choices are in one and the same stroke interpretive moves that inspire readers to interpret further.

14

TOWARDS A TRANSLATION CULTURE

A diagnosis of a profession

Today anglophone literary translators, if they choose to take the initiative and submit a proposal to publishers, inevitably face multiple rejections. Few translators enjoy the luxury of a steady stream of commissions, so that if they want to translate, they must necessarily develop their own projects and hope to locate a receptive editor. Yet so many factors conspire against them. Since the Second World War, the volume of English-language translations published annually has averaged a tiny fraction of total book output, 2–4 percent (Venuti 2008: 11–12), and the figure is likely to decrease in view of the less than sanguine prospects of book publishing in competition with other cultural industries, especially those involving electronic media. Behind these factors lies an unfavorable cultural situation. As English achieved global hegemony during the past century, anglophone cultures grew increasingly insular, complacent in the awareness that English was the most translated language worldwide, less interested in foreign cultural traditions and trends (except, perhaps, fashion and food), and much less hospitable to literary translation.

There is also the persistent financial problem. Since 1900, literary translations have not been consistently profitable for publishers in the United Kingdom and the United States. Most translations of fiction, poetry, and other literary genres have incurred a loss within one or two years of publication, even in the case of writers who later entered the modern canon, and relatively few translations have been retained on backlists. Proust, Mann, Svevo, Rilke were all commercial failures when the first English translations of their work were published (see chapter 9: 160). Imagine, then, the myriad foreign writers whose works have been translated but quickly faded into oblivion. Robin Healey's bibliography listing English translations of twentieth-century Italian literature includes roughly 1,400 works published between 1929 and 1997 (Healey 1998). Most of these translations cannot be found anywhere except in the British Library and the Library of Congress. The occasional success of a contemporary foreign novelist like Roberto Bolaño or Stieg Larsson is misleading. The current situation has not really changed enough to indicate any across-the-board upsurge in sales of translations or any expansion of the readership for them.

Hence most translators will be fortunate if they are able to translate a handful of literary works during their careers and even more fortunate if the translation projects that they themselves initiate see print. A translator like Ralph Manheim published over one hundred translations, Richard Howard over one hundred and fifty, Joachim Neugroschel and Anthea Bell each over two hundred. Those days are gone, however, and whether they will return seems doubtful, certainly not in the foreseeable future. The fact is that too many translators are vying for too few projects. After publishing fifteen book-length translations over the past three decades, I can testify that a track record does not matter. It might even work against you, if your work has provoked controversy. I find it just as difficult to publish a translation today as I did when I was starting out.

This state of affairs, however, is not only to be recorded and lamented. It must also be interrogated. What, I want to ask, can a translator learn from rejections? I will present two recent instances from my own experience, although I have chosen to preserve the anonymity of the editors in question. What follows is not a personal attack on these particular editors, but a critique of current editorial methods and their assumptions about translation. My account, therefore, should not be dismissively reduced to sheer sour grapes. What happened to me can and does happen to many other translators. I have decided to go public in an effort to engage issues that urgently need to be discussed by both translators and readers of translations alike.

Tales of rejection

In the spring of 2009, I was translating a book by a contemporary Catalan poet named Ernest Farrés, and, as I had done in the past with other projects, I was submitting the poems to magazines. My aim was to create a readership for a foreign writer who was entirely unknown in the anglophone world. I had received a number of acceptances, but as typically happens they were outnumbered by the rejections, which were couched in form letters or the most laconic of handwritten notes and emails.

After an editor with whom I was acquainted had rejected some poems, I questioned the decision. I didn't expect the rejection to be reconsidered. No, I wanted to force the magazine to do what magazines rarely do: to make explicit the standards by which it judged the translations or, if not this particular submission, then translations in general. Editor X was kind enough to reply, explaining that the poems "didn't make us feel as if the tops of our heads were taken off." I pressed further: had Editor X ever considered that translations, by their very nature, should be judged differently from original compositions in English, or that the standard might include but should nonetheless differ from a visceral reaction that is evidently rooted in a homegrown sensibility? After all, Emily Dickinson was being quoted at me. Editor X thought my view novel and promised to give it some thought, but the conversation stopped there.

Yet I could have taken it much further. Should an English translation of a twenty-first-century Catalan poet, I would have asked, be judged according to a concept of poetry formulated by a nineteenth-century poet in the United States? Why should we hold a poet who writes in a minor language and whose literature is under-represented in English to a standard articulated by a poet who, after a shaky initial reception, now occupies an unshakeable position in the canon of American literature? Are the values enshrined in that canon inimical to Catalan and possibly other foreign poetries? Can a poem that took the top off the head of a reclusive, self-absorbed woman in nineteenth-century New England do the same to an anglophone reader today? How appropriate or fair is the application of that metaphor to translations of poems written by a Catalan man who works as a cultural editor for a Barcelona-based newspaper? Or is the problem that my translations seem too foreign, requiring a response that is not visceral but less immediate or spontaneous, more thoughtful, especially since the poems are ekphrastic, all based on paintings by Edward Hopper? Does not the use of this painter offer a basis for understanding what is distinctive and perhaps culturally specific in the foreign poet's writing by foregrounding his take on an American cultural icon? Or was the magazine pursuing a universality that few foreign poetries can – or, I would add, should – support in translation?

My questions obviously possess a critical edge, designed to provoke debate. Editor X may have been willing to treat them as worthy of consideration, if only I had gotten the opportunity to ask them. The problem, however, was that this editor seemed entirely unable to formulate such questions, let alone provide answers. The kind of speculative thinking from which the questions derive seems never to have entered into the editorial process of the magazine, even though it regularly publishes translations. For me, the most disheartening aspect of the experience was not the rejection. It was rather the knowledge that Editor X has published ten book-length translations, fiction, nonfiction, and poetry. The translating seems to have done nothing to deepen this editor's thinking about translation.

Consider another but somewhat different rejection, in this case from an editor who was producing an anthology of essays in which translators discuss their own work. Editor Z described the audience as "the translation workshops that are burgeoning all over the university landscape." The editor was interested in using an essay I had published in an academic journal which occasionally prints literary translations along with research articles and reviews. My essay introduced my translations from the work of a medieval Italian poet, Jacopone da Todi (see chapter 4). The editor's interest was encouraging: I had written the essay to argue for the value of a theoretical approach, and the editor, I believed, supported my agenda. I wanted to challenge the prevalence of belletristic commentary on translation, the tendency among contemporary translators to make fairly impressionistic remarks on their practice, on its literary and cultural value, on the equivalence they believe to have established between their translations and the source texts. To consider the problems raised by translating an archaic poetry such as Jacopone's for modern anglophone readers,

I drew on Ezra Pound's 1929 essay "Guido's Relations," in which he provided a rationale for his translations of the thirteenth-century Italian poet Guido Cavalcanti. My discussion was not merely theoretical but also methodological: the concepts it formulated were used later in the essay to analyze previous English versions of Jacopone's poetry and to explain my own rather different translation strategies.

Editor Z, however, wanted me to cut the theoretical section entirely. I was told that it "takes away from the subtlety of the trains of thought developed in the latter portions and encourages students to overlook them, since you've already provided an abstract summa." The mention of "already" is telling: the editor apparently regarded the theory as redundant and so treated it as unnecessary, not just distracting. I could only wonder about this judgment because the essay had gone through the referee process typical of academic journals: it had been scrutinized by three anonymous readers, but none of them had pointed to any redundancy or found that any section undermined or somehow detracted from the argument. Why couldn't Editor Z reach the same conclusion?

I might have attributed the problem to cursory reading if the editor didn't also include a revealing comment: "I'm a great fan of theoretical approaches embodied in practice." This view struck me as questionable: *every* literary and critical practice embodies theoretical concepts as assumptions that at once enable and constrain the practice. Such concepts make possible a translation, determining what form it will take. Translators routinely assume a concept of good literature in choosing source texts for translation, as well as a concept of good writing in making certain verbal choices while excluding others during the translation process. These concepts constitute a theory, even if they remain inchoate, unarticulated, or unconscious. They depend on more fundamental assumptions about the nature of authorship and textuality and their relationship to the world, which in turn rest on even more basic ideas of human subjectivity, of what it is to be human.

If theoretical concepts are always embodied in a practice, Editor Z must have been objecting to my insistence that these concepts, as they related directly to translation, be presented to the reader. The editor seemed to assume a one-to-one correspondence between theory and practice (thus a description of translation strategies would make a theoretical statement redundant), whereas the relations between them are usually uneven, disjunctive, and far from predictable, open to interpretation and revision during the translation process. In translating Jacopone, I was inspired by Pound's caveats, but the result was quite different from his versions of Cavalcanti. A theoretical concept can drive diverse practical applications. The editor's misunderstanding, I concluded, must have expressed an antipathy towards theory itself along with an uncritical emphasis on practice.

When I suggested as much, Editor Z asserted that the planned anthology sought "to go beyond the simplistic theory/craft or theory/belletrism opposition that polarizes much contemporary discourse about translation." But in wishing to cut the theoretical section of my essay, was not the editor merely repressing the "theory" part of those oppositions, while I was attempting to move beyond them by joining a theoretical discussion to a discussion of translation practice? "Craft" and "belletrism" involve theories too, but they are different from mine. Why shouldn't those competing theories be articulated and examined independently of the practices they make possible? Editor Z did not seem to understand that, without the formulation of theoretical concepts, commentary about translation remains imprecise and quickly turns impressionistic. I declined to allow the theoretical discussion to be cut, and the debate ended there.

The editor was in effect adopting an anti-intellectual attitude towards translation, resisting the sort of theoretical self-consciousness that might allow translators to criticize and to improve their own work as well as to provide an illuminating account of it to their readers. The most disheartening aspect of the experience, once again, was not the rejection, but the knowledge that Editor Z has published more than fifteen book-length translations of fiction and nonfiction.

The rise of belletrism in translation

The experiences I have been describing reflect the continuing dominance of a belletristic approach to translation among literary translators, whether they are affiliated with academic institutions or work independently, whether their writing also includes poetry and fiction or focuses on translation, and whether or not they also write about translation in the form of reviews and commentary. The belletrism stretches back to the early twentieth century: it originated in modernist literary practices, particularly in the insertion of translations or adaptations into original compositions, but also in the polyglossia that characterizes many modernist texts, the use and quotation of foreign languages, whereby the reader is turned into a translator. These practices erased the distinctions that can usually be drawn between first- and second-order creations, permitting a translation or adaptation to be regarded as an original composition.

Pound sketches this view in "Guido's Relations," which he concludes by distinguishing between two kinds of translation. One he calls "interpretative": it functions as a "metrical gloze" that adheres closely to the source text, which is printed across the page from the translation (Anderson 1983: 251). "The 'other sort'," he continues,

> I mean in cases where the "translater" is definitely making a new poem, falls simply in the domain of original writing, or if it does not it must be censured according to equal standards, and praised with some sort of just deduction, assessable only in the particular case.
>
> *(Ibid.)*

Remarkably, Pound makes no mention of the source text when he describes the sort of translation that is "original writing" or aspires to be such through adaptation. He assigns it an aesthetic autonomy from the source text and judges it not according to a concept of equivalence, but according to the "standards" by which he judges original compositions.

I call this approach belletristic because it emphasizes the aesthetic qualities of the translated text itself. It is also impressionistic in the sense that it is vague or ill-defined. Pound's essay is filled with intriguing ideas, but it is the statement of a practitioner, not a theoretical formulation, and he does not make explicit exactly what the standards might be. They could be inferred from his practice, it might be argued, although any inference would constitute an interpretation, dependent on and varying with the theoretical assumptions that different readers bring to the interpretive act. Besides, Pound's translation practices themselves varied widely: his close but abbreviated rendering of "The Seafarer" (1911) differs from the imagistic versions of Chinese poetry he wrote for *Cathay* (1915), and both translation projects differ even more from his poem "Homage to Sextus Propertius" (1919), although all these works are second-order creations that take foreign texts as their source materials. What remains constant in Pound's translations and adaptations is their modernist experimentalism, regardless of whether they are interpretative or original in his terms. He was relentlessly innovative, deploying various concepts of equivalence and cultivating a stylistic range that encompasses the clarity and precision of Imagism as well as such nonstandard linguistic forms as poetical archaisms and colloquialisms. Belletrism in translation may be impressionistic, but it always carries a literary agenda, which can remain implicit, be deliberately concealed, or be presumptuously taken for granted.

In Pound's wake, translations came to be regarded as literary works in their own right, although his experimentalism was largely abandoned. In 1938, Dudley Fitts published *One Hundred Poems from the Palatine Anthology in English Paraphrase* with New Directions, announcing in his preface that "my purpose has been to compose, first of all, and as simply as possible an English poem," but a poem, he indicated, that avoided "poeticisms" and "archaisms" (Fitts 1956: xvii–xviii). Modern usage, specifically the current standard dialect of English, became the hallmark of anglophone translation. In his 1958 essay, "The Poetic Nuance," Fitts was bolder, confidently asserting that "The translation of a poem should be a poem, viable as a poem, and, as a poem, weighable" (Fitts 1959: 35). His confidence should be taken as a sign that the belletristic approach had become canonical by that point. His essay appeared in Reuben Brower's pioneering collection *On Translation*, published by Harvard University Press in 1959. Here such important translators as Rolfe Humphries, Richmond Lattimore, Jackson Mathews, and Edwin Muir argued for the aesthetic autonomy of the translated text, regardless of whether the translator was a poet or a scholar. Lattimore concluded his essay with the statement that

> Among the multiple objects which the translator of Greek poetry must keep simultaneously in mind, the chief one is perhaps this: to make from the Greek poem a poem in English which, while giving a high minimum of the meaning of the Greek, is still a new English poem, which would not be the kind of poem it is if it were not translating the Greek which it translates.
>
> *(Lattimore 1959: 56)*

Lattimore displays a scholar's interest in scrupulously maintaining a semantic correspondence to the source text, but he is insistent that the translation must stand on its own as a poem in the translating language.

Belletrism stops short of examining its own assumptions, which are usually presented as an undefined notion of literature or literary taste. Not surprisingly, then, explicit formulations of the belletristic approach to translation grew increasingly rare as the twentieth century unfolded. Comments were restricted to brief essays, prefaces, and interviews, and they tended to be contradictory, professing an antipathy towards translation theory or claiming its irrelevance while laying out theoretical concepts to describe a translation practice. In a 1976 interview, Christopher Middleton, the noted translator from German who was also as an academic for over four decades, adamantly declared:

> I have no theory. The thing is, I don't like theorizing about it, pressed as one is to theorize about literature when one is teaching. Translation is for me an intimate, secret, and intuitive activity, and I've never risked thinking out how I do it or why I do it. I'd rather it be a spontaneous, unconscious, nontheoretical thing.
>
> *(Honig 1985: 186)*

Middleton doesn't see that an "activity," even though "intuitive" and "unconscious," can still be grounded on a theory. Nor does he specify what he might have "risked" by reflecting on his practice, although his very use of the word "risk" indicates a worry that "theorizing" would produce a negative impact on the "how" and "why" of his translating. Here belletrism verges on irrationalism, possibly paranoia.

Yet when Middleton describes his practice later in the interview, his account does, in fact, assume a set of divergent concepts:

> I've always tried to translate poetry – in terms of service to the letter of the original text, the word as something ultimate, despite the provisional nature of all language – and at the same time the translation as a poem in its own right: the kind of poem the author would have written in my language.
>
> *(Ibid.: 190–91)*

Sharing the belletristic approach of his many predecessors, Middleton asserts the aesthetic autonomy of the translation: it is "a poem in its own right." But he also values close adherence to the source text, a strategy that as a Germanist he may have derived from romantic theorists like Friedrich Schleiermacher who argued that such a strategy produces a foreignizing effect: "the more precisely the translation adheres to the turns and figures of the original," wrote Schleiermacher (in Susan Bernofsky's English), "the more foreign it will seem to its reader" (Schleiermacher 1813: 53). Middleton ends, however, with an implicit advocacy of free, domesticating translation: his last phrase is an unacknowledged quotation of Dryden's famous pronouncement that in his version of the *Aeneid* he "endeavour'd to make *Virgil* speak such *English*, as he wou'd himself have spoken, if he had been born in England, and in this present Age" (Dryden 1958: 1055). In between, Middleton refers to "the provisional nature of all language," a point that would call into question both Dryden's and Schleiermacher's views on translation. The phrase seems to quote the 1968 English version of Roland Barthes's *Writing Degree Zero* (1953) (where the passage, in Annette Lavers and Colin Smith's English, reads: "the mobile and ever-provisional nature of language"), although it could just as well allude to Jacques Derrida's thinking about the instability of meaning (Barthes 1968: 12; see Derrida 1972). Far from lacking a translation theory, Middleton has gathered some extremely heterogeneous assumptions which are likely to prove irreconcilable, whether in theory or in practice.

Middleton is a British citizen who emigrated to the United States. But his status as a native anglophone doesn't give him any special purchase on the belletristic approach or its problems. In a 1982 essay called "Some Thoughts on Translating Poetry," Jonas Zdanys, a Lithuanian-born poet and translator, similarly dismissed any use of theory because "questions of art, by definition, are subjective, relative, and personal." He acknowledged that translation theories existed at that time, identifying a "'Western' school" in the United States and an "'Eastern' school" in the Soviet Union. But he insisted that "makers of translations should adhere to neither theory and to no other predetermined theory." His dismissal did rest on a theory, however, a belated romanticism in which "art" is construed individualistically as a form of self-expression. And he proceeded to stake out a theoretical position for translation in which the individual is paradoxically subsumed in a literary tradition:

> Translation, it seems to me, ought to involve a search for and, when necessary, a substitution not of linguistic equivalents but of "affective equivalents," images which, like Eliot's "objective correlatives," capture emotion and as many of the cognitive *implications* of the original as possible. If this search entails changing the "literal" meaning – as defined by some compiled listing of linguistic "equivalents" – then [... t]hat change should be undertaken in the search to create a poem which reads like and shares the tonal inflections and qualities of the prevailing poetic tradition of the new language. That is, poetry translated into contemporary American English becomes part of a tradition – or prevailing literary condition – in which rhythms are easy and in which there is no sense of linguistic stress or forced collocation of image. The reader of the translation must feel that he is reading an original contemporary American poem.
>
> *(Zdanys 1982)*

Zdanys's dismissal of theory, except for the concepts that make possible his own translation practice, leaves him unable to examine his position critically. With T. S. Eliot, he assumes that every reader's response to the "objective correlatives" in a poem or to the "affective equivalents" in a translation will be exactly the same, regardless of the "subjective, relative, and personal" factors he had associated with "questions of art." He also articulates a deeply conservative view of translation, whereby foreign poetries must be assimilated to "the prevailing poetic tradition of the new language." We are very far from Pound's experimentalism here, from the modernist impulse to challenge literary traditions. Still, Pound's notion of translation as original composition underlies Zdanys's belletrism.

Today the dominance of this approach among literary translators has resulted in their general inability to comment insightfully on their own work. A recent clash between a translator and a reviewer is a case in point. In July 2010, the *London Review of Books* published Michael Wood's negative review of two new collections of Jorge Luis Borges's poems, *Poems of the Night* and *The Sonnets*. Wood built his case against Borges the poet through detailed comments on the Spanish texts. He also quoted the translations, but he used them primarily to illustrate his points for readers lacking Spanish. Only in a few cases did he remark on the accuracy or poetic effect of a translator's work. Early on, he indicated his preference for closer versions by referring to particular translations as "loyal" or "faithful," although by the end he simply inserted the parenthetical phrase "slightly modified" to indicate that he had revised a translation so as to bring it closer to the Spanish.

One of the translators, Stephen Kessler, took issue with Wood's modification of his translation in a letter to the editor, arguing that it not only "violates critical ethics" but "displays a rather serious misunderstanding of what a translator does" (Kessler 2010: 5). Yet when Kessler formulated what he saw as the proper understanding, he restated the familiar belletristic approach:

> The translation of a poem is an independent work of art created by the translator, not a transcription. Wood's "modified" citations do not serve as a direct critique of the translations – a legitimate reason to offer alternate readings – but seem to be small attempts to improve on otherwise acceptable versions. Such tampering with a published text is tantamount to altering any other text under review as a way of "correcting" what the author has actually written.
>
> *(Ibid.)*

Even though Kessler's English version appears in *Poems of the Night* with Borges's Spanish text printed *en face*, here he erases the distinction between translation and original composition, arrogating to himself a notion of authorial originality. He apparently thinks that viewing a translation as "an independent work of art" is sufficient justification for his verbal choices, and so he doesn't need to explain what concept of equivalence he applied to make his version "acceptable." Unfortunately, this stance led to a missed opportunity to offer such an explanation in his letter.

The material at issue is a sixteen-line extract from the poem "Amanecer," translated as "Break of Day." Wood modified two lines of Kessler's English translation. Here is Borges's Spanish with Wood's revised version:

> la imagen de las calles
> que definirán después con los otros.

the image of the street
that later they will define with others.

Kessler's version reads: "the image of the streets/that later others will define." In Wood's closer rendering, the word "they" refers to an earlier mention of people "who have been up all night." Why Kessler departed from the Spanish is not at all clear, particularly since to omit "they" significantly changes the meaning by removing the group of people that Borges had singled out and by shifting the emphasis to the "others." A reader who knows Spanish might regard the departure as an error. Kessler's rendering does establish a metrical regularity in the line, making it consistently iambic. And a reader inclined to speculative interpretations could certainly fill a word like "others" with a conceptual density, especially given the attention that the term "otherness" has received in recent years in cultural theory and philosophy. But Kessler's belletrism prevents him from providing an account that would illuminate what he has done. Claims of the aesthetic autonomy of the literary work have never been as anti-intellectual as they have come to be among contemporary translators.

The translation workshop and its limitations

During the 1960s, the belletristic approach was decisive in improving the cultural status of translators because it characterized translation as a writing practice. As Edmund Keeley has observed, "translators began to be accepted as legitimate creative artists during the mid-1960s and, eventually, as legitimate teachers of translation in the various university workshops that came into existence as part of the rapidly expanding field of study called Creative Writing" (Keeley 1990: 292). In 1963, Paul Engle, then director of the Writers Workshop at the University of Iowa, invited Keeley to teach what was the first translation workshop in the United States (Weissbort 2006: 610). The pedagogy was belletristic, emphasizing the translation as an independent literary text. When in September 2010 I interviewed Keeley about his work at Iowa, he recalled that Engle instructed him to "treat [the translation workshop] like a poetry or fiction workshop" and to "focus on the product in English." The students were master's candidates in poetry or fiction who translated from a variety of foreign languages. They were asked to present their translations to the workshop by explaining why they chose the source text, what rival translations they might have worked with or against, and what specific problems the text posed for translation into English. The content of the course consisted solely of the students' translations. Keeley saw no need for readings in translation theory and commentary. In the interview, in fact, he described himself "as ardently against the idea of translation theory. You don't read the theory of poetry to learn how to write a poem or to teach the writing of one."

A belletristic pedagogy was widely adopted in the translation workshops that began to proliferate at universities in the United States from the 1960s onwards, initially in creative writing programs, both undergraduate and graduate. The orientation was resolutely practical, focusing on specific translation problems, discussing solutions, and excluding readings in translation theory and commentary or using only those readings that had some direct bearing on practice. Frank MacShane, who in 1966 instituted the translation workshop in the Writing Division of the School of the Arts at Columbia University, noted that he "presented the students with a number of ideas about translations of the sort collected and edited by Reuben Brower," but he made clear that "we were not interested so much in the theory of translation as in the practice of it" (MacShane 1971: 234). In 1973, Daniel Weissbort was hired in the Department of Comparative Literature at Iowa to direct a program leading to a Master of Fine Arts degree in translation, and although it included a course that surveyed translation history and theory from antiquity to the twentieth century, Weissbort was later careful to remark that "Our primary interest was in the production of translated texts, rather than in the consideration of the theoretical dimension of translation" (Weissbort 2006: 610–11).

By the 1980s, the belletristic approach had firmly linked translation to creative writing in academic institutions, even when the workshops were taught in literature departments and programs. This link insured that the workshop became the dominant curricular form for teaching translation. As with poetry and fiction workshops, the content of the translation workshop was primarily the students' own work, occasionally combined with professional translations, and the pedagogy was practically oriented towards the production of a literary text in English. The relations between the translation and the source text might actually receive little attention, in some workshops none at all. And with rare exceptions translation theory and commentary were absent or given limited attention.

What qualified as theory and commentary, moreover, differed with the instructor, but in most cases the readings did not include material in which theoretical concepts were formulated abstractly with or without illustrations drawn from translations. According to Weissbort, Engle "was particularly adamant" about the need for "a theoretical/historical component" in the graduate translation program at Iowa, although what he had in mind was "a historically focused rather than theory-based" course to supplement the workshop (Weissbort 2006: 610). When Weissbort taught the course, he tended to stop at Pound because he "found contemporary translation theory, especially that which drew on French critical theory (Derrida, for instance), rather daunting" (ibid.). By the mid-1990s, as former student Christopher Mattison recalled, Weissbort's reading list had been narrowed mostly to essays by practitioners (email: 29 September 2010).

In 1987, in an article that appeared in the magazine of the American Literary Translators Association, *Translation Review*, Jonas Zdanys listed the readings that "best suit the introductory nature of an undergraduate translation workshop" such as he taught in the Department of Comparative Literature at Yale University (Zdanys 1987: 10). The list is dominated by belletristic and practically oriented material to the exclusion of theoretical statements. It includes the essays by Fitts and Mathews from the Brower anthology as well as essays by two poets, T. S. Eliot and Yves Bonnefoy. Zdanys had clearly selected readings that could be useful in solving the translation problems he found most urgent, problems that hinged on recreating the formal features of the source text. Such readings can certainly be helpful to beginning translators, but they will not enable students to examine critically the authors' underlying assumptions about translation – or their own.

The Brower anthology, long out of print, was eventually superseded by John Biguenet and Rainer Schulte's edited volume *The Craft of Translation* (1989), which has come to be a frequently assigned textbook in translation workshops, especially those housed in creative writing programs. It contains essays by such distinguished translators as Edmund Keeley and Christopher Middleton, Gregory Rabassa and William Weaver, Margaret Sayers Peden and Burton Raffel. The focus is, according to the editors, "the reconstruction of the translation process," where "thinking grows out of the situation within a text; it is not brought to the text from the outside" (Biguenet and Schulte 1989: vii, xii). The emphasis on practice thus characterizes the translation process as free of the translator's preconceptions, as if translators did not bring to their work an ensemble of values, beliefs, and representations which include theoretical concepts. The translator is portrayed as a writer whose reflection is limited to specific verbal choices. Biguenet and Schulte subsequently drew a sharp distinction between theory and practice by editing another volume, *Theories of Translation* (1992). Here, too, they finally reduce thinking about translation to the production of a translated text ("Translation thinking is always concerned with the reconstruction of processes"), mystifying the cultural and social conditions that figure into the translator's decisions, and that are examined by several of the theorists and commentators whose work they included in their book (Schulte and Biguenet 1992: 9).

The translation workshop as it has been conducted for some fifty years reveals what is most harmful about the belletristic approach. With limited and often no consideration of theoretical readings, students do not acquire a conceptual vocabulary to describe, explain, and evaluate their translations and those of the professional translators whose work they might be asked to read in the course. MacShane's account of his workshop is typical: "I thought that such general principles as there are would emerge more forcefully if they came out of a visible problem in a student's work than if they were considered abstractly" (MacShane 1971: 234). MacShane's pedagogy, however, is actually based on "general principles," on that most hallowed of British and American cultural traditions, the epistemology known as empiricism: he assumes that a real object or process is not constructed for knowledge but given, independent of the knowing subject, and upon observation that object or process yields a knowledge that is free of illusion and prejudice (see Easthope 1999a: 88–90). MacShane's empiricism means that his teaching rests on a theory which excludes other theoretical concepts while rendering invisible the application of its own.

Hence he does not see that translation problems do not simply appear in a translator's work, whether student or professional. The problems need to be formulated as such, and the formulations can occur only on some conceptual basis. Theory, especially abstract speculation, creates conceptual parameters within which certain problems become visible while others do not. Once a problem is formulated, a solution can be developed, but only within the parameters set up by specific concepts.

This process can be seen in a rare detailed account of a translation workshop. Although Zdanys insisted that the aim of his Yale workshop was "to understand the necessary organic unfolding of each translation apart from the constraints of pre-determined aesthetic theories," he described the theoretical concepts that governed his teaching (Zdanys 1987: 9). "The best translations of any given time," he would tell his students at the first class meeting,

> were those that were most fluent and idiomatic in the new language, and those qualities depended not just on the translator's eye and ear but also on the aesthetic qualities of the original poem. I suggested that it would be most inter-esting for all of us if students would avoid translating work more than a generation old [...] and concentrate on more contemporary poets, who might in many ways be rendered into contemporary American English easily.
>
> *(Ibid.: 11)*

A serious problem with these prescriptions is their lack of precision. Zdanys seems to be defining fluency or easy readability as the use of current standard English in a translation, but the term "contemporary American English" can embrace many different Englishes, not only the standard dialect but also a range of nonstandard forms, including regional and social dialects, slang and colloquialism, obscenity and jargon. In referring to "the aesthetic qualities of the original poem," he evidently assumes a concept of equivalence. But what if the source text is not "fluent and idiomatic"? What if it isn't written in the current standard dialect of the source language? Should the translator deviate from current standard English to create an analogous style in the translation? Zdanys's prescriptions insure that students will analyze and judge translations within rather narrow parameters. He also forces them to adopt a thoroughgoing presentism by excluding the possibility of translating earlier poetries as well as any consideration of past theories and practices.

Here the crucial problem with treating translation merely as creative writing becomes apparent. The typical translation workshop is staffed by a poet-translator or a professional translator who inexorably and often unwittingly imposes his or her own aesthetics on student-translators. This imposition happens in two ways: (1) by discriminating among verbal choices, not according to relations to the source text or to the receiving culture, but according to unexamined notions of good writing and literary taste, and (2) by emphasizing practical problems, which are solved according to the instructor's aesthetics. As a result, student translators lack the conceptual resources that might allow them not only to comment incisively on translations, their own and those of other translators, but also to assess the ideas advanced by the instructor, if not the belletrism which supports them. An instructor usually commands authority through experience, but if the teaching simply doles out a product, here an obscure notion of literary value or a ready-made translation solution, the authority becomes repressive and counterproductive. Students may develop certain translation skills, but they do not learn to think about translation critically or to translate independently.

Imagining a translation culture

The dominance of the belletristic approach has severely limited the development of literary translation, not only thinking about translation but translation practice as well. This is perhaps especially true of the United States, where translation workshops have long been offered in creative writing programs, but it applies to anglophone cultures generally, even if in varying degrees, because belletrism remains the dominant discourse about translation in reviews and commentary. Despite recent generations of highly accomplished translators, despite the existence of awards and cultural organizations that recognize and support the work of translators, despite the creation of presses and publishing series devoted to translations, despite the emergence of translation studies as an area of research and teaching in academic institutions, the fact is that literary translation continues to be grossly misunderstood, undervalued if not discounted or neglected, and persistently exploited. The belletristic approach has proven useless to change this situation.

Nonetheless, to submit an idea or practice to critique, to interrogate its assumptions and consequences, is not to dismiss it entirely. I am not arguing, then, that belletrism should be simply abandoned. Insofar as literary translation is a writing practice, any approach must be writerly to a significant extent, acknowledging that a translated text is *relatively* autonomous from its source text, and that the relative autonomy consists, at least in part, of a certain aesthetic independence. To advance translation at the present time, however, this idea is insufficient: translation must rather be conceived, practiced, and taught according to a hermeneutic model, as an act of interpretation.

We must leave behind the instrumentalism that still dominates thinking about translation. According to this view, an acceptable translation reproduces or transfers an invariant contained in or caused by the source text, whether its form, its meaning, or its effect, usually a combination of these features. Varieties of instrumentalism prevail among literary translators, as can be seen whenever they comment on their work or on translation in general.

In *Translating Style* (1998), for example, the novelist-translator Tim Parks analyzes in detail the prose style of such fiction writers as D. H. Lawrence, James Joyce, and Virginia Woolf and then compares Italian translations to the English texts, repeatedly finding some "divergence between original and translation" (Parks 1998: 118). Throughout, he assumes an instrumental model of translation: he treats the yield of his stylistic analysis as a formal invariant contained in the source. Yet his comparisons are never actually made to the English texts, but rather to *his interpretations* of those texts. This becomes apparent on the few occasions when he suddenly questions his analysis. Thus in discussing a passage from Lawrence's *Women in Love* Parks adds the qualification that "no precise interpretation is possible" and immediately reiterates this point ("leaving aside the thorny question of exactly what any expression might mean") (ibid.: 12). All the same, he faults the translation for failing to reproduce the stylistic effect that he perceives in the English text: "Quite apart from any particular semantic sense, it is this fullness that is lost in the Italian, a fullness that can easily be assessed by comparing translation against original" (ibid.). How easy can the assessment be if the source text is admittedly indeterminate? Parks is always ready to allow his own interpretations to function as incontrovertible standards of judgment, but he refuses the Italian translators the same right to interpret, preferring instead to locate "a tendency, perhaps, to distort the text to fit in with the translator's own individual interpretation" (ibid.: 92). The problem, evidently, is that the translator did not agree with *his* interpretation.

In *Why Translation Matters* (2010), similarly, the translator Edith Grossman formulates the instrumental concept of equivalent effect. "The most fundamental description of what translators do," she asserts,

> is that we write – or perhaps rewrite – in language B a work of literature originally composed in language A, hoping that readers of the second language – I mean, of course, readers of the translation – will perceive the text, emotionally and artistically, in a manner that parallels and corresponds to the esthetic experience of its first readers.
>
> *(Grossman 2010: 7)*

But which "first readers"? Readerships are notoriously fragmented today, regardless of the language and culture: readers bring the most diverse kinds of knowledge and taste to their reading, so that their responses are difficult, if not impossible, to predict. Later, Grossman suggests that the linguistic and cultural differences a translator must negotiate are ultimately insurmountable: "Languages," she observes, "even first cousins like Spanish and Italian, trail immense, individual histories behind them, and with all their volatile accretions of tradition, culture, and forms and levels of discourse, no two ever dovetail perfectly or occupy the same space at the same time" (ibid.: 68). How, then, can the translation produce an effect on its reader that is the same as or similar to the effect that the source text produces on the source-language reader? Grossman responds that "a translator's fidelity is not to lexical pairings but to context – the implications and echoes of the first author's tone, intention, and level of discourse" (ibid.: 70–71). But how can a translator be sure that the translation realizes the source-text author's intention when that author did not intend to write in the translating language? And when the translator possesses an indisputable record of the author's intention – for instance, in the use of a particular genre – that record might be ignored. Take the sonnet: the meter and rhyme scheme are undoubtedly deliberate. Yet in translating Spanish Renaissance sonnets Grossman chooses to avoid any re-creation of these formal features. She does write that translators do no more than "hope" to produce an equivalent effect, so perhaps we should regard this concept as a convenient fiction, consoling to the translator who at every point confronts the sheer impossibility of any instrumental understanding of translation.

What recommends the very different hermeneutic model is both its explanatory power and its practical application. The interpretive activity begins with the choice of a source text and continues in the development of a strategy to translate it. These stages in the translation process are determined not merely by the source text and culture but also by values, beliefs, and representations in the receiving culture. Translators should be able to give an account of their work that is cognizant of these cultural conditions. They should be able to show how, given these conditions, their translation aims to fix the form and meaning of the source text so as to inscribe a particular interpretation. The inscription can never be more than provisional, one interpretation among several different possibilities, and it is always subject to further interpretation by the range of cultural constituencies in the receiving situation. Nonetheless, translators should be capable of articulating the interpretants that make possible their translations. By "interpretants," I mean the various factors that every translator applies to transform the source text into a translation. Interpretants can be formal, including a concept of equivalence, such as a semantic correspondence based on dictionary definitions, or a concept of style, a set of linguistic features linked to a particular genre (as when a foreign crime novel might require a suitably hardboiled prose in the translating language). Interpretants can also be thematic, meanings or codes. Examples include an interpretation that was presented elsewhere in commentary (such as scholarly research) or an ideological standpoint affiliated with a specific social group (as when a feminist or queer translator encodes a political agenda).

In interpreting the source text, the translator alters it in the most material way. It is detached from its originary context where it supported meanings, values, and functions specific to the source language and culture, and it is simultaneously inserted in a different context, created by the translation, where it supports meanings, values, and functions specific to the translating language and culture. To assert that translation is transformation does not mean that no correspondence, formal or semantic, exists between the source and translated texts. The point is rather that a literary work is much more than any such correspondence: it is a complex cultural artifact that never survives intact the move to another language and culture where it comes to signify, to be valued, and to function differently. My idea of translation as interpretation is thus very different from George Steiner's "hermeneutic motion," where the translator is imagined as performing a "restitution" to "compensate" for the "aggression" of interpreting the source text, establishing, "ideally, exchange without loss" (Steiner 1975: 297, 300, 302–3). I am arguing that a ratio of source loss and translating gain cannot be avoided or resolved, and the only way that a translation can do right abroad, in relation to the source text and culture, is to do wrong at home, making an appreciable difference in relation to the cultural norms and institutions of the receiving situation, contributing to a change, for instance, in how a foreign work or a foreign literature is perceived in translation.

To translate according to the hermeneutic model and to be capable of addressing translations as interpretive acts, translators must be equipped with an array of qualifications that they do not receive from the prevalent workshop pedagogy. These qualifications start with advanced proficiency in a source language, but include the ability to write a variety of styles in the translating language with clarity, precision, and resonance. Translators must also possess a broad and deep knowledge of translation traditions in the translating language and culture, i.e., a historical grasp of theoretical concepts and practical strategies. And they must be specialists in the fields in which they translate, as those fields have developed in both the source and the translating cultures. A translator of French poetry into English should be not only proficient in the French language, but also learned in French literary traditions, proficient not only in the English language but also in English literary traditions, capable of imitating and assessing English poetries and knowledgeable in translation traditions both in anglophone cultures and in the cultures, past and present, that have informed the theories and practices which constitute anglophone traditions. The promise of theory is self-consciousness and self-criticism, as well as an expansion of the translator's stylistic repertoire. But the teacher must be able and willing to move between the theoretical concept and the verbal choice, to show how the verbal choice is at once writerly and interpretive, productive of cognitive and literary effects, to start with, and ultimately cultural and social in its potential impact. The more deeply immersed in these kinds of knowledge translators are, the greater the command they will exercise over their translating, and the more articulate and judicious they will be in describing, explaining, and evaluating translations.

The current state of literary translation, particularly in anglophone countries, indicates the urgent need for the kind of translator I am fashioning here. Belletrism has long been rampant in translation commentary, and this has led, on the one hand, to an unreflective impressionism that has not illuminated what a translator does and, on the other hand, to an aggressive anti-intellectualism that discourages thinking about translation. As a result, a continuing public discussion has yet to materialize, and the consequence for publishing has been catastrophic, since an understanding of the translator's work is essential to the creation of an informed readership who can appreciate translated literature. Too many translators are as guilty of this problem as their teachers and readers are. They naively believe that theory can be divorced from practice in any kind of writing or research, that translation practices can be assessed simply by comparing the translation to the source text instead of taking into account the cultural conditions of the translating, and that a historical knowledge of translation is unnecessary when without such knowledge translators have no sure basis on which to understand and criticize the cultural status quo and so they wind up reaffirming it. Recently, translators have claimed that translation is de facto a form of scholarship, but they remain so deeply invested in a belletristic approach that they can't – some say they won't – provide a scholarly account of their translating. Merely to assert that translation is scholarship will not compel scholars to abandon romantic concepts of original authorship that have long been entrenched in the academy, and that have either stigmatized translation as hackwork or restricted it to a derivative form of creative writing. Such an attitude towards translation will not be changed simply by putting a translation of a novel or of a poetry collection before a scholar, especially when it might be accompanied by commentary that lacks incisive thinking and scrupulous research. Translators should be able to write well, without a doubt. But today they also need to think, write, and speak about their translations with a high degree of critical sophistication.

We lack a discourse about translating that can foster and sustain what I would like to call a translation culture, a culture where translated texts are knowledgeably written and read, taught and studied, recognized as works that are not simply distinct from the source texts they translate but also vital to the receiving culture and to its ongoing exchanges with various foreign cultures. If we lived in a translation culture as I am imagining it, translators would simultaneously learn how to translate and how to comment on translations in compelling ways. Their commentary would be grounded in a body of knowledge that is literary and historical, theoretical and critical, a knowledge of translation as well as of the fields in which translations are produced and used. Translators would be capable not only of situating their projects in relation to past theories and practices but also of assessing the appeal of those projects to readers in the present. They would be capable of sharing their knowledge with the diverse readerships who use and depend on their work, and this sharing would take an equally diverse range of forms: research monographs and articles in translation theory and history intended for scholars, evaluative reports on translations to help publishers, reviews of translated novels and poetry collections for periodicals large and small, prefaces to translations written by themselves and others, interviews about their projects and their careers, and blogs on current issues in translation. It is only with the emergence of a translation culture that readers will learn how to appreciate translations as translations without reducing them to their source texts, that the practice of translation will be understood and valued in academic institutions as both a creative form of writing and a rigorous form of scholarship, and that, as a result of these developments, publishers will see a financial return that motivates and supports their continued investment in translations. If translators want to change the cultural marginality of translation, they need to change the ways that they themselves think about and represent their work.

[2011]

BIBLIOGRAPHY

Aleramo, S. (1908) *A Woman at Bay*, trans. M. H. Lansdale, New York and London: G. P. Putnam.

——(1979) *A Woman*, trans. R. Delmar, London: Virago.

Allain, M.-F. (1983) *The Other Man: Conversations with Graham Greene*, trans. G. Waldman, London: Bodley Head.

Althusser, L., and Balibar, E. (1970) *Reading Capital*, trans. B. Brewster, London: New Left Books.

Amati Mehler, J., Argentieri, S., and Canestri, J. (1990) *La Babele dell'inconscio: Lingua madre e lingue straniere nella dimensione*, Milano: Raffaello Cortina Editore.

Anderson, B. (1991) *Imagined Communities: Reflections on the Origin and Spread of Nationalism*, rev. ed., London and New York: Verso.

Anderson, D. (1983) *Pound's Cavalcanti: An Edition of the Translations, Notes, and Essays*, Princeton, NJ: Princeton University Press.

Arrojo, R. (1998) "The Revision of the Traditional Gap between Theory and Practice and the Empowerment of Translation in Postmodern Times," *The Translator* 4/1: 25–48.

Bacardí, M. (1998) "Joan Sales i els criteris de traducció," *Quaderns: Revista de Traducció* 1: 27–38.

Badiou, A. (2001) *Ethics: An Essay on the Understanding of Evil*, trans. P. Hallward, London: Verso.

——(2004) *Theoretical Writings*, ed. and trans. R. Brassier and A. Toscano, London: Continuum.

——(2008) *Conditions*, trans. S. Corcoran, London: Continuuum.

Baker, M. (1992) *In Other Words: A Coursebook on Translation*, London and New York: Routledge.

——(2000) "Linguistic Perspectives on Translation," in P. France (ed.) *The Oxford Guide to Literature in English Translation*, Oxford: Oxford University Press, pp. 20–26.

——(2006) *Translation and Conflict: A Narrative Account*, London and New York: Routledge.

Bakhtin, M. (1984) *Problems of Dostoevsky's Poetics*, trans. C. Emerson, Minneapolis, MN: University of Minnesota Press.

Balcells, A. (1996) *Catalan Nationalism: Past and Present*, ed. G. J. Walker, trans. J. Hall, New York: St. Martin's Press.

Barsky, R. F. (1994) *Constructing a Productive Other: Discourse Theory and the Convention Refugee Hearing*, Amsterdam: John Benjamins.

——(1996) "The Interpreter as Intercultural Agent in Convention Refugee Hearings," *The Translator* 2/1: 45–64.

Barthes, R. (1968) *Writing Degree Zero*, trans. A. Lavers and C. Smith, New York: Hill and Wang.
——(1974) *S/Z*, trans. R. Miller, New York: Hill and Wang.
Bass, A. (1985) "On the History of a Mistranslation and the Psychoanalytic Movement," in Graham (1985), pp. 102–41.
Baudrillard, J. (1983) *In the Shadow of the Silent Majorities … or The End of the Social*, trans. P. Foss, P. Patton, and J. Johnston, New York: Semiotext(e).
Belitt, B. (1978) "The Translator as Nobody in Particular," in *Adam's Dream: A Preface to Translation*, New York: Grove Press, pp. 45–53.
Belsey, C. (1980) *Critical Practice*, 2nd edition, London and New York: Methuen, 2002.
Benjamin, A. (1989) *Translation and the Nature of Philosophy*, London and New York: Routledge.
Benjamin, W. (1923) "The Translator's Task," trans. S. Rendall, in Venuti (2012b), pp. 75–83.
Berman, A. (1999) *La Traduction et la lettre, ou l'auberge du lointain*, Paris: Seuil.
Bernofsky, S. (1997) "Schleiermacher's Translation Theory and Varieties of Foreignization: August Wilhelm Schlegel vs. Johann Heinrich Voss," *The Translator* 3/2: 175–92.
Bettarini, R. (1997) "Jacopone da Todi e le laude," in C. Segre and C. Ossola (eds) *Antologia dela poesia italiana: Duecento*, Torino: Einaudi, pp. 278–332.
Bhabha, H. (1994) *The Location of Culture*, London and New York: Routledge.
Biguenet, J., and Schulte, R. (eds) (1989) *The Craft of Translation*, Chicago: University of Chicago Press.
Billiani, F., and Sulis, G. (eds) (2007) *The Italian Gothic and Fantastic: Encounters and Rewritings of Narrative Traditions*, Madison, NJ: Farleigh Dickinson University Press.
Blanchot, M. (1988) *The Unavowable Community*, trans. P. Joris, Barrytown, NY: Station Hill Press.
Bloch, E. (1988) *The Utopian Function of Art and Literature: Selected Essays*, ed. and trans. J. Zipes and F. Mecklenburg, Cambridge, MA: MIT Press.
——(1991) *Heritage of Our Times*, trans. N. Plaice and S. Plaice, Oxford: Polity.
Bloom, H. (1994) *The Western Canon: The Books and School of the Ages*, New York: Houghton Mifflin Harcourt.
Blum-Kulka, S. (1986) "Shifts of Cohesion and Coherence in Translation," in J. House and S. Blum-Kulka (eds) *Interlingual and Intercultural Communication: Discourse and Cognition in Translation and Second Language Acquisition Studies*, Tübingen: Narr.
Borges, J. L. (1949) *El Aleph*, Buenos Aires: Losada.
——(1964) *Labyrinths: Selected Stories and Other Writings*, ed. D. A. Yates and J. E. Irby, New York: New Directions.
Bourdieu, P. (1984) *Distinction: A Social Critique of the Judgement of Taste*, trans. R. Nice, Cambridge, MA: Harvard University Press.
——(1988) *Homo Academicus*, trans. P. Collier, Stanford, CA: Stanford University Press.
——(1990) *The Logic of Practice*, trans. R. Nice, Stanford, CA: Stanford University Press.
——(1993) "The Field of Cultural Production, or: The Economic World Reversed," trans. R. Nice, in R. Johnson (ed.) *The Field of Cultural Production: Essays on Art and Literature*, New York: Columbia University Press, pp. 29–73.
——(1998) *Practical Reason: On the Theory of Action*, trans. S. Farage, R. Johnson, R. Nice, G. Sapiro, and L. Wacquant, Stanford, CA: Stanford University Press.
Brisset, A. (1996) *A Sociocritique of Translation: Theatre and Alterity in Quebec, 1968–1988*, trans. R. Gill and R. Gannon, Toronto: University of Toronto Press.
Brook, P. (1972) Introduction, in T. Hughes, *Seneca's Oedipus*, Garden City, NY: Doubleday, pp. 5–9.
Brower, R. (ed.) (1959) *On Translation*, Cambridge, MA: Harvard University Press.
Brown, P., and Levinson, S. (1987) *Politeness: Some Universals in Language Usage*, Cambridge: Cambridge University Press.
Bruckner, D. J. R. (1995) "They're Speaking English Up There Now," *New York Times Book Review*, 22 October, p. 37.

Buck, T. (1995) "Neither the letter nor the spirit: Why most English translations of Thomas Mann are so inadequate," *Times Literary Supplement*, 13 October, p. 17.

Bunker, E. (1998) *No Beast So Fierce*, Harpenden: No Exit Press.

——(2001) *Come una bestia feroce*, trans. S. Bortolussi, Torino: Einaudi.

Busquets, L. (1977) *Aportació lèxica de Josep Carner a la llengua literària catalane*, Barcelona: Fundació Salvador Vives Casajuana.

Buzzati, D. (1971) *Le notti difficili*, Milano: Arnoldo Mondadori.

——(1983) *Restless Nights: Selected Stories*, ed. and trans. L. Venuti, San Francisco: North Point Press.

Calvino, I. (1965) *Le Cosmicomiche*, rpt. Milano: Arnoldo Mondadori, 1993.

——(1968) *Cosmicomics*, trans. W. Weaver, San Diego, New York, and London: Harcourt Brace and Company.

Camus, A. (1942) *L'Étranger*, Paris: Gallimard.

——(1946) *The Stranger*, trans. S. Gilbert, New York: Alfred Knopf.

——(1988) *The Stranger*, trans. M. Ward, New York: Alfred Knopf.

Carloni, M. (1994) *L'Italia in giallo: Geografia e storia del giallo italiano contemporaneo*, Reggio Emilia: Diabasis.

Carlotto, M. (2000) *Arrivederci, amore, ciao*, Roma: Edizioni E/O.

——(2006) *The Goodbye Kiss*, trans. L. Venuti, New York: Europa Editions.

Carner, J. (1986) *El reialme de la poesia*, ed. N. Nardi and I. Pelegrí, Barcelona: Edicions 62.

Carroll, L. (1927) *Alícia en terra de maravelles*, trans. J. Carner, Barcelona: Editorial Joventut, 1987.

Carsaniga, G. M. (1974) "Realism in Italy," in F. W. J. Hemmings (ed.) *The Age of Realism*, Harmondsworth: Penguin, pp. 323–55.

Cary, J. (1983) Review of Buzzati (1983), *Parabola* (Fall): 120–21.

Casacuberta, M. (1989) "*Quaderns de l'Exili* (Mèxic 1943–47), una revista d'agitació nacional," *Els Marges* 40: 87–105.

Casanova, P. (2004) *The World Republic of Letters*, trans. M. B. DeBevoise, Cambridge, MA: Harvard University Press.

——(2010) "Consecration and Accumulation of Literary Capital: Translation as Unequal Exchange," trans. S. Brownlie, in M. Baker (ed.) *Critical Readings in Translation Studies*, London and New York: Routledge, pp. 287–303.

Castiglione, B. (1972) *Il libro del Cortegiano*, ed. E. Bonora. Milano: Mursia.

Catford, J. C. (1965) *A Linguistic Theory of Translation: An Essay in Applied Linguistics*, London: Oxford University Press.

Cecchetti, G. (1959) Review of Mandelbaum (1958), *Comparative Literature* 11: 262–68.

Chamberlain, L. (1988) "Gender and the Metaphorics of Translation," *Signs* 13: 454–72.

Chesterman, A. (2009) "The Name and Nature of Translator Studies," *Hermes* 42: 13–22.

Clancy, T., and Pieczenik, S. (1998) *Tom Clancy's Op-Center: Balance of Power*, New York: Berkley.

——(1999) *Op-Center: Equilibrio de poder*, trans. V. Pozanco, Barcelona: Planeta.

Clowse, B. B. (1981) *Brainpower for the Cold War: The Sputnik Crisis and National Defense Education Act of 1958*, Westport, CT: Greenwood.

Cohen, S. (2001) "*Critical Inquiry*, October, and Historicizing French Theory," in S. Lotringer and S. Cohen (eds) *French Theory in America*, New York and London: Routledge, pp. 191–216.

Colina, S. (1999) "Transfer and Unwarranted Transcoding in the Acquisition of Translational Competence: An Empirical Investigation," in J. Vandaele (ed.) *Translation and the (Re)Location of Meaning: Selected Papers of the CETRA Research Seminars in Translation Studies, 1994–1996*, Leuven: Research Centre for Translation, Communication and Cultures, pp. 375–92.

Collison-Morely, L. (1919) "Souls Divided," *Times Literary Supplement*, 27 November, p. 689.

——(1921) "Tozzi's 'Tre Croci,'" *The Athenæum*, 31 December, p. 903.

Coll-Vinent, S. (1998) "The French Connection: Mediated Translation into Catalan during the Interwar Period," *The Translator* 4/2: 204–28.

Comay, R. (1991) "Geopolitics of Translation: Deconstruction in America," *Stanford French Review* 15/1–2: 47–79.

Conte, G. B. (1999) *Latin Literature: A History*, trans. J. B. Solodow, rev. D. Fowler and G. W. Most, Baltimore, MD: Johns Hopkins University Press.

Contini, G. (ed.) (1960) *Poeti del Duecento*, Milano-Napoli: Ricciardi, vol. 2.

Cortázar, J. (1959) "Las babas del diablo," *Las armas secretas*, Barcelona: Planeta, 1984, pp. 56–71.

——(1967) "Blow-Up," in *End of the Game and Other Stories*, trans. P. Blackburn, New York: Pantheon, pp. 114–31.

Cotroneo, R. (1995) "Sostiene Tabucchi," *L'Espresso*, 2 June, pp. 104–8.

Cronin, M. (2003) *Translation and Globalization*, London and New York: Routledge.

——(2006) *Translation and Identity*, London and New York: Routledge.

Damrosch, D. (2003) *What Is World Literature?*, Princeton, NJ: Princeton University Press.

Daniell, D. (2003) *The Bible in English: Its History and Influence*, New Haven, CT: Yale University Press.

Dante (1954) *The Inferno*, trans. J. Ciardi, New York: Mentor.

De Certeau, M. (1984) *The Practice of Everyday Life*, trans. S. Rendall, Berkeley, CA: University of California Press.

De Gámez, T. (ed.) (1973) *Simon and Schuster's International Dictionary: English/Spanish, Spanish/English*, New York: Simon and Schuster.

Deledda, G. (1905) *After the Divorce*, trans. M. H. Lansdale, New York: Henry Holt.

——(1984) *After the Divorce*, trans. S. Ashe, London: Quartet.

Deleuze, G., and Guattari, F. (1987) *A Thousand Plateaus: Capitalism and Schizophrenia*, trans. B. Massumi, Minneapolis, MN: University of Minnesota Press.

Derrida, J. (1967) *L'écriture et la différence*, Paris: Seuil.

——(1972) "Freud and the Scene of Writing," trans. J. Mehlman, *Yale French Studies* 48: 74–117.

——(1978) *Writing and Difference*, trans. A. Bass, Chicago: University of Chicago Press.

——(1982a) "Différance," in *Margins of Philosophy*, trans. A. Bass, Chicago: University of Chicago Press, pp. 1–28.

——(1982b) "Signature Event Context," in *Margins of Philosophy*, trans. A. Bass, Chicago: University of Chicago Press, pp. 307–30.

——(1987) "The Laws of Reflection: Nelson Mandela, In Admiration," trans. M. A. Caws and I. Lorenz, in *For Nelson Mandela*. New York: Seaver Books, pp. 13–42.

——(1992) "Onto-Theology of National-Humanism (Prolegomena to a Hypothesis)," *Oxford Literary Review* 14/1–2: 3–23.

——(1993) *Spectres de Marx: l'état de la dette, le travail du deuil et la nouvelle internationale*, Paris: Galilée.

——(1994) *Specters of Marx: The State of the Debt, the Work of Mourning, and the New International*, trans. P. Kamuf, London and New York: Routledge.

——(1996) *Le monolinguisme de l'autre: ou la prothèse d'origine*, Paris: Galilée.

——(1998) *Monolingualism of the Other; or, The Prosthesis of Origin*, trans. P. Menash, Stanford, CA: Stanford University Press.

——(1999) "Qu'est-ce qu'une traduction 'relevante'?" in *Quinzièmes Assises de la Traduction Littéraire (Arles 1998)*, Arles: Actes Sud, pp. 21–48.

——(2001) "What Is a 'Relevant' Translation?" trans. L. Venuti, *Critical Inquiry* 27: 174–200.

——(2005) *Rogues: Two Essays on Reason*, trans. P.-A. Brault and M. Naas, Stanford: Stanford University Press.

Devi, M. (1997) *Breast Stories*, ed. and trans. G. C. Spivak, Calcutta: Seagull.

Diemert, B. (1996) *Graham Greene's Thrillers and the 1930s*, Montréal and Buffalo: McGill-Queen's University Press.

Dostoevsky, F. (1912) *The Brothers Karamazov*, trans. C. Garnett, London: Heinemann.
——(1990) *The Brothers Karamazov*, trans. R. Pevear and L. Volokhonsky, San Francisco: North Point Press.
Dryden, J. (1956) *The Works of John Dryden*, ed. E. N. Hooker and H. T. Swedenberg, Jr., Berkeley, CA: University of California Press, vol. I.
——(1958) "Dedication of the *Æneis*" (1697), in J. Kinsley (ed.) *The Poems of John Dryden*, Oxford: Clarendon Press, vol. III.
Dunford, M., and Holland, J. (1998) *New York City: The Rough Guide*, 6th ed., trans. J. Deinema, E. Ottens, E. Schreuder and C. Smit, Houten: Nederlandstalige editie.
——(2000a) *New York City: The Rough Guide*, 7th ed., London: Rough Guides Ltd.
——(2000b) *New York: The Rough Guide*, trans. A. Barella Sciolette and C. Scandone, rev. G. Penazzi, Bologna: FuoriThema.
During, S. (ed.) (1999) *The Cultural Studies Reader*, London and New York: Routledge.
Easthope, A. (1983) *Poetry as Discourse*, London and New York: Routledge.
——(1991) *Literary into Cultural Studies*, London and New York: Routledge.
——(1999a) *Englishness and National Culture*, London and New York: Routledge.
——(1999b) *The Unconscious*, London and New York: Routledge.
Ebel, J. G. (1969) "Translation and Cultural Nationalism in the Reign of Elizabeth," *Journal of the History of Ideas* 30: 593–602.
Eber, I. (1980) *Voices from Afar: Modern Chinese Writers on Oppressed Peoples and Their Literature*, Ann Arbor, MI: University of Michigan Center for Chinese Studies.
Eliot, T. S. (1950) *Selected Essays*, New York: Harcourt, Brace and World.
Eminem (2000) *The Marshall Mathers LP*, Interscope Records.
Enright, D. J. (1968) "Effrontery and Charm," *New York Review of Books*, 21 November, pp. 22–24.
Evans, A. B. (2000) "Jules Verne and the French Literary Canon," in E. J. Smyth (ed.) *Jules Verne: Narratives of Modernity*, Liverpool: Liverpool University Press, pp. 11–39.
Even-Zohar, I. (1990) "Polysystem Studies," *Poetics Today* 11/1.
Faas, E. (1980) *Ted Hughes: The Unaccommodated Universe*, Santa Barbara, CA: Black Sparrow.
Falk, R. (1999) *Predatory Globalization: A Critique*, Cambridge: Polity.
——(2002) *La Globalización depredadora: Una crítica*, trans. H. Bevia and A. Resines, Madrid: Siglo XXI.
Farrés, E. (2006) *Edward Hopper: Cinquanta poemes sobre la seva obra pictòrica*, Barcelona: Viena.
——(2009) *Edward Hopper: Poems*, trans. L. Venuti, Minneapolis, MN: Graywolf; Manchester: Carcanet, 2010.
Feeney, D. (1998) *Literature and Religion at Rome: Cultures, Contexts, and Beliefs*, Cambridge: Cambridge University Press.
Feinstein, E. (2001) *Ted Hughes: The Life of a Poet*, London: Weidenfeld and Nicolson.
Fish, S. E. (1980) *Is There a Text in This Class? The Authority of Interpretive Communities*, Cambridge, MA: Harvard University Press.
Fitts, D. (1959) "The Poetic Nuance," in Brower (1959), pp. 32–47.
——(ed. and trans.) (1956) *Poems from the Greek Anthology*, New York: New Directions.
Fitzgerald, A. (2012) "In Conversation: Jonathan Galassi with Adam Fitzgerald," *The Brooklyn Rail*, May. http://brooklynrail.org/2012/05/books/ Accessed 24 June 2012.
Freud, S. (1953) *The Interpretation of Dreams*, trans. J. Strachey, Harmondsworth: Penguin, 1976.
——(1960) *The Psychopathology of Everyday Life*, trans. A. Tyson, New York: Norton, 1965.
Frota, M. P. (2000) *A singularidade na escrita tradutora: linguagem e subjetividade nos estudos da tradução, na lingüística e na psicanálise*, Campinas: Pontes.
Fulton, R. (2007) Letter to the editor, *Times Literary Supplement*, 9 February, p. 17.
Gavronsky, S. (1977) "The Translator: From Piety to Cannibalism," *SubStance* 16: 53–61.
Gentile, A., Ozolins, U., and Vasilakakos, M. (1996) *Liaison Interpreting: A Handbook*, Melbourne: Melbourne University Press.
Gibbons, R. (1985) "Poetic Form and the Translator," *Critical Inquiry* 11/4: 654–71.

Giddens, A. (1979) *Central Problems in Social Theory: Action, Structure, and Contradiction in Social Analysis*, Berkeley and Los Angeles, CA: University of California Press.

Gill, B. (1955) "The Uses of Love," *New Yorker*, 5 March, pp. 114–15.

Golino, C. (1959) Review of Mandelbaum (1958), *Italian Quarterly* 3: 76.

Gouanvic, J.-M. (1999) *Sociologie de la traduction: la science-fiction américaine dans l'espace culturel français des années 1950*, Arras: Artois Presses Université.

——(2005) "A Bourdieusian Theory of Translation, or the Coincidence of Practical Instances: Field, 'Habitus,' Capital and 'Illusio'," trans. J. Moore, *The Translator* 11/2: 147–66.

——(2007) *Pratique social de la traduction: le roman réaliste américain dans le champ littéraire français, 1920–1960*, Arras: Artois Presses Université.

Graham, J. (1985) *Difference in Translation*, Ithaca, NY: Cornell University Press.

Greenberg, J. (ed.) (2008) *Side by Side: New Poems Inspired by Art from Around the World*, New York: Harry Abrams.

Grossman, E. (2010) *Why Translation Matters*, New Haven, CT: Yale University Press.

Gutt, E.-A. (1991) *Translation and Relevance: Cognition and Context*, Oxford: Blackwell.

Habermas, J. (1998) *On the Pragmatics of Communication*, ed. M. Cooke, Cambridge, MA: MIT Press.

Hallett, G. (1971) "The Bottle and the Fly," *Thought* 46/1: 83–104.

Harvey, D. (1989) *The Condition of Postmodernity: An Enquiry into the Origins of Social Change*, Oxford: Blackwell.

Harvey, K. (1995) "A Descriptive Framework for Compensation," *The Translator* 1/1: 65–86.

Hass, V. P. (1955) Review of Ash (1955), *Chicago Sunday Tribune*, 24 April, p. 6.

Hatim, B., and Mason, I. (1997) *The Translator as Communicator*, London and New York: Routledge.

Healey, R. (1998) *Twentieth-Century Italian Literature in English Translation: An Annotated Bibliography, 1929–1997*, Toronto: University of Toronto Press.

Heidegger, M. (1947) "Letter on Humanism," trans. F. A. Capuzzi, in D. F. Krell (ed.) *Basic Writings*, New York: Harper and Row, 1977, pp. 193–242.

——(1962) *Being and Time*, trans. J. Macquarrie and E. Robinson, New York: Harper and Row.

——(1975) *Early Greek Thinking*, ed. and trans. D. F. Krell and F. A. Capuzzi, New York: Harper and Row.

Heilbron, J., and Sapiro, G. (2007) "Outline for a Sociology of Translation: Current Issues and Future Prospects," in M. Wolf and A. Fukari (eds) *Constructing a Sociology of Translation*, Amsterdam: Benjamins, pp. 93–107.

Hermans, T. (1999) *Translation in Systems: Descriptive and System-oriented Approaches*, Manchester: St. Jerome.

Hoby, Sir T. (trans.) (1900) B. Castligione, *The Book of the Courtier*, ed. W. Raleigh, New York: AMS Press, 1967.

Holmes, J. S. (1988) "The Name and Nature of Translation Studies," in *Translated! Papers on Literary Translation and Translation Studies*, Amsterdam: Rodopi, pp. 67–80.

Homer (1951) *The Iliad of Homer*, ed. and trans. R. Lattimore, Chicago: University of Chicago Press.

Honig, E. (1985) *The Poet's Other Voice: Conversations on Literary Translation*, Amherst, MA: University of Massachusetts Press.

Hooley, D. M. (1988) *The Classics in Paraphrase: Ezra Pound and Modern Translators of Latin Poetry*, Selingsgrove, PA: Susquehanna University Press.

Hughes, S., and Hughes, E. (ed. and trans.) (1982) *Jacopone da Todi: The Lauds*, New York: Paulist Press.

Hughes, T. (1969) *Seneca's Oedipus*, London: Faber and Faber.

——(1970) *Crow: From the Life and Songs of the Crow*, London: Faber and Faber.

Hugo, V. (1985) *Œuvres Complètes: Critiqué*, ed. J.-P. Reynaud, Paris: Laffont, vol. 11.

Hutcheon, L. (1989) *The Politics of Postmodernism*, London: Methuen.

Hu Ying (2000) *Tales of Translation: Composing the New Woman in China, 1899–1918*, Stanford, CA: Stanford University Press.

Ibarz, M. (1984) "El pensament fermat de Joan Sales," *L'Avenç* 67: 15.

Inghilleri, M. (2011) *Interpreting Justice: Ethics, Politics and Language*, London and New York: Routledge.

Jakobson, R. (1959) "On Linguistic Aspects of Translation," in Brower (1959), pp. 232–39.

James, H. (1901) "Matilde Serao," *North American Review*, 172: 367–80.

Jameson, F. (1981) *The Political Unconscious: Narrative as a Socially Symbolic Act*, Ithaca, NY: Cornell University Press.

——(1991) *Postmodernism, or The Cultural Logic of Late Capitalism*, Durham, NC: Duke University Press.

Jones, A. B. (1997) *Women in Contemporary Spain*, Manchester: Manchester University Press.

Kastelic, N. S. (2010) *Publishing, Slovenia, 2009: Final Data*. Ljubljana: Statistical Office of the Republic of Slovenia, *www.stat.si/eng/novica_prikazi.aspx?id=3529* Accessed 2 January 2011.

Keeley, E. (1990) "The Commerce of Translation," *Journal of Modern Greek Studies* 8/2: 291–97.

Kessler, S. (2010) "Letter to the Editor," *London Review of Books* 32/14 (22 July): 5.

Klein, N. (2000) *No Logo*, London: Flamingo, 2001.

Kleinberg, S. J. (1999) *Women in the United States, 1830–1945*, New Brunswick, NJ: Rutgers University Press.

Kuh, K. (1962) *The Artist's Voice: Talks with Seventeen Artists*, New York: Harper and Row.

Lacan, J. (1977) *Écrits: A Selection*, trans. A. Sheridan, New York: Norton.

Lash, S., and Urry, J. (1994) *Economies of Signs and Space*, London: Sage.

Lattimore, R. (1959) "Practical Notes on Translating Greek Poetry," in Brower (1959), pp. 48–56.

Lecercle, J.-J. (1990) *The Violence of Language*, London and New York: Routledge.

Lee, L. O. (1973) *The Romantic Generation of Modern Chinese Writers*, Cambridge, MA: Harvard University Press.

——(1987) *Voices from the Iron House: A Study of Lu Xun*, Bloomington, IN: Indiana University Press.

Lefevere, A. (ed. and trans.) (1977) *Translating Literature: The German Tradition from Luther to Rosenzweig*, Assen: Van Gorcum.

——(ed. and trans.) (1992) *Translation/History/Culture: A Sourcebook*, London and New York: Routledge.

Levin, G. (1995) *Edward Hopper: A Catalogue Raisonné*, New York: Whitney Museum of American Art and Norton, vol. 3.

——(2007) *Edward Hopper: An Intimate Biography*, New York: Rizzoli.

Levine, S. J. (2005) "The Latin American Novel in English Translation," in E. Kristal (ed.) *The Cambridge Companion to the Latin American Novel*, Cambridge: Cambridge University Press, pp. 297–317.

Lewis, C. T., and Short, C. (1879) *A Latin Dictionary*, Oxford: Clarendon Press.

Lewis, P. E. (1985) "The Measure of Translation Effects," in Graham (1985), pp. 31–62.

Llobera, J. R. (1983) "The Idea of the *Volksgeist* in the Formation of Catalan Nationalist Ideology," *Ethnic and Racial Studies* 6: 332–50.

Logue, C. (2001) *War Music: An Account of Books 1–4 and 16–19 of Homer's Iliad*, London: Faber and Faber.

Longenbach, J. (2008) *The Art of the Poetic Line*, Saint Paul, MN: Graywolf.

Loomba, A. (1998) *Colonialism/Postcolonialism*, London and New York: Routledge.

Lowell, R. (1961) *Imitations*, New York: Farrar, Straus and Giroux.

Lucarelli, C. (2001) "Quella iena di Bunker non diverrà mai un angelo," *La Stampa Tuttolibri*, 8 December, p. 3.

Luke, D. (1970) "Introduction," in T. Mann, *Tonio Kröger and Other Stories*, ed. and trans. D. Luke, New York: Bantam, pp. ix–xxxviii.

——(1995) "Translating Thomas Mann," *Times Literary Supplement*, 8 December, p. 15.

Lyotard, J.-F. (1984) *The Postmodern Condition: A Report on Knowledge*, trans. G. Bennington and B. Massumi, Minneapolis, MN: University of Minnesota Press.

MacIntyre, A. (1988) *Whose Justice? Which Rationality?*, Notre Dame, IN: University of Notre Dame Press.

MacLehose, C. (2004–05) "A Publisher's Vision," *EnterText* 4/3 Supplement: 103–16.

MacShane, F. (1971) "The Teaching of Translation," in *The World of Translation*, New York: PEN American Center, pp. 231–40.

Mahony, P. (1980) "Toward the Understanding of Translation in Psychoanalysis," in *Psychoanalysis and Discourse*, London: Tavistock, 1987, pp. 3–15.

Mair, A. (1957) "Seneca, Lucius Annaeus," in *Encyclopedia Britannica*, ed. W. Yust, 14th edition, Chicago: Encyclopedia Britannica.

Mandel, E. (1975) *Late Capitalism*, trans. J. De Bres, London: Verso.

Marías, J. (2003) *The Man of Feeling*, trans. M. J. Costa, New York: New Directions.

Massardier-Kenney, F. (2010) "Antoine Berman's Way-making to Translation as a Creative and Critical Act," *Translation Studies* 3/3: 259–71.

May, E. T. (1988) *Homeward Bound: American Families in the Cold War*, New York: Basic Books.

May, R. (1994) *The Translator in the Text: On Reading Russian Literature in English*, Evanston, IL: Northwestern University Press.

McEwan, I. (1981) *The Comfort of Strangers*, London: Jonathan Cape.

——(1982) *El placer del viajero*, trans. B. Gómez Ibáñez, Barcelona: Editorial Anagrama.

——(1983a) *Cortesie per gli ospiti*, trans. S. Bertola, Torino: Einaudi.

——(1983b) *Étrange séduction (Un bonheur de rencontre)*, trans. J.-P. Carasso, Paris: Seuil.

——(1997) *El confort dels estranys*, trans. M. Trias, Barcelona: Ediciones Destino.

McGann, J. (1991) *The Textual Condition*, Princeton, NJ: Princeton University Press.

Mena, E. (2010) Review of Farrés (2009), *Three Percent*, 10 January. *http://www.rochester.edu/College/translation/threepercent/index.php?id=2438* Accessed 9 January 2012.

Mengaldo, P. V. (1991) "Aspetti della lingua di Calvino," in *La tradizione del Novecento. Terza serie*, Torino: Einaudi, pp. 227–91.

Meschonnic, H. (1973) *Pour la poétique II*, Paris: Gallimard.

Mitchell, J. (1975) *Psychoanalysis and Feminism*, Harmondsworth: Penguin.

Mitchell, J. and Rose, J. (eds) (1982) *Feminine Sexuality: Jacques Lacan and the École Freudienne*, trans. J. Rose, London: Macmillan.

Moliner, M. (1994) *Diccionario de uso del español*, Madrid: Editorial Gredos.

Moretti, F. (2000) "Conjectures on World Literature," *New Left Review* n.s. 1 (January–February): 54–68.

Muir, W. (1968) *Belonging: A Memoir*, London: Hogarth Press.

Nabokov, V. (1955) "Problems of Translation: *Onegin* in English," *Partisan Review* 22: 496–512.

Nagid, N. L. (1955) "The Decadent Life," *Commonweal*, 13 May, pp. 163–66.

Nash, M. (1983) *Mujer, familia y trabajo en España (1875–1936)*, Barcelona: Anthropos.

Neruda, P. (1972) *The Captain's Verses*, trans. D. D. Walsh, New York: New Directions.

——(1973a) *Residence on Earth*, trans. D. D. Walsh, New York: New Directions.

——(1973b) *Incitement to Nixonicide and Praise for the Chilean Revolution*, trans. S. Kowit, Madison, WI: Quixote.

New Yorker (1988) "Briefly Noted," 2 May, p. 119.

Nida, E. (1964) *Towards a Science of Translating, with Special Reference to Principles and Procedures Involved in Bible Translating*, Leiden: Brill.

Niedecker, L. (2002) *Collected Works*, ed. J. Penberthy, Berkeley and Los Angeles: University of California Press.

O'Doherty, B. (1973) *American Masters: The Voice and the Myth*, New York: Random House.

O'Gorman, N. (1959a) "Language and Vision," *Poetry* 93: 329–32.

——(1959b) *The Night of the Hammer*, New York: Harcourt Brace.

Olson, C. (1960) "Projective Verse" (1959), in D. M. Allen (ed.) *The New American Poetry*, New York: Grove Press, pp. 386–99.

Ortín, M. (1996) *La prosa literària de Josep Carner*, Barcelona: Quaderns Crema.

——(2001) "Els Dickens de Josep Carner i els seus crítics," *Quaderns: Revista de Traducció* 7: 121–51.

Parks, T. (1998) *Translating Style: The English Modernists and their Italian Translations*, London: Cassell.

Paterson, D. (1999) *The Eyes: A Version of Antonio Machado*, London: Faber and Faber.

——(2006) *Orpheus: A Version of Rilke's Die Sonette an Orpheus*, London: Faber and Faber.

Payne, J. (1993) *Conquest of the New Word: Experimental Fiction and Translation in the Americas*, Austin, TX: University of Texas Press.

Peresson, G. (2010) *Rapporto sullo stato dell'editoria in Italia, 2010*, Milano: Ediser/Associazione italiana editori.

Peresson and Mussinelli, C. (2009) "The Sale and Purchase of Translation Rights in the Italian Market," *Publishing Research Quarterly* 25: 254–63.

Peretti, J. (2001) "My Nike Media Adventure," *The Nation* 272/14 (April 19): 19–22.

Pericay, X., and Toutain, F. (1996) *El malentès del Noucentisme: Tradició i plagi a la prosa catalana moderna*, Barcelona: Proa.

Perloff, M. (1996) *Wittgenstein's Ladder: Poetic Language and the Strangeness of the Ordinary*, Chicago: University of Chicago Press.

Polk, W. R. (2004) "Los neoconservadores en las alturas del poder," trans. J. G. L. Guix, 24 January, on-line edition.

Pound, E. (1929) "Guido's Relations," in T. S. Eliot (ed.) *The Literary Essays of Ezra Pound*, New York: New Directions, 1954, pp. 192–200.

Pozzi, A. (1998) *Parole*, ed. A. Cenni and O. Dino, 2nd ed., Milan: Garzanti.

——(2002) *Breath: Poems and Letters*, ed. and trans. L. Venuti, Middletown, CT: Wesleyan University Press.

Prat de la Riba, E. (1906) *La nacionalitat catalana*, Barcelona: Edicions 62, 1998.

Pratt, M. L. (1986) "Interpretive Strategies/Strategic Interpretations: On Anglo-American Reader-Response Criticism," in J. Arac (ed.) *Postmodernism and Politics*, Minneapolis, MN: University of Minnesota Press, pp. 26–54.

——(1987) "Linguistic Utopias," in N. Fabb, D. Attridge, A. Durant, and C. McCabe (eds) *The Linguistics of Writing: Arguments between Language and Literature*, Manchester: Manchester University Press.

Pusey, J. R. (1983) *China and Charles Darwin*, Cambridge, MA: Harvard University Press.

Rafael, V. (1988) *Contracting Colonialism: Translation and Christian Conversion in Tagalog Society under Early Spanish Rule*, Ithaca, NY: Cornell University Press.

——(2009) "Translation, American English, and the National Insecurities of Empire," *Social Text 101* 27/4 (Winter): 1–23.

Raymond, J. (1955) "Two First Novels," *New Statesman and Nation*, 21 May, pp. 727–28.

Reichert, K. (1996) "'It Is Time': The Buber-Rosenzweig Bible Translation in Context," in S. Budick and W. Iser (eds) *The Translatability of Culture: Figurations of the Space Between*, Stanford, CA: Stanford University Press, pp. 169–85.

Riba, C. (1979) *Clàssics i moderns*, ed. J. Molas, Barcelona: Edicions 62.

Ricoeur, P. (1970) *Freud and Philosophy: An Essay in Interpretation*, trans. Denis Savage, New Haven, CT: Yale University Press.

Rigby, K. (2010) "Ernest Farrés's 'Edward Hopper'," *Words without Borders*, March. http://wordswithoutborders.org/book-review/ernest-farress-edward-hopper Accessed 4 February 2012.

Rolo, C. J. (1955) Review of Ash (1955), *Atlantic*, April, pp. 84–86.

Sagan, F. (1954) *Bonjour Tristesse*, Paris: Julliard.

——(1955) *Bonjour Tristesse*, trans. I. Ash, New York: Dutton.

Sales, J. (1956) *Incerta glòria*, Barcelona: Club Editor.

——(trans.) (1961) "Nota dels editors Catalans," in F. Dostoievski, *Els germans Karamàzov*, Barcelona: Club Editor.

Sanders, M. (1992) "Training for Community Interpreters," in C. Picken (ed.) *ITI Conference 6 Proceedings*, London: Aslib.

Sapiro, G. (2010) "French Literature in the World System of Translation," trans. J. Gladding, in C. McDonald and S. R. Suleiman (eds) *French Global: A New Approach to Literary History*, New York: Columbia University Press, pp. 298–319.

Saussy, H. (2006) *Comparative Literature in an Age of Globalization*, Baltimore, MD: Johns Hopkins University Press.

Schleiermacher, F. (1813) "On the Different Methods of Translating," trans. S. Bernofsky, in Venuti (2012b), pp. 43–63.

——(1890) *Selected Sermons*, ed. and trans. M.F. Wilson, New York: Funk and Wagnalls.

Schroeder, S. (2006) *Wittgenstein: The Way Out of the Fly-Bottle*, Cambridge: Polity.

Schulte, R., and Biguenet, J. (eds) (1992) *Theories of Translation: An Anthology of Essays from Dryden to Derrida*, Chicago: University of Chicago Press.

Schwartz, B. (1964) *In Search of Wealth and Power: Yan Fu and the West*, Cambridge, MA: Harvard University Press.

Schweda Nicholson, N. (1994) "Professional Ethics for Court and Community Interpreters," in D.L. Hammond (ed.) *Professional Issues for Translators and Interpreters*, Amsterdam: John Benjamins.

Sellent Arús, J. (1998) "La traducció literària en català al segle XX: alguns títols representatius," *Quaderns: Revista de Traducció* 2: 23–32.

Semanov, V. I. (1967) *Lu Hsün and His Predecessors*, trans. C. Alber, White Plains, NY: M. E. Sharp, 1980.

Shackman, J. (1984) *The Right to be Understood: A Handbook on Working with, Employing and Training Community Interpreters*, Cambridge, England: National Extension College.

Shuttleworth, M., and Cowie, M. (1997) *Dictionary of Translation Studies*, Manchester: St. Jerome.

Sigmund, P. E. (1977) *The Overthrow of Allende and the Politics of Chile, 1964–1976*, Pittsburgh, PA: University of Pittsburgh Press.

Skelton, J. (1983) *The Complete English Poems*, ed. V. J. Scattergood, Harmondsworth: Penguin.

Smith, B. H. (1988) *Contingencies of Value: Alternative Perspectives for Critical Theory*, Cambridge, MA: Harvard University Press.

Smith, W. (1875) *A Dictionary of Greek and Roman Antiquities*, London: John Murray.

Spanos, W. (1993) *Heidegger and Criticism*, Minneapolis, MN: University of Minnesota Press.

Sperber, D., and Wilson, D. (1986) *Relevance: Communication and Context*, Oxford: Blackwell.

Spivak, G. C. (1985) "Subaltern Studies: Deconstructing Historiography," in D. Landry and G. MacLean (eds) *The Spivak Reader*, London and New York: Routledge, pp. 203–36.

——(1992) "The Politics of Translation," in *Outside in the Teaching Machine*, London and New York: Routledge, 1993, pp. 179–200.

——(ed. and trans.) (1995) *Imaginary Maps: Three Stories by Mahasweta Devi*, London and New York: Routledge.

Spunta, M. (2004) *Voicing the Word: Writing and Orality in Contemporary Italian Fiction*, Bern: Peter Lang.

Starr, W. H., Thompson, M. P., and Walsh, D. D. (1960) *Modern Foreign Languages and the Academically Talented Student*, Washington D. C. and New York: National Education Association and Modern Language Association of America.

Steiner, G. (1975) *After Babel: Aspects of Language and Translation*, New York and London: Oxford University Press.

Tabucchi, A. (1994) *Sostiene Pereira: Una testimonianza*, Milan: Feltrinelli.

——(1995) *Declares Pereira: A True Account*, trans. P. Creagh, London: Harvill.

Tennyson, A. (1972) *Selected Poetry*, ed. C. Ricks, London: Longman.

Testa, E. (1997) *Lo stile semplice: Discorso e romanzo*, Torino: Einaudi.

Thompson, J. (1954) *A Hell of a Woman*, New York: Vintage, 1990.

Times of London (1958) "Perplexities and Poetry," 6 November, p. 13C.

Timpanaro, S. (1976) *The Freudian Slip: Psychoanalysis and Textual Criticism*, trans. K. Soper, London: NLB.

Toury, G. (1980) *In Search of a Theory of Translation*, Tel Aviv: Porter Institute for Poetics and Semiotics.

——(1986) "Monitoring Discourse Transfer: A Test-Case for a Developmental Model of Translation," in J. House and S. Blum-Kulka (eds) *Interlingual and Intercultural Communication: Discourse and Cognition in Translation and Second Language Acquisition Studies*, Tübingen: Narr, pp. 79–94.

——(1995) *Descriptive Translation Studies and Beyond*, Amsterdam: John Benjamins.

Tranströmer, T. (2006) *The Deleted World: Versions by Robin Robertson*, London: Enitharmon.

Trueblood, A. (1982) *Antonio Machado: Selected Poems*, Cambridge, MA: Harvard University Press.

Turi, G. (1997) "Cultura e poteri nell'Italia repubblicana," in G. Turi (ed.) *Storia dell'editoria nell'Italia contemporanea*, Firenze: Giunti, pp. 383–448.

Tymoczko, M. (1999) *Translation in a Postcolonial Context: Early Irish Literature in English Translation*, Manchester: St. Jerome.

——(2000) "Translation and Political Engagement: Activism, Social Change and the Role of Translation in Geopolitical Shifts," *The Translator* 6/1: 23–48.

Underhill, E. (1919) *Jacopone da Todi, Poet and Mystic—1228–1306: A Spiritual Biography*, London: J. M. Dent.

Ungar, S. (2006) "Writing in Tongues: Thoughts on the Work of Translation," in Saussy (2006), pp. 127–38.

Ungaretti, G. (1953) *Les cinq livres*, trans. J. Lescure, Paris: Editions de Minuit.

——(1958) *Life of a Man*, ed. and trans. A. Mandelbaum, Milan: Scheiwiller, London: Hamish Hamilton, and New York: New Directions.

——(1975) *Selected Poems of Giuseppe Ungaretti*, ed. and trans. A. Mandelbaum, Ithaca, NY: Cornell University Press.

Unwin, S. (1960) *The Truth about Publishing*, 7th ed., London: Allen and Unwin.

Vallverdú, F. (1968) *L'escriptor català i el problema de la llengua*, Barcelona: Edicions 62.

Van Gogh, V. (1888) "Letter to Theo van Gogh," trans. Mrs. J. van Gogh-Bonger, ed. R. Harrison, 8 September, no. 533. *http://www.webexhibits.org/vangogh/letter/18/533.htm* Accessed 15 January 2012.

Van Ham, P. (2001) "The Rise of the Brand State," *Foreign Affairs* 80/5 (September/October): 2–6.

Venuti, L. (1982) "The Art of Literary Translation: An Interview with William Weaver," *Denver Quarterly* 17/2: 16–26.

——(1991) "Simpatico," *SubStance* 65: 3–20.

——(1995) "Translating Thomas Mann," *Times Literary Supplement*, 22 December, p. 17.

——(1998) *The Scandals of Translation: Towards an Ethics of Difference*, London and New York: Routledge.

——(2005) "Translation, History, Narrative," *Méta: Journal des Traducteurs* 50/3: 800–817.

——(2008) *The Translator's Invisibility: A History of Translation*, 2nd ed., London and New York: Routledge.

——(2009) "Translation, Intertextuality, Interpretation," *Romance Studies* 27/3: 218–34.

——(2010) "Ekphrasis, Translation, Critique," *Art in Translation* 2/2: 131–52.

——(2012a) "Genealogies of Translation Theory: Jerome," in Venuti (2012b), pp. 483–502.

——(ed.) (2012b) *The Translation Studies Reader*, 3rd ed., London and New York: Routledge.

Vermeer, H. (1989) "Skopos and Commission in Translation Action," trans. A. Chesterman, in L. Venuti (2012b), pp. 191–202.

Vickers, N. (1981) "Diana Described: Scattered Women and Scattered Rhyme," *Critical Inquiry* 8: 265–79.

——(1986) "This Heraldry in Lucrece' Face," in S. R. Suleiman (ed.) *The Female Body in Western Culture: Contemporary Perspectives*, Cambridge, MA: Harvard University Press, pp. 209–22.

Vincent, G. T., and Lees, S. (2006) "A Life with Art: Stephen Carlton Clark as Collector and Philanthropist," in *The Clark Brothers Collect: Impressionist and Early Modern Paintings*, Williamstown, MA: Sterling and Francis Clark Art Institute, pp. 123–99.

Von der Lippe, G. B. (1999) "Death in Venice in Literature and Film: Six 20th-Century Versions," *Mosaic* 32/1: 35–54.

Wadensjö, C. (1998) "Community Interpreting," in M. Baker (ed.) *Encyclopedia of Translation Studies*, London and New York: Routledge, pp. 33–37.

Ward, A. (1974) *Book Production, Fiction and the German Reading Public, 1740–1800*, Oxford: Oxford University Press.

Warmington, E. H. (ed. and trans.) (1936) *Remains of Old Latin*, vol. 2, London: William Heinemann.

Watling, E. F. (ed. and trans.) (1966) *Seneca: Four Tragedies and Octavia*, Harmondsworth: Penguin.

Weaver, W. (1989) "The Process of Translation," in Biguenet and Schulte (1989), pp. 117–24.

Weissbort, D. (2006) "Postface," in D. Weissbort and A. Eysteinsson (eds) *Translation Theory and Practice: A Historical Reader*, Oxford: Oxford University Press, pp. 609–15.

Wesley, J. (1983) *A Collection of Hymns for the Use of the People Called Methodists*, ed. F. Hildebrandt, O. A. Beckerlegge and J. Dale, vol. 7 in *The Works of John Wesley*, Oxford: Clarendon Press.

Westbrook, V. (1997) "Richard Taverner Revising Tyndale," *Reformation* 2: 191–205.

White, H. (1973) *Metahistory: The Historical Imagination in the Nineteenth Century*, Baltimore, MD: Johns Hopkins University Press.

Whittle, N. (2010) "Dialogues with the Dead," *Financial Times*, 23 January, p. 16.

Willcox, L. C. (1920) "A Famous Mystic of the 13th Century," *New York Times*, 11 April, p. BR166.

Williams, G. (1999) *French Discourse Analysis: The Method of Post-Structuralism*, London and New York: Routledge.

Wills, G. (1997) "Homer's Women," *New Yorker*, 27 January, pp. 74–78.

Wilson, E. (1946) "Books," *New Yorker*, 13 April, pp. 99–100.

Wittgenstein, L. (2009) *Philosophical Investigations*, trans. G. E. M. Anscombe, P. M. S. Hacking, and J. Schulte, Chichester: Wiley-Blackwell, rev. 4th ed.

Wong, L. (1998) "Lin Shu's Story-retelling as Shown in His Chinese Translation of *La Dame aux camellias*," *Babel* 44: 208–33.

Wood, M. (2010) "The Unreachable Real," *London Review of Books* 32/13 (8 July): 26–28.

Yao, S. G. (2002) *Translation and the Languages of Modernism: Gender, Politics, Language*, New York: Palgrave Macmillan.

Zdanys, J. (1982) "Some Thoughts on Translating Poetry," *Lituanus*, 28/4 (Winter), online.

——(1987) "Teaching Translation: Some Notes toward a Course Structure," *Translation Review*, 23: 9–13.

Zhang, S., and Schmitt, B. H. (2001) "Creating Local Brands in Multilingual International Markets," *Journal of Marketing Research* 38 (August): 313–25.

INDEX